Cameroon

the Bradt Travel Guide

Ben West

edition
2

www.bradtguides.com

Bradt Travel Guides Ltd, UK
The Globe Pequot Press Inc, USA

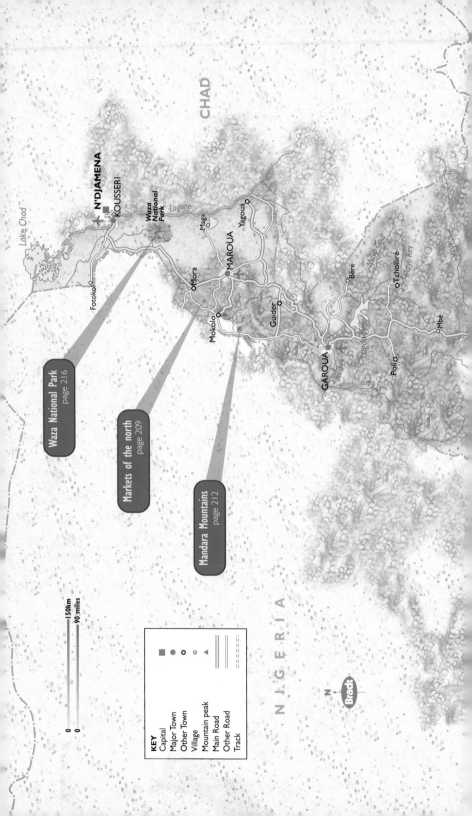

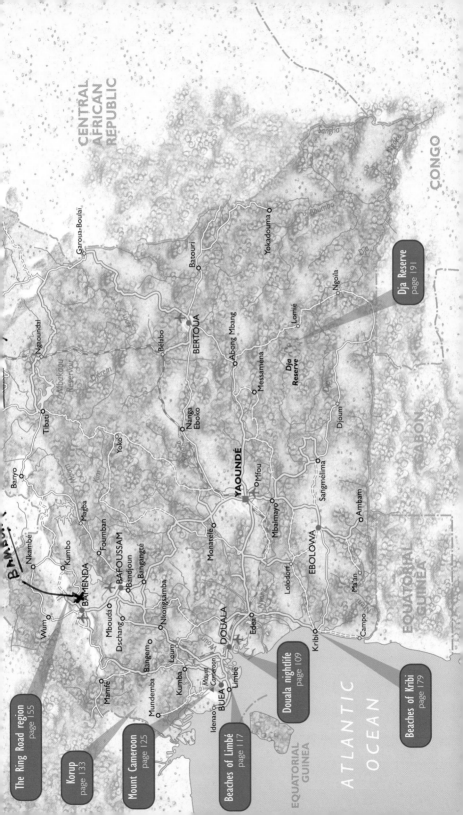

CENTRAL AFRICAN REPUBLIC

CONGO

GABON

EQUATORIAL GUINEA

EQUATORIAL GUINEA

ATLANTIC OCEAN

Dja Reserve page 191

The Ring Road region page 155

Korup page 133

Mount Cameroon page 125

Beaches of Limbé page 117

Douala nightlife page 109

Beaches of Kribi page 179

Sangha

Ngoko

Boumba

Dja

Garoua-Boulaï

Batouri

Yokadouma

Ngoïla

Lomié

BERTOUA

Bélabo

Abong Mbang

Messaména

Dja Reserve

Djoum

Djerem

Mbakaou Reservoir

Ngaoundal

Tibati

Yoko

Nanga Eboko

Mfou

YAOUNDÉ

Sangmélima

Ambam

Banyo

Magba

Foumban

Mount Mbam

BAFOUSSAM

Bandjoun

Bangangté

Monatélé

Mbalmayo

EBOLOWA

Ma'an

Campo

Nkambé

Kumbo

BAMENDA

Mbouda

Dschang

Bangem

Nkongsamba

Loum

Edéa

Kribi

Wum

Mamfé

Mundemba

Kumba

Mount Cameroon

BUEA

Limbé

DOUALA

Idenao

Nianga

Lokoundjé

Lolodorf

Nyong

BAMBUI

Cameroon
Don't miss...

Colourful markets
Tourou market, Extreme North Province
(SLV) page 215

Wildlife
Elephant at Kalamaloué National Reserve, Extreme North Province
(SLV) page 217

**Spectacular
landscapes**
Rhumsiki Peak,
Extreme North
Province
(SLV) page 213

Beaches
Kribi, South
Province
(SLV) page 179

**Ancient
kingdoms
and cultures**
Palace of
Bandjoun,
West Province
(MB) page 142

top   **Foumban market, West Province**
(SLV) page 145

above   **Road to Fon's Palace, Bafut, Northwest Province**
(RB) page 157

left   **Traditional dome-shaped houses of the Mousgoum people, Pouss, Extreme North Province**
(AA) page 215

top	Mosque, Nkongsamba, Littoral Province (SLV) page 114
above left	Douala, Littoral Province (MB) page 103
above right	Yaoundé, Centre Province (MB) page 163
below	Cathedral, Kribi, South Province (SLV) page 179

top   **Childen playing football, Bandjoun** (MB) page 142
above left   **Peul girl, Manengouba Hills** (SLV) page 16
above right   **Woman wearing a traditional wooden** *calabash*, **Tourou** (SLV) page 215
below   **Children in Douala, Littoral Province** (MB) page 103

AUTHOR

Ben West has written on a wide variety of subjects for numerous newspapers and magazines including *The Guardian*, *The Independent*, the *Daily Telegraph*, *The Times*, the *Daily Mail*, *Vogue* and *Reader's Digest*. Travel writing has taken him to more than 20 countries, including five in Africa, and his first trip to Cameroon netted him four tropical diseases. He was chief property correspondent of the *Daily Express* and the *Sunday Express* from 1999 to 2001, at which time penning one too many features on the joys of bungalow living became too much. His books include *London for Free* (Pan, 1996), *Buying a Home: The Virgin Guide* (Virgin Books, 2003), *The Rough Guide to Family Fun in Ireland* (Rough Guides, 2004) and *Buying a Property Abroad* (Cadogan, 2004). His theatre show featuring Prunella Scales, *Gertrude's Secret*, has been touring a number of London and regional UK theatres since September 2006.

AUTHOR'S STORY

My first visit to Cameroon was my first contact with Africa, leading to a fascination for a continent that remains unabated. In 1986 I joined a friend who was visiting his father in the Cameroonian capital, Yaoundé.

I was instantly captivated by the country, not least due to its diversity, and the great contrasts to the way of life I knew. That first trip was certainly eventful. After an excursion to the north of the country I returned to Britain with two types of malaria, blackwater fever and another tropical illness, filariasis. My friend ended up in a Yaoundé hospital, also having contracted malaria and dysentery. Despite this, the strong effect Africa seems to have on many people took hold of us, and we've both returned to Africa a number of times.

Some years later I was surprised to learn that no English-language guide dedicated to Cameroon existed, which was the impetus for asking Bradt whether they would like one. Whilst writing it was certainly a daunting task, it was always a fascinating one, and I hope that the book leads others to discover and grow to love the country too.

Inexplicably, Cameroon seldom features on travellers' plans despite the huge wealth of cultural and geographical treasures it possesses. To non-travellers it also remains a little-known country and indeed the impressive performance of its football team, the Lake Nyos tragedy of 1986 (where volcanic toxic gas claimed hundreds of Cameroonian lives) and celebrated *socassa* musician Manu Dibango are about the only things many people can associate with it.

Much of the year – during the rainy season especially – there are very few travellers (as most people like to call themselves) or tourists (as others call most travellers). In September, for example, in many areas you may only see one tourist a week, if that.

To enjoy it most, accept that life in Cameroon, as in the whole of Africa, runs at a slower pace than most of us are probably used to. Patience is a massive virtue here. Cameroonians do not pay as much attention to time and punctuality as the typical Westerner, as they feel that one need not be enslaved by a clock. So slow down, and you'll take it all in and enjoy it so much more.

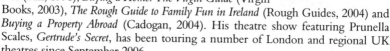

Second edition July 2008   First published 2004

Bradt Travel Guides Ltd, 23 High Street, Chalfont St Peter, Bucks SL9 9QE, England
www.bradtguides.com
Published in the USA by The Globe Pequot Press Inc, 246 Goose Lane,
PO Box 480, Guilford, Connecticut 06475-0480

Text copyright © 2008 Ben West
Maps copyright © 2008 Bradt Travel Guides Ltd
Illustrations © 2008 Individual photographers and artists (see below)

ISBN-13: 978 1 84162 248 4
British Library Cataloguing in Publication Data
A catalogue record for this book is available from the British Library

Photographs Anthony Asael/Art in All of Us (AA), Martin Barlow (MB), Keith Barnes (KB), Richard Bonneville (RB), Christophe Courteau (CC), Rowena Quantrill (RQ), Steven Le Vour'ch (SLV)
Front cover Group of West African giraffes (*Giraffa camelopardalis peralta*) (CC)
Back cover Child in 'Pygmy' camp, Lobé; beach at Kribi (both SLV)
Title page White throated bee-eater (SLV); Traditional houses, Pouss (AA); Ngondo Festival of the Sawa (SLV)

Illustrations Annabel Milne
Maps Terence Crump and Dave Priestley (based on source material from Macmillan Educational (Oxford) Ltd
Typeset from the author's disk by Wakewing
Printed and bound in Italy by L.E.G.O. Spa – Lavis (TN)

Acknowledgements

I would most like to thank my wife, Bryony, for her great patience and tolerance of my obsession with Cameroon. I would also like to thank my children, Josh, Jerusha and Jethro, for stoically managing to listen again and again to my accounts of various African wonders, tropical diseases and sub-Saharan frustrations.

There are a couple of people I would very much like to thank for introducing me to the country in the first place, helping with research and being of great assistance while I was there, but I cannot mention them by name for reasons too complicated to mention here. They know who they are.

I would particularly like to thank J and Geeta Ravikumar. Not only were they so welcoming in Cameroon, but they were remarkably helpful and generous when it was needed. Thank you also to Hester Brown and Arun Muttreja, who introduced me to them.

The excellent contributions by Keith Barnes and Christian Boix concerning birding in Cameroon must of course receive prominent acknowledgement, as also should further information kindly provided by Colin Workman and Andrew Pape-Salmon. Brian Cruickshank's information and suggestions have been very helpful, as have those from David J Dixon and Marta Sabbadini. I am also grateful for helpful suggestions and updates from Jarret Cassaniti, Anne-Marie Legare, Heather Talbot, Dan Barthmaier, Ard Berge, Conal Ho and Robbie Whytock.

Lastly I would like to thank the staff at Bradt Travel Guides for their enduring support for this book.

FEEDBACK REQUEST

The African continent is always in a state of change and some information can obviously become rapidly out of date. Border regulations change, buses re-route, hotels close, prices rise. Asking locally for updates can really make travelling easier and more enjoyable; please help keep this book up to date by sending us your views and any new information. We'd love to hear from you. Please send information and comments to Ben West, c/o Bradt Travel Guides Ltd, 23 High Street, Chalfont St Peter, Bucks SL9 9QE; e ben@benwest.info.

Contents

LIST OF MAPS

Introduction

Cameroon is often described as being 'the melting pot of Africa' or 'Africa in miniature' or 'Africa in microcosm'. This is because it encompasses much from elsewhere on the continent: from every type of African people to every form of landscape. The contrasts are spectacular. In geography (from lush rainforest in the south to the near-desert of the north); in climate (the coastal city of Douala has on average about ten times as much rainfall in July than the nearby capital, Yaoundé); in the peoples (there are over 275 ethnic groups in Cameroon); in language (officially bilingual, and with around 160 African dialects); and religion (a Catholic and Protestant south and Muslim north, with a good dose of traditional African religions thrown in).

Touristically, the country is so attractive it is perplexing that it is so little known or visited. Blending magnificent scenery – from the arid plains in the north to verdant mountains in the south – and impressive national parks with an exceptional richness of culture, a visitor can experience the whole African gamut from 'pygmy' hunting camps deep in the rainforest in the south to Arabic-speaking trading towns in the near desert of the north as well as the colourful ancient tribal kingdoms and striking mountain scenery in the Ring Road region near Bamenda in the western highlands. In this region the town of Foumban has a market, a royal palace and museum to explore.

Cameroon also has many gloriously unspoilt, empty, relaxing beaches. Kribi, a popular resort in the south, has beautiful white beaches, while Limbé, northwest of Douala, has black volcanic ones.

Limbé is also ideal for climbing Mount Cameroon, west Africa's highest peak but still a relatively easy hike, best started from the mountainside town of Buéa.

To the northwest, the country is beautiful, with further volcanic peaks covered by bamboo forest rising to over 2,000m (6,500ft), and with picturesque waterfalls and villages scattered over the lower slopes. This region boasts Korup National Park, which has adequate facilities to allow visitors to explore spectacular rainforest.

Cameroon's two biggest towns, Yaoundé, the capital, and the port of Douala, both boast luxury hotels, a good range of restaurants, as well as nightclubs and vibrant markets.

Cameroon has a large number of lakes including crater lakes created by volcanic activity. The largest include Lake Barombi at Kumba, Lake Baleng near Bafoussam, lakes Tison and Mbalang around Ngaoundéré, the twin lakes of Manenguba as well as lakes Oku, Nyos and Wum in the northwest.

There are also lakes formed from basins such as gigantic Lake Chad and Lake Fiango, and also tectonic lakes, formed by large depressions caused by tectonic movements in the earth's crust. These include Lake Ejagani near Mamfé, Lake Ossa near Edea and Lake Dissoni near Kumba.

In addition, there are lagoons made from the accumulation of sand, on the Wouri and Ndian basins, and artificial lakes at Edea and Songloulou on the Sanaga

River, Lagdo on the Bénoué River, Mape on the Mbam River, Mbakaou on the Djerem and Bamendjin on the Noun.

Highlights for a visitor would also include Waza National Park with its abundance of wildlife, the mountains and pretty villages around laidback Islam-influenced Maroua with its tree-lined streets as well as Mora's colourful Sunday market.

In addition to fabulous beaches, southeast Cameroon is greatly made up of virgin forest that is home to abundant wildlife including lowland gorillas and so-called pygmies. This region has the lowest density of services and lowest-quality roads and therefore is the most challenging to travel through.

SPELLINGS

There is wide variety and inconsistency of spellings in Cameroon and where there is choice those in this book are either the most prevalent or randomly chosen. In some cases French spellings are adopted, in others those that are more easily recognisable to English speakers.

Part One

GENERAL INFORMATION

Location West coast of Africa

Neighbouring countries Nigeria, Chad, Central African Republic, Congo, Gabon, Equatorial Guinea

Size/Area 475,440km^2 (183,639 square miles)

Status Republic

Population 19 million

Life expectancy 54.59 years

Capital (& population) Yaoundé, 1.1 million

Other main towns Douala, Garoua, Maroua, Ngaoundéré, Bamenda

GDP US$580–650

Languages/Official languages English and French

Religion Islam (20%), Christianity (40%), indigenous beliefs (40%)

Currency CFA franc

Exchange rate (June 2008) £1 = 829CFA, US$1 = 425CFA, €1 = 656CFA

National airport Douala

International telephone code +237

Time GMT +1. No daylight saving time.

Electrical voltage 220V

Weights and measures Metric

National flag Tri-coloured, with vertical strips of red, yellow and green, adorned with a star at its heart

National anthem *Chant de Ralliement* (*The Rallying Song*)

Public holidays 1 Jan – New Year's Day; 11 Feb – Youth Day; 1 May – Labour Day; 20 May – National Day; 15 Aug – Assumption Day; 25 Dec – Christmas Day

Background Information

FACTS AND FIGURES

REPUBLIC OF CAMEROON/REPUBLIQUE DU CAMEROUN The country is often referred to as Cameroon, Cameroun, and The Cameroons. *Cameroon* is the English spelling, while *Cameroun* is the French one. *The Cameroons* is an obsolete expression dating from the time when the country was split into separate British and French territories. The name is derived from *camaroes*, the Portuguese word for prawns, which were found in great quantities in the Wouri River by the first European explorers.

LOCATION Situated on the west coast of Africa, running north to south from the Sahara Desert to the Atlantic Ocean, Cameroon is bounded by the Gulf of Guinea, Nigeria, Chad, the Central African Republic, Congo, Gabon and Equatorial Guinea.

Like most African countries, Cameroon was created by Europeans drawing arbitrary lines on a map. These boundaries did not coincide with any pre-existing geographic or cultural divisions.

SIZE Cameroon covers an area totalling 475,440km^2 (183,638 square miles), which is larger than California and about twice the size of the UK. It comprises 469,440km^2 of land and 6,000km^2 of water, and has a coastline of 402km.

ELEVATION EXTREMES Lowest point: Atlantic Ocean 0m; Highest point: Mount Fako (Mount Cameroon) 4,095m.

CAPITAL The capital of Cameroon, and home of the government, is Yaoundé, a city set in a lush region at an altitude of about 750m. Built upon seven hills, it is more relaxed than Cameroon's largest city, the economic and industrial capital, Douala.

POPULATION A 1999 estimate of Cameroon's population settled upon just under 15.5 million with about 50% living in rural areas. According to the UN Department of Economic and Social Affairs in 2007 the estimated figure has risen to just under 19 million – a hefty increase. Migration from rural areas to the cities is increasing all the time.

Yaoundé is estimated to have a population of around 1.2 million, Douala 1.8 million, Garoua 290,000, Maroua over 200,000, Bafoussam 145,000, Bamenda 220,000, Nkongsamba 110,000 and Ngaoundéré approximately 150,000. In ethnicity, the diversity of the population has regularly seen Cameroon dubbed Africa's most socially artificial country.

Nearly a third of the population lives in Littoral and Central provinces, not least because they contain the two largest cities in the country, Yaoundé and Douala.

(2001 estimates)

Infant mortality rate 76.88 deaths per 1,000 live births

Life expectancy at birth Total population 54.59 years; male 53.76 years; female 55.44 years

Fertility rate 4.8 children born per woman

Age structure 0–14 years 42.37%, 15–64 years 54.28%, 65 years and over 3.35%

Population growth rate 2.41%

Birth rate 36.12 births per 1,000 population

Death rate 11.99 deaths per 1,000 population

Adult prevalence rate of HIV/AIDS 7.73% *(1999 estimate)*

About 11,000 Europeans (predominantly French) and 1,200 Americans live in the country, including around 150 Peace Corps volunteers stationed throughout the country. There are also sizeable immigrant populations of Nigerians, Chadians, Congolese and Senegalese.

Each region has distinct societies: from the Muslim traders and pastoralists in the north, to the farmers and craftspeople of the west and the forest peoples of the south.

RELIGION Estimates of the population observing traditional animist African beliefs (the base of most traditional religions in Africa, where there is the belief in and worship of a spirit in all natural things) stand at about 40%, with the remainder made up of around 40% Christian and 20% Muslim. Yet such statistics are misleading as they fail to take into account the overlapping of Christianity with pre-colonial beliefs.

Many Cameroonians are Christian and yet follow traditional beliefs, such as taking part in a traditional dance at a funeral or wedding. Also, the above statistics for Christianity relate mainly to those practising rather than simply professing their religion, a figure far higher than that in the UK.

Particularly strong observance of traditional African beliefs comes from the 'Pygmy' communities of the southern rainforests. They typically believe in a forest spirit, where the forest is seen as a mother, father and guardian. There is also a sizeable community of non-Muslim animists known as Kirdi in the north.

WITCHCRAFT AND SUPERSTITION Traditional beliefs are still very much alive and well throughout many of the more rural parts of Cameroon.

In early 2001, for example, an average of ten people a week were dying in the town of Baba in northwest Cameroon. Although reports in the press attributed the deaths to meningitis, most people in the town believed the cause to be from witches and wizards.

The traditional ruler, Fon Fuekemshi II, decided to suspend all funerals in the town in an attempt to reduce the high death rate. He believed that the disease was being spread when large numbers of people gathered to pay their respects to the dead.

The villagers hired a 'witch-hunter' from a nearby village but he was soon expelled by local officials when local people started refusing to attend hospital on his instructions. One report claimed that people took dead bodies to him to be resurrected after rumours spread that he had made a dead man speak and reveal his killer.

LAND USE

- Arable land: 13%
- Permanent crops: 2%
- Permanent pastures: 4%
- Forests and woodland: 78%
- Other: 3%
- Irrigated land: 210km^2

NATURAL HAZARDS Recent volcanic activity with release of poisonous gases.

PORTS, HARBOURS AND WATERWAYS Cameroon's ports and harbours are Bonaberi, Douala, Garoua, Kribi and Tiko. Cameroon has 2,090km of waterways.

PROVINCES AND DISTRICTS Cameroon is divided into ten administrative provinces (see map overleaf). These are listed below, with both their English and French names and with their capitals in brackets:

- Adamawa/Adamaoua (Ngaoundéré)
- Centre/Centre (Yaoundé)
- East/Est (Bertoua)
- Extreme North/Extrême Nord (Maroua)
- Littoral/Littoral (Douala)
- North/Nord (Garoua)
- Northwest/Nord-Ouest (Bamenda)
- West/Ouest (Bafoussam)
- South/Sud (Ebolowa)
- Southwest/Sud-Ouest (Buéa)

EDUCATION Cameroon does well compared with its neighbours as far as education goes. Compulsory between ages 6–14, attendance is more than 70%, literacy is around 63% and nearly 90% of children receive primary education.

LITERACY Of those aged 15 and over, 63.4% can read and write according to a 1995 estimate.

LEGAL SYSTEM The legal system is based upon the French civil law system, with a common law influence. Traditional courts are still very important in domestic, property and probate law. Tribal laws and customs are recognised in the formal court system when they do not conflict with national law. Traditional kingdoms and organisations also exercise other functions of government, while traditional rulers receive a government allowance.

TIME The time in Cameroon is one hour later than Greenwich Mean Time, therefore when it is noon in Cameroon it is 11.00 in London, 06.00 in New York, noon in Paris and 21.00 in Sydney. Cameroon does not observe daylight saving time.

OPENING TIMES Government offices and banks are generally open from 07.30–15.30 from Monday to Friday and shops and businesses vary from around 08.00–15.00 daily, or 09.00–12.30 and 15.30–19.30, or 08.00–noon and 14.30–17.30. Pharmacies tend to open from 08.00–20.00, markets from approximately 07.00–18.00, and post offices from Monday to Friday 08.00–15.30 and Saturday 08.00–13.00. Restaurant opening hours frequently change so haven't been included in the guide.

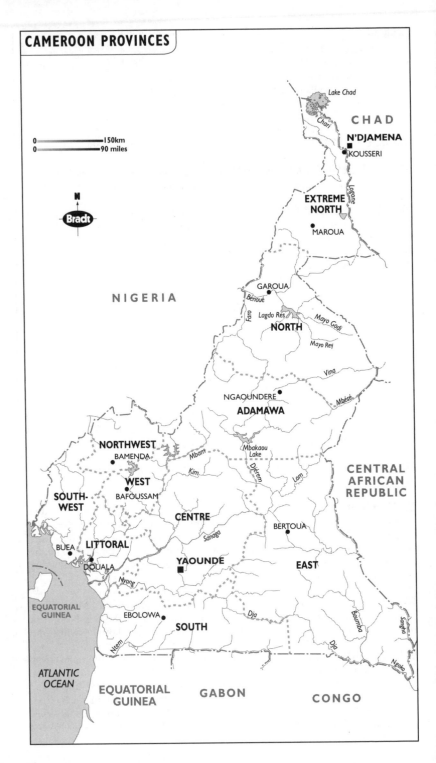

CAMEROON PROVINCES

CURRENCY Cameroon's currency is the Central African economic zone's (Communauté Financière Africaine/the African Financial Community) CFA franc. In this book, £1 = 829CFA, US$1 = 425CFA, €1 = 656CFA based on exchange rates in June 2008.

ELECTRICITY The electricity supply is 220V and plugs are usually of the European two-pin type, although the British three square-pin variety may be occasionally found in anglophone regions.

WEIGHTS AND MEASURES The metric system is used.

GEOGRAPHY

Cameroon has an extremely diverse terrain, but its variety should come as no surprise in a country which encompasses the edges of the Sahara in the north to more than 20 million hectares of dense equatorial rainforest in the south and east, with every African landscape in between including dry grassy plains, volcanic ranges punctuated by crater lakes, rocky mountainous tracts and savanna.

It possesses four distinct, diverse geographical regions. To the west and the northwest are rolling hills and volcanic mountains draped in lush vegetation fed by heavy rainfall; the low coastal plains of the south are blanketed with thick equatorial rainforest extending to the Sanaga River; in central Cameroon, this rainforest yields to the vast, sparsely vegetated Adamaoua Plateau; extending northwards from this plateau to Lake Chad at the most northerly point of the country are the northern plains, where savanna contrasts strikingly with unusual rock formations in the Mandara Mountains.

Much of the south of the country is a low-lying coastal plain dominated by dense rain-fed lowland forest (or rainforest) where trees can grow as high as 50m, their upper branches forming a canopy preventing light from reaching the forest floor. This prevents plants from flourishing in such regions, apart from vines and other epiphytes.

At the centre of the country is a dissected plateau, the Adamaoua, averaging 1,300m above sea level, which does much to separate the north from the south of the country.

As a striking contrast to the rough vegetation of the south, the landscape of north Cameroon is characterised by a semi-arid region dotted with rocky escarpments. The region begins with huge grassy plains of the Adamaoua Plateau, extending further to the north between Maroua and Kousseri into extensive dry flat plains and steppes spotted with patches of grain plants on the border of the Sahel.

About 150 million years ago, when South America pulled away from Africa, the rifting caused volcanic activity in west Africa, notably in the Highlands of Cameroon, which comprise the Rumpi Hills, Mount Kupe and the Bamenda Highlands, and which extend into Nigeria's Obodu Plateau. A series of volcanic mountains lead from Bioko Island (part of Equatorial Guinea) off the coast and which continue as part of a volcanic intrusion that roughly follows the Nigerian border. The mountain chain extends inland as far as the Adamawa Plateau and the wild, unfertile Mandara Mountains in the north of the country. The biggest is the active volcano Mount Cameroon, at 4,095m/13,353ft the highest peak in west Africa and the sixth highest in Africa. There are a number of volcanic crater lakes in this area.

CLIMATE

This part of the world is often assumed to be constantly very hot. A glance at a climate chart would show that this belief is something of a myth.

The climate of Cameroon varies greatly with terrain, from tropical along the coast to semi-arid and hot in the northern plains and the Sahel region with a seven-month dry season.

The great variations in rainfall from one region to the next are astonishing – from hardly enough rain to support agriculture in the Extreme North to over 500cm (200 inches) per annum in the southwest.

Debundscha, near Limbé in the southwest, is the second-wettest region in the world, after Mawsynvan in Maghalaya State, India.

THE SOUTH Generally, the south has a dry season from approximately November to February, light rains from March to May and a rainy season from June to October. Humidity rises greatly in the south in July and August.

Great disruption can be experienced during this time, with roads and tracks washed away and towns including Douala, which is warm and humid all year round, become overrun by floods (not surprising, considering that the average rainfall in July is around 750mm compared with 50mm in January). Mamfé especially can be difficult to reach. The temperature is highest from March to May (around 30°C/86°F in Yaoundé) and stays around a minimum (in the night) of 19°C and a maximum (in the day) of around 28°C in Yaoundé throughout the year, while in Douala the minimum temperature hovers around 23°C, the maximium nearer 28°C.

THE NORTH Northern Cameroon has a long, less dramatic rainy season from around May or June to September (peaking at around 320mm rainfall in August compared with no rainfall from November to March) and although travel is easier than in the south, the national parks are generally closed from May to December. The temperature in Kousseri ranges from a minimum of 14°C or so (in the night) from December to February rising to 23°C upwards from April to June. During the day, a maximum of 33°C is reached from December to February and a blistering 42°C/104°F from March to May.

HISTORY

From as long ago as around 8000BC, Cameroon has received countless human migrations and become home to a very varied range of cultural, tribal, linguistic and cultural groups – such as Puels from the coast of Guinea; Fulani and Arab people from western Sudan; and Bantus from the Congo.

The earliest inhabitants of the country were likely to have been the Bakas and other ethno-linguistic groups of short stature (commonly but strictly incorrectly known as 'Pygmies'), some of whom still inhabit the forests of the South and East provinces. They were forced into the forests by Bantu-speaking peoples originating from the Cameroonian western highlands, the Sahel and Nigerian plateau in around 200BC.

While Bantu peoples settled in the south and east of the country, the north became inhabited by a combination of Arabic and Hamitic peoples, and the indigenous peoples of central and southern Africa.

In the north of the country, around the Chad basin, a series of important African civilisations originated including the Kanem, Bornou and Sao peoples, the Sao having migrated from the Nile Valley. Sao archaeological finds from this period have been recovered including jewellery, terracotta and bronze sculptures, and coins.

At the start of the 15th century the Fulani, a pastoral, nomadic Islamic people, started migrating from the western Sahel and by the end of the 16th century had a strong presence in the north of the country.

Portuguese explorers, led by Fernando Po, arrived on Cameroon's coast in 1472 and became the first Europeans to sail up the estuary of the Wouri River, which Po dubbed the Rio dos Camaroes (River of Prawns) because of the high number of giant shrimps it contained, and which gave the country its name.

The Portuguese set up sugar plantations and began a 400-year slave and goods trade with local chiefs (especially around Douala, Limbé and Bonaberi) which would later also involve the British, Dutch, French and Germans. The chiefs also traded ivory against European goods. Despite Cameroon's new relationship with these countries, there would be no attempt made to colonise the country until the 19th century.

As the coastal region grew in influence it overtook that of powers in the north such as the Bornou Empire, which extended as far as the Adamawa region in the 16th century.

Between the late 1770s and early 1800s, the Fulani conquered much of what is now northern Cameroon, conquering or displacing its largely non-Muslim inhabitants. A slave trade developed here also.

Increasingly during the first half of the 19th century British missionaries established a presence in Cameroon (starting with the Baptist Missionary Society of London's first station in Cameroon at Bimbia in 1844) and protested against the slave trade. American Presbyterians also sent missionaries and the result was not only the Christianisation of the country but the introduction of European culture and education.

Significant European settlement and conquest of the interior then followed, especially from the late 1870s, when supplies of the malaria suppressant, quinine, became plentiful. At this time feudal northern Cameroon was under the control of the Fulani Empire in Sokoto (Nigeria), while in the south trade in slaves switched to so-called legitimate trade, in things like gold and ivory between the coastal chiefs and German, French and British trading companies. In return they received European manufactured items such as cloth, metals, firearms and alcohol.

At this time the whole continent was being transformed by the influx of European powers, known as the 'Scramble for Africa'. In 1880, around 90% of Africa was ruled by Africans. Twenty years later, European powers had seized almost all of the continent.

The chiefs located around Douala became increasingly concerned that tradesmen in the interior of the country would deal directly with the Europeans, side-stepping them, and therefore pressed for British guarantees that would have led to the creation of a protectorate. Queen Victoria delayed doing anything about the issue and when at last she sent an envoy to solve the matter in 1884 Germany had already signed a treaty with Douala and Bamiléké chiefs where they gave over their sovereignty to Germany to receive trade advantages.

Cameroon as a political unit was thus created, replacing numerous states, nationals, chiefdoms and political entities which each had its own history, culture, economy and government.

All of present-day Cameroon and sections of several of its neighbours became the German colony of Kamerun, with a capital at Buéa which later switched to Yaoundé.

From 1885 Baron von Soden, the first governor of the colony, concentrated on putting down rebellions in the interior of the country. The German intention was initially to establish an increased presence inland before British or French officials and traders did so. There were serious conflicts, especially with the Bafut, Bulu and Kpe.

A decade later von Soden's replacement, von Puttkamer, built the country's first railway line using forced labour. German rule brought further infrastructure of practical value like public buildings, roads and other engineering projects. But German rule was harsh: at one plantation a fifth of the labourers died in a single year from overwork. In 1899 German forces attacked the Adamawa region and conquered Tibati. At this time, according to analysis of the available information, the population of Kamerun stood at around 2,650,000, including around 150 European missionaries and 50,000 African Christians.

World War I stopped German expansion. Soon after the war began British, Belgian and French colonial troops, made up principally of Africans, invaded Cameroon and in 1916 forced the Germans to leave.

In 1919 a League of Nations mandate divided the colony between Britain and France with a British administrative zone, which took up 20% of the land, divided into Northern and Southern Cameroons, and a French one taking up the remaining 80%.

France ruled from Yaoundé while Britain's territory, a strip bordering Nigeria from the sea to Lake Chad, was governed from Lagos in Nigeria. In 1922 the League of Nations formally conferred mandates on Britain and France for their respective administrative zones.

In 1946 the French and British mandates were renewed as United Nations trusteeships and on the whole the British territory was still governed from Nigeria. Two groups began to emerge in the British sector, one wanting reunification with French Cameroon, the other wanting to merge with Nigeria.

The exportation of products like cocoa, timber and palm oil increased greatly in the years after the war, but the French imposed taxes and used forced labour to build roads, plantations and other facilities, which caused resentment to build up in the country.

The French territory had increasing calls for reunification and anti-British/French political parties formed and grew in strength, including the Union of Cameroonian Peoples (UPC), based largely among the Bamiléké and Bassa ethnic groups, and French-educated Fulani northerner Ahmadou Ahidjo's Bloc Démocratique Camerounais.

The UPC demanded unification of the two Cameroons and for independence from France. With these demands not met, in 1955, the UPC began an armed struggle for independence in French Cameroon. This rebellion, which caused thousands of deaths and much damage, continued with a weakening intensity, even after independence.

In 1958 Ahidjo formed a new, more conservative party, l'Union Camerounaise, and French Cameroon was granted self-government with Ahidjo made prime minister. French Cameroon achieved independence on 1 January 1960 as the Republic of Cameroon, from UN trusteeship under French administration.

In 1961, following a UN-sponsored referendum, the largely Christian (British) Southern Cameroons joined the Republic of Cameroon to become the Federal Republic of Cameroon, while the largely Muslim Northern Cameroons voted to join Nigeria.

At this time – with a multi-ethnic and multi-religious population impatient for development and change, weary of its chequered colonial past, increasingly disillusioned by a weak economy heavily reliant on a few exports, little industrial production and an undeveloped infrastructure – Cameroon seemed to be a typical African nation ripe for a period of significant political, social and economic problems. Yet, it soon established a stable footing avoiding debt, diversifying its economy, avoiding political instability and working towards producing enough food to feed its nation.

The formerly French and British sectors each continued to maintain substantial autonomy. From 1961–63 there was large-scale unrest, believed to have been orchestrated by the UPC. Ahidjo quelled this with the help of French forces. He then outlawed all political parties but his own in 1966 and successfully suppressed the UPC rebellion, censoring the press, imprisoning thousands of political opponents and capturing the last important rebel leader in 1970.

In 1972, following a national referendum, a new constitution replaced the federation with a unitary state and was renamed the United Republic of Cameroon, to the great consternation of anglophone Cameroon. Economically Cameroon was growing stronger at this time, successfully exploiting its copious natural resources such as coffee, cocoa and oil. Ahidjo resisted borrowing heavily and instead concentrated on developing the agricultural and industrial sectors and investing in health, education and roads. School enrolment reached 70%, the country became self-sufficient in food, and exported a growing range of commodities.

Despite such successes, Ahidjo resigned as president in 1982 and allowed his prime minister Paul Biya, from the Bulu-Beti ethnic group in the south, to succeed him. Yet a year later Ahidjo went into exile after Biya accused him of masterminding a coup against the government. Biya also dismissed the prime minister and several of his cabinet because of this. Biya was elected to his first full term as president and changed the name of the country to the Republic of Cameroon.

In 1984 members of the Presidential Guard, who had originally been appointed by Ahidjo and who remained loyal to him, initiated a revolt in the capital and three days of fighting ensued that may have caused as many as a thousand deaths.

In 1985 Biya announced that there would be no legal opposition to the ruling party, which he renamed the Rassemblement Démocratique du Peuple Camerounais (RDPC).

In 1986 Cameroon was international news when it experienced its worst-ever natural disaster, a discharge of toxic underwater volcanic gases from Lake Nyos, a crater lake in the Northwest Province. More than 2,000 people were killed. Cameroon also received international recognition after the national football team did exceptionally well in the 1990 World Cup.

As the economy remained buoyant when compared with Cameroon's neighbours, elections were held in 1988 giving Biya more than 99% of the vote, helped no doubt by him being the only presidential candidate.

The early 1990s were characterised by episodes of unrest and growing discontent from certain elements of the population. A pro-democracy demonstration with 35,000 participants in Bamenda in 1990 resulted in six deaths and many injured when troops intervened. Anglophone regions increasingly felt neglected by the francophone majority and groups like Amnesty International questioned Cameroon's record on political detentions and torture.

Opposition parties increasingly demanded a multi-party political system but instead their meetings were banned, the independent press and media were restricted and seven out of the ten provinces were put under military rule. It took a five-month strike in 1991 that greatly disrupted the cities and industry for the ban on opposition meetings to be lifted, for political prisoners to be released and for a multi-party presidential election to be set for the next year. The election saw Biya re-elected after he exerted control on the media and instigated other anti-democratic measures. Demonstrations followed, a state of emergency was declared in the west of the country and detainment, torture and deaths of demonstrators, political opponents and journalists brought international attention as a national debt crisis loomed.

Clashes between Cameroon and Nigeria broke out from 1993 over border disputes, chiefly the 'oil-rich' Bakassa Peninsula and hostilities in 1996 led to Cameroon and Nigeria agreeing to UN mediation over the peninsula. The situation eased two years later when both countries exchanged more than 200 prisoners of war. Some observers see the dispute as a political red flag to be waved to direct public attention away from internal problems rather than being caused by economic greed by either country over still unconfirmed oil in the area.

International support for Cameroon slowly grew again and in 1995 it joined the Commonwealth, while maintaining a close relationship with France. In 1997 Biya's party, the Cameroon National Democratic Movement (formerly the National Cameroonian Union) won a majority of seats in parliament amid further allegations of irregularities and Biya was re-elected president despite the election being boycotted by the main opposition parties.

Corruption is still present at all levels of government, even though the continuous presidency by Paul Biya since 1982 has given the country considerable political stability and the country enjoys a functioning relationship with its African neighbours and with the West, most notably with the United States of America.

Indeed, in recent years Cameroon has been classed repeatedly as one of the most corrupt countries in the world by Berlin-based research organisation Transparency International, and in 2006 it rated the country 138th out of 163 countries in its Corruptions Perceptions Index. The Roman Catholic Church in Cameroon denounced corruption in the country in 2000 saying that it had permeated all levels of society. In the 2005 Global Corruption report Cameroon ranked with Iraq, Azerbaijan, Ethiopia and others as being one of the most corrupt countries in the world.

Cameroon remains characterised by state ownership of key industries and corporations, significant government intervention in the economy, relatively high taxes and widespread over-regulation. There have been ongoing problems concerning unpaid public sector salaries, a poor health and education infrastructure and rising violent crime.

However, the economy was boosted in 2000 when the World Bank approved funding for a massive oil and pipeline project stretching from the oilfields of southern Chad through Cameroon to Kribi on the coast despite strong criticism from environmental and human rights activists. Now operational, the pipeline generates an estimated US$500 million annually for the country although precious few new jobs have been created for Cameroonians and the man in the street is unlikely to have seen any benefits of significance as yet.

Concerns for the country's environment remain high and in 2001 Global Forest Watch reported that 80% of the country's indigenous forests have been allocated for logging.

From that year on, tensions grew between Biya's government and separatists lobbying for the country's five million English-speakers in the west. Unrest reached serious levels in 2002, spreading north among Muslim communities. Presidential elections in 2004 swept Biya into power again, and council and parliamentary elections followed in July 2007, with international observers questioning the legitimacy of both. Dissatisfaction remains, peaking in February 2008 with widespread protests throughout the country.

POLITICS

Politically the country is relatively stable by African standards, yet increasing demands for a more democratic system and the restoration of human rights has led to regular discontent including waves of strikes and violence in all sections of the country.

President Paul Biya has been chief of state since 6 November 1982 as head of the Rassemblement Démocratique du Peuple Camerounais (RDPC), which was the only political party until opposition parties were permitted by law in 1990.

The president is elected by popular vote for a seven-year term with the election next due to be held in October 2011. Article 6 of Cameroon's 1996 Constitution states that, 'The President of the Republic shall be elected for a seven year term of office and is eligible for re-election once.' Yet while talking to reporters in Paris in October 2007 after meeting French President, Nicolas Sarkozy, Biya avoided stating whether he would run the 2011 presidential race, suggesting that he was possibly considering using his party's parliamentary overwhelming majority to extend the presidential mandate through a constitutional amendment.

The head of government is Prime Minister Peter Mafany Musonge, who has held the post since 19 September 1996. The cabinet and prime minister are appointed by the president; he appoints and dismisses judges, ratifies treaties, leads the armed forces, and has considerable authority in other areas. The president appoints the governors of Cameroon's ten provinces and his government can re-organise electoral districts in ways that would benefit itself.

The right to vote is from 21 years of age. Now having a multi-party system, recent elections have been dogged by allegations of vote-rigging by Biya's party, which holds the overwhelming majority in the 180-member national assembly. The chief opposition party is the Social Democratic Front (SDF), which is predominantly anglophone.

One dominant ongoing problem the country has endured for many years is the clash between the anglophone and francophone regions. Many in the minority English-speaking population advocate restoration of the decentralised federal structure which consisted of separate anglophone and francophone regions that was in place until unification in 1972. Some anglophone groups advocate secession of the two English-speaking provinces. The government is opposed to both of these proposals.

Other problems include Cameroon's conflict with Nigeria over the Bakassi Peninsula, and opposition to government plans to privatise public enterprises and reduce the number of civil servants. A dysfunctional judicial system also hampers development, as does personal political rivalry between Biya and the leader of Gabon. As Cameroon and Gabon represent more than half of central Africa's population and commerce, the development of positive initiatives like a workable economic community, a viable customs union, a securities exchange and a single market have been held back in this region.

ECONOMY

Compared with most Western industrial nations, which typically have per-capita gross domestic products (GDPs) of at least US$30,000, Cameroon is poor. Yet compared with its neighbours, Cameroon's economy is quite buoyant. According to the International Monetary Fund in 2007, the per-capita GDP (nominal) in Cameroon was estimated at US$1,110, coming in 127th out of 180 countries which, compared with many other African countries like Burundi at US$127 and the Democratic Republic of the Congo at US$161 (the two lowest GDPs on the list), is very good.

Cameroon is helped by its varied natural resources, which include petroleum and timber. There are sizeable but unexploited deposits of iron ore, bauxite, copper, chromium, uranium and other metals.

Agriculture, mainly subsistence and small-scale farming, is the country's principal economic activity, employing about 80% of the population. The main agricultural products are cocoa (of which Cameroon is one of the world's largest producers), robusta and arabica coffee, bananas, cotton, palm oil, wood, tobacco and rubber. Hydro-electricity covers almost all of Cameroon's energy needs so that oil and gas are largely treated as export products.

Yet Cameroon faces many of the serious problems facing other under-developed countries, including a top-heavy civil service and a generally unfavourable climate for business enterprise. International oil and cocoa prices have considerable impact upon the economy. Widespread poverty exists, with about half the population living below the poverty line (according to Purchasing Power Parity, the International Monetary Fund's World Economic Outlook Database of April 2007, 50% of the population are living on less than US$2 a day) and significant social problems persist as does widespread corruption at all levels of society. Unemployment, the infant mortality rate and population growth remain high. According to the United Nations in 2006, 25% of the population is malnourished.

In the 1990s the government opened up much of the economy to competition. France and the Netherlands are the major export markets followed by Germany, the USA and fellow members of the Central African Customs and Economic Union.

From 1990 the government embarked upon IMF and World Bank programmes intended to encourage trade and business investment, improve efficiency in agriculture and recapitalise the nation's banks. Yet coffee and cocoa prices dropped in the early 1990s, while less and less was being manufactured and much was imported.

A major setback occurred in January 1994 when the currency was massively devalued. Overnight it went from CFA100 to CFA50 equalling one French franc. This was the main reason around 20,000 French expatriates living in Cameroon in 1994 reduced to 5,000 in 1995.

The year 1997 saw the initiation of a government, IMF and World Bank economic reform programme aimed to reduce government control over the economy and stimulate more private-sector investment and growth. In 1997, 1998 and 1999, the country's economy grew at a 4–5% annual rate, while the government reduced its spending.

Low world prices for cocoa and coffee in 1999 again threatened the economy, while banana exporters faced increased competition from Latin American producers.

Banks that had become insolvent following the devaluation crisis by the end of the decade had been closed and the government privatised all state-owned banks. Today, Cameroon has nine banks, the majority owned by foreign banking companies. The government has also been privatising large state-owned companies such as utilities and those in the food sector.

WORK The minimum wage is currently CFA23,514 per month (approximately £25/US$44). To give an idea of typical wages, domestic staff working for an expatriate would expect to earn between CFA27,000–81,000 (£28–86/US$50–150) per month depending upon qualifications, duties and hours worked. A 54-hour week with one day off is the official workweek in Cameroon. The minimum age for the employment of children is 14.

The law prohibits forced or compulsory labour, yet it occurs in practice. For example, prison inmates can be contracted out to private employers or used as communal labour for municipal projects. In rural regions it is not uncommon for children to work from an early age on family farms and relatives often employ rural youth, especially girls, as domestic helpers. Many urban street vendors in the country are less than 14 years of age. Cameroon has also been known in the past to be a source, destination and transit point for trafficked children.

Cameroon is very diverse culturally, and contains more than 275 ethno-linguistic groups. The ethnic distinctions include the Bantoid-speaking inhabitants of the kingdoms of the western highlands, the hunting and gathering 'Pygmies' of the southern forests, and the Muslim sultanates and non-Muslim people of the north.

According to the US Department of State in 1999, the population is made up of Cameroon Western Highlanders (including Bamiléké and Bamoun) 31%; Equatorial Bantu 19%; Kirdi 11%; Fulani 10%; Northwestern Bantu 8%; Eastern Nigritic 7%; other African 13%; non-African less than 1%.

The population can roughly be separated into groups occupying the south, west and north.

PEOPLES OF THE SOUTH

The 'Pygmies' The first settlers in Cameroon were the so-called 'Pygmies', who have one of the oldest cultures on earth. They have long fascinated Western academics and theologians because so many of their legends correspond with Old Testament stories. Their complex pattern of nomadic life, established over thousands of years, is threatened more than ever by outside influences like politics and commerce and those that remain increasingly live sedentary lives.

The incorrect term 'Pygmy' has long been used to identify such people of short stature living in central African rainforests. These people would never call themselves pygmies as they believe the word is based on roots that show a great ignorance and misunderstanding of them. It could imply that there is something wrong or laughable about their size. These people instead see themselves as members of their own very distinct ethnic groups.

In Cameroon they are predominantly from the Baka ethnic grouping and to a lesser extent the BaAka, BaKola, Bagyeli, Bofi, and Medzan, living in the dense forests of the south and southeast. Bantu farmers commonly associate closely with them. They still practise their traditional hunting and gathering way of life, trading resources of the forest with neighbouring farming villages for cultivated foods and other goods. This can be a fair exchange but is increasingly less so as the forest peoples lose more and more control of the forest and its resources.

Being forest dwellers, they know the forest, its plants and animals intimately. They live by hunting animals such as pigs, antelopes and monkeys as well as fishing and gathering yams, berries and other edible plants. They see the forest as a generous god who provides for all their needs.

According to Survival International, there are now about 250,000 of these forest peoples living in central Africa (ie: the Democratic Republic of Congo, Republic of Congo, Cameroon, Gabon, Central African Republic, Rwanda, Burundi and Uganda) today.

The southeastern rainforests of Cameroon where many of these people live are pretty impenetrable and you need copious time and determination to meet them there. But if you visit Kribi, where the beach leads directly into rainforest, there is a good chance of meeting some, who may be found hollowing out a canoe by the shore or scaling the trees for avocados. Many are very obliging, and may be happy to exchange a few coconuts, vegetables and fruits for a packet of cigarettes.

Conservation organisations such as the World Wide Fund for Nature (WWF) encourage the needs of these forest people being met. For example, in the Lobéké National Park, Bakas were recently granted access to some forest areas so that they could participate in shrimp fishing, harvesting and gathering of mangoes, honey and other non-timber forest products.

The Baka are largely nomadic, often moving from one area to another. Their traditional festivity to celebrate their forest spirit, Jengi, and enshrine young men into their secret society is still widely honoured. Jengi celebrations used to usually involve the killing of an elephant, but this is no longer the case.

In the summer of 2002 disturbing memories of Belgium's imperfect colonial past were reawakened by an exhibition at a private zoo in Yvoir in southern Belgium in which eight 'pygmies' from Cameroon performed for tourists: the 'pygmies' sang and danced in a mock-up of a pygmy village, which critics dismissed as a racist, neo-colonial, discriminatory, money-making scheme no different from those held in 19th-century Belgium and France where Africans went on show like animals in a zoo.

Bantu-speaking groups The Bantu-speaking groups generally spread from the Adamawa range to settle along the northwest coastal region, such as the Bassa, Douala, Bakweri, Batanga, Malimba, Mbos and Bakoko from the 15th century onwards, to be followed in the 19th century by the Ewondo, Bulu, Yezum, Ntumu, Fang, Eton and others, who settled around Yaoundé and the equatorial region.

PEOPLES OF THE WEST A semi-Bantu population became established from the 16th century onwards in the west of the country, including the Tikar and the Bamoun who both are now settled in the chiefdoms of the Grassfields and who now dominate in the northwest, and the Bamiléké, a mixture of peoples from all directions and now the country's biggest and most economically dominant ethnic group.

The Tikar This is a British designation encompassing a number of ethnic groups. Having largely migrated from Nigeria, they generally occupy the Mbam and Bamenda regions.

The Bamoun Famous for their royal dynasty, which goes back to 1394, this ethnic group are centred around Foumban and known for their wood carvings and other artwork.

The Bamiléké Population density is greatest in the south and southwest of the country and most widespread in this region are the Bamiléké. They are spread around Yaoundé and Bafoussam, and Douala especially. In their rural homelands in the southwest, they have around 75 political units governed by *chefferies* (chiefs) and secret societies within these organisations keep their many traditional rituals alive. The Bamiléké retain the skulls of their dead ancestors in order to continue to pay homage to their spirits. Known for being good farmers, their traditional homes are made from a variety of local materials, including sun-baked soil bricks.

PEOPLES OF THE NORTH

The Fulani The Fulani (or Fula, Foulbé or Peul) tend to be tall, thin and lightly built people with aquiline noses, oval faces and a light complexion. Dominant in the north and northwest, they are an Islamic population that have been settling across the savanna of west Africa for centuries but who first arrived in Cameroon in the 19th century. Originally nomadic (*bororo* or *wodaabe*) cattle herders, many are now settled farmers and merchants. Those that remain cattle herders see cattle as central to their lives, and the health of their cattle is often seen as a bigger priority than their own.

The nomadic Fulani have an initiation ceremony involving boys being lashed with sticks, which scars them, against a backdrop of drumming.

Their homes differ: in the Mandara Mountains in the northwest they live in hamlets of thatched huts, while around Pouss, in the northeast, their huts are made completely from dried mud.

The Kirdi Even further north, in the Mandara Mountains of the northwest, can be found Kirdi (the word comes from 'pagan' from the Fulani), known as 'mountain peoples'. They are made up of Chadic- and Adamawa-speaking peoples such as the Fali, Kapsiki, Mafa, Massa, Mousgoum, Mofou, Matakam, Toupouris, Guidar, Bata, Fata and Podoko, whose main occupation is farming. Looked at from afar, their cliffside villages around the Mora, Mokolo, Tourou and Mabas regions have almost a hobbit-like appearance, with their round homes with pointed roofs, which are covered with grass.

The Kirdi are non-Muslim peoples, instead retaining their traditional religious beliefs. They were originally driven by the Fulani into the inhospitable and isolated rocky areas near the Nigerian border. Life expectancy for them is generally under 30 years.

The Choa Even further north, around Lake Chad, are the semi-nomadic Choa, of Arabic origin. The Choa arrived in Cameroon around 300 years ago from Sudan.

The Kotoko Also living in the Lake Chad region, and relying on subsistence farming and fishing, the Kotoko are descendants of the Sao peoples, one of the earliest cultures to populate Cameroon.

LANGUAGE

Cameroon's official languages are English and French. Arabic is also widely spoken, in the north. French is by far the most prevalent, with English spoken by around 20% of the population. The staffs of the major hotels and restaurants are predominantly bilingual. Spanish is also very occasionally spoken.

West Africa is the most linguistically intricate region in the world and Cameroon alone has more than 275 African languages and dialects still spoken, including Fulfulde (the language of the Fulani), Douala (language of the Douala people) and Ewondo (the dialect of a Beti clan near Yaoundé). Broadly speaking, the south of the country speaks semi-Bantu, Ewondo and Fang, while the north speaks Adamwala, Fulani and Chadic. Other African languages commonly spoken are Bamiléké, Bamoun and Arabic.

Around 10% of the country relies upon pidgin English, spread across about half the provinces of the country, but primarily in the west, near Nigeria.

If you log onto www.ethnologue.com it has details (including region, alternative language names and classification) of 279 living languages, three second languages without mother-tongue speakers and four extinct languages in the country.

THE EAST–WEST LINGUISTIC DIVISION Superimposed upon the north–south divisions of the country – the large geographical and climatical differences as well as the religious ones (a largely Muslim north and Christian south) – is an east–west division resulting from European colonialism.

After World War I the westernmost region of Cameroon became controlled by the British, while the larger central and eastern portion was under the rule of the French. Consequently, Cameroonians are divided linguistically into English- and French-speakers with francophones dominating both because they are a numerical majority and because the most important centres, Douala and Yaoundé, are French-speaking.

TRADITIONAL FESTIVALS Annual festivals provide an occasion for carnivals and colourful dances. In much of the country, there are ceremonies and feasting because of births, deaths, sowing the seeds and harvesting as well as the commemoration of ancestors. Many of these festivities feature vibrant musical ceremonies.

They include the **Ngondo** Festival of the Sawa, the coastal dwellers of Cameroon from Limbé to Kribi, with the Wouri River being the focal point of the festival in Douala. The ritual and feast, held in the first week of each December, celebrates the unity of the Sawa peoples and their ancestors, who are believed to live in the waters. The festival, beginning on the banks of the river Wouri, features traditional dances, choral music, handicraft exhibitions, a canoe parade and race, a carnival, and the collection of the ancestors' message by a diver, from the bottom of the river, contained in a calabash.

Originally organised to resolve land disputes, the **Ngouon** Festival of the Bamouns takes place once every two years in Foumban and features horse parades.

The **Nyem-Nyem** annual festival in the Adamaoua, centred around Ngaoundéré, traces back the heroic resistance of the people against German penetration into their land. Each January traditional festivities are held around caves on the top of Mount Djim, about halfway between Tignere and Tibati, near Galim, about 65km from Tignere.

The **Medumba Festival** in Bangangte is held every two years, usually in July, to promote both the Medumba language and the artworks of the 13 villages in the locality.

MARRIAGE The current marriage rate for 15–19-year-old girls in Cameroon is 41%, which compares with 72% in Mali and 26% in Ivory Coast.

Especially in more rural areas, a young girl often does not have a say in whether, when and whom she will marry. Instead, both sets of parents make such decisions. The girl may be subordinate in important decisions, such as when to have children and how many to have.

A dowry of some kind is usually very important. When a couple get married in villages in northwest Cameroon, for example, the bridegroom is expected to present bushmeat to his in-laws as part of his dowry. In Batibo, for example, where the bulk of Cameroon's palm wine is produced, suitors wishing to marry a girl from the region must provide a mandatory 10 litres of palm wine. The bride shares this with the groom to demonstrate that they will share everything as married partners. Her suitor is required to give his future in-laws other goods, such as beer, salt and oil.

ARTS AND CRAFTS The arts and crafts of Cameroon reflect the great ethnic diversity of its peoples. Ancestral traditions form the basis for most art forms, with wood sculpture prominent. Each ethnic group typically translates wooden decorative panels, furniture and doors into a multitude of expressions in wood.

Some crafts, such as weaving baskets, embroidering cloth, batik works, the painting and carving of calabashes and bas-relief sculpture, show the presence of art in the daily lives of Cameroonians.

The peoples of the western highlands are known for their bronzework, brasswork and wooden sculptures embroidered with glass beads. The regions around Bafoussam, Foumban and Bamenda in the west are renowned for their masks, embroidered costumes, miniature figures, thrones, pipes and statues made from earthenware, bronze or wood.

Because of the high quality of the clay in the region, villages near Bamenda, such as Bali, and around Foumban have a rich tradition of producing ceramics. Masks (usually depicting animals) and wood carvings are also in abundance here.

Detailed figurative artworks and distinctive, long tobacco pipes made from brass and bronze are also to be seen in Tikar areas north and east of Foumban.

Bamum beadwork is renowned. Cowrie shells (*mbuum*) were traditionally used as money and today *mbuum* remains the Bamum word for money. When the Bamum Kingdom enlarged at the beginning of the 19th century, beads were very rare and small glass beads were brought from Nigeria and the coast. The Bamum started a tradition of producing royal costumes decorated with beads.

In the northern provinces cloth weaving, leather goods and decorative brasswork are prevalent. Fulani women wear large copol amber beads, which are opalescent rather than transparent. Such beads are increasingly rare and are highly valuable.

Maroua and nearby villages in the north are known for their colourful markets where embroidered tablecloths, bracelets, swords, mats and other decorative objects are available.

DANCE The huge number of ethnic groups in Cameroon provide more than 200 distinctive dances. Local festivals and public holidays offer an excellent opportunity to experience Cameroon's lively dance traditions.

In the south, there are 'Bafia' or 'Bikutsi' ballets and other dances led by the *mvet* (or zither) player, a bard and epic poet. In the west, Bamiléké dancers wearing picturesque costumes display striking masks.

In 2000 an overtly sexual dance from neighbouring Ivory Coast, *mapouka*, performed either naked or with few clothes in public places, was banned in southwest Cameroon, on the grounds that it was causing public immorality. The dance features a woman bending almost double while a man supports her waist from behind.

TRADITIONAL AND FOLK MUSIC The large number of ethnic groups in Cameroon provide a huge variety of musical types. Local festivals and public holidays offer a good opportunity to experience Cameroon's lively music traditions.

In the north of the country, the Toupouri people perform the *gourna*, where dancers form a circle and carry long sticks vertically. The Bamiléké perform war dances including the *lali*, protecting the village against invaders, and the *tso*, where the dancers wear panther skins. The *motio* dance, in the southwest, features the slaughtering of a goat in one blow of a blade, to signify the bravery and strength of the men.

The folk music of the south of the country is particularly varied, with mainly drum- and xylophone-based compositions of the Bakweri, Bamoun, Beti and Bamiléké, often performed by accompanying masked dancers.

The rare bird, Bannerman's turaco, is important to the culture of the Kom people, from the highlands of the northwest. They use its feathers to decorate their traditional costumes, called *chindohs*. The turaco's song is mimicked using a *njang*, which is similar to a xylophone. When there is a death in the village, *njang* music is played for three days continuously.

A greater variety of instruments is played in the south by the Fang, Eton, Bulu and Mvele, including a small xylophone called the *mendzan*, zithers, lutes and the *ngkul*, a traditional drum.

Traditional music of the Baka peoples ('Pygmies') of the rainforest typically consists of instrumentally simple music made from drums, rattles and chants that can be divided into either long, percussive dirges or earthy, polyphonic a cappella chants.

An audio CD that is available showcasing the music of the Baka is *The Baka Forest People: Heart Of The Forest* (Hannibal, 2002) performed by Baka Pygmies in the rainforests of Cameroon.

Other musical styles Cameroon's most well-known musician by far has to be saxophonist, pianist and singer **Manu Dibango**, who has done much to promote the infectious, slick *makossa* dance rhythm of Cameroon and who can be considered an African international superstar. *Makossa* evolved from the 1930s and originated from the Douala region. Fusing soul and high-life, it was influenced by Congo dance music and today makes great use of the electric guitar. You are likely to often hear *makossa* blaring out of clubs and discos.

Born Emmanuel Dibango N'Djocke in 1933 in Douala, Dibango's father was of the Yabassi people, his mother of the Douala. Dibango has always felt that he is a divided man, being born of two antagonistic ethnic groups.

His training and career began when he was just 15, when his parents sent him to Paris. Here he met **Francis Bebey** (who died in 2001), another African expatriate and another of Cameroon's most successful musicians, who played a wide range of instruments and styles including traditional Cameroonian music, jazz, pop, classical guitar and *makossa*. *Nandolo/With Love – Works 1963–1994* (Original Music) is one of over 20 of his very varied albums.

Both Dibango and Bebey explored the Calais jazz scene together and started a band, learning how to play the instruments as they went along. Bebey explained 12-bar blues to Manu, who studied classical piano before taking up the saxophone in 1954.

Dibango's albums include *Afrijazzy* and *Mboa'Su*, while his album *Wakafrika* features a Nigerian juju guitarist (King Sunny Ade) and Dibango's jazzy saxophone performing a tune by Benin composer Wally Badarou.

Makossa was further popularised by **Moni Bile** in the 1980s, whose albums include *10th Anniversary: Best of Moni Bile* (Sonodisc, France).

The mid-1980s also saw the emergence of **Sam Fan Thomas**, who has enjoyed considerable success with a lighter form of *makossa*, *makassi*, giving the sound an even more commercial bent. Albums include *The Best of San Fan Thomas* (TJR, France) and *African Typic Collection* (Virgin Earthworks).

Petit-Pays became Cameroon's most popular *makossa* band, taking off in the late 1980s, since when they have had several big hits. Albums consist of dance music influenced by *makossa*, *sokous*, the more slow and sensual *zouk* and sometimes a little touch of salsa.

Bikutsi, the war music of the Beti people, is another popular dance music, and which is typically sung in Ewonde. In the late 1980s a group called **Les Têtes Brûlées** briefly enjoyed international attention with their quick-rhythmed *Bikutsi* music style.

Henri Dikongue's recording, *C'est La Vie*, integrates Afro-Parisian, Latin, Caribbean and other styles.

Les Nubians are French/Cameroonioan sisters Helene and Celia Faussart. Their album *Princesses Nubiennes* (1999) is a mix of hip hop, r&b and soul mixed with the rhythms of Africa.

Cameroonian artiste **Wes** has recorded *Welenga*, which combines traditional instruments, synthesizers and rock guitars into a style that touches both the Western pop charts and the Bantou villages of his upbringing.

CINEMA One of Cameroon's earliest film-makers was **Jean-Paul Ngassa**, noted for his *Aventures en France* (1962) and *La Grand Case Bamilékée* (1965).

Producer and director **Daniel Kamwa** later found success with a prize-winning short film, *Boubou Cravatte* (1972), which he followed with a very successful *Pousse Pousse* (1977), dealing with the clash between tradition and modern city living, and then *Notre Fille* (1980).

One of Cameroon's most widely recognised cinematographers is **Jean Pierre Dikongue-Pipa**, who produced *Muno Moto* (1975), *Prix de la Liberté* (1978) and *Badiaga* (1983).

Another emerging talent at that time was **Arthur Si Batar**, whose debut feature, *Les Cooperants* (1978), focused on the common theme of city and village life.

One of musician Francis Bebey's novels, *Les Trois Petits Cireurs* was successfully made into a film by **Louis Balthazar Amadangoleda** in 1985.

Claire Denis's film, *Chocolat* (1988), was an international success and is about a young white girl (pointedly named France) growing up in the Cameroons and learning the ways of colonialism. Scenes were filmed at Limbé.

Jean-Marie Teno examines political regimes since independence in his documentary, *Afrique, Je te Plummerai* (1992) and his feature film, *Clando* (1996).

Quartier Mozart (1992), directed by **Jean-Pierre Bekolo**, is a lively, modern film dealing with a girl given magical powers that allow her to transform into a male.

Sisters in Law (2005) is an excellent FilmFour documentary that gives a real insight into the legal system in Cameroon. It follows the state counsel and court president of Kumba in southwest Cameroon as they deal with some shocking cases, for example, abused and raped children and a wife trying to divorce her violent husband. Both officials are women, and indeed around 37% of the Cameroonian judiciary are women, a healthy figure that puts many 'first world' countries to shame. When I saw this film at the London Film Festival the audience was primarily a mix of Londoners and Cameroonians. It was strange to see the different cultures laughing in completely different places in the film, demonstrating a real difference in the perception of the world. Yet the crimes the two wise, effective judges came up against were universal.

FOOTBALL For many people, the word 'Cameroon' conjures up football. Cameroon enjoyed feverish, instant worldwide attention when they defeated World Cup holders Argentina in the first game of the 1990 World Cup finals tournament. Despite this, they were knocked out of the competition in the quarter-finals when they lost 3–2 to England after extra time.

Cameroon has also done remarkably well in the African Cup of Nations. The country won the cup in 1984, 1998, 2000 and 2002, a record only shared with Ghana and Egypt.

Roger Milla, born on 20 May 1952, is undoubtedly Cameroon's most famous player, known and loved the world over. His achievements are astounding. Representing Cameroon internationally from 1972 to 1994, he won the accolade of being African Footballer of the Year both in 1976 and 1990. He is the oldest player to appear in a World Cup finals tournament, as well as being the oldest ever to score a goal, which happened when he was aged 42, during a game against Russia in the 1994 World Cup.

2

Natural History

Because of its outstanding geographical and climatic features, Cameroon has some of Africa's richest and most varied fauna and flora with more than a thousand species of tree alone. Not only does the country offer some of the best wildlife reserves in west Africa, but there are plenty of opportunities to view birds and mammals in all of Africa's natural habitats including desert, swamp, woodland, rainforest and savanna.

Forested regions are home to colourful spiders, ants and termites, and large centipedes and millipedes. Many types of butterfly are prevalent, especially in lowland forest areas.

RESERVES, NATIONAL PARKS AND CONSERVATION AREAS

Hunting, overgrazing, deforestation and human population pressure means that in many areas Cameroon's reserves are the best bet by far for seeing the biggest range of wildlife. Even then, the animals can be secretive and solitary, and in the rainforest areas lack of infrastructure for visitors and the dense vegetation can make viewing difficult. A great variety of birds, on the other hand, are widespread.

The game parks of northern Cameroon may not have the diversity and density of animals found in East and southern Africa but can nevertheless guarantee some spectacular wildlife.

Waza National Park, in the far north of the country wedged between the borders of Chad and Nigeria, is Cameroon's most visited national park, not only because it is most geared to visitors both in infrastructure and facilities like accommodation, guides and transport, but because it contains some of west and central Africa's most impressive wildlife. Its forest and huge expanse of grassy and wet plains contain a good variety of wildlife including lion, hippopotamus, monkey, giraffe, buffalo, herds of elephant and a wide variety of birdlife.

Korup National Park, in the southwest of the country and bordering Nigeria, is the most accessible of the country's protected tropical rainforest areas. Scientists estimate that it is more than 60 million years old. It contains an exceptional variety of flora and fauna. Although reasonably geared to visitors, access to the park can be difficult in the rainy season.

To the north of Korup National Park, and in reality a continuation of Korup, is the **Ejagham Forest Reserve**. Around both Korup and Ejagham are spread the sizeable **Banyang Mbo Wildlife Sanctuary** near Nguti, as well as three more forest reserves, the **Mawne River**, **Nta-ali** and **Rumpi Hills**, the last's terrain peaking with the 1,769m Mount Rata.

Three parks lie in a row roughly between Garoua and Ngaoundéré – **Faro Reserve**, **Bénoué** and **Bouba Ndjida national parks**. A combination of hunting and poaching in this region mean that Waza, further north, is a better bet for observing wildlife, although Faro's forested savanna, hills and mountains, the

Guinea woodlands of Bénoué and Bouba Ndjida, on the banks of the Mayo Lidi River all have a good range of animals to search out.

Kalamaloué National Reserve, by Chad just outside Kousseri at Maltam in the extreme north, is small yet offers opportunities for viewing wildlife including antelope, giraffe, monkey and warthog, and some elephants cross the reserve.

Bafut-Nguemba Forest Reserve is easily reached from Bamenda but unfortunately has been substantially destroyed. Despite that, it is rich in birdlife.

The remote **Dja Reserve** southeast of Yaoundé, is difficult to get to and has virtually no facilities. Declared a World Heritage Site by UNESCO for its outstanding natural significance, it shelters many hundreds of species of plant, bird, mammal and other wildlife. Dja is one of the few remaining gorilla sanctuaries in the world and is also home to significant numbers of 'Pygmies' and other traditional forest dwellers.

Between Douala and Kribi is the **Douala-Edea Reserve**, bordered on its northern edge by the Sanaga River and on its western edge by the Atlantic Ocean. It features a wide variety of fauna, flora and habitats.

Campo-Ma'an National Park, bordering Equatorial Guinea and the coast near Kribi, is a virtually unmanaged patch of rainforest and has few facilities for visitors although there is basic accommodation and guides are available.

Nki and **Boumba Bek forest reserves** and **Lobéké National Park** in the southeastern corner of Cameroon lie within the thick and extensive Congo Basin rainforest. Reaching them involves a lot of time, planning, persistence and patience and the wildlife can be very difficult to see because of the dense vegetation. Although rich in wildlife and home to a significant 'Pygmy' population, this region has suffered considerably from logging and poaching, notably within Lobéké (the most accessible of the three) and to some extent Boumba Bek. Much of Nki, on the other hand, remains unexplored and is devoid of human habitation.

Cameroon is scattered with further small reserves, notably the **De Bafia Reserve** near the beaches of Sanaga and town of Monatélé, north of Yaoundé; the 1,700ha **Mozogo-Goko Reserve** north of Maroua; the **Kalfou Reserve**, east of Maroua; as well as the very sizeable **Pangare Djerem Reserve** (also called the Mbam and Djerem National Park), southeast of Tibati. But unless you have a particular or specialist interest in wildlife or are spending a great deal of time in the country, those most easily accessible, best geared to visitors and with the most and easily seen animals should be focused upon, such as the very contrasting Waza and Korup.

CONSERVATION OF THE NATURAL WORLD

Conservation of the natural world, especially in Africa, remains more urgent than ever before. For example, in 2003 only 23,000 lions remained in Africa compared with 230,000 twenty years before, and many of these that have survived harbour feline Aids and bovine tuberculosis. According to wildlife experts, this means that the lion is frighteningly close to extinction. When you add the unprecedented variety of other flora and fauna that are fast depleting and disappearing, it paints a particularly sad picture for the natural world.

DEFORESTATION The greatest threat to biodiversity in Cameroon comes from deforestation. According to the World Resources Institute, more than 80% of the earth's natural forests has already been destroyed, and as much as 90% of west Africa's coastal rainforests has disappeared since 1900.

As well as the loss of wildlife habitats – 70% of the earth's land animals and plants live in forests – rainforest helps generate rainfall in drought-prone countries elsewhere. Studies have found that destruction of rainforests in Cameroon may have caused droughts in the interior of Africa. This is in addition to the catastrophic global effects, such as the increase in global warming.

Logging has led to vast areas of the forest being cleared through unsustainable methods, and timber exploitation in the country tripled in the early 1990s, triggered somewhat by devaluation of the local currency, the CFA franc. Currency devaluations effectively halved the cost of hauling 800-year-old trees through the hundreds of miles of forest to the parquet-flooring and furniture-making markets of Europe and Japan.

Also, logging was boosted by a sharp fall in prices of agricultural products such as cocoa and coffee that beforehand were a big part of the national economy. In Cameroon, wood production soared 50% between 1992 and 1997, the last years for which figures are available. It is little surprise when logging currently creates a US$60-million-a-year revenue for the Cameroonian government.

The wood is exported mainly to Europe and almost all is known to have been felled illegally, with little or no monitoring of the logging industry. The scale of destruction in the Congo Basin, for example, is now thought to be so serious and rapid that up to 20% of the forest could be lost within 15 years, with potential implications for climate control, flooding, and loss of plant species.

A recent report by Global Witness, an official monitor of the Cameroon government, found that almost all companies working in the country had been acting illegally. Some were working in protected areas, others were falsely declaring how much timber they were taking and bribing officials.

Logging is mainly done by international companies (presently more than 15 European-owned logging companies operate in southeast Cameroon alone, with around a third being multi-national conglomerations), which provides few benefits to local people, and currently is practised in an ecologically unsustainable manner. The logging roads facilitate access to sensitive areas by poachers. Illegal logging has caused great damage as thousands of protected tree species are cut down. Logging (along with mining) also threatens the way of life of the so-called 'Pygmy' peoples of the forest like the Baka and the Kola.

In a survey conducted in 1993, nearly 70% of respondents from Lobéké in southeastern Cameroon considered that the timber companies had an overwhelmingly negative impact on the forest and its people, despite some short-term economic benefit. The most critical problem is the easy access to forested areas: as timber companies open new roads in search of exploitable trees, vast tracts of previously unreachable forest become accessible.

There are encouraging signs though. In 2002, for example, the US, France, Germany, Japan and the EC working with the World Bank, international conservation groups and giant logging companies pledged to invest up to US$100m into trying to save the forests of the Congo Basin.

POACHING AND HUNTING Poaching is another great threat to biodiversity in Cameroon. Bushmeat is the main source of protein for many impoverished villagers in Cameroon's forests, as well as a delicacy for rich city dwellers. Hunting is further promoted because it is also financially attractive: hunters can easily earn CFA600,000/£680/US$1,335 a year, much more than most Cameroonians. A collapse of cash crops like coffee and cocoa in recent years also made sales of bushmeat of increasing importance to local people.

Experts increasingly believe that numerous animals might be exterminated within a decade if bushmeat hunting is not stopped. Though habitat loss is often seen as the main cause of wildlife extinction, commercial bushmeat hunting has become the most immediate threat.

Though the selling of bushmeat is illegal, it is widely on sale. At a central Yaoundé market, for example, without much difficulty you could find fresh snake, monkey, pangolin and lizard, even elephant and gorilla. Endangered gorillas can currently reach around US$100 on the wild-meat market while chimpanzee is worth almost as much. There are only about 125,000 common chimpanzees left in central Africa's rainforests, and thousands are shot every year.

At the same time elephant hunting for ivory trade has hit an all-time high as tonnes of ivory have been shipped out by expatriate workers. Many opportunists have also turned to poaching after being encouraged by rumours of rich mineral deposits in the southeastern rainforests.

Even the smallest small-scale farmer can think killing predators like lion or leopard is of personal benefit, even though more and more species are reaching the brink of extinction. A study in the Laikipia region of Kenya in 2003 found that on average a lion attacks livestock worth £200 a year, equivalent to one cow or three sheep. With better husbandry, a night guard or strong fencing and gates, losses can plummet, but using poison and bullets is always a cheaper option.

Poaching remains a considerable threat to animal species populations in the reserves. Some of the hunting is done for subsistence by local inhabitants, some to provide meat for timber company employees, but widescale commercialised hunting is carried out mostly by outsiders to cash in on the booming bushmeat trade. The indigenous population has noted a decline in the densities of animals suitable for bushmeat, necessitating longer forays into the forest for their traditional subsistence activities.

Bushmeat markets thrive in many rainforest regions, especially in the logging towns. Animals are also taken to feed the exotic animals trade, gorillas, chimpanzees and parrots, for example. It is no surprise there is such a trade considering that African grey parrots commonly sell for £500 to £1,000 abroad, and other types sell for as much as £3,000. Exotic skins and other trophy items (bongo and leopard, for instance) are also in demand.

The savannas of the north have also not escaped the effect of hunting. At one time this region supported a large and diverse ungulate community, but almost a century of habitat loss and uncontrolled over-hunting with modern firearms and vehicles has decimated animal populations.

Much bushmeat hunting is carried out by use of wire snares, especially for forest antelopes; .458 calibre guns are used for big-game hunting of elephants. Also, several European-based safari companies operate in the forests, usually from December to June, catering to wealthy foreign clients interested in hunting trophy animals. Some of these companies have been operating in Cameroon for more than 20 years, although their legal status is questionable. They receive government permission to hunt, but have no clearly defined concessions.

Local people are typically upset with the hunting companies, which have apparently never consulted with local chiefs or the population in general. Some are even known to intimidate local residents by burning their hunting camps and possessions, and have even directly threatened to shoot people found in the forest. There are also instances where professional hunters take many more animals than they officially report, often burying those not considered trophy specimens.

'Pygmies' still use traditional hunting techniques such as the use of poisoned arrows, especially for primate hunting, but recent increased instability in neighbouring countries has led to a wide circulation of firearms and ammunition and an increasing number of Bakas being used by local big-game hunters.

Fortunately, there are some encouraging signs. In 2003 Nigeria and Cameroon announced plans to create a cross-border park to protect rare birds and a type of endangered chimpanzee threatened by the bushmeat trade. The park would

Keith Barnes

IMPORTANT BIRD AREAS (IBAS) – CONSERVING CAMEROON'S BIRDING HOTSPOTS

The IBA programme aims to identify and protect a network of sites throughout the world that are critical for naturally occurring bird populations.

WHAT ARE IBAS? Put simply, IBAs are sites, either protected or unprotected, that are vital for the conservation of the world's birds. Because IBAs target specific suites of birds, normally threatened, rare or range-restricted birds, they often double as some of the finest birding destinations on the continent, particularly for those birders seeking more elusive species. Korup National Park, Ngoundaba Ranch, the Bakossi Mountains, Mount Cameroon and Dja Faunal Reserve are all IBAs. What makes them IBAs is that they are well-defined sites with boundaries – it is possible to demarcate and conserve them – and they each hold one or more of a particular set of special birds, worthy of conservation attention. Also, because IBAs are selected using identical and standardised criteria, an IBA in Cameroon is the same as an IBA in Liberia, Malawi, Iraq or England; as a result they form a global conservation currency. Cameroon holds 33 IBAs that support an excellent cross-section of the country's threatened and unique avifauna. Often these sites double as key birdwatching areas, with ecotourism-based initiatives alongside them.

HOW ARE IBAS PROTECTED? Selecting IBAs according to the criteria is probably the easiest part of the process. The publication of the directories documenting the sites is only a beginning. The directories serve to highlight certain areas requiring additional conservation attention, as an alarming proportion of the sites fall outside the official protected area network. The most difficult job is to get people to sit up and listen. The members of the BirdLife Partnership have been most influential in this regard, liaising with government officials, international conservation bodies and key global decision-makers to further the ends of the programme.

Cameroon's national IBA programme stands to benefit from concerned individuals taking an interest in their local IBAs, as volunteers or custodians. If you would like to become involved, please contact the Cameroon Biodiversity Conservation Society, formerly the Cameroon Ornithological Club (*PO Box 3055, Messa, Yaoundé, Cameroon;* ℡ *221 16 58;* e *cbcs@iccnet.cm*) or the BirdLife International Secretariat (*Wellbrooke Court, Girton Rd, Cambridge CB3 0NA, United Kingdom;* f *01223 277200;* e *birdlife@birdlife.org.uk; www.birdlife.net*) for more information.

encompass the mountain forests, savanna and grasslands of the Gashaka Gumti National Park in eastern Nigeria and Tchabal-Mbabo in Cameroon. The area hosts 28 bird species, including 13 only found in the mountain chain. The area is also home to a subspecies of endangered chimpanzee found only in eastern Nigeria and western Cameroon and the African wild dog, the continent's second-most endangered carnivore.

In May 2003 the Cameroonian authorities announced that any restaurant owner caught serving meat from endangered animals could face up to three years in prison and a fine of more than US$16,000, which will further discourage the bushmeat trade.

In December 2003 international conservation group WWF and Traffic, a group which monitors the trade in endangered species, 'named and shamed' Nigeria, Senegal and Ivory Coast for allegedly sustaining the illegal ivory trade.

Having largely destroyed their own elephant populations, the three countries were found to have been importing and selling tonnes of ivory poached in nearby countries, including Cameroon. Poachers, using machine guns, can kill a herd easily in a day.

The WWF, which has an office in the Bastos district of Yaoundé (\ *221 62 67; www.wwfcameroon.org*) is working with the Cameroonian government to increase protected areas of the forest, discourage logging and poaching and support the continuing traditional lifestyles of the communities living in the forest.

The Lobéké, Boumba-Bek and Nki forest reserves have become national parks in recent years, with the increased environmental protection this brings.

Increased protection of the wilder regions of Cameroon cannot come soon enough, especially as many have great biodiversity. The remarkable biodiversity of the country is coupled with a high number of animals and plants that are endemic to their localities. More than 40 plant species are thought to be unique to Mount Cameroon, for example, as well as numerous birds. The mountain is also home to monkeys and forest elephants.

Rarities found in the rainforests of the southwest include chimpanzees, red-capped mangabeys and the drill, one of the rarest primates in Africa, which can only also be found in Equatorial Guinea's Bioko Island and southeastern Nigeria. Rainforest areas are also home to elephants, gorillas and buffaloes, although the thick vegetation can make it very difficult to spot them.

WILDLIFE GUIDE

MAMMALS

Elephants Cameroon has a number of the most distinctive large mammals of the continent. Both forest (*Loxodonta africana cyclotis*) and savanna (*Loxodonta africana africana*) African elephant (the latter having larger bodies, ears and tusks and less hair) are present in Cameroon, in Waza and Bénoué national parks in the north, Korup and Faro national parks in the west and, most noticeably, the reserves and

African elephant

numerous other sites in the southeast of the country. Indeed, Lobéké, Boumba Bek and Nki, with their extensive swampland and forest vegetation, are important elephant habitats and have an elephant population estimated at nearly 10,000. Elephant also pass through the Kalamaloué Reserve, near Lake Chad in the far north.

Unfortunately, elephant hunting remains a significant problem in the country, especially in the southeast where logging roads have opened far more forest in recent years and provide easy access to bushmeat poachers.

Rhinoceros The north of Cameroon contains the most northerly surviving population in Africa of the endangered black rhinoceros (*Diceros bicornis*), notably in Bénoué and Bouba Ndjida national parks. However, recent surveys have failed to confirm whether or not this species is now extinct in Cameroon. The only surviving examples of *D. b. longipes*, the rarest of the black rhinos, are believed to be in northern Cameroon. Confusingly, like the white rhinoceros, the black rhinoceros is actually grey in colour and therefore the way it can be distinguished from the white is its striking prehensile hooked upper lip that helps it grab leaves and grass.

Black rhino

Hippopotamus The common hippopotamus (*Hippopotamus amphibius*) is found in the southwest of the country and in the north in lakes and waterways. It spends much of the day under water, to emerge at night to graze. Beware: hippos kill more people in Africa than any other mammal. The mangroves of the coastal regions by the Nigerian border and either side of Douala also provide the habitat for isolated populations of pygmy hippopotamus (*Hexaprotodon liberiensis heslopi*).

African buffalo

Buffalo Cameroon has good populations of African buffalo (*Syncerus caffer*). Particularly adaptable to different habitats, it lives both in the forests and savanna regions. The red forest buffalo (*Syncerus caffer nanus*) lives in small herds in the forests of the south, while the savanna variety (*Syncerus cafer caffer*) of the north tends to live in large herds.

Antelope The savanna and woodland regions in the north of the country contain the biggest range and species of antelope. These include the Lord Derby's eland (*Taurotragus derbianus*), which is also known as the giant eland, which is misleading as although it has larger horns than the common eland (*Taurotragus oryx*), it is a lighter animal. Cameroon is now the only country where Lord Derby's eland remains common.

Eland

Other species prevalent in the north include the handsome roan antelope (*Hippotragus equines*) which has a light red-brown coat, the large, robust, shaggy-coated waterbuck (*Kobus ellipsiprymnus*) and Buffon's kob (*Kobus kob kob*), which is similar to but smaller than the Uganda kob (*Kobus kob thomasi*), absent in Cameroon.

Roan antelope

The large and ungainly looking hartebeest (*Alcelaphus buselaphus*), the gazelle-like oribi (*Ourebia ourebi*) and the red-fronted gazelle (*Gazella rufifrons*), a gazelle with deep-reddish-brown upperparts and white underparts, are also present.

Hartebeest

Now restricted to tiny pockets in northern Cameroon are the hartebeest-like korrigum (*Damaliscus lunatus korrigum*) and, more widespread, the similar-looking tiang (*Damaliscus lunatus tiang*).

Around Korup and the forest regions straddling the Nigerian border forest elephants create paths used by a variety of antelope species such as the secretive bushbuck (*Tragelaphus scriptus*), the most widely distributed of the African tragelaphines.

Bushbuck

The forests east and southeast of Yaoundé provide a suitable habitat for larger forest antelopes such as the semi-aquatic sitatunga (*Tragelaphus spekei*), which is similar in appearance to its near-relation the bushbuck, and the bongo (*Tragelaphus euryceros*). When under threat, bongos hold their spiral horns against the backs of their necks as they run, to prevent them from tangling in vegetation.

Sitatunga

Reedbuck

The Mandara Mountains in the north of the country harbour a population of the endangered western subspecies of mountain reedbuck (*Redunca fulvorufula adamauae*), a grey-brown antelope with crescent-shaped horns.

Over-hunting in the extreme north of the country has greatly reduced numbers of such species as the scimitar-horned oryx (*Oryx dammah*), dama gazelle (*Gazella dama*), dorcas gazelle (*Gazella dorcas*) and red-fronted gazelle (*Gazella rufifrons*). The subspecies of the common hartebeest, the bubal hartebeest (*Alcelaphus busephalus buselaphus*), is now extinct.

Eight types of duiker, a group of about 16 small antelope species, are commonly found in Cameroon. The common, grey or bush duiker (*Sylvicapra grimmia*) and red-flanked duiker (*Cephalophus rufilatis*) are found in the savanna regions in the centre and north of the country, the white-bellied (*Cephalophus leucogaster*), Peters' (*Cephalophus callipygus*), Weyns' (*Cephalophus weynsi*), and black-fronted duikers (*Cephalophus nigrifrons*) in the south and east, while the bay (*Cephalophus dorsalis*), the blue (*Cephalophus monticola*) and the yellow-backed (*Cephalophus silviculter*) duikers are found everywhere but the north. All but the common (grey) · duiker is forest-dwelling. Duikers are distinguished by having arched backs, skulking habits and tufts of hair between the ears, and the forest-dwellers have a stocky, squat appearance.

Common duiker

Giraffe Typically living in herds of between five and 15, there used to be good-sized populations of West African or Nigerian giraffe (*Giraffa camelopardalis peralta*) in the north, but now these are generally absent outside protected areas such as Waza, Bénoué and Kalamaloué, and even here, they are still significantly threatened by poaching.

Gorillas Cameroon is one of the few countries where lowland gorillas (*Gorilla gorilla*) still occur. The others are neighbouring Gabon and the Democratic Republic of Congo. (The other subspecies is the mountain gorilla, or *Gorilla gorilla berengei*, which lives high in the mountain rainforests of Rwanda and Uganda.)

Growing up to 1.8m high and weighing up to 210kg, they actually thrive on an unstable environment, whether it be caused by volcanic disturbance, landslides, fires or tree-felling, as they contribute to generating the growth of the low-level herbs they need. Primarily vegetarian, much of their diet consists of plants like wild celery, galium vines and lobelias. They often eat unpleasant-tasting leaves that other animals avoid.

The vast Congo Basin rainforest, of which the southeast of Cameroon is part, is one of the richest areas in the world for primates, and contains possibly more gorillas than any other area. Here, the vast tracts of lowland forest harbour thousands of western lowland gorillas (*Gorilla gorilla gorilla*), smaller than either mountain or eastern lowland species, with around 5,000 believed to be in Lobéké National Park alone.

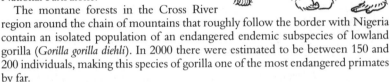

Mountain gorilla

The montane forests in the Cross River region around the chain of mountains that roughly follow the border with Nigeria contain an isolated population of an endangered endemic subspecies of lowland gorilla (*Gorilla gorilla diehli*). In 2000 there were estimated to be between 150 and 200 individuals, making this species of gorilla one of the most endangered primates by far.

Southern Cameroon represents one of the few remaining gorilla sanctuaries left in the world, although widespread logging, bushmeat hunting and agricultural expansion increasingly threaten the region.

Viewing gorillas in the wild in Cameroon invariably involves persistence and perseverance, but is well worth the effort: they share many attributes with humans, living in groups, the male acting as family head, the female cuddling her offspring. They even have fingerprints!

Their groups are typically made up of up to 30 individuals, living in a territory of around 10–15km². The group is always headed by a male, known as a 'silverback' due to the grey hair that develops as he reaches maturity. He shows his strength by tearing up plants, throwing branches and shaking trees.

The silverback leads the group and deals with arguments that may come up. There are usually nearly two females for every male in the group, which regularly groom each other to remove pests and parasites.

Groups of gorillas have until recent years seldom come into contact with other gorillas, but destroying the rainforest, as has happened so much in recent years through logging, farming and building, has caused different gorilla groups to clash.

In some cases a rival male may challenge the group leader and if succeeding, typically kills the young gorillas not related to him so that he can then breed with the females of the group, who would have otherwise not bred again until their offspring were independent.

Chimpanzees Though not as common as gorillas, chimpanzees (*Pan troglodytes*), the closest relation to humans of all other animals, are widely present throughout the forested areas of southern Cameroon, and especially where human disturbance is minimal or non-existent. Chimpanzees have been confirmed at Mount Cameroon, Korup National Park, Bwombi-Mwo Forest Reserve and Mount Kupe, as well as the Douala-Edea and Campo reserves. In southeastern Cameroon a small number of chimpanzees are present near Yokadouma. They are present in greater numbers in the evergreen forest of Dja, and Lobéké, Boumba Bek and Nki in the southeast.

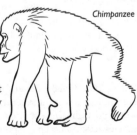

Chimpanzee

Chimps are hunted for their meat throughout Cameroon and their habitats are increasingly threatened by human activities like timber extraction, the pet trade and laboratory testing.

In the Nigerian border region the forests of the mountains support the endangered chimpanzee subspecies, *Pan troglodytes vellerosus*.

Monkeys, drills, guenons

Around 20 species of monkey are found in Cameroon, including the crowned, the red-capped and the grey-cheeked mangabey in the south, the vervet (green) monkey, found everywhere but the south, the mona monkey (southwest, including mounts Cameroon and Kupe), the endangered red-eared guenon (also in the southwest, by the Nigerian border) and the Satanic colobus in the southeast.

Vervet monkey

The lowland forests in the vicinity of the Nigerian border, the Cross and Sanaga rivers and Mount Cameroon play a key role in the conservation of primates. The strictly endemic hill-loving Preuss's red colobus monkey (*Procolobus pennanti preussi*) and the quiet, shy near-endemic red-eared guenon (*Cercopithecus erythrotis*), which has a red tail, a red spot on the nose and red-tipped ears, are present here.

Crowned guenons (*Cercopithecus pogonias*), a slim and graceful monkey which sits upright while sleeping in the trees, is also present here, as is the highly endangered drill (*Mandrillus leucophaeus*), which differs from other monkeys because of the male's large size and short tail. This region is also the habitat of the black colobus monkey (*Colobus satanas*).

The mangroves of the coastal regions by the Nigerian border and around the coast at Douala provide a suitable habitat for both the near-endemic Sclater's monkey (*Cercopithecus sclateri*) and the talapoin monkey (*Miopithecus talapoin*).

Patas monkey

North of Yaoundé and as far as Ngaoundéré sees the presence of the patas monkey (*Cercopithicus patas*), a slender, light reddish-brown monkey with a black stripe above the eyes, distinguished for being one of the few ground-dwelling primates. Feeding on grass, fruit, insects and new shoots, these monkeys can run at speeds of up to 35mph (55km/h).

The savanna olive baboon (*Papio anubis*) is present in the centre and north including Waza, with the baboon-like mandrill found in the south.

Otter and civet

Both the smallest of the sub-Saharan otters, the Spotted-necked otter (*Lutra maculicollis*), and the largest African otter, the Cape clawless otter (*Aonyx capensis*), are present throughout the country. The Congo clawless otter (*Aonyx congica*), very similar to the Cape clawless otter, is in the southeast.

Cape clawless otter

The long and sleek, nocturnal grey/brown tree civet (*Nandinia binotata*) can be found in the forests of the south, while the more adaptable, heavier and longer African civet (*Civettictas civetta*) is present throughout the country.

African civet

Genet and linsang

Several genet species – with their long, slender bodies, long tails and short legs and similarity to the African civet – are present in Cameroon, although only the experienced observer would find it easy to identify them to species level. The large-spotted genet (*Genetta tigrina*) is generally found north of

Ngaoundéré and south of Maroua, while the servaline genet (*Genetta servalina*) can be found in the tropical forests of the south, from west to east. The thinly distributed panther genet (*Genetta maculata*) is found at Korup and the forests of the west of the country. Additionally, the African linsang (*Poiana richardsoni*), a genet-like species found in the rainforests of the southeast of Cameroon, is also present.

Mongoose A rich variety of mongoose also inhabits Cameroon. These include the long-nosed mongoose (*Herpestes naso*) and the black-footed mongoose (*Bdeogale nigripes*), both found only in the forested areas of the south of the country. Conversely, the slender mongoose (*Galerella sanguinea*), the white-tailed mongoose (*Ichneumia albicauda*) and large grey mongoose (*Herpestes ichneumon*), only inhabit the centre and north, with the water (marsh) mongoose (*Atilax paludinosus*), similar to an otter, found in well-watered habitats throughout the country. The flat-headed cusimanse (*Crossarchus platycephalus*), a species of small mongoose of which little is known, is also present in the lowland forests of the southwest.

Jackal, wild dog, polecat, weasel and hyena

The nocturnal side-striped jackal (*Canis adustus*) inhabits well-watered and wooded pockets of the north, as does the wild dog (*Lycaon pictus*). The striped polecat (*Ictonyx striatus*) and the Libyan striped weasel (*Poecilictis libyca*) are only found in the extreme north. The heavily built spotted hyena (*Crocuta crocuta*), the best-known of the hyenas, and the striped hyena (*Hyaena hyaena*) are both present in low densities in the extreme north.

Spotted hyena

African wild dog

Cats Sightings of big cats are generally a rarity. Lions (*Panthera leo*) are present in the centre and north, but outside protected areas such as Waza, Bouba Ndjida and Bénoué national parks, their numbers have declined dramatically. The cheetah (*Acynonix jubatus*) populates the north, including Waza, but numbers have dropped significantly in recent years. More encouragingly, the leopard (*Panthera pardus*) is found all over the country. Caracals (*Caracal caracal*), with their distinctive long tufts of hair at the tips of their pointed ears, servals (*Leptailurus serval*) and African wild cats (*Felis silvestris*) are to be found in northern areas, while golden cats (*Felis aurata*) are domiciled in the tropical forests of the south, east and west.

Cheetah

Leopard

Serval

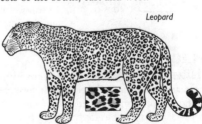

Hedgehog, hare, squirrel, porcupine The white-bellied hedgehog (*Atelerix albiventris*) is present in Cameroon, restricted to the centre and north, while the almost-grey Cape hare (*Lepus capensis*) is only found in the extreme north. The centre, west and north support the western ground squirrel (*Xerus erythopus*), which sports white side stripes. The north African porcupine (*Hystrix cristata*) is present throughout the country. The African brush-tailed porcupine (*Atherurus africanus*), on the other hand, is only found in the south and southwest. The long, black-and-white-banded quills of these porcupines lie flat unless the animal is threatened, when they become raised and allow the animal to appear far larger.

Hogs Several kinds of hog blanket the country: the warthog (*Phacochoreus africanus*), which Lydekker unkindly desribed in 1908 as being 'incarnations of hideous dreams'; the bushpig-like red river hog (*Potamochoerus porcus*); and the giant forest hog (*Hylochoerus meinertzhageni*), which lives up to its name being Africa's largest pig species, ranging from about 1.5–2.5m in length and 130–240kg in weight.

Warthog

Hyraxes, aardvarks, galagos and bushbabies The stoutly built and tail-less diurnal guinea pig-like rock hyrax (*Procavia capensis*) is found in the north, with the nocturnal tree hyrax (*Dendrohydrax dorsalis*) found in the forests of both the west and south. The unmistakable insectivore, the aardvark (*Orycteropus afer*), with its elongated pig-like snout, is found everywhere but in the south, although seldom seen because of its nocturnal lifestyle.

Aardvark

Rock hyrax

Of the galago species, the bushbaby (*Galago senegalensis*), is most often seen, identification aided by its distinctive big round eyes, highly mobile ears and long fluffy tail. It is found north of the centre of the country. In the south the smoke grey-furred Allen's galago (*Galago alleni*) is found, as is the western needle-clawed galago (*Galago elegantulus*), which sports red-hued dorsal fur and a white-tipped tail.

Lesser bushbaby

Pangolins Three rare species of the striking, scaly pangolin are found in Cameroon: the giant ground pangolin (*Manis gigantea*) throughout the country, and the smaller long-tailed tree pangolin (*Manis tetradactyla*) and white-bellied tree pangolin (*Manis tricspis*) found in the lowland forests of the south. Scouring the forest floor for termites and ants, when frightened pangolins curl into a ball, so that their tough scales can act as a deterrent against predators.

Pangolin

INSECTS
Butterflies and moths Whilst the majority of Cameroon's overwhelming variety of many thousands of species of invertebrate life are overlooked by most visitors, butterflies and moths (order Lepidoptera), constituting around 1% of all named insects, seldom fail to capture the attention of those visiting Cameroon.

This is not surprising, considering their comparatively large size and bright colours, and the wide variety of species prevalent. More than 1,000 species of butterfly inhabit Cameroon, compared with just 56 in the UK. That represents more than a quarter of the total number of species found in tropical Africa.

The forests of the Nigeria–Cameroon border region are especially rich in butterflies, including the striking creamy white *Charaxes superbus* and powerful *Charaxes acraeoides*. In all, around 950 species are present in this region, more than in any other forests in Africa. Of these, around 100 species are found nowhere else. The area around Mount Cameroon and the forests of the southeast of the country are also particularly important regions for butterflies, including the endemic *Charaxes musakensis*.

AMPHIBIANS AND REPTILES

Frogs and toads Cameroon's frogs are of all sizes, including the goliath frog, which at 1ft long (over 2ft with legs extended) is the biggest frog in the world. It was allowed to evolve because of the perrenial wetness of the region. As heavy as a domestic cat, it feels like a balloon filled with wet sand if you hold it. Found only along isolated rainforest rivers in Cameroon and Equatorial Guinea, this is just one of many species threatened by logging destroying its habitat and locals slaying it for its exotic, sweet meat.

The species richness of amphibians and reptiles is particularly high in the rainforests of the southeast of the country. Here there are two endemic clawed frog species, *Xeropus boumbaensis* and *Xeropus pygmaeus*. The Mount Cameroon region harbours one strictly endemic toad, *Werneria preussi*, with the four-digit toad (*Didynamipus sjotstedti*), Tandy's smalltongue toad (*Werneria tandyi*) and the frog, *Athroleptis bivittatus,* near-endemics. Around the Korup region on the border with Nigeria the amphibian fauna is very diverse and endemic species include Dizangue reed frog (*Hyperolius bopeleti*), Schneider's banana frog (*Afrixalus schneideri*) and Werner's river frog (*Phrynobatrachus werneri*). The savanna and grasslands north of Yaoundé and Ngaoundéré yield such endemic amphibians as the Bouda River frog (*Phrynobatrachus scapularis*) and the Bamiléké Plateau frog (*Rana longipes*).

Turtles If you are lucky, turtles can be seen on the coast, with the females laying their many eggs on the beaches. The mangroves of the coastal regions situated by the Nigerian border and either side of Douala provide habitat to the threatened west African manatee (*Trichechus senegalensis*) and the soft-skinned turtle (*Trionyx triunguis*). In the summer, several species of marine turtle appear. These include the green (*Chelonia mydas*), leatherback (*Dermochelys coricea*), loggerhead (*Caretta caretta*) and hawksbill turtle (*Eretomychelys imbricata*).

Lizards Lizards are plentiful in many areas, with chameleons and geckos a common sight. Of more than 170 species of reptiles and amphibians in Korup, the forest chameleon (*Chamaeleo camurunensis*) and two worm lizards (*Cynisca schaeferi* and *C. gansi*) are endemic. In the forested areas south and southeast of Yaoundé, endemics include the Cameroon stumptail chameleon (*Rhampholeon spectrum*), the grey chameleon (*Chameleo chapini*) and crested chameleon (*Chameleo cristatus*). There are also endemic skinks (small, long-tailed lizards): Fuhn's five-toed skink (*Leptosiaphos fuhni*) and Peter's lidless skink (*Panaspis breviceps*). The Mandara Mountains region in the north of the country contains a couple of endemic reptile species, the Mount Lefo chameleon (*Chamaeleo wiedersheimi*) and the African wall gecko (*Tarentola ephippiata*).

Crocodiles The Nile crocodile (*Crocodylus niloticus*) which grows to about 6m in length, is the most widespread species present in waterways both north and south

2

around the country, and notably around the Mount Cameroon area and the mangroves of the coastal regions by the Nigerian border and around Douala. The nocturnal dwarf crocodile (*Osteolaemus tetraspis*) lives in the rivers and streams of the rainforests of the south of the country. The smallest of African crocodiles, it grows up to 2m in length.

Snakes Snakes, both venomous and harmless varieties, are also common in Cameroon though can be difficult to spot, and thankfully most fear humans and scurry away.

The Gabon viper (*Bitis gabonica*), the largest viper in Africa, growing to almost 2m in length, is present in the rainforests of the south and notably the Mount Cameroon region. It has the largest fangs (up to 5cm) of any venomous snake worldwide. In the densely forested areas south and southeast of Yaoundé, Grant's African ground snake (*Gonionotophis grantii*) and Zenker's worm snake (*Typhlops zenkeri*) are present. In the savanna and grasslands north of Yaoundé the strictly endemic Sudan beaked snake (*Rhinotyphlops sudanensis*) is present.

BIRDS Cameroon's diversity of habitats supports some of the best birding in Africa, having over 900 species in about 75 families, with about 18 endemic species, 20 speciality species and 18 endangered species. Eight of the ten families endemic to the mainland of Africa are present in the country. In a two-week trip you could expect to see around 250–300 species. Some birders manage far more in a longer trip, taking in more areas.

For the greatest success, research the region thoroughly before the trip: www.wildsounds.co.uk has a selection of CDs and cassettes of bird calls. Online natural history, environment and science bookstore www.nhbs.com can help you select field guides, while www.birdingpal.com may be able to help with finding an experienced local bird guide.

The coastal lowlands on the outskirts of Douala make a good start to a birding holiday and on the mangroves and mudflats of the Wouri River, off the Limbé Road, you may see such birds as the black tern, white-fronted plover, grey parrot, purple heron, black heron, little egret, western reef-egret, intermediate egret, Carmelite sunbird and great egret. Moving west from Douala, Limbé is a good spot for searching out the western reef egret, western bluebill and Carmelite sunbird.

In an article in *Travel Africa*, Keith Betton, vice-chairman of the African Bird Club, cited Mount Kupe as second in the top ten birding sites in Africa. More details follow on this and other sites in Keith Barnes's excellent section on birding in Cameroon.

Birding Cameroon *Keith Barnes*
Rainforest birding in west Africa can be slow and frustrating. Most species occur at low densities, others are frequently heard and rarely seen, and many of those that show up, may do so once only. When species do show themselves, it is often fleetingly and generally in poor light. But for those who are persistent and patient, the rewards are endless, and when a rockfowl finally leaps into view, the frustration vanishes and it becomes plainly obvious why you do it – the rainforest offers the most exotic and sought-after species in Africa, from blue cuckooshrikes to ant-thrushes and alethes. It is all well worth the persistence. Birding the savanna is much easier and much more productive in short time spells; the weather and conditions are also more conducive to seeing more birds. Many of the larger and more spectacular species Africa is renowned for are absent or exceptionally rare in west Africa. However, what west Africa lacks in quantity it more than makes up for in quality; in fact the region probably holds more desirable bird species than any other part of Africa.

Christian Boix

Discovered in 1949, at Mount Kupe near Nyasoso, the Mount Kupe bush shrike was only seen twice between 1949 and 1984 and believed to be endemic to Mount Kupe. More recently, however, particularly since its highly distinctive vocalisations have been described, it has been recorded more frequently. This is not to suggest it is common, with an estimated seven pairs known to occur on the whole of Mount Kupe. However, two new localities have been discovered, Lake Edib (Bakossi Mountains) where habitat available is eight times larger than that of Mount Kupe, and Banyang Mbo wildlife sanctuary, where a single bird was seen in 1999. The entire world population lives scattered in three apparent nuclei of less than 200km².

It is considered critically threatened by BirdLife International, with a global population of some 50–249 individuals. Its apparent scarcity is hard to explain and commonly attributed to habitat degradation. This is unlikely, given that its preferred habitat is well protected and the species generally occurs far from human settlements, using only primary forest with relatively open understorey at 950–1,450m above sea level at Mount Kupe and 1,000–1,250m above sea level at Lake Edib. Despite this altitudinal isolation it seems to be a species that is naturally very scarce, and perhaps on the edge of natural extinction.

The French call it the 'Gladiator of Mount Kupe', and indeed this stunning gem has become a stalwart flagship species for forest conservation in Cameroon and it is just plain unmistakable when sighted. The Mount Kupe bush shrike is a forest bush shrike with a green back, grey belly, yellow vent and unique head pattern, capped with a broad black mask that extends to its front, a slate-grey crown and nape. A clear, pure-white throat rimmed by a narrow jet-black breast band, gives this bird away. Such a conspicuous throat appears to be used for advertising, although some of the adverts are poorly understood. For example, some adult individuals show a stylish maroon medallion in the centre of the throat. Speculation has suggested it may be an age-related marking distinguishing breeding birds from non-breeders, perhaps just a geographical morph or even a secondary sexual character? The only consensus seems to be that it is not sex specific. Furthermore, females during breeding appear to develop a yellow tinge surrounding the black patch, speculation suggesting a physiological consequence or an advert of receptiveness?

It's been confirmed as a monogamous territorial breeder, yet in the non-breeding season they are often sighted in trios, which could explain the need for distinctive throat markings to avoid aggression. But as with many other unstudied facets of this species, it still remains a mystery. Studies to understand what is limiting this species' total numbers or work to better understand the biology of this declining gem are needed urgently. Fortunately, the fact that the Cameroon government and Post Office have immortalised this species in the national stamp collection suggests that they are aware of the conservation significance this species deserves.

For those wishing to catch a glimpse of this highly enigmatic species, the best chances are along the shrike trail on Mount Kupe above Nyasoso and in the Bakossi forests near the village of Kodmin. Speak to the WWF project officers at Nyasoso to arrange a guide (and vehicle) for the day. But be warned that a libation ceremony at 06.00, involving a fair amount of beer, whisky and Cola nuts at the chief's palace in Kodmin, is an unavoidable prerequisite to start your hunt!

Natural History **WILDLIFE GUIDE**

2

Despite being the richest country in west Africa for birds, ornithologically speaking, Cameroon remains little known. It is probably the most accessible country in west-central Africa with many exceptionally exciting and interesting

Christian Boix

Cameroon is probably the best place in the world to see grey-necked rockfowl which, along with the yellow-necked rockfowl of Upper Guinea comprise the family Picathartidae, arguably the most difficult family of birds to see in the world. The rockfowl is an avian oddity – an ornithological understatement – and it has been since its discovery in Cameroon in 1899. The poor beast has suffered a century of chronic taxonomic identity crises, being initially described as a crow (*Corvidae*), later as a starling (*Sturnidae*) and not long ago as a flycatcher (*Muscicapidae*), with some workers considering its closest relatives being babblers (*Timaliidae*) and others the thrushes (*Turdidae*). Recent DNA and anatomical work supports a 'crow-like' ancestry, but others suggest that another African oddity, the South African rockjumpers (*Chaetops*) are more likely cousins. Such confusion stems from the fact that rockfowls are probably remnants of an archaic avian lineage. Fortunately, both species of rockfowl presently enjoy some phylogenetic stability by being placed within a separate family.

The grey-necked rockfowl is a medium-sized bird (200–250g) with a strong broad tail (c180mm long) to balance its weight on vines, stems and branches. A pair of long, muscular, silver-grey legs are responsible for its rapid catapulting motion and are used as powerful leaf-litter rakes for foraging. Despite an apparent reluctance to fly, the bird is endowed with enough wing load both for take-off and sustained flight. Its large black bill gives it the appearance of a crow and is a powerful tool used to forage along the forest floor. However, what never fails to mesmerise the observer is its tri-coloured, bald, bulbous head with a double-lobed blue-grey fore-crown and bulging crimson nape, separated on either side by a sinister-looking triangular black mask. The underparts, including throat and belly, are soft lemon-yellow with a grey wash on the throat and upper chest. The bird's primaries form a distinct black band that separates the yellow underparts from the slate-grey upperparts. The combination of its equivocal past and its unusual appearance make it arguably the most sought-after bird in Africa.

The Rockfowl is lightning fast, its fluid motion almost shadowless, bounding silently in Gollum-like fashion through the forest undergrowth leaving only a trail of quivering stems and vines for the ill-prepared birder. They generally occur in groups of three to five birds scouring the forest floor and undergrowth in search of 'creepy crawlies' such as insects, earthworms, millipedes, centipedes, frogs and lizards.

Rockfowls are restricted to the lushest Guinea–Congolian primary and secondary rainforests of west Africa. The grey-necked rockfowl is found mainly in lowland rainforests of Cameroon, Gabon, Nigeria and Bioko. Within Cameroon, colonies have been found at Korup National Park, Dja Reserve and Campo Reserve. There are even rumours of a small colony on the outskirts of Yaoundé. Colonies are generally small (two to five nests)

bird species. Cameroon supports 915 bird species if we include the golden nightjar discovered by Ian Sinclair et al. (April 2003). Of these, 704 are resident, 218 are seasonal migrants (145 from the Palaearctic and 73 intra-African). Seven species are endemic to geographical Cameroon.

Key birds There is no doubt that Cameroon's potential popularity as a birding destination is bolstered by it containing some of Africa's and indeed the world's most highly desirable bird species. The grey-necked rockfowl (Picathartes) is chief amongst these (see box, above, *Finding grey-necked rockfowl*). Along with the rockfowl, the Mount Kupe bush shrike (see box on page 37), Arabian bustard and Egyptian plover were all included in *Birdwatch* magazine's 2003 poll of the world's 50 most desirable birds. Other highly sought-after specialities include quail plover, with the exception of a very large colony at Dja Reserve that is blessed with 47 nests of which at least 20 are believed to be active! Nests are made of mud, and are akin to a very large swallow's nest.

From a conservation perspective, the rockfowl's bizarre nature and reluctance to take to the wing have been its downfall. It is sought after for local cuisine, zoos, museums and the bird trade, resulting in it being considered globally threatened by BirdLife International. Unfortunately, the Cameroon birds are not protected by folklore, as are its congeners in Sierra Leone, where their presence around rocks (preferred burial places of many forest tribes) have earned them a mythical respect by all worshipping visitors. Although law in Cameroon protects the rockfowl, hunting, the bird trade and conversion of forest into farmland and logging operations are challenging its survival.

WHERE TO FIND A ROCKFOWL By far the most reliable site to see grey-necked Picathartes in Cameroon is in Korup National Park. Chief Adolf at the WWF office in Mundemba will be able to help arrange such trips. Other breeding sites in Cameroon include the rocks around Mount Kupe, although it is seldom seen there anymore. The onset of the wet season is the best time to find them (March–May).

TIPS TO SEE ROCKFOWL To say that rockfowl loathe surprises is a gross understatement. The bird is extremely skittish and any sudden movement or noise will result in it beating a rapid retreat. However, they can be fairly bold, curious and confiding around breeding sites if the observer behaves cautiously, silently and respectfully.

- Do not wear any material that may rustle such as nylon or plastic.
- Avoid brightly coloured garments: choose dark and sombre clothing for the occasion.
- Avoid hanging or dangling items off your clothes, belt, binoculars, etc, especially if they are shiny, noisy or may get caught in the vegetation.
- Wear good walking shoes and walk cautiously.
- Do not disturb rockfowl at the nest once they have commenced breeding.
- Pre-empt your next step and move, avoiding snapping twigs and branches to push out of the way. Bear in mind that getting to the rock/cave is no assurance of success. How silently you get there will!
- Before your final approach, rest and drink. Coughing, sneezing and throat clearing are likely to alert the birds to your presence and result in disappointment.
- As you are likely to be sitting for a long time choose your favourite sitting position.
- Once you have bagged the 'beast' retreat as silently as you arrived; respect the bird, the silence and the moment.

stone partridge, violet turaco, Sudan golden sparrow and scissor-tailed kite in the northern savannas and grey pratincole, bare-cheeked trogon, grey-sided and red-sided broadbills in the forested southwest. Alongside these rare and spectacular species, well-represented members of the avifauna include hornbills, turacos, kingfishers, illadopsis, and bee-eaters in the forests and seedeaters, cisticolas, raptors and starlings in the northern woodlands and semi-desert.

Access Although occasionally frustrating, Cameroon is a well-connected country with a road and air network that can (and usually does) get one from A to B very effectively. Regular flights connect the two main birding zones in the north (Maroua–Garoua) and south (Yaoundé–Douala) of the country and the roads in the north are good year-round. In the south, it is best to avoid the rainy season

OPTICAL EQUIPMENT Binoculars that are sealed and waterproof are the most essential piece of equipment. Someone who has been thrifty on binoculars will soon realise that they have wasted their time and money, because once your bins fill with water or mist, they become useless. In the rainforest 8x32 magnification is normally the safest bet as this tends to gather more light and pinning down the bird in your viewfinder is easier. In open areas (eg: savanna) 10x40s are more useful as the image is larger. Telescopes can be useful, particularly in the savannas, or when watching waterbirds on an open lake. In the rainforest a telescope is a personal preference, but in my experience their use is limited and they are cumbersome to carry. Finally, if you use glasses, be warned: most birding is done watching straight into the canopy, and this means that invariably your glasses will steam up and you will end up seeing very little when the frantic flock moves past. If you can afford using contact lenses this is perhaps the best environment to use them; if you can't use contact lenses, be sure to have several cleaning devices handy to demist your glasses and binoculars (binos in birder parlance).

RAINGEAR The only thing worse than your binoculars being filled with water is you being soaking wet. Be sure to get waterproof and sturdy boots, ponchos and rainproof trousers. Boots also double as protective ant-swarm gear, and ponchos make excellent makeshift hides. Peaked or broad-rimmed hats keep rainwater out of your eyes and binos.

SOUND GEAR Seeing much in the rainforest often depends on your ability to recognise, follow, locate and reproduce bird sounds. These days, mini-disk (MD) recorders, with an

between May and August when the roads become mudpaths and places such as Korup are virtually inaccessible. For most of the year however, although the roads are poor, most sites can be visited.

Timing March and early April are the optimal times to visit Cameroon. This is before the heavy rains come, but many birds in the south are actively setting up territories and many of the seasonal migrants are still present in the far north. Avoid going to the south in May to August when rain can severely impact your chances of making it to your destination of choice, and even if you get there you may still be rained out.

Major birding biomes/habitats The diversity of habitats in Cameroon is staggering and is replicated nowhere else in west Africa. Far north Cameroon comprises the low sparse thorn-dominated woodlands and grasslands of the Sahel biome. This biome extends from just north of Bénoué to Lake Chad. There are many species characteristic of this dry woodland–grassland mosaic, although these are shared with many other west African nations. To the south, Cameroon is covered by Guinea savanna, which is a broad-leaved woodland. The third major habitat is Afromontane forest. Within Cameroon, this habitat is found on Mount Cameroon, Mount Kupe and the Bamenda-Banso Highlands. According to BirdLife International two vital Endemic Bird Areas (EBA) form a major part of Cameroon: the first is the Cameroon Mountains (EBA 086). This holds some 29 restricted range endemics that are confined to Cameroon, and a small portion of Nigeria (Obodu Plateau). Undoubtedly, Cameroon remains the country of choice to see these, and many other birds. The remainder of the country, particularly in the far south and west comprises attached amplified speaker are the norm. For bird recording, I recommend the Sony TC-D5 Pro II analogue cassette deck and Sennheiser MKH-70 RF-condenser microphone with Sennheiser blimp windscreen, pistol grip/shockmount and power supply. For more information on bird vocalisation recording in the tropics see Nick Athanas's informative article *Making sense of the sounds: learning tropical bird vocalizations* at www.thebirdindex.com. West Africa has a superb set of bird sounds in the form of Claude Chappuis's *African Bird Sounds* CDs available from Wildsounds (*www.wildsounds.co.uk*).

WATCHES Watches with both compass and altimeter can be extremely useful. Birders are known to wander off the path of forest trails and a compass could be invaluable in helping you find your way home. Certain birds in the Cameroon highlands are specific to certain altitudinal bands and here the altimeter can be extremely helpful in finding your most sought-after quarry.

GPS In recent years, GPS has revolutionised both birding specifically and travel off the beaten track generally. Prices of GPS equipment have plummeted, making their use far more widespread. Not only do they let you record exactly where you saw a sought-after species, but they allow you to wander freely, safe in the knowledge that you will be able to find your way back. But beware of thick rainforest canopies such as at Korup National Park, where acquiring satellite signal maybe tricky at times.

FLASHLIGHTS A Maglite is useful, both as a torch and to be able to spot owls, nightjars and roosting birds at night.

lowland Guinea–Congo forests. Another vital Endemic Bird Area forms this part of Cameroon, the Cameroon and Gabon lowlands (EBA 085), which has six bird species found nowhere else in the world, including the mythical grey-necked rockfowl (see box on pages 38–9).

Independent birding Independent birders need to plan well and expect a few surprises *en route*. The best area for independent birders is Mount Kupe, where transport, accommodation, good guides and sound advice are all available from the WWF office at Nyasoso.

Birding tours A list of specialist birding tour operators appears in the *Tour operators* section in *Chapter 3*.

Further ornithological information

Cameroon Ornithological Club BP 3055; Messa, Yaoundé; e coc@iccnet.cam
African Bird Club BirdLife International, Wellbrook Court, Girton Rd, Cambridge CB3 ONA; www.africanbirdclub.org. The leading organisation concerning the conservation & study of African birds. It provides bi-annual newsletters & other benefits. Membership currently costs £18 (£10 for students) per year. Its website has recently been improved & the 'country resources' section has information on birds of each country, including Cameroon. There are bird images.

West African Ornithological Society 1 Fishers Heron, East Mills, Fordingbridge, Hants SP6 2JR. Has regular bulletins.
Foreign Birdwatching Reports and Information Service 5 Stanway Cl, Lackpole, Worcester WR4 9XI; 🕾 01905 454541
Dutch Birding Travel Report Service PO Box 737, 9700 AS Groningen, The Netherlands; 🕾 315 014 5925
www.worldtwitch.com Has very informative reports on Cameroonian birding tours, most in search of rare birds.

Online updated versions of the site guide that appears in this book and trip reports and recent information about birding Cameroon may be found at www.tropicalbirding.com and www.thebirdinginn.com. Birders are also recommended to consult the following online series of articles on top birding sites in Cameroon: www.africanbirdclub.org/feature/cameroon1.html and cameroon 2.html. Updated Cameroon birding trip reports can also be found on www.birdingafrica.com.

When you return from your trip, be sure to sign up for a free account to create your own Cameroon checklist and submit your valuable data to the WOBAP (World Bird Atlas Project) at www.thebirdindex.com.

Some relevant field guides for birding are listed in *Appendix 4* (see page 238).

3

Planning Your Trip

WHEN TO VISIT

Overall, from a climatic point of view, the best time to visit is during the cooler, drier months between November and February. December and January are most ideal, although dust from the *harmattan* winds that blow sand south from the Sahara from around November to March can turn the skies a sandy grey and greatly restrict visibility. This can cause flights to be delayed or cancelled, and can spoil views and give photographs an overcast look.

The rainy season, generally from May to November, but generally worst from July to October, can make many roads almost impassable and travel very difficult in many regions.

HIGHLIGHTS AND SUGGESTED ITINERARIES

Cameroon's rich history and widely variable geography means that a visitor is spoilt for choice:

HIGHLIGHTS
- Mount Cameroon – West Africa's highest peak (see page 125)
- Mandara Mountains – a magical volcanic landscape of conical peaks peppered with beautiful rural villages (see page 212)
- The sleepy, palm-fringed beaches of Kribi (page 179) and Limbé (page 117)
- Ring Road – a particularly scenic 367km circular route with traditional kingdoms, lakes, waterfalls, green hills and mountains (see page 155)
- Waza National Park – elephants, hippos and giraffes at one of the best national parks in the region (see page 216)
- Douala – if you have the energy and courage to brave one of Africa's most vibrant cities (see page 103)

SUGGESTED ITINERARIES
One week With little time to spare, the most rewarding option is to head west. After typically arriving in Douala or Yaoundé, spend a day or two relaxing on the beach at Limbé. The more adventurous and energetic, depending on weather conditions, could follow this up by an assault on Mount Cameroon or a visit to Korup National Park, one of Cameroon's more accessible patches of rainforest. If you want a less strenuous, more cultural experience, the Ring Road region, with its ancient kingdoms, would be equally unforgettable.

Two weeks With an extra week to play with you could either spend more time in the west of the country, perhaps finishing with a couple of days sampling Kribi's sandy beaches, or head for the capital, Yaoundé, for a flight to Maroua in the north to discover the Mandara Mountains and fascinating villages scattered around. Be sure to build in extra time to absorb possible lengthy flight delays. Travelling by road would be too difficult.

Three weeks An extra week gives you the luxury of experiencing all the above at a more sedate pace, visiting Waza National Park and travelling to and from the north by both train and on road.

Four weeks or more With this amount of time available you can consider seeing more of the southwest of the country when going to Kribi, or going really off the beaten track by tackling the seldom-visited rainforests of the southeast.

PUBLIC HOLIDAYS, SPECIAL EVENTS AND FESTIVALS

If you are lucky you may stumble upon a traditional event such as a wedding, naming ceremony, thanksgiving to a diety or celebration of the end of the harvest, and be invited to watch or take part. Many such events involve music, singing, dancing and colourful, striking costumes and are a truly memorable spectacle.

1 January	New Year's Day
Late January	Mount Cameroon Race, a gruelling 27km (17 mile) race up and down the 3,000m (10,000ft) mountain
11 February	Youth Day
March/April	Easter
1 May	Labour Day
20 May	National Day, especially well celebrated in Maroua
21 May	Sheep Festival
15 August	Assumption Day
Mid-November	Nso Cultural Week, Kumbo, western Cameroon, where horses are raced through the streets
Mid-December	Ngoun Festival, Foumban
Mid–late December	Lela Festival, Bali
25 December	Christmas Day

ISLAMIC HOLIDAYS Northern Cameroon is broadly Islamic (whereas the south is basically Christian), and therefore Islamic holidays have significantly greater significance here. Islamic holidays depend upon local sightings of phases of the moon and therefore vary from year to year and region to region. Because the Islamic calendar is based upon 12 lunar months that total 354 or 355 days, these holidays fall around 11 days earlier than in the previous year.

During the lunar month of **Ramadan** (predicted to start on 1 September in 2008, 24 August in 2009 and 10 August in 2010), Muslims fast during the day and feast at night and normal business hours may be interrupted. Restaurants often close during the day and there may be restrictions on smoking and drinking.

The end of Ramadan (**Djoulde Soumae/Eid al-Fitr/Id al-Sighir**) typically lasts from two to as many as ten days (and is estimated to end on 30 September in 2008, 23 September in 2009 and 9 September in 2010). Celebrated all over Cameroon, the festival is perhaps most noticeable in Foumban, where there are horse races, processions and dances.

Muslims in northwestern and northern Cameroon also widely celebrate **Tabaski** (or Eid al-Kabir) near the start of the year. In 2008 this is predicted to be 8 December, in 2009 27 November, and in 2010 16 November. The celebrations coincide with the end of the pilgrimage to Mecca and commemorate Abraham's willingness to sacrifice his son as commanded by God. During the event a ram is sacrificed instead. Celebrations typically include a parade of *marabouts* (Muslim holy/wise men and fortune-tellers) and great feasts.

New Year's Day in the Islamic calendar is expected to be on 29 December 2008, 18 December 2009 and 7 December 2010, while **Ashoura**, celebrating the meeting of Adam and Eve after leaving Paradise, is predicted to be on 7 January 2009, 16 December 2010 and 5 December 2011.

Just over 12 weeks after Tabaski is a smaller celebration, **Eid al-Moulid** (or Mawlid or Milad), commemorating the birth of the Islamic Prophet Mohammed. It is predicted to be around 9 March 2009, 26 February 2010 and 15 February 2011.

TOUR OPERATORS

TOUR OPERATORS WITH ITINERARIES THAT INCLUDE CAMEROON Organised tours can make a lot of sense, especially as in Cameroon many interesting places can be difficult to reach by public transport, or even with your own vehicle.

UK

African Trails 93 Leyland Rd, Preston, Lancs PR1 9QJ; 01772 741600; e sales@africantrails.co.uk; www.africantrails.co.uk. North to south 22- or 29-week tours of Africa pass through Cameroon. There are agents for the company in Australia, New Zealand, Austria, Belgium, Denmark & Kenya.

Dragoman Overland Camp Green, Kenton Rd, Debenham, Stowmarket, Suffolk IP14 6LA; 01728 861133; e info@dragoman.co.uk; www.dragoman.com. Offering several overland trips that visit Cameroon.

Earthwatch 267 Banbury Rd, Oxford OX2 7HT; 01865 318831; e info@earthwatch.org.uk; www.earthwatch.org/europe. The Earthwatch Institute engages people worldwide in scientific field research & education to promote the understanding & action necessary for a sustainable environment. It sometimes offers Cameroon tours although none were available at the time of going to press. Earthwatch has offices worldwide.

USA

Access Africa Suite 914, 80 Wall St, New York, NY 10005; 212 785 0130; e info@accessafrica.com; www.accessafrica.com. Access Africa offers various west African tours including one to Cameroon that covers Limbé, Mount Cameroon, the Kribi region, Foumban & Waza National Park.

Bicycle Africa 4887 Columbia Dr South, Seattle, WA 98108-1919; 206 767 0848; www.ibike.org/bikeafrica. Bicycle Africa specialises in ecotourism bike holidays for small groups. There are currently 2 tours in Cameroon, a 15-day 570km/340 mile bicycle tour of the west, & a 15-day 480km/220 mile tour of the north.

DreamWeaver Travel 1185 River Dr, River Falls, WI 54022; 715 425 1037; e dudley@ dreamweavertravel.net; www.dreamweavertravel.net. Organises 'ecologically & culturally appropriate'

scheduled trips to Cameroon usually in Oct & Dec. Also builds trips around other dates & offers custom trips for individuals. Visits cover anything from southeastern Cameroon's equatorial rainforest & meetings with Baka 'Pygmies' to northern Cameroon's arid moonscape & nomadic culture.

Explore Africa 445 Anglers Dr, Suite 2E, Steamboat Springs, CO 80477; (970) 871-0065; e info@ exploreafrica.net; www.exploreafrica.net. This company offers an itinerary that includes Gabon, the Central African Republic & Douala, Bafut, Koutaba & Foumban in Cameroon. Price dependent upon tour size.

Turtle Tours Box 1147, Carefree, AZ 85377; 480 488 3688; e turtletours@earthlink.net; www.turtletours.com. Offers custom-made tours of Cameroon.

TRAVEL AGENTS AND TOUR OPERATORS IN NORTH AMERICA These agents can organise discount flights and may be able to help with overland tours and advice.

Air Hitch www.airhitch.org. A rather long-winded system offering discounted tickets from the US to Europe, currently from US$167 one-way.

Nomad Travel Bazaar 127 Harmon Cove Towers, Secaucus, NJ 07094; (201) 770 0120; www.travelbazaar.com

Travel Cuts 124 MacDougal St, New York, NY 10012; ☏ (212) 674 2887; www.travelcuts.com. Specialises in budget & student travel.

LOCAL TOUR OPERATORS AND TRAVEL AGENTS These operators can generally organise tours, internal and international flights, car hire and hotel bookings, and can often help in other ways, such as currency exchange. Tours tend to be pricey.

Yaoundé

Cameroon Tours and Safaris (CAMTOURS) BP 1198; immeuble La Patience 273, Rond-point Nlongkak; ☏ 2220 50 70; e info@camtours.org; www.camtours.org. The extremely well-established CAMTOURS specialises in birdwatching & safari tours, the latter concentrating on the most popular national parks, Waza, Korup & Bénoué. Tours are also organised to rainforest sanctuaries, & there are cultural tours of the grasslands region as well as beach vacations to Kribi & Limbé. Car & minibus hire can also be organised.

Safar Tours BP 5855; Hilton Hotel, Bd du 20 Mai; ☏ 2222 87 03/2223 36 46; e safar@safartours.com; www.safartours.com. Books domestic/international air tickets & organises tours.

Jully Voyages BP 6064; 385 Rue Mvog-Fouda Ada, Quartier Elig-Essono; ☏ 2222 14 48/2222 39 47; www.jullyvoyages.com. Can organise trekking, tours & safaris.

MTA (Mouwayoue Travel Agency) BP 3176; 272 Av J F Kennedy, Centre Ville; ☏ 2223 97 65/2323 44 44

Inter-Voyages BP 127; 71 Rue Valéry Giscard d'Estang; ☏ 2223 10 05/2222 03 01

Cameroon Travel Center BP 6977; 139 Rue Joseph Omgba Nsi, Quartier Elig-Essono; ☏ 2222 62 21

Moabi Voyages BP 2374; 1061 Av de l'Indépendance; ☏ 2222 87 37

Inter Tour Rte Mvog-Mbià; ☏ 2223 97 62; e intertour@hotmail.com

Camvoyages BP 606; Av de l'Indépendance; ☏ 2223 22 12

Douala

Ebene Voyages BP 446; ☏ 3342 29 85; e info@ebene-voyages.com; www.ebene-voyages.com. This highly recommended, established tour operator is based in the Bali neighbourhood of Douala. Ebene offers personalised tours including trekking, canoeing & travel by railway, taxi & 4x4 minibus. In the north, tours often cover the Mandara Mountains & Lake Chad, while in the southeast there are trips to see the Baka 'Pygmies' & Dja Reserve. In the west trips are organised to Mount Cameroon, crater lakes & various chiefdoms.

Jet Cam Tour BP 5301; Res-de-chaussée, Res La Fala, junction of Bd de la Liberté & Rue Gallieni, Akwa, by Résidence La Falaise; ☏ 3343 30 78. Changes money as well as booking flights & arranging tours.

Souad Travel Agency BP 4200; Av de la Liberté, by Hotel Parfait Garden; ☏ 3342 65 50. Arranges excursions throughout Cameroon.

Prestige Tours Cameroon BP 1766; ☏ 3342 11 64. Prestige can help with flight bookings & car hire as well as organise tours.

Globe Travel BP 4855; Rue Joss, Bonanjo; ☏ 3343 12 79. Excursions that can be arranged include visits to Mount Cameroon, Foumban, the villages of the Mandara Mountains in the north & 'Pygmy' villages in the southeast rainforests. Other services include car hire, hotel & flight reservations.

Trans Africa Tours BP 15435; ☏ 3342 90 04. Offers various excursions as well as car hire, air ticket reservation, etc.

Jully Voyages BP 1868; Rue Boué de Lapeyrère, Akwa; ☏ 3342 32 09

Cameroun Horizon BP 3237; 758 Rue Tobi Kuoh, off Pl du Governement; ☏ 3342 94 24; e camhoriz@camnet.cm; www.cameroun-plus.com

Cameroon Rev'Tour ☏ 3342 10 05; m 7774 94 46

Bafoussam

Tandel Voyages Sarl BP 994; Rue Entrée de la Ville, Ndiengdam; ☏ 3344 65 81

MTA (Mouwayoue Travel Agency) BP 1240; Bd Pachoin Adolphe-Tamdja; ☏ 3344 49 21

Ngaoundéré

Alto Agence de Tourisme By the Grand Marché; ☏ 2225 11 29. Various trips including horseriding.

Garoua

Cameroon Safari Agency BP 1050; Bd Dr Jamot, town centre; ☎ 2227 23 26; m 9997 92 40; e camsafagency@yahoo.fr

Maroua

Fagus Voyages BP 352; Djarengol-Pitoare; m 9986 18 71; e fagusvoyages@bluewin.ch; www.fagusvoyages.com. Organises safaris in Boubandjida, Waza & Bénoué reserves, fishing trips in lakes & rivers, hiking & trekking in the Mandara & Atlantika mountains. Also offers car hire.

Safari Kirdi BP 90; Siege-Office; m 77 644831; e safarikirdi@yahoo.fr; www.oasereisen.de. The owner of this company offering tours, Mr Dabala, is very reliable & speaks French, English & German.
Cameroun Extreme Nord Safaris BP 508; ☎ 2229 33 56/2229 15 32; e deliteri@hotmail.com
Jean-Remy Zra Teri BP 507; ☎ 2229 26 23

SPECIALIST BIRDING TOUR OPERATORS

Birding Africa 4 Crassula Way, Pinelands 7405, Cape Town, South Africa; ☎ +27 21 531 9148; e info@birdingafrica.com; www.birdingafrica.com. This group of biologists, bird-book authors & conservationists have been leading birding tours in Africa for international tour companies & small groups since 1997. They have acted as consultants for the BBC Natural History Unit & showed Bill Oddie his very first Cape rock-jumpers. Offers 10-day tours in both northern Cameroon & southern Cameroon, a Picathartes Quest & tailor-made tours.
Bird Quest Two Jays, Kemple End, Stonyhurst, Lancs BB7 9QY, UK; ☎ 01254 826317; e birders@birdquest.co.uk; www.birdquest.co.uk. 15/18-day tours of Cameroon for £3,490/US$6,561/€5,165 excluding flights.

Rockjumper Birding Tours PO Box 13972, Cascades 3202, South Africa; ☎ +27 33 394 0225; e info@rockjumper.co.za; www.rockjumper.co.za. Tours of 21 days duration covering both north & south.
Sarus Bird Tours 12 Walton Dr, Walmersley, Bury, Lancs BL9 5JU; ☎ 0161 761 7279; www.sarusbirdtours.co.uk. Covering the main birding sites in the country on a CFA2,588,250 (£2,820/US$5,700) tour, excluding flights.
Tropical Birding 17 Toucan Tropics, 26a Willow Rd, Blouberg Rise 7441, South Africa; ☎ +27 21 556 4124/+27 82 400 3400; e tropicalbirding@telkomsa.net; www.tropicalbirding.com. Both set-departure trips in Mar & Apr as well as customised trips for small groups in search of mega-specials such as grey-necked rockfowl & Mount Kupe bush shrike are available.

In addition, the **Cameroon Biodiversity Conservation Society**, formerly the Cameroon Ornithological Club (*PO Box 3055, Messa, Yaoundé, Cameroon;* ☎ *2221 16 58;* e *cbcs@iccnet.cm*) also offers guiding tours of limited duration.

And Cameroonians who have worked with **BirdLife International** carrying out surveys in the Bamenda Highlands are able to act as guides to visitors wishing to see a general range of species or to focus on the endemics. Contact can be made via Taku Awa II (m *7745 44 44;* e *takuawa@yahoo.co.uk*).

The website, **www.mount-cameroon.org/birdwatching.htm**, includes contact details of local guides in the forests in Cameroon. If you hire one of these guides, you will make a contribution to the community which will help in biodiversity conservation. If you intend to visit Mount Cameroon, please make sure you go through The **Mount Cameroon Ecotourism Organisation** (MCEO) (*PO Box 66, Buéa, SWP;* ☎ *3332 20 38;* m *7758 45 93;* e *mountceo@yahoo.co.uk; www.mountcameroon.org*). They are the only official tour operator on the mountain.

SPECIALIST TRAVEL AGENTS AND TOUR OPERATORS IN BRITAIN
These agents can organise flights to and from Cameroon and may be able to help with overland tours and advice. It is also worth trying online booking agents/discounters like www.lastminute.com, www.cheapflights.com and

www.priceline.co.uk in the UK, www.cheaptickets.com and www.priceline.com in the US, and www.travelshop.com.au in Australia.

African Travel Specialists 229 Old Kent Rd, London SE1 5LU; ☏ 0870 345 5454
Bridge the World ☏ 020 7911 0900; www.bridgetheworld.com
Cameroon Holidays 14 Market Pl, Hornsea HU18 1AW; ☏ 01964 536191; e sales@capeverdetravel.com; www.cameroonholidays.com
Ebookers 178 Tottenham Crt Rd, London W1P 9LF; ☏ 020 7757 2000; www.ebookers.com

Global Village 102 Islington High St, London N1; ☏ 0844 844 2540 (UK local rate); ☏ +44 207 704 5700; www.gvillage.co.uk
STA Travel www.statravel.co.uk. Look online to find your nearest branch.
Student Travel Centre 1st Floor, 24 Rupert St, London W1D 6DQ; ☏ 020 7434 1306; www.www.student-travel-centre.com
Trailfinders www.trailfinders.com. Look online to find your nearest branch.

SPECIALIST TRAVEL AGENTS AND TOUR OPERATORS IN FRANCE

Capital Tours 54 Rue du Brave Rondeau, 17000 La Rochelle; ☏ 05 46 68 24 58
Club Aventure 18 Rue Seguiler, 75006 Paris; ☏ 01 44 32 09 30; www.clubadventure.com
Go Voyages 14 Rue Clery, 75002 Paris; ☏ 01 53 40 44 00; www.govoyages.fr

Nouvelles Frontiers 87 Bd de Grenelle, 75015 Paris; ☏ 01 45 68 70 00; www.nouvellesfrontieres.fr
Vie Sauvace 24 Rue Vignon, 75009 Paris; ☏ 01 44 51 08 00

DISABLED TRAVELLERS

Facilities are very few and far between for disabled travellers in Cameroon, and private transport arrangements may be required. Many streets are unpaved or pot-holed, wheelchair ramps are very rare, and accommodation is likely to have few facilities such as a lift, except in the most expensive hotels.

General advice is available from **Tripscope** (☏ *0845 7585 641; www.justmobility.co.uk/tripscope*) in the UK; the **Irish Wheelchair Association** (☏ *01 818 6400; www.iwa.ie*) in the Republic of Ireland; the **Australian Council for the Rehabilitation of the Disabled** (☏ *02 6282 4333; www.acrod.org.au*) in Australia, and the **Society for the Advancement of Travelers with Handicaps** (☏ *212-447 7284; www.sath.org*) in America.

i TOURIST INFORMATION

CAMEROON
Ministry of Tourism (Ministère du Tourisme) BP 266; Bd Rudolf Manga Bell, Yaoundé; ☏ 2223 29 36;
e mintour@camnet.cm; www.camnet.cm/mintour/tourisme/

EUROPE
Tourism Information Bureau for Europe 26 Rue de Longchamps, 75016, Paris, France; ☏ (0) 1 45 05
96 48; e office@cameroun-infotourisme.com; www.cameroun-infotourisme.com

RED TAPE

ENTRY REQUIREMENTS

Passport All visitors to Cameroon require a full passport which should remain valid at least six months beyond the end of the trip.

Foreigners are required to carry their passport (or an officially certified photocopy) with them at all times while in the country and will be asked to produce this at the various roadside checkpoints.

It is a good idea to have photocopies made of the title and visa pages of your passport, as well as the page showing your arrival date in Cameroon, and getting these certified, so that you both safeguard against loss or having your passport confiscated while in the country, and can keep your passport in a safe place.

Main police stations in Cameroon can certify for free the photocopies if you provide them with your passport, visa and a CFA500 (95 cents/53p) fiscal stamp (*timbre*) purchased from the Ministry of Finance (Minefi), which has offices in the bigger towns.

Yellow fever certificate All visitors require a valid yellow fever certificate, which becomes valid ten days after the vaccine is administered and lasts for ten years. Many UK GP surgeries do not offer yellow fever vaccinations any more so check in plenty of time as you may have to visit a specialist travel clinic.

Cholera certificate Although the cholera jab is not considered to be very effective, the certificate may be requested by officials, especially if there is a cholera epidemic in the region or, more probably, they are after a bribe. Many travel clinics are happy to provide a certificate misleadingly stating that you *haven't* had the jab, but which tends to do the trick at borders.

Return ticket If you arrive by air, this is required for entry into the country.

Visa Apart from nationals of Central African Republic, Congo, Mali and Nigeria for a stay not exceeding 90 days, all passport holders must have a tourist visa issued by a Cameroonian high commission or embassy unless there is no representation in the country of departure. In west Africa there are Cameroonian embassies or consulates in Dakar, Lagos, Abidjan and Calabar, but these offices may refuse to issue a visa.

Passengers in transit continuing their journey out of Cameroon on the first or same aircraft within 24 hours and holding onward tickets and not leaving the airport do not require a visa.

Obtaining a visa is an example of how haggling and vague bureaucracy can affect all areas of African life. Strictly speaking, visitors without a visa may be required to leave Cameroon on the next available flight, particularly if they are coming from a country where there is a Cameroonian embassy. Unofficially, visas are usually available at the airports at Douala and Yaoundé.

For passengers arriving from countries without Cameroonian diplomatic representation, airport visas are usually available.

Visas can take more than three weeks to obtain by post or two or three days if applied for and collected in person. In the UK, tourist visas for three months currently cost £60 (about US$120) and in theory it's double for six months, although when I last applied the High Commission in London would only grant one-month visas, costing the same amount.

Be prepared that documents required and stipulations can vary (and website information can be out of date) and therefore applying for a visa can take several visits or telephone calls, and can be far more time-consuming than you would first assume.

Ask whether you can submit photocopies of documents like air tickets, travellers' cheques or bank statements, rather than the originals. I have submitted original bank statements in the past and did not get these returned, to the consternation of my accountant.

Required documents to be submitted are a full passport valid for at least six months, two completed application forms (available from the high commission or embassy), two passport-sized photographs, a yellow fever vaccination certificate and the visa application fee.

You would need to show a return or continuation air ticket (or possibly a receipt with flight details from a tour operator) and proof of means of subsistence (for example a bank statement, but failing that travellers' cheques or a credit-card statement should normally suffice) unless a tour operator or travel agency is organising the trip.

Last time I applied for a visa, because I was travelling independently, I was asked to also provide a legalised letter of invitation with the Cameroonian police from my host or contact in Cameroon. From London this seemed a bit of a time-consuming, logistical headache to say the least, so I politely remonstrated and the official then said proof of a hotel reservation would do. There are numerous websites that allow you to book a Douala or Yaoundé hotel for a night for this purpose so that you can print out a reservation, which you can cancel at a later stage at no cost, if required.

If you are applying by post you will also need to supply a pre-paid special delivery envelope in order to get your passport returned. Contact the embassy a few days after applying as they will not contact you if something is wrong with your application.

Visas are valid from the date you are entering Cameroon, not from date of issue, and must be activated within a month of issue. A visa only represents permission to apply to enter and does not guarantee entry into Cameroon. You can be refused entry, for example for not having a yellow fever certificate or for having only a one-way ticket.

Visas can be extended, which is easiest to do in Yaoundé, although often possible in the regional capitals. In Yaoundé, go to the Ministry of Immigration, Avenue Mdug-Fouda Ada (✎ 2222 24 13).

Apart from the mandatory visa you need to enter Cameroon, it is generally easiest and best to obtain any further ones you may need before you leave home rather than in Cameroon.

Some travellers have found, for example, that requesting a visa for a neighbouring country has initially been refused while in Cameroon, and they have had to take further measures, such as obtaining a general letter of recommendation from their own consulate.

Visa service companies Visa service agents such as Corporate Visa Services (✎ 020 7336 0101; visa4travel.com) in the UK and Travisa (✎ 202 463 6166 or ✎ 1 800 222 2589; www.travisa.com) in North America can obtain a visa on your behalf for a fee.

Sufficient funds When you enter the country, you may have to convince immigration officials that you have what they consider to be sufficient funds for your time in Cameroon.

Ⓔ EMBASSIES

CAMEROONIAN EMBASSIES, CONSULATES AND DIPLOMATIC MISSIONS

Australia 65 Bingara Rd, Beecroft, NSW 2119; ✎ 02 9876 4544; www.cameroonconsul.com

Belgium Av Brughmann 131-133, 1060 Bruxelles; ✎ 02 345 1870

Canada 170 Clemow Av, Ottawa, Ontario KIS 2B4; ✎ 613 236 1522/865 16 64; www.haut-commissariat-cameroun-ottawa.ca

Central African Republic BP 935, Av de la France, Bangui; ✎ 61 16 87

Chad Rue des Poids Lourds, N'djamena; ✎ 51 28 94

Congo BP 2136, Rue General Bayardelle, Brazzaville; ✎ 83 34 84

Equatorial Guinea 19 Calle Rey Boncoro, Malabo; ✎ 24 64

Ethiopia Bole Rd, Addis Ababa; ☎ 44 81 16
France 73 Rue d'Auteuil, 75016 Paris; ☎ 01 47 43 98 33
Gabon BP 14001, Bd Leon Mba, Libreville; ☎ 73 29 10
Germany 532 Bad Godesberg, Rheinallee 76, Bonn 53; ☎ 0228 356 038
Italy 282 Corso Vittorio Emmanuelle, 00186 Rome; ☎ 654 71 50

Ivory Coast (Côte d'Ivoire) Immeuble le General, Rue Botreau-Roussel; ☎ 20 21 33 31
Netherlands Amalistraat 14, The Hague; ☎ 70 346 97 15; www.cameroon-embassy.nl
Switzerland 6, Rue Dunant, Geneva; ☎ 022 736 2022
United Kingdom 84 Holland Pk, London W11 3SB; ☎ 020 7727 0771
United States 2349 Massachusetts Av, N.W, Washington, DC 20008; ☎ 202 265 8790

FOREIGN DIPLOMATIC REPRESENTATION IN CAMEROON
Yaoundé

Canada BP 572; Immeuble STC-TOM, Pl de l'Hôtel de Ville; ☎ 2223 23 11
Central African Republic BP 396; off Rue Albert Ateba Ebe; ☎ 2220 51 55
Chad BP 506; Rue Joseph Mballa Eloumden, Bastos; ☎ 2221 06 24
Congo Rue 1815, Bastos; ☎ 2221 24 58
Democratic Republic of Congo BP 632; Bd de l'URSS, Bastos; ☎ 2220 51 03
Equatorial Guinea BP 277; Rue 1805, Bastos; ☎ 2221 08 04
France BP 1631; Plateau Atemengue, Av de France, near Pl de la Réunification; ☎ 2223 40 13/2222 17 76

Gabon BP 4130; Rue 1816, off Bd de l'URSS, Bastos; ☎ 2220 29 66
Germany Av Charles de Gaulle; ☎ 2221 00 56
Ivory Coast (Côte d'Ivoire) BP 11357; Rue 1805, Bastos; ☎ 2221 74 59/2221 74 59
Liberia BP 1185; Bd de l'URSS, Bastos; ☎ 2221 54 57
Nigeria BP 448; off Av Monseigneur Vogt; ☎ 2222 34 55
United Kingdom BP 547; British High Commission, Av Winston Churchill; ☎ 2222 07 96/2222 05 45; e bhc.Yaoundé@fco.gov.uk; www.britcam.org
United States of America PO Box 817; Rue de Nachtigal; ☎ 2223 05 12; www.usembassy.state.gov/Yaoundé

Douala

Benin Bepanda College Maturite, Bepanda; ☎ 3340 13 41/3340 21 53
Canada BP 2373; 68 Av Charles de Gaulle, Bonanjo; ☎ 3343 29 34/342 31 05
Central African Republic Rue Castelnau, Akwa; ☎ 3343 45 47
China ☎ 3342 62 76
Democratic Republic of Congo BP 690; 70 Rue Sylvanie, Akwa; ☎ 3343 20 29
Denmark ☎ 3342 64 64
Equatorial Guinea BP 5544; Rue Tokoto, Bonapriso ☎ 3342 96 09
France BP 869; Av des Cocotiers, Bonanjo; ☎ 3342 62 50
Greece ☎ 3342 81 09
Italy ☎ 3342 95 37

Nigeria BP 1553; Bd de la Liberté, Akwa; ☎ 3343 21 68
Norway ☎ 3342 52 6.
Senegal Galerie MAM, Bonanjo; ☎ 3342 28 63
Spain ☎ 3342 72 40
Sweden ☎ 3342 52 69
Switzerland ☎ 3342 21 70
Togo BP 828; 490 Rue Dicka Mpondo, Akwa; ☎ 3342 11 87
Tunisia ☎ 3342 70 37
United Kingdom BP 1784; British Consulate, 3rd Floor, Standard Chartered Bank Bldg, Bd de la Liberté, Akwa; ☎ 3342 36 12/3342 21 77
United States of America BP 4006; Immeuble Flatters, off Av Charles de Gaulle, Bonanjo; ☎ 3342 03 03

GETTING THERE AND AWAY

✈ BY AIR
Yaoundé or Douala? Almost all visitors to Cameroon fly to Douala, which for many years has been Cameroon's principal international air transport hub. Yet several airlines also fly to Yaoundé and landing here to an extent avoids the bigger crowds and more chaotic city-of-a-developing-country reception you will invariably receive at Douala.

Although Yaoundé is further east than Douala you can get to most of the key tourism areas in the south and west almost as easily. Yaoundé is more convenient for the north, as you can hop off the plane onto the train to Ngaoundéré, and it will also save hassle if you are visiting the rainforests of the east.

Prearrange and relax Because arrival at Douala Airport can be rather hectic, even a bit hostile if you're an unseasoned traveller in Africa, and reliable onward transport can be difficult to secure, it is a good idea to prearrange being picked up, for example by your hotel if it offers this service, or an established tour operator, such as Ebene Voyages (↘ 3342 29 85; m 9999 66 31; e ebene.voyages@camnet.cm), which could also prearrange some activities for the start of your time in Cameroon. A few days lazing on the beach at Kribi, or at a laidback nifty little Cameroonian beach community like nearby Ebodje, before commencing touring or trekking, is a great antidote to a punishing schedule of long-haul flights, visa applications and the rest.

Flights to Cameroon Flights to Cameroon from Europe (either to Yaoundé, or far more frequently, to Douala) are currently via Paris, Brussels, Amsterdam, Zurich or London. The Air France flight from Paris to Douala, for example, is 3,150 miles and takes about six hours, and the connecting flight to London takes around 50 minutes.

Some African airlines offer flights to Cameroon via another African country. These are listed below. There are currently no direct flights to Cameroon from North America and visitors have to make a connection in Europe.

At the time of writing, a return trip from London to Douala or Yaoundé typically costs from about £525 to £850 economy class including taxes, and up to £3,000 first class although newcomers to Cameroon routes, Royal Air Maroc and Afrqiyah Airways, have been offering flights for as little as £360 return.

Another option, especially if you are heading for the north, is to fly to Ndjamena in Chad and travel the last 30 miles to Cameroon on land. Although, at the time of writing the Foreign Office advises against all travel around the area bordering Chad because armed banditry is common.

January to April is generally the cheapest time of year for flights. These are the current carriers, all with connections from London.

Afriqiyah Airways ↘ +32 2 788 2020; www.afriqiyah.be. Flies to Douala via Brussels & Tripoli.

Air France ↘ 0845 0845 111; www.airfrance.com/uk. Flies from London to Douala (daily) & Yaoundé (3 times a week) via Paris.

Cameroon Airlines ↘ 020 833 0386 (London), ↘ 01 43 12 30 12 (Paris). Flies from London (on an Air France flight) to Paris Charles de Gaulle Airport & then to Yaoundé & Douala several times a week. At the time of writing all flights (international & domestic) were currently suspended. Moreover, all Cameroon Airlines websites were out of date & should be ignored.

Ethiopian Airlines ↘ 020 8987 7000; www.flyethiopian.com. Flies from London to Douala via Addis Ababa twice a week & although it often offers the cheapest fares, you typically have to spend a day in Addis Ababa on the outward journey & a night on the way back (although accommodation is usually provided free on the return).

Kenya Airways ↘ 01784 888222; www.kenya-airways.com. Flies to Douala from London via Nairobi & is generally one of the cheapest airlines for the route but the stopover in Nairobi often makes the journey one of the longest.

KLM Royal Dutch Airlines ↘ 0870 243 0541; www.klm.com. Flies to Douala & Yaoundé via Amsterdam with connecting London flights.

Royal Air Maroc ↘ 020 7307 5800; www.royalairmaroc.com. Flights to Douala & Yaoundé from the UK via Casablanca.

SN Brussels Airlines (previously Sabena) ↘ 0870 735 2345; www.brusselsairlines.com. Flies twice a week to Douala & once a week to Yaoundé via Brussels with connecting London flights.

Swiss International Airlines ☏ 0845 601 0956; www.swiss.com. Flies to Douala twice weekly & Yaoundé once weekly via Zurich, again with connecting London flights.

Virgin Nigeria ☏ +44 844 412 1788; www.virgin.nigeria.com. Offers flights to Douala via Lagos, & Virgin Atlantic from London to Lagos.

🚌 BY LAND

Border crossings Ensure all your paperwork is completely in order to satisfy customs and immigration staff. Accept that, especially at quiet borders, there may be a considerable wait. An official may have to be summoned from their home or another location before you have the required stamp to proceed, and the matter may not be treated with the same degree of urgency as you would like. Borders may close in the afternoon, evening, on national holidays, at weekends, and in Muslim areas on Fridays. If there is a wait, don't get impatient or lose your temper with border officials, which could make matters worse, but instead make the most of your time, for example by reading a book or writing a letter.

Travelling overland on these routes can be rough and a 4x4 vehicle is recommended. It is inadvisable to attempt these routes at night or during the rainy season.

The principal border crossings are Kousseri for Chad; Banki or Ekok for Nigeria; Ambam to Bitam for Gabon; Campo or Ebebiyin for Equatorial Guinea; Garoua-Boulai or Kenzou, near Gamboula, for the Central African Republic; and Ouesso for Congo.

Overland from Nigeria The two most popular routes from Nigeria lead to Mora in the north of Cameroon and Mamfé in the west of the country.

If you take the northern route a good road takes you from Maiduguri to Bama and then to the border post at Banki. This takes about 90 minutes by minibus. Taxis and minibuses are available on the Cameroon side to take you across the plains to Mora and Maroua, the latter taking around 90 minutes and typically costing CFA2,000 (£2.15/US$3.80).

If you take the western route, you can take a three-hour bush taxi from Calabar to Ikom and then one from Ikom to the Nigerian border village of Mfum, which is 25km. Here you go through Nigerian customs and red tape and continue towards Ekok, walking across the bridge over the Cross River, up a hill to the Cameroonian border post at Ekok. The border post closes at 19.00. You have a choice then of taking a 60km taxi ride from Ekok to Mamfé through the mountains, or you can go by *pirogue* from Ekok down the Cross River to reach Mamfé. An alternative *pirogue* route takes you from Calabar to Mamfé.

Visas currently cost CFA30,000–40,000 (£32–42/US$56–75) depending on nationality and are available from the Nigerian Embassy in Yaoundé or consulates in Douala and Buéa.

Overland from Chad At the time of writing the Foreign Office advises against all travel around the area bordering Chad because armed banditry is common, but if it appears safe to enter Cameroon this way a relatively new bridge links Ndjamena, Chad's capital, with Kousseri in Cameroon. You can take an inexpensive taxi or motorcycle taxi from Ndjamena or Nguele to the Cameroonian side of the bridge. Minibuses operate from Kousseri to Maroua and the CFA4,500 (£4.82/US$8.50) journey, which is very beautiful, takes around four hours.

Because of the increasing levels of crime along this route in recent years minibuses in this area may have an armed escort. Check the security situation locally.

You can also enter Cameroon from Lere and Bongor in southern Chad, the latter by canoe over the Logone River.

One-month visas currently cost CFA35,000 (£37/US$66) and are available from the Chad Embassy in Yaoundé.

Overland from the Central African Republic At the time of writing the Foreign Office advises against all travel around the area bordering the Central African Republic because armed banditry is common. But if it appears safe to enter Cameroon this way the Cameroonian border post at Batouri can be reached from the road leading from Berberati and Gamboula in the Central African Republic, while the border point at Garoua Boulai is reached by a road from Bouar.

There are some buses or you can hitch a lift on a truck. From Garoua Boulai you can head north for Ngaoundal via Meidougou, a 270km journey, where you can catch the Yaoundé–Ngaoundéré train, or take a minibus for Bertoua (93km from Batouri, 255km from Garoua Boulai) where you can take a 90km taxi trip to Belabo train station. There is also at least one bus daily from Garoua Boulai to Ngaoundéré, which takes around ten hours.

A one-month visa is CFA35,000 (£37/US$66), available from the CAR Embassy in Yaoundé.

Overland from Equatorial Guinea The main road from Bata in Equatorial Guinea leading to the main Cameroon entry point (as well as one for Gabon) at Ebebiyin has been improved by the building of a paved road. The Ntem River is crossed by ferry. The road continues to Ambam, where it meets the main road to Ebolowa.

Alternatively, taking the coastal route, take the track from Bata to Elende on the border with Cameroon, where you can take a boat to Ipono, just south of Campo. Bear in mind that there is no accommodation on either side of the border. At Campo you can get a minibus for the 90km journey to the coastal beach town of Kribi, which takes about four hours and costs CFA1,500 (£1.60/US$2.83).

Visas are CFA36,000 (£38/US$67), valid for a month, and available from the embassy in Yaoundé and the consulate in Douala.

Overland from Congo At the time of writing the border with Congo was closed. When it is not, entering Cameroon from Congo is time-consuming and strenuous. You need to head for Ouesso. Barges for Ouesso leave Brazzaville infrequently and you may be waiting for a week or two. At Ouesso you can take a minibus to the border where a *pirogue* transports you over the Ngoko River to the village of Kika. You then need to hitch eastwards as far as the town of Moloundou where, during the dry season, you can take the 212km route to Yokadouma by bus, which takes about eight hours and costs CFA5,000 (£5.35/US$9.45).

Visas for Congo are for three months and available from the Congo Embassy in Yaoundé.

Overland from Gabon You can enter Cameroon by taking the main road from Libreville to Oyem, continuing to Bitam for the exit formalities, and heading for Ambam in Cameroon, where you get your entry stamp. At Kye Ossi a ferry takes you across the Ntem River. Both the 90km journey by minibus from Ambam to Ebolowa and the 170km trip from Ebolowa to Yaoundé take about three hours each.

Visas cost CFA40,000 (£42/US$75)and last a month.

BY SEA

From the UK Grimaldi Line sails from Tilbury, near London, and several other European ports, and stops at a number of major ports in west Africa including Douala. Strand Voyages (*Charing Cross Shopping Concourse, Strand, London WC2N*

4HZ; ℄ 020 7836 6363) and Freighter World Cruises (*180 South Lake Av No. 335, Pasadena, CA 91101, USA;* ℄ *626 449 3106*) both can provide further details.

From Nigeria It is possible to take a boat from Calcemco Beach just north of Caabar in Nigeria, or alternatively from Oron, south of Calabar, which goes to Limbé and Idenao in Cameroon. These boats are not regulated. A passenger speedboat costs anything from CFA20,000 to CFA40,000 and takes around four hours. Cargo boats are another option but these are not recommended as they are often not safe.

There are also boats that go from Ikang in Nigeria to Mundemba in Cameroon.

If you are considering arriving by boat, check the current security situation as you pass the Bakassi Peninsula, which is under dispute by Nigeria and Cameroon and which has been subject to serious unrest in recent years.

Visas currently cost CFA30,000–40,000 (£32–42/US$56–75) depending on nationality and are available from the embassy in Yaoundé or consulates in Douala and Buéa.

From Equatorial Guinea There are sometimes boats connecting Douala, Limbé and Ngueme, a village near Limbé, with Malabo on Bioco Island (Equitorial Guinea). Enquire at the shipping offices around Limbé and Douala's port.

Pirogues operate across the Ntem River from Equatorial Guinea to Cameroon.

Visas for Equatorial Guinea are available from the embassy in Yaoundé or the consulate in Douala and are currently CFA36,000 (£38/US$67).

WHAT TO TAKE

SOME SUGGESTIONS
- Pocket French dictionary/phrasebook
- Lightweight, easily erected mosquito net – essential to help avoid malaria
- Extra passport photos for photographic permits, visa extensions, etc
- International drivers' licence
- Insect repellents
- Water purifying tablets/water filter
- Dental floss: as well as cleaning your teeth with it, it can double as string, a washing line, can secure a mosquito net, can be used as thread for repairing clothes
- Sewing kit
- Disposable razors
- Tampons
- Contraceptives
- Binoculars
- First-aid kit
- Alarm clock
- Map distance measurer
- Torch (flashlight) and spare bulb and batteries, useful during electricity cuts
- Small towel for cheaper hotels that have none
- Earplugs (for noisy hotels)
- Calculator (for working out exchange rates)
- Padlock (for hotel doors without a lock and for securing luggage)
- Compass
- Hand-held Global Positioning System (GPS) unit, costing from under £100/US$175 is a consideration if you will be in remote areas
- Waterproof bag (to protect your luggage if you take boat trips)

- Plastic bags
- Plastic rain poncho/lightweight windproof waterproof jacket, which can double as a ground mat and is easier than carrying an umbrella.
- Hat
- Penknife or Swiss Army Knife
- Short-wave radio for listening to local broadcasts or BBC World Service, etc
- Sheet sleeping bag/sleeping sheet/travel liner (for cheap hotels with unappealing or non-existent bedding)
- Compressible sleeping bag
- Novels – for those interminable waits at roadblocks and bus stations

$ MONEY AND INSURANCE

TRAVEL INSURANCE In this part of the world a good travel insurance policy covering possible medical complications is essential, including an emergency flight home, with coverage of theft and loss a bonus. Shop around, as policies can vary widely in price, and check the small print. 'Dangerous activities', which could even include trekking, may be excluded. Bear in mind that you may have to pay for medical treatment on the spot and claim later, so keep all documentation. STA Travel Insurance (*www.statravel.co.uk*) provides good cover, including laptops.

CURRENCY Cameroon's currency, along with most of the francophone countries in west Africa is the central African economic zone's (Communauté Financière Africaine or the African Financial Community) CFA franc guaranteed by the French Treasury. To complicate things, there is also a west African CFA (used by Burkina Faso, Senegal, Guinea Bissau, Ivory Coast, Togo, Benin, Mali and the Comoro Islands) which although identical in value, cannot be used in Cameroon.

Note that although the value of the central African CFA is exactly the same as the west African CFA, one incurs a loss of money when changing from either of the currencies.

There are no limits on the importation or export of foreign currencies, but the importation limit of the local currency is CFA20,000. Tourists may export up to CFA20,000 per journey, while those on business may take out up to CFA45,000.

Any amount of CFA can be exported to other central African CFA countries (Gabon, Equatorial Guinea, Congo, Central African Republic, Chad).

Currency is available in CFA10,000, CFA5,000, CFA2,000, CFA1,000 and CFA500 notes, and 500, 100, 50, 25 10 and 5 CFA coins.

It is a good idea to try and avoid being given high denomination notes at the bank as they may be difficult to get rid of – many shops will not carry sufficient change to accept them.

EXCHANGE, TRAVELLERS' CHEQUES, CREDIT CARDS, ATMS AND TRANSFERS It is advisable to ensure that you have more than enough hard currency in cash to cover all of your expected expenses. Exchange rates for cash are much more favourable than for travellers' cheques or credit cards. Euros are the best currency to travel with. Those with dollars and sterling are likely to have problems changing them, especially outside Douala and Yaoundé, and especially in the north.

Banks – although not all branches – with a foreign exchange service include Crédit Lyonnais, Société Générale de Banque au Cameroun (SGBC), Amity, Standard Chartered Bank and Banque International du Cameroun pour l'Epargne et le Crédit (BICEC). The first three are perhaps most geared up for changing money, and the first two can also provide Western Union international money transfers.

Exchange rates for the prices in this book (June 2008) £1 = 829CFA, US$1 = 425CFA, €1 = 656CFA.

Those used to the convenience of using travellers' cheques, credit cards, debit cards and obtaining cash from hole-in-the-wall machines will get quite a shock in Cameroon. Changing money can generally be a very frustrating experience. It is important to plan ahead especially outside Douala and Yaoundé as opportunities to obtain cash easily and inexpensively can be rare.

Whilst some banks are open on Saturdays, this does not include foreign exchange services. Banks are typically open from 07.30 to 15.00 or 15.30 from Monday to Friday, and outside Douala and Yaoundé may at times run out of money.

The moral arguments of using the black market aside, changing money through the black market is not really an option as in many African countries, because the CFA is easily converted and pegged to the euro.

Many hotels will allow you to exchange money at a fair rate.

Travellers' cheques It is common for banks, even in Douala and Yaoundé, not to accept travellers' cheques and when they do they are likely to request to see your purchasing receipt, offer poor exchange rates and charge a very high commission.

Euro travellers' cheques are the most widely used but service can be slow, especially outside Douala and Yaoundé. Commission rates for foreign currencies start at around 2% although exchange rates, especially for less common currencies, can be 25% below the official exchange rates and a commission of around 20% is not uncommon on US dollars or sterling.

I gave up on bringing travellers' cheques to the country after spending a fruitless afternoon in Douala trying unsuccessfully to change some euro travellers' cheques, despite visiting virtually every bank in the city. Even if a bank takes euro travellers' cheques, it is likely that it will only accept ones issued by certain bank, rather than all banks – and invariably not from the issuer of your cheques.

Credit cards Although credit and debit cards can be used for a few more expensive hotels and restaurants, and occasionally for tourist services such as tours, car hire and flights, it is best to assume that you will not be able to use them. The high incidence of credit-card fraud in Africa means that even organisations like Air France will not accept credit cards in their Cameroon offices.

If you do find that you can make use of a credit card, a 2–15% commission may be charged. It is seldom possible to draw cash against credit cards at banks or hotels. If you are able to, you will almost certainly need to use your PIN number. MasterCard credit cards are often not useable but Visa credit cards are far more common. When taking credit cards overseas inform your card issuer of the dates you will be in Africa otherwise transactions may be blocked due to suspected fraudulent misuse.

ATMs Automated teller machines (ATMs), or hole-in-the-wall cashpoint machines, are few and far between. They include a secure one at Douala Airport in a glass cabin (taking Visa, not MasterCard) and ones at SGBC bank branches: at Rue Joss, Bonanjo, Douala; on Avenue Charles de Gaulle, Yaoundé; and off Rue Centrale in Garoua, as well as branches in Bafoussam and Limbé.

Look out for any tampering with the ATM machine. I put a credit card in a Douala machine and the next day the credit-card company fraud department was onto my home telephone enquiring whether I really wanted to buy £666-worth of toys from a lock-up in Nigeria.

International money transfers Cities and most bigger towns in Cameroon have at least one Western Union office that can wire money from abroad. Thankfully the transfer of money from abroad now takes only a few minutes rather than several days, as it used to do, and the person abroad wiring you the money can do so by telephone, giving their credit card details. Unfortunately, the service is expensive. For example, the Western Union service charge to send £200/US$352 from the UK to Cameroon by credit card is currently around £25/US$44, for £300/US$528 is £32/US$56, and for £400/US$704 is £39/US$68. The service charge using a debit card instead of a credit card is approximately 15% less. The exchange rate on the amount received in CFA is also several per cent less favourable than if money had instead been changed from euros to CFA at a bank in Cameroon.

You can also have money wired from your own bank at home, but this is usually slow and more complicated.

Western Union ➘ 0800 833 833 (UK); ➘ 1 800 325 6000 (US & Canada); ➘ 1800 501 500 (Australia); ➘ 1800 395 395 (Republic of Ireland); www.westernunion.com

BUDGETING You can live both extremely cheaply and at great cost in Cameroon. While road transport, simple hotels and market food can cost a fraction of what a Westerner is used to, conversely, international-standard hotels, car hire and top restaurants can cost far more. Public transport increases in cost the more remote and difficult the route, and can be higher during the rainy season, but is generally a bargain.

Although Douala and Yaoundé have the most expensive hotels by far, they also have some of the cheapest as well and it is in the more remote areas, especially in the north, where budget-priced accommodation can be hard to come by, and standards of accommodation for the money you are paying plunge.

Generally, locally produced items like food, drink and transport are cheap, while imported items can cost twice what they do in the West. Reckon on around CFA470 (50p/88c) for a litre of petrol, CFA375 (40p/70c) for a 50cl bottle of beer and around CFA500 (53p/94c) for a 66cl bottle of beer in a bar. A packet of cigarettes varies from local concoctions like 'Business Class' for CFA300 (32p/56c), CFA500 (53p/94c) for Lambert and Butler, CFA1,000 (£1.07/$1.89) for Benson and Hedges and CFA1,500 (£1.60/US$2.83) for Dunhill.

A city taxi ride is around CFA1,000 (£1.07/US$1.89), a night in a simple hotel to be under CFA10,000 (£10/US$18), in an air-conditioned one around CFA15,000 (£16/US$29) and comfortable hotels with extras like television or a pool from CFA30,000 (£32/US$58). Hiring a car and driver for the day will cost from CFA45,000 (£48/US$87), easily double if you use one of the international agencies. Food from street vendors and simple cafés is easily obtainable for around CFA4,000 (£4.20/US$7.56) per day.

TIPPING See page 81 for details.

4

Travelling in Cameroon

GETTING AROUND

Possibly the easiest and cheapest way of getting around the country is to use **buses** to take you to the main centres. Once you are dropped off in the town or city by these buses you can then use taxis, share taxis or minivans for shorter, more localised trips. These can be ludicrously cramped and the cheaper the service the more likely you may have to wait a few hours for the vehicle to fill up.

An exception to this rule would be travelling between Yaoundé in the south and Ngaoundéré in the north, which is far quicker, easier and more comfortable by **train**.

The buses are cheap and generally efficient, and some routes, such as the route passing the verdant anarchy of forest from Douala to Yaoundé, have operators that offer luxury air-conditioned buses with drinks and snacks on board and the attractive bonus of providing a whole seat to yourself. Even this option is comparatively cheap.

Share **taxis** on set routes to other towns and within the city or town itself are very cheap, and even if you have a taxi to yourself in town it is good value. For optimum flexibility you could consider hiring a taxi for the day.

Flying is by far the most expensive way of getting around and can be subject to delays, and **car hire** is another expensive option.

Travel around Cameroon can be taxing at the best of times, and can be well nigh impossible in some areas during the rainy season. Even so, main cities and towns enjoy a comparatively good network of tarmac roads.

At times you may be subjected to incessant, seemingly inexplicable delays, cancellations and roadblocks.

✈ BY AIR

Internal flights Cameroon Airlines (CAMAIR), the national carrier, operates a regular domestic air service between Douala, Yaoundé, Ngaoundéré, Bafussam, Bertoua, Garoua and Maroua (see page 52 for contact details). There are sometimes flights to Batouri, Kribi, Dschang, Mamfé, Bali and Koutaba. At the time of writing, however, all flights had been suspended due to financial problems.

Douala–Yaoundé flights cost around CFA30,000 (£32/US$56); Yaoundé–Garoua CFA68,000 (£72/US$128); Yaoundé–Bafoussam CFA21,000 (£22/US$39); Yaoundé–Maroua CFA85,000 (£91/US$160); Douala–Ngaoundéré is CFA61,000 (£65/US$115), Douala–Bertoua, CFA50,000 (£53/US$94). All prices are one-way. Currently flights run once or twice each week.

Be prepared for delays, cancellations and overbooking of internal flights. Arrive at the airport early to improve your chances of receiving a boarding pass. The *harmattan* (see page 43) can cause visibility problems at Ngaoundéré and Maroua and therefore causes delays.

Air travel times from Yaoundé are approximately 50 minutes to Bafoussam; 70 minutes to Bamenda; 30 minutes to Douala; 50 minutes to Dschang; 150 minutes to Garoua; 90 minutes to Koutaba; 45 minutes to Kribi; 60 minutes to Mamfé; 230 minutes to Maroua; and 160 minutes to Ngaoundéré.

Cameroon imposes a domestic airport departure tax of CFA500 (53p/95c) on domestic flights.

If you take an interest in the safety record of airlines, you will be interested to know that from 1981 to 2003 Cameroon Airlines has had five accidents with 77 fatalities, 71 of which died in a crash on 3 December 1995. In 2005 the French civil aviation authority banned flights to France by Cameroon Airlines for an indefinite period because of safety concerns. Bellview, previously regarded as a safe airline by Western expatriates in Cameroon, had a crash on 22 October 2005 where all 117 on board were lost.

Though unusual outside Africa, many African airlines require reconfirmation of flights 72 hours in advance.

Flights from Cameroon to other destinations in Africa When Cameroon Airways was operational (not the case at the time of writing) it flew to destinations that included Bamako, Lagos and Dakar. There is an ever-changing range of regional airlines, almost always flying from Douala. Presently they include Bellview (to Libreville and Lagos), Air Gabon and Air Service (Libreville), Hewa Bora (Brazzaville), Benin Golf Air (Malabo, Abidjan, Cotonou), Tourmai Air Chad (Ndjamena, Bangui, Brazzaville), Trans Air Congo (Brazzaville), Air Ivoire (Lomé, Cotonou, Lagos, Accra and others), Equato Guineana de Aviacion (Malabo), Virgin Nigeria (Lagos), Ethiopian Airlines (Addis Ababa), and Kenya Airways (Abidjan, Nairobi).

Airline offices in Cameroon
Yaoundé
Air France BP 14335; 528 Rue de Nachtigal; ☎ 2223 43 78; www.airfrance.com/cm
Cameroon Airlines Av Monseigneur Vogt; ☎ 2223 03 04/2223 40 01
Kenya Airways Nsimalen Airport; ☎ 2223 36 02

SN Brussels Airlines BP 13812; Av Foch; ☎ 2223 47 29/2223 47 35; www.brusselsairlines.com
Swiss International Airlines BP 14710; Av Foch; ☎ 2222 97 37/2223 94 52, airport: ☎ 2222 97 30; www.swiss.com

Douala
Air France BP 4076; 1 Pl du Gouvernement, Bonanjo; ☎ 3342 15 55, airport: ☎ 3342 28 78; www.airfrance.com/cm
Air Gabon BP 371; off Av Charles de Gaulle; ☎ 3342 49 43
Air Ivoire BP 1313; Bd de la Liberté, Akwa; ☎ 3342 06 95; e airivoiredla@airivoire.com; www.airivoire.com
Cameroon Airlines BP 4092; 3 Av Charles de Gaulle, Bonanjo; ☎ 3342 32 22/3342 25 25/☎ 3342 01 11, Hotel Akwa Palace: ☎ 3342 26 01, airport: ☎ 3342 25 25

Equato Guineana de Aviacion BP 11673; represented by Hila Hotel; ☎ 3342 15 86/996 46 66
Kenya Airways Rue de Trieste, Bonanjo; ☎ 3342 96 91
SN Brussels Airlines BP 2074; 100 Av Charles de Gaulle, Bonapriso; ☎ 3342 05 15; www.brusselsairlines.com
Swiss International Airlines BP 2959; Av Charles de Gaulle, Bonanjo; ☎ 3342 29 29, airport: ☎ 3342 10 40; www.swiss.com

Airports
Yaoundé Nsimalen International Airport BP 13615; ☎ 2223 17 44/2223 06 11
Douala International Airport BP 3131; ☎ 3342 36 30

Garoua International Airport BP 987; ☎ 2227 23 46
Maroua-salak Airport BP 271; ☎ 2229 19 49
Ngaoundéré Airport BP 279; ☎ 2225 11 57
Bertoua Airport ☎ 2224 14 86

Douala International Airport Like the airports of other large African cities, Douala's international airport can be quite chaotic, with the excessive heat and porters, hustlers and taxi drivers all touting for business.

When you arrive you will invariably have to work through this procedure: inspection of hand luggage, health (yellow fever card) check, filling out an immigration card, passport control, handing in completed disembarkation card, showing return ticket if requested, getting health slip stamped, baggage hall check, and at exit from customs you hand in your baggage registration slips from your ticket before being allowed to take away your luggage and show your passport.

If you have checked your baggage through to Yaoundé, you now collect it, and go through customs. For connecting flights enter the domestic flights section of the building. Baggage is checked in at the far end of the hall where you will receive a boarding card if you do not already have one. The departure lounge is down on the lower ground floor. Facilities include a duty-free shop, bar, post office, bank, shops and a buffet/restaurant.

Expect to pay around CFA3,500 (£3.75/US$6.61) for a taxi from the airport for the 10km/6-mile journey to the centre of Douala.

Connecting flights and overland to Yaoundé Onward flights to Yaoundé can be unreliable and overbooked and a boarding card is not a guarantee of a seat or of departure. It is often quicker and more reliable to drive or take a bus from Douala to Yaoundé (allow three hours). Centrale Voyages operates a service that takes around three hours and costs CFA3,600 (£3.95/US$7.90). The first bus from Douala leaves at 06.30. Recent visitors have advised against using Guaranti Express, whose buses are inferior to those of Centrale Voyages. Another option is Bucca Voyages. Taking a taxi from Douala Airport to the Centrale Voyages bus office is about 3,600 CFA (£3.95/US$7.90) also.

If you miss a connecting flight through delays in the arrival of your flight from Europe, the carrier airline should arrange hotel accommodation in Douala and onward transport free of charge. See ground staff of the airline on arrival to obtain the necessary vouchers.

Yaoundé (Nsimalen) International Airport Arrival procedures are the same as for Douala. Nsimalen Airport is about 25km (15½ miles) from the city. There is no public transport system and the 20-minute taxi ride costs approximately CFA4,500 (£4.82/US$8.50) and the Hilton and Mount Fébé hotels operate a hotel express bus service.

Departure procedures: reconfirm your ticket Confirm your onward or return flight as soon as possible after arrival. There is a departure tax of CFA10,000 (£10.71/US$18.90) for international flights. It is payable in CFA, euros or US dollars.

Air safari If you are fortunate enough to have the funds to finance a private air tour of Cameroon, or need to charter a flight to an unusual destination in the country, there follows a list of Cameroon's towns with civil airport facilities. Most of the runways are unpaved.

Abong-M'Bang, Akonolinga, Ambam, Bafia, Bafoussam, Bali, Bamenda, Banyo, Batouri, Bertoua, Betare-Oya, Dimako, Dizangue, Djoum, Douala, Dschang, Ebolowa, Eseka, Foumban (alternative name Koutaba), Garoua, Kribi, M'bakaou, M'bandjock, Mamfé, Maroua (two), Mokolo, Moloundou, Ngaoundéré, Nkongsamba, Nanga-Eboko, Ngaoundal, Nguti, Tibati, Tiko, Waza, Yaoundé (two).

🚗 **BY ROAD** Driving around Cameroon is not for the novice. Of the country's 37,000km of roads, only about 15% are paved. Broken bridges, pot-holes, general decay and overturned vehicles may close roads (especially the smaller dirt roads) temporarily. During the rainy season many roads have washed away or are passable only with 4x4 vehicles.

In the cities, as well as the huge pot-holes to navigate, driving is something of a free-for-all, a sort of military campaign, with cars, trucks, bikes and motorbikes going in all directions, especially at junctions. Strangely, it all seems to work, though – most of the time. In theory, Cameroon drives on the right.

On many roads, as well as hazards like pot-holes and ditches, road and traffic signs are infrequent, while livestock and pedestrians regularly create dangers – livestock inadvertently, while some Cameroonian pedestrians have an unnerving habit of standing in the middle of a road with their arms outstretched to force cars to stop, in an attempt to hitch a lift. Many drivers drive too fast, drive when overtired, and overtake on blind bends.

Although the bad condition of the roads can be a safety concern, the best roads, such as the main road from Douala to Yaoundé, can be a concern for the opposite reason – being in such good condition they encourage speeding. The Douala–Yaoundé road, for example, has a bad safety record (more than 70 coach passengers died in a crash in January 2003, for instance) but then this should be put in context with the multiple pile-ups that occur on our motorways in the West.

Good roads connect Cameroon's other southern cities and both Yaoundé and Douala are easily accessible from Bamenda, Foumban and Bafoussam and from Cameroon's two main seaside towns of Kribi and Limbé.

But many roads are in not such good condition. In places the road between Ekok and Mamfé, for example, is no more than a mound of red mud, about 5ft wide, the sides sloping steeply down into the forest on either side of the road. In the rainy season this surface becomes very slippery when wet.

Travel in the east of the country is hampered by dense rainforest and a lack of paved roads, and in the south, south of Yaoundé, apart from paved roads to Ebolowa, Kribi and Sangmélima, the network is mainly made up of tracks and dirt roads.

A paved 510km road from Ngaoundéré to Maltam connects the three major northern cities of Ngaoundéré, Garoua and Maroua, but they are cut off from the south by long stretches of unpaved road. Roads around the Adamawa Plateau are particularly problematic. It is easier to take the train, which can transport vehicles, although this costs around CFA100,000 (£107/US$189).

Gangs of armed carjackers have also been a problem in recent years, especially in the Adamawa and Northern provinces, and the golden rule here, if you are unlucky enough to be stopped by one, is to offer absolutely no resistance and simply give them your valuables (and vehicle if they want it). These gangs tend to target the more expensive vehicles like top-of-the-range 4x4s rather than clapped-out bangers.

Along with malaria, road safety is likely to be your biggest safety concern. Early morning is safest to be on the roads, with drivers most refreshed and least likely to be drunk, and travelling after dark is not to be recommended at all. Apart from the lack of visibility you will have of pot-holes and other hazards: both wild and domestic animals often spend the night by the roadside and maybe even on the road itself.

If you are in a bus, minibus or share taxi and want to complain about dangerous driving, it is often better to say you feel nauseous rather than simply ask the driver to slow down, as he will generally be more concerned to keep vomit off the seats than avoid an accident.

On the positive side, the roads in rural areas, which constitute most of Cameroon, have very little traffic.

Road travel times from Yaoundé are approximately 3 hours 30 minutes to Bafoussam, 4 hours 30 minutes to Bamenda, 3 hours to Douala, 20 hours to Garoua, 24 hours to Maroua and 12 hours to Ngaoundéré.

In Cameroon there is little point trying to deduce journey times from looking at maps. Even if the road is good and there is little traffic, long delays can be caused by police and military roadblocks.

Roadblocks Police and military roadblocks are a frequent factor of travelling by road and are often situated on the edge of towns. The roadblock can be anything from a piece of rope to a plank of wood studded with nails, a wooden barrier or a row of oil drums. To deal with them ensure you have all your required documents to hand and remain polite and courteous, however rude and obstreperous the police you encounter may be.

Foreigners are allowed to carry a certified photocopy of the first five pages of their passport, which safeguards having your passport confiscated along the way. Main police stations can certify the photocopies if you provide them with your passport, visa and a CFA500 (53p/94c) fiscal stamp purchased from the Ministry of Finance.

Car hire You can cover a lot of ground by taking your own vehicle, but fuel, insurance and maintenance tend to make this option expensive, while security and breakdowns can be a real headache.

Car hire is most commonly available in Douala, Yaoundé, Bafoussam, Ngaoundéré, Maroua and Garoua. Saloon cars with the international agencies typically cost from around CFA20,000 (£21/US$37) per day plus further charges per kilometre (around CFA250/26p/47c), for insurance and taxes, plus petrol. If you plan to leave the surfaced roads, you may be required to take a 4x4 vehicle, and costs can be very high, typically around CFA50,000 (£53/US$94) per day with further charges per kilometre (around CFA350/37p/66c), for insurance and 18.7% taxes, plus petrol. There is usually a deposit to be paid of at least CFA500,000 (£530/US$940). You may also be required to hire a driver if you are hiring an expensive car or leaving the main routes.

Considering all this, it is likely to be cheaper to hire a taxi on a daily basis (see below). Generally speaking, hire cars cannot be driven into neighbouring countries, and the minimum age for renting a car is 21.

Foreign licences and International Driving Permits are not valid in Cameroon, but a Cameroonian licence is usually obtainable within 24 hours upon production of the foreign licence and payment of the prescribed fee.

International car hire agencies operate in Cameroon through local licensed offices and there are various local companies, which are generally cheaper. Car hire can also be arranged through the better hotels and tour operators.

International car-hire companies in Cameroon

Avis 🕾 0870 606 0100 (UK), 🕾 1 800 272 5871 (Canada), 🕾 01 605 7500 (Republic of Ireland); www.avis.com

Europcar 🕾 0845 722 2525 (UK), 🕾 01 614 2800 (Republic of Ireland); www.europcar.co.uk
Hertz 🕾 0870 844 8844 (UK), 🕾 1 800 263 0600 (Canada), 🕾 01 660 2255 (Republic of Ireland); www.hertz.com

Douala car hire

Auto Joss BP 1265; 20 Rue Monoprix, near Score supermarket, Bonapriso; 🕾 3342 86 19; e autojoss@cyberix.cm. A Nissan Sunny is

CFA22,000 (£23/US$41) per day plus CFA200 (21p/37c) per km, with insurance CFA6,750 (£7.23/US$12.75) per day plus 18.7% taxes.

4

Marta Sabbadini, English teacher and trainer in Cameroon

Taxi rides are the easiest and most common way of getting around Cameroonian cities and towns and can often prove to be quite an experience. Though a real hazard to anyone else on the road, taxi drivers are remarkably efficient at finding passengers and getting them to their destinations. Yellow cars in all conditions circulate the streets, often unashamedly with no windscreen or back seats. But if you choose your taxi carefully, it can be an excellent way of getting to know a city. Only by taking a taxi can you discover the names of landmarks that you will never find on any street map.

Yellow taxis circulate the streets at all times, hooting at anyone they think may be a potential passenger. The standard taxi ride involves paying CFA175 for '*1 place*' and sharing·the taxi – that is, one or two passengers at the front and three at the back. Taxi drivers are incredibly skilled at working out routes which incorporate all their passengers' stops, and although this makes the trip a little longer, they only take on people that fit a general route. Luggage can be kept at your feet or put in the boot. Where this is very large, the driver may ask for an extra CFA100 or so.

Alternatively, if you are in a hurry, have a long way to go, or simply don't fancy squeezing in with everyone else, you can get a taxi for yourself. This is called a *depot* and can be negotiated at CFA1,000, regardless of whether you are alone or with company. If you need to do various stops, or perhaps need a taxi all afternoon, better to negotiate a *taxi course*, usually at around CFA3,000, which basically provides you with a private car and driver. Make sure to be clear about times and destinations before setting off. Taxis from Douala Airport into the centre of town cost a flat fare of CFA3,000 per vehicle, though drivers may well try to tell you otherwise.

The ritual for hailing a taxi involves standing on the roadside in the direction of where you are going, preferably in a sensible place for a taxi to see you and stop. You then wave at every taxi that passes, shouting your destination and number of people travelling (for example '*Rond-point Deido, 2 places*'). If your destination suits the driver, he will grind to a halt and indicate for you to get in (often without speaking or even looking at you) simply by hooting. If not, he will ignore you and drive on by.

It is taxi etiquette to say a general '*bonjour*' to the driver and other passengers as you get in the car. You will find that the windows usually have no handles. If you want to

Avis Hotel Akwa Palace, Bd de la Liberté, Akwa; ☎ 3342 03 47. A small 4x4 is CFA40,000 (£42/US$75) per day plus CFA285 (30p/53c) per km plus CFA9,500 (£10/US$18) insurance per day. A larger 4x4 such as a Land Cruiser is CFA58,000 (£62/US$109) per day plus CFA350 (37p/66c) per km plus CFA11,800 (£12/US$22) per day. A driver is obligatory for the latter, at around CFA15,000 (£16/US$28) per day.
Avis Douala Airport; ☎ 3330 02 01
Europcar Rue Njonjo; ☎ 3343 21 26
Auto Rent ☎ 3342 40 46
Auvergne Auto ☎ 3342 94 55
Sam Auto ☎ 3343 03 31

Yaoundé car hire

Avis Rte de Douala; ☎ 2230 22 85/2230 20 88
Avis Hilton Hotel; ☎ 2223 36 46
Europcar Near Cameroon Airlines office, off Av Vogt; ☎ 2223 08 11
Jully Voyages Av Mvog-Fouda Ada, near train station; ☎ 2222 39 47

Eurovoyages Rue Narvick; ☎ 2222 66 10
Auverne Auto Bd du 20 Mai; ☎ 2222 57 06
Hertz Near the centre, on the road to the airport; ☎ 2230 41 88
ADA c/o Safar Tours, Hilton Hotel, Bd du 20 Mai; ☎ 2222 87 03

Bafoussam car hire

Avis BP 1045; Rte de Foumban; ☎ 3344 13 71

open or close your window, indicate this to the driver ('*chaffeur*') who will hand over the handle.

On arriving at your destination, indicate to the driver exactly where you want him to leave you, passing him your fare as you get out. He will give any change to you once you have left the car, through the window. In situations where you do not have small change, you should tell the driver at the start of your journey so he can find the necessary change *en route*.

Occasionally drivers decide to change route because several passengers ask to go to the same place. He can thus ask you to change taxis, or more commonly, will find you a taxi and negotiate with them to take you, before you even have time to protest. In this case, you pay nothing to the old driver, paying the full fare to the new driver on arrival.

In the rare case where the car breaks down, it is up to you whether to wait around or find a new one, and do not expect any apologies on the driver's behalf. If it is just a flat tyre, it is probably better to wait, as the drivers can change them in a minute. If it looks like it is going to take longer, give the driver some of the fare, say half, and ask him to find you a new taxi.

As at all times when travelling in Cameroon, safety should be borne in mind. It is always worth taking a look at the other passengers before getting in, avoiding vehicles that are carrying only men, or seem to be already full. Incidents have been heard of whereby a seemingly innocent group of passengers are in fact a group of crooks who, in collaboration with the driver, try to distract you with some story (such as asking you to help them find their way or change a dollar note), only to then drive down a quieter street so as to threaten and rob you.

Make a point of letting the driver know that you are checking their ID (which should be hanging from the rear view mirror) as you get in. I generally prefer sitting in the front seat, or, if at the back, avoid the middle seat from which it is more difficult to get out. After dark it is better to avoid share taxis and pay for a *depot*. Fares can go up to around CFA1,500 after 22.00.

Finally, trust your instinct and if a taxi doesn't feel right – because the other passengers are paying you unnecessary attention or because the driver seems to be deviating from the route without reason – simply ask to get out immediately, pay the fare and find a new car.

Ngaoundéré car hire
Vina Voyages Av Ahidjo; ℡ 2225 25 25

Garoua car hire
Avis Near the port; ℡ 2227 12 98
Auto Location Rue Ahmadou Ahidjo; ℡ 2227 20 38

Lasal Voyages Rue des Banques; ℡ 2227 21 37/2227 12 98

Road accidents If you are a motorist involved in a road accident, by law you are not permitted to move your vehicle until the police have inspected the scene and given the go-ahead. This can mean lengthy traffic delays for everyone else.

Before setting off Before setting off on a journey, especially to areas off the beaten track, check the vehicle thoroughly, including the spare tyre, battery, water, oil and engine, and be sure there are enough tools at least to change a wheel. You should carry jerrycans of water and fuel at all times as well as all the required documents.

Buses, minivans and share taxis Buses, minibuses and share taxis cover most of Cameroon's towns and vary from super-efficient, air-conditioned minibuses with waitress service that ply popular routes like Yaoundé to Douala, to cheaper, tatty but relatively safe buses, inexpensive, licensed minibuses. Unregulated, overcrowded vehicles including minibuses, seated vans and oversized saloon cars cover the widest range of destinations.

A vehicle due to leave at 08.00 may not leave until noon, and the driver may wait an hour just to get a last passenger. Typically there are innumerable stops for passengers, police roadblocks and, in the north, praying. At stops you are likely to be offered things like fruit, *brochettes* and boiled eggs by locals. As accidents are quite frequent, travel – especially at night – should be avoided when possible.

Embarkation systems can be puzzling, or even alarming, but generally are no cause for concern. Your luggage may be spirited away the moment you agree to buy a ticket, for example, and you are left to wait luggage-less for a couple of hours until it miraculously appears again and the vehicle is on its way. Centrale Voyages, for instance, sells you a ticket, writes your name on it and then keeps it while your luggage is taken from you by porters in green coats. Despite passengers having no luggage and no ticket, when the bus is ready to leave their names are read out and are given their tickets back so that they can board the bus.

Popular routes, such as Douala to Limbé or Douala to Kribi, will have a large choice of carriers, and it can seem quite alarming when you get stormed by about 20 men eager to sell you a ticket. Even more alarming though, can be a cramped ride at breakneck speed: very generally, the less you pay, the less attention paid to safety.

Agency buses Private, agency-run (*agence de voyages*) long-distance coaches and buses (or *car, grand car, 'big bus'*) and minibuses to many destinations operate in the absence of a national bus network. They include Guaranti Express, Centrale Voyages, Alliance Voyages and Binam and are generally very good value.

The buses usually run from outside the agency's office. Finding out destinations, timetables (which frequently change) and where a particular bus departs from can be a challenging business. The easiest way is to ask at your hotel which agency to recommend for your destination. Taxi drivers generally know all of the agencies and the destinations they offer.

Regular bus services run between main towns and cities like Yaoundé, Douala, Limbé, Kribi, Bafoussam and Bamenda, and in the north, Ngaoundéré, Garoua and Maroua. There are no bus services across the Adamawa Plateau from Yaoundé to Ngaoundéré, where the train service is the best option.

Share taxis and minibus taxis Share taxis, or bush taxis (*taxi brousse* in French) are a very common way to get around and are commonly saloon cars (often Peugeot 504s and 505s seating seven passengers, the most comfortable), less comfortable minibuses (*minicars*) seating from around 12–20 passengers, and station wagons and covered pick-ups (*bâchés*) with benches down the sides seating around 15 or 16 and crammed in to the point of discomfort.

The advantage is that they are licensed passenger vehicles, their low rates and routes fixed by the government. They can be found at the town's or city's bus, bush taxi/motor parks (*gare routière, autogare*) although many towns have several of these, which complicates things. They almost always leave when full rather than run to a timetable, and are likely to pick up further passengers along the way even though they are not registered for extra passengers.

Often there is a choice of operators. If more than one is competing for the route, unsurprisingly usually the one that is most full will leave first, whatever the touts claim. The best seats are behind the driver, or near a window, and on the side with most shade. The place not to be is in the row of seats directly beside the sliding door as it will be musical chairs the whole way, and any passengers picked up on the way will invariably have to cram themselves in here.

You can buy two seats for more comfort, or even charter the whole vehicle by multiplying the price of each seat by the number available. Luggage is generally charged at about 10% of the fare per item.

Clandos Clandos are similar to share taxis and minibus taxis, except that they are unregistered, but tend to cover destinations the agencies and registered share taxis do not. They tend to be not as well maintained and can be even more overcrowded. They can also be found at the town's or city's taxi or motor parks or touting for business near agency offices.

Taxis Taxis are available in most of the towns and cities and the official hire rate is CFA2,300 (£2.46/US$4.34) per hour from 06.00 to 22.00 and CFA2,800 (£3/US$5.29) per hour from 22.00 to 06.00.

In urban areas many taxis operate as share taxis where you flag the taxi down, tell the driver where you want to go, and if this is on the route he is already taking with his other passengers, you jump in (see box on pages 64–5). Agree the price before doing so. In urban areas the fare is generally set at CFA175 (19p/39c: I know; crazy) per drop within the town from 06.00 to 22.00 and CFA200 (22p/44c) from 22.00 to 06.00.

For longer journeys, taxis are considerably cheaper than in the West, but far more expensive than other options by road. For example, Douala to Limbé by taxi is likely to cost in the region of CFA25,000 (£26.79/US$47.25), compared with around CFA1,000 (£1.07/US$1.89) by minibus.

In Douala and Yaoundé at the top hotels there is also the option of taking a luxury, air-conditioned taxi where the starting price is in the region of CFA7,000 (£7.67/US$15.68).

Hiring a taxi instead of car rental Hiring a taxi by the day can be a better bet than car hire. Not only is it likely to be a similar price or even cheaper (expect to pay around CFA30,000/£32/US$64 per day) but if it breaks down it is not your problem. Also, a knowledgeable driver may show you things you would have otherwise missed.

But a hired taxi is more likely to break down than a rental car. Therefore, have a good look at the condition of the vehicle before hiring. Is there a spare tyre? Are the tyres bald? Are the lights and windscreen intact?

Before hiring, agree all aspects of the hire with the driver, such as the driver's bed and board and whether petrol is included in the price.

Motorcycle taxis In northern towns and increasingly in the south are *moto taxis* (motorbikes) taking one or two passengers on the back on short journeys. The fare is generally CFA100 (11p/18c) per trip during the day and double at night, although it is common for the rider to try it on and ask for more. This means of transport is popular and cheap, but safety is more of an issue and it is probably better to pay a little extra for a conventional taxi or share taxi.

Hitching In some rural regions, especially in the southeast of the country, where your only option may be a logging truck, hitchhiking may be the only way of getting around unless you have your own hire car or motorbike. Even so, it is not completely safe and therefore cannot be recommended. If you do hitchhike, don't do it alone and take advice from other hitchers and reliable locals beforehand.

Waving down a vehicle is a common way of travelling in Cameroon, but you are usually expected to pay, unless an expat, aid worker, volunteer, tourist or missionary picks you up. This is understandable, as roads may be in poor condition and public transport may be non-existent, rare or infrequent, and therefore any traffic can be seen as potential 'public transport'. If you cannot pay anything, say so at the outset.

Vehicles with markings for international aid and relief agencies can be a good bet, so look out for markings for organisations like UNESCO.

Cycling Cycling can be an excellent way of exploring as you can discover areas inaccessible by car or motorbike. If you need a rest from riding, bikes can be strapped to the top of a bus or minibus.

Cycling is best avoided in urban areas and is best done in the early morning and late afternoon. Food and water needs should be planned carefully in advance as there may not be many opportunities to restock.

Staff at hotels and bicycle repair stands should be able to find you a bike to hire. Mountain bikes are most suitable in this region but often not available so consider bringing your own. Check with your airline whether you have to dismantle it for the flight and whether there is an extra charge. Carry ample spares including a puncture repair kit, inner tubes and a spare tyre.

BY RAIL Cameroon has a total of 1,104km of railway and there are services from:

- Douala to Yaoundé
- Yaoundé to Ngaoundéré via Belabo
- Douala to Mbanga
- Mbanga to Kumba
- Ngoumou to Mbalmayo

The 622km Yaoundé to Ngaoundéré service is by far the most popular and most useful for travellers and there is a daily overnight service in each direction. It is scheduled to take around 12 hours but recently passengers have been reporting a journey of around 16 to be more typical. It can sometimes, thankfully very occasionally, take over 30 hours. However, it is a good travel option as it covers an area, the Adamawa Plateau, where road travel can be very slow and difficult. It passes superb rainforest scenery.

I am sure my trip on the line is typical: interminable queues and struggling through a scrum to get a ticket, a struggle to find the sleeping car, being turfed out by the guard despite the sleeping car cabin (*couchette*) being reserved in my name, crisp white sheets and an immaculate basin yet no water emanating from the taps in the couchette I was eventually given after a lengthy protest, a ceiling fan that did not work and a train that arrived a couple of hours late. Still, it was a great experience.

The route is via Belabo and Ngaoundal (for road travel to the Central African Republic). In theory it leaves Yaoundé at 18.00 and Ngaoundéré at 18.20, arriving the next morning around 06.30, although in practice if you arrive by 09.00 you are doing well. If you have time to kill at Yaoundé, there is a row of wooden shacks serving beer and food, such as grilled fish and plantain for CFA500 (53p/94c).

Tickets are only available on the day of departure. Beware, the ticket office opening hours can vary enormously. Tickets cost CFA18,000 (£19/US$34) in a first-class couchette sleeping two or four, CFA9000 (£10/US$17) in a first-class seat and CFA6000 (£6/US$11) second class. Only the couchettes can be recommended because theft can be a problem with the cheaper options. Meals are available on the train, such as fish, rice and paw paw for CFA2,500 (£2.67/US$4.72), and an omelette and tea/coffee breakfast for CFA1,000 (£1.07/US$1.89).

As far as safety goes, although in February 1998 two petroleum tanker trains crashed near Yaoundé, killing at least 200 people, the railway has a good record. Remember to take drinking water. Street vendors will usually offer food such as boiled eggs, oranges, lemons, *brochettes* and bread rolls through the windows whenever the train stops.

Taking photographs can attract unwanted attention in Cameroon, and this is especially so on trains. Also beware of thieves and keep your baggage buried well away from the windows and door. Close windows at night and do not store luggage in the overhead racks. There is a restaurant car.

As for the other routes, the 305km Douala to Yaoundé service typically takes around four or five hours and therefore going by road is a quicker option. This service leaves Douala and Yaoundé at approximately 07.00 and 13.30 daily and first class costs CFA6,700 (£7.18/US$12.66), second class CFA3,000 (£3.21/US$5.67).

The service between Douala and Nkongsamba in the west, passing Yaoundé, has deteriorated in recent years with delays more common. This 170km route can take over eight hours. However, the short branch line on this route from Mbanga to Kumba can often be a good travel option, rather than going by road, as the road conditions can be bad, especially in the rainy season.

As schedules often change, enquire in advance by calling the train operator, Camrail (*BP 766, Gare de Bessengue, Douala; ☎ 3340 49 40/3340 60 45/3340 30 80*).

ACCOMMODATION

HOTELS In Douala and Yaoundé and generally in other big cities there are hotels of an international standard. The luxury hotels are expensive when compared with Europe, Australia or North America.

The better hotels in Cameroon are officially rated from one to five stars. All other accommodation is not officially rated, but tends to be better value. Often the price is negotiable at all levels of standard. There are almost no luxury wildlife lodges or tented camps as you would find in southern or east Africa.

The best hotels will generally have clean rooms with air conditioning and a private bathroom. Lower-priced options may have fans rather than air conditioning, may or may not have a bathroom and there will not necessarily be hot water, while the cheapest accommodation may be unclean, have few working facilities, shared bathrooms, a broken window and little or no security for your belongings.

Mid-range hotels, where they exist, are generally acceptable and good value, while the cheaper hotels often double as the local brothel and drinking den and can mean a disruptive night. *Auberges* (guesthouses) are sometimes available at a wide range of standards, and in rural areas there are often *campements*, which are not campsites, but simple inns, lodges or motels with basic accommodation with shared facilities, although there are a few more upmarket exceptions.

Generally, there is plenty of good-value accommodation in the cities, while in rural areas, the north especially, if an average hotel off the beaten track has a virtual monopoly on accommodation in the region, this is likely to be reflected in the prices.

Off the beaten track you may be able to stay in resthouses, in missions or with local people. Ask around when you arrive. Missions are an exception in the budget range, often providing clean, good, safe accommodation, but priority goes to mission or aid workers and in recent years travellers have often been discouraged and therefore obtaining a room can be more difficult.

When choosing a hotel, see the room beforehand and ask for a discount if the air conditioning cannot be used because there is no electricity, or the taps are not all working. Rates are often quoted per room rather than per person, but get this straight at the start.

If you pay under CFA5,000 (£5.35/US$9.45) per night for a room with two beds you can expect a basic hotel or *auberge* with few, basic amenities. From CFA5,000–10,000 (£5.35–10.70/US$9.45–18.90) you may get a self-contained room with a bathroom and more facilities, such as a fan. For CFA10,000–20,000 (£10.70–21.40/US$18.90–37.80) expect the hotel and room to be of a better standard, perhaps with a restaurant and bar. Spend CFA20,000–40,000 (£21.40–42.87/US$37.80–75.61) and expect a standard business- or tourist-class hotel, perhaps with extra amenities like a swimming pool, tennis court and secure parking. If you spend over CFA40,000 (£42.87/US$75.61) per night you are approaching luxury class and top international standards. Even so, some rooms in hotels in Yaoundé and Douala exceed CFA200,000 (£214/US$378) per night.

⚠ CAMPING Campsites are almost non-existent, but away from the cities, towns and beaches of Limbé and Kribi, where theft could be a problem, and apart from the wildlife parks and natural reserves which may have restrictions (although often have camping facilities), there's plenty of wild countryside to pitch up in. Outside the parks ask the village chief or local landowner for permission to camp on their land.

Avoid camping on anything resembling a path through the bush, however indistinct, as it could be a game trail. If a lightening storm is on the cards, ensure that there are higher things nearby than your tent. Don't camp too near water, which animals may visit to drink from, but again don't camp so far away that water is difficult to get to.

STAYING WITH LOCAL PEOPLE Offers of accommodation in people's homes are unusual except in villages in the north that are used to travellers, such as Mokolo and Roumsiki, where there are often few accommodation options anyway. Agree prices and terms clearly at the outset.

LONG-TERM RENTALS Villas and houses are available for rent in most towns in Cameroon while apartments are commonly available for rent in Douala and Yaoundé. Estate agents (*agent immobiliers*) may be able to help.

✖ EATING AND DRINKING

EATING Cameroon offers some of the best cuisine in the whole of west Africa. The country's great geographical differences influence the crops grown around the country. In the south the cuisine is dominated by starch staples like yam and cassava (or manioc, or *batons de manioc*, often appearing as *feuille* on menus) and plantain (a large green unsweet banana that requires cooking, that is normally boiled when unripe and sometimes mashed into an edible glob, or fried when

HOTEL PRICE CODES		
Double room per night:		
$$$$$	Exclusive	above 70,000CFA
$$$$	Upmarket	40,000–70,000CFA
$$$	Mid-range	20,000–40,000CFA
$$	Budget	10,000–20,000CFA
$	Cheap	up to 10,000CFA

yellow and black and ripe). In the north meals are far more likely to have maize and millet. Peanut (groundnut) sauces and palm oil sauces are commonly added to many dishes.

Douala and Yaoundé both have a good choice of restaurants, serving a variety of cuisines including Cameroonian, French, Chinese, Italian, Lebanese, Cambodian, Vietnamese, Indian and Japanese. The most expensive restaurants and hotels tend to serve French dishes, although quality can be quite poor despite the high prices.

You may occasionally find restaurants and cafés serving something substantially more exotic than that, such as snake, giant land snail, pangolin, antelope, gorilla, chimpanzee, elephant, cat or dog. The grasscutter (or agouti, or cane rat), a rodent of the porcupine family, is sometimes found in stews. Less likely to be found on menus are Cameroonian dishes such as fried grasshoppers, ants and termites.

Yet menus are likely to adjust somewhat since the Cameroonian authorities announced in May 2003 that any restaurant caught serving meat from endangered animals could face up to three years in prison and a fine of more than CFA8,000,000/£8,500/US$16,000.

Less formal than restaurants, 'chicken' and 'fish' houses abound, especially in the main cities. They serve chicken, fish, plantains and chips. Most are good and more reasonably priced than full-service restaurants.

The smallest, simplest restaurants are called *chantiers* ('worksites') and serve inexpensive traditional Cameroonian dishes. There are also chop houses (basic eating houses) serving 'chop' (simple local-style dishes) and simple eateries often just consisting of a couple of tables and benches. At a street café you could typically expect to buy an omelette, bread or chips and a drink for under CFA1,000 (£1.07/US$1.89).

Street food is very widely available, typically served on a stick, wrapped in paper or a plastic bag, and is cheap, clean, freshly cooked and tasty. Commonest is the *brochette* or *soya*, a CFA100 (10p/18c) stick of kebabbed meat or fish, usually accompanied by a sauce such as peanut or spice. Although the meat or fish may not have been up to strict hygienic standards when raw, it is normally very thoroughly barbecued and often a far better bet than the frequently reheated pots of food in many restaurants. Spicy maggi sauce is often on hand as a dressing. In the south, grilled fish is often sold at street stalls with fried plantain and cassava.

Beware, though, that in some towns and villages off the beaten track a kebab may consist of less attractive animal parts: sinews and rubbery intestines, tripe and strips of hide.

For snacks, street vendors often sell doughnuts, and peanuts sold in plastic bags. There are good breads, pastries and chocolate commonly available. Chestnut-sized dark red, white and pink kola nuts are widely popular. A mild stimulant that also suppresses hunger, they are chewed for their bitter juices rather than swallowed. Commonly exchanged between friends, they are good when travelling to offer to other passengers as well as to pep yourself up.

RESTAURANT PRICE CODES

Average price of a main course:

$$$$$	Expensive	above 15,000CFA
$$$$	Above average	10,000–15,000CFA
$$$	Mid-range	5,000–10,000CFA
$$	Inexpensive	2,000–5,000CFA
$	Cheap	up to 2,000CFA

Miondo, sticks made of pounded cassava wrapped in plantain leaves and steamed, can be bought ready-to-eat in places offering roasted fish, with three *miondo* (6 rings) typically costing around CFA100 (11p/22c) or one *baton* (a thicker stick) for CFA50.

Coffee stalls are also common, often open only in the morning and typically serving instant coffee with a hunk of bread and butter or mayonnaise and perhaps various fillings.

Fish is popular throughout the country, caught on the coast and in the lakes and rivers. Mackerel, sole and prawns are common.

Eggs and bread are easy to obtain, but cheese far rarer. Fresh milk is rarely available and only dried and sterilised (UHT) long-life milk are easily obtained.

Along the coast are coconuts, commonly covered in a green shell.

Sweetcorn (or corn on the cob) is commonly sold roasted or boiled, and peanut butter is often sold at markets.

Cameroon's great differences in climate and altitude also ensure a wide variety of fruit and vegetables being available, such as avocado, onion, sweet grapefruit, cucumber, mango, guava, paw paw, oranges (often green, yet ripe), sugar cane, tomato, various varieties of banana (including red-skinned), pineapple and papaya. Many are commonly available at markets. When potatoes are on a menu, they usually refer to sweet potatoes rather than normal potatoes. Aubergine (eggplant) is quite common, and can often be yellow, white or red.

Dishes like soups, casseroles and stews are accompanied by rice or a thick, stodgy, bland, mashed dough, either couscous or *fufu* (or *foufou* or *foutou*) made from cassava, rice, banana, yam, plantain or corn.

Cowpeas (*wake*), black-eyed beans, are often mashed and cooked as deep-fried balls called *akara*. Little brown-and-white beans known as pigeon peas are also widespread.

When ordering chips (*frites*) there is often a choice, such as potato, yam or plantain.

Vegetarianism Vegetarianism is little-known and vegetarian restaurants almost non-existent, although Indian and Chinese restaurants in the cities often have vegetarian dishes. Pizzas, omelettes and chips made from root crops like potatoes or yam, are commonly available in towns and cities and boiled eggs and bread are commonly sold on the street. You can stock up on vegetables, fruit and nuts at the markets.

Some Cameroonian dishes *Ndole* (or *ndola*), is made from a slightly bitter leaf that is similar to spinach, which is shredded and made with spices, groundnuts or melon seeds into a thick sauce often accompanying meat, shrimp or fish, and is especially popular around Douala and the south.

Mbongo (or *bongo*) is a dish with a blackish sauce made from crushed and burnt spices and added to meat or fish, and especially popular in Littoral Province.

Popular in the northwest is *njama-njama* (or *ama jama*), made from the huckleberry leaf and commonly eaten with *corn chaff* (maize cooked with beans, tomatoes, spices and palm oil).

Mintumba is a type of cassava-based bread.

Miondo are rather sticky sticks made of pounded cassava wrapped in plantain leaves and steamed. A real staple food in Cameroon, being cheap and filling, and usually eaten with fish or meat.

In the west a popular dish is *condreh*, plantains cooked with palm oil, meat and spices. Another dish of this region is *khokki*, a maize pudding cooked with yam leaves and palm oil.

Popular in the East Province is *Ouinga*, a traditional dish of meat with a sauce made from local herbs and lots of pepper.

In the Extreme North, *folere* is a popular dish of sauce with meat or fish accompanied by *fufu*. Baobab leaves are also prepared with meat or fish and eaten with *fufu* in this region. In the north, goat is the most popular meat used.

Bobolo, a southern dish, is baguette-shaped and made from cassava. Another southern dish, *ebandjea*, a dish prepared with fish, lemon, tomatoes and pepper, is popular around the coast.

Around Buéa *eru* is popular: *ekok* leaves cooked with smoked fish in palm oil and served with cassava *fufu*.

In the coastal areas of the South Province, *ndomba*, a highly spiced fish cooked in banana leaves, is popular.

Kwem (or *nkwem*) is a dish that is especially popular in the Centre Province and contains pounded cassava leaves and groundnuts cooked in palm oil. It is generally eaten with yam, plantain or cassava tubers.

Ekok, a finely chopped forest leaf, is often prepared in palm nut pulp and then grilled, and is also popular in the centre of the country.

Nbomba is steamed meat or fish wrapped in banana leaves, popular in the Yaoundé region.

Charwarmas, a Lebanese snack of grilled meat in bread with salad and sesame sauce, is also popular.

DRINKING Coffee is often of the instant variety, and both tea and green tea are far more popular.

When sealed bottles of mineral water are not available, you could opt for soft drinks like Coca-Cola, Sprite, Fanta and lemonade, and various similar local concoctions, although there is no guarantee that the water used is clean. (Make sure you take the glass bottles back to the shop or stall as they are often returnable.)

Buvettes, small drinks stalls or simple bars, are common. Drinking beer is an extremely popular pastime in Cameroon; indeed bars, often no more than a wooden shack, spring up all over the place. Lagers are common, such as the ever popular Le 33 Export, Castel, Gold Harp and Beaufort are others. A strong version of Guinness is also popular.

A 50cl bottle of a common beer like 33, Castel or Beaufort will generally set you back around CFA400–500 (42–53p/75–94c) in a typical Cameroonian bar, ie: likely to be little more than a wooden shack, rising to CFA1,000 (£1.07/US$1.89) in a mid-range bar or restaurant and CFA1,500 (£1.60/US$2.83) in an expensive tourist hotel or restaurant. The prices are similar in the few places that sell draught beer (*pression*). Maddeningly, many bars have televisions blasting out the likes of *Hawaii Five-O* in French, so don't always count on a quiet drink.

You may get an opportunity to try a homemade beer, often made from maize, millet or sorghum, often strong, and cloudy in appearance. The millet beer found in the north is called *bilibili*, while a popular corn beer of the region is called *kwatcha*.

Potent palm wine (*matango* or *white mimbo*) made from palm sap, is also popular, especially in the south and west. It is often distilled into something resembling gin and known as *afofo*. Beware of the strong alcohol content, and also be aware that unpurified water is often added to the wine.

SHOPPING

Bigger towns often have a *centre artisanal* or *marché artisanal* where arts and crafts can be purchased. The main market in the town will often not sell them.

Bafoussam, Foumban and Bamenda in the west are cities renowned for their masks, wood carvings, embroidered costumes, miniature figures, thrones, pipes and statues made from earthenware, bronze or wood.

Maroua in the north is known for its multi-coloured market where colourful textiles and embroidered tablecloths are sold together with bracelets, swords, mats and other decorative objects.

The Bamoun/Bamiléké region in the West and Northwest provinces is rich in art, which includes bas-reliefs, masks and statues. The distinctive, long tobacco pipes used by the Tikar are widely available to buy in the area. In the north of the country, Fulani jewellery and leather goods are easily found.

A good selection of Cameroon's arts and crafts are available to buy in Douala and at Yaoundé's *marché artisinale*, although quality can be very variable.

Government permission must be sought to remove certain artworks and antiques out of the country. If you are in doubt, check the position by contacting the Delegation Provinciale du Tourisme located in Douala (↘ *3342 14 22*) and Yaoundé (↘ *2223 50 77*).

Although haggling is often expected when purchasing something, don't bargain too hard. Each penny you save is likely to be of far more consequence locally than to you, and a bargain may be obtained because of low wages paid to the producer. Don't of course purchase products made from local wildlife, particularly from endangered species.

SPORTS AND ACTIVITIES

Many areas of Cameroon are excellent for **hiking**, often affording beautiful scenery and varied terrain. The northern area between the towns of Rhumsiki and Mora, home of the Mandara Mountains, and around the Ring Road north of Bamenda in the southwest of the country are especially excellent areas for hiking.

Mount Cameroon offers an excellent opportunity for **mountaineering** and hiking and for those with the required stamina, Mount Cameroon hosts an international mountain race each February.

There is also good **rock climbing** in the Mindif area, about 35km south of the northern town of Maroua, where there is a huge, challenging rock known as La dent de Mindif ('Mindif's tooth'), jutting up out of nowhere.

The beautiful white beaches by the southern coastal town of Kribi and volcanic black ones of Limbé are popular for **swimming**, although beware the strong currents. The safety of swimming at a particular beach should always be sought locally from a reliable source.

Some beaches along the coastline of Cameroon slope steeply and waves can therefore cause a strong undertow. If safety is an issue, many of the better hotels have pools that non-guests can use for a small fee, and there are also public swimming pools in Yaoundé and Douala. Only swim or take a boat in waters that you are absolutely sure are safe – not only from hazards like hippos and crocodiles, but water-borne diseases like bilharzia as well.

Cycling is a good way to travel in rural areas, and encourages interaction with the locals. Possibly the best cycling is in the western and northern provinces of the country. Football and basketball are very popular, and, if you bring your own ball, a game can be easy to initiate in many villages.

Jogging is popular with expatriates, spearheaded by the Hash House Harriers, a group founded by some beer-swilling Australians in Malaysia in 1939, that expanded and which has been running around Cameroon for decades. Yaoundé, Douala, Bamenda and Garoua all have Hash groups, and the local expat communities should be able to advise of the starting point of the latest run.

There are many opportunities to **fish** in rivers and coastal areas, while **golf** lovers will find a spectacular 18-hole course in Yaoundé and another course at Tiko, near Douala.

Douala and Yaoundé both have **equestrian clubs**, and numerous tour operators and travel agents can organise horseriding and trekking trips.

PHOTOGRAPHY

In the past a photography permit was required, but this is no longer the case although it is worth visiting the Ministry of Information and Culture in one of the capitals of the ten regional provinces and requesting a slip with official confirmation that a permit is *not* required. Although this will incur a small fee, it should lessen the chance of delays later on.

Buy film and camera batteries beforehand as in Cameroon these tend to be either expensive, damaged by the heat or hard to find. UV/skylight filters not only protect the lens but block haze. Keep your camera in a dust-proof bag. Local photo processing services can be very variable in quality.

Many Cameroonian people can be suspicious, resentful or hostile of you taking photographs or videos, because of taboos relating to their traditional beliefs and for other reasons, or they may expect payment if they are to be photographed and therefore it is always best to ask people first before photographing them. Offer to pay a small fee or to send them a copy of the photograph, or, if you plan to take a lot of photos, consider taking a Polaroid camera also so that you can furnish your subject with an instant portrait as a thank you. Bear in mind that local people may not wish you to take pictures of their places of worship or of a natural feature that has religious significance to them.

To avoid attention, from anyone from a policeman on the make to senior security officials, avoid taking photographs or videoing anything that could even vaguely be considered governmental, military, strategic or official in any way. This includes things like airports, harbours, railway stations, army, police and prison buildings, police, soldiers, bridges, dams, ferries and members of the government. To complicate matters, many such public facilities are unmarked, and even photographing something as innocuous as a shopfront or field can spark problems with officials.

Indeed, it is best not to bring out your camera wherever there are police, soldiers or other officials. Photography of parades and festivals, photography in Douala and Yaoundé, and any photography an official could deem likely to harm the country's reputation are also not recommended.

MEDIA AND COMMUNICATIONS

MEDIA Cameroon Radio and Television Centre (CRTV) broadcasts on one television channel and some programmes are in English. There is also one national radio station and a station geared to each of the ten provinces of the country (again with some programmes in English), and several commercial stations. Satellite television is increasingly common, especially in better hotels. Cameroonian television, radio and press can be very patchy about international current affairs.

The country's only daily newspaper, the *Cameroon Tribune* (*www.cameroon-tribune.cm*), is published in both French and English, but heavily influenced by the government, which owns it. *The Herald*, published in English, is largely concerned with representing anglophone interests in the west of the country. There is a thrice-weekly independent newspaper in French, *Le Messager*, as well as a very variable number of privately owned newspapers including *La Nouvelle Expression, La Voix du Paysan* and the *Cameroon Post*.

English-language newspapers can be difficult to obtain and a good alternative is to bring a small shortwave radio which will pick up Voice of America (*www.voa.gov*;

MHz 15.58, 11.98, 6.035, 0.909), European stations and the BBC World Service (*www.bbc.co.uk/worldservice*; MHz 17.83, 15.40, 11.77, 7.160), the last of which broadcasts programmes that include *Network Africa* and *Focus on Africa*.

Copies of British, European and North America newspapers and magazines may be available in the lobbies of the expensive hotels in Douala and Yaoundé and some street vendors also sell international publications.

✉ **MAIL** Many roads and streets in Cameroon do not have names or numbered addresses. Consequently, the majority of businesses, government offices and individuals do not have street addresses. Mail is generally sent to a 'boite postale' (BP) or post office box (PO Box).

Post office opening hours are Monday–Friday 08.00–15.30 and Saturday 08.00–13.00.

The central post offices in Douala and Yaoundé (PTT, standing for Postes, Télécommunications et Télédiffusion) operate a quite reliable post restante service. When you collect mail you will be required to show your passport and each letter collected costs CFA150 (16p/28c).

People sending you mail should address their letters to you in this way, with their address on the back:

Ben WEST
Poste Restante
PTT (Grande Poste)
Yaoundé
CAMEROON

International airmail letters typically take from 8–15 days to arrive from Europe or the US. Allow at least a week for airmail from Cameroon to reach Europe and two weeks elsewhere. International surface mail can take from three to six months.

Important correspondence and parcels should be sent using an express mail service such as Federal Express (*www.fedex.com*) or DHL Worldwide Express (*www.dhl.com*).

📞 **TELEPHONE** Telephoning abroad from Douala and Yaoundé is generally not a problem, but can be difficult elsewhere in the country although the availability of international direct-dial telephones and mobile telephone coverage is increasing all the time.

When telephones are scarce you could try asking someone locally such as a member of hotel staff, whether you can top up their mobile with a card bought by you, using some of the credit on the card yourself.

Most major towns have IntelCam offices at post offices which can provide international calls at a price, and there are shops and telephone booths throughout the country (*téléboutiques* or *cabines téléphoniques*) where you can telephone and fax from, also usually at a high rate. You may be able to receive incoming calls or faxes for a small charge or use an internet telephone service like Skype for far less than a conventional phone.

Currently telephoning the US averages around CFA2,235 to CFA3,575 (£2.45–£3.90/US$5–8) per minute, for example, and it is much cheaper to telephone Cameroon from the US.

It is often cheaper and easier to correspond by fax if this is possible, and instead of calling collect or reverse charging calls (to do so ask for 'PCV', pronounced '*pay say vay*') it is better to arrange in advance to receive calls at a certain time and number.

From 1 June 2007 all numbers gained a digit to increase the capacity of the numbering system from eight million to 80 million. Subscribers of CamTel, the fixed landline provider, saw a 2 added to the start of their numbers beginning 2, and a 3 to those beginning 3. Mobile customers gained an extra 7 if with numbers beginning 7 with MTN, or a 9 if with numbers beginning 9 provided by Orange.

Dialling codes The international direct dialing code for Cameroon is 237 followed by the eight-digit number.

To call from Cameroon, dial the international access number (usually 00) and then the country code followed by the area code (dropping the initial 0 if there is one) and then the number.

Therefore, to dial the UK from Cameroon, dial 00 44 and then the area code and number, dropping the first 0 of the area code.

Other international access codes: North America and Canada (00 1), Ireland (00 353), Australia (00 61), South Africa (00 27), New Zealand (00 64).

When telephoning Cameroon from abroad, add 00 before the 237 country code.

Mobile telephone There is mobile telephone coverage of variable quality in Cameroon, but often excellent around Douala and Yaoundé and bigger towns. Currently the cost to make calls to the UK is around £1.30 per minute and 80p per minute to receive them, but of course depends upon the network and payment method. Mobile telephones can be hired on a daily, weekly or monthly basis.

Satellite telephone If you need a telephone that will work in even the most remote areas of Cameroon, consider hiring an Inmarsat satellite phone. It is not cheap (typically £75 per week or £225 per month, plus £3 per minute for calls plus a big deposit) but you can rest assured you should be able to get the football results even if you're deep in the rainforest. Web addresses for satellite telephone rental companies include www.adam-phones.co.uk, www.phone-rentals.co.uk, www.cellhire.com and www.mobell.co.uk.

Emergency telephone numbers Cameroon emergency services can be very patchy, especially outside major cities.

Police: ☎ 17
Fire: ☎ 18
Ambulance: ☎ 112

EMAIL AND INTERNET There are numerous cyber cafés and shops with email and internet services in city centres, far less so in towns. There are several on Boulevard de la Liberté in Douala alone, for example. The costs typically vary from around CFA500 to CFA1,000 (53p–£1.07/94c–US$1.89) per hour for internet access. Service is often slow and unreliable.

BUSINESS

OPENING HOURS
- Government offices, public services: 07.30–15.30
- Banks: 07.30–15.30
- Pharmacies: 08.00–20.00
- Shops: vary from around 08.00 to 15.00 daily, or 09.00–12.30 and 15.30–19.30, or 08.00–noon and 14.30–17.30
- Markets: approximately 07.00–18.00

- Post offices: Monday–Friday 08.00–15.30 and Saturday 08.00–13.00
- Restaurants: opening times are often very flexible and are therefore not included in the listings.

PERSONAL SAFETY

African travellers, travel books and government advice sheets for African countries are full of shocking stories of violent car hijackings, muggings and terrifying diseases. While such things do happen on the continent, the dangers need to be put in perspective.

I was once in conversation with the pilot of a small plane in Botswana while we were dipping and diving, doing the loop the loop and flying just above the elephants and trees of the stunning Okavango Delta. It was certainly a white-knuckle ride as impressive as one you would find at a state-of-the-art leisure park, and it was unfortunate that I was aware that he was barely sober after a heavy drinking session the night before.

A Zimbabwean, he told me of how he used to carry a gun to school during the Rhodesian war, and how various snakes and spiders had nearly claimed his life over the years. I said his life sounded incredibly dangerous, that he was lucky to still be alive.

He then said, 'Tell me again, you live in a house next to five lanes of traffic?'

At that time I lived on one of the busiest roads in London, so wide it was almost a motorway. He said my life in Britain sounded fraught with danger and indeed as I write, this week a 13-year-old schoolboy was stabbed outside my London house.

Often, even when things seem to be as dangerous as things get, in reality the danger is negligible. I know a man who was living in Yaoundé during a coup attempt during the late 1980s. Gunfire was all around him for several days yet he just stayed at home and read a book. The danger soon subsided.

Certainly, Africa has armed robbers and maniacs, but there's more chance of being shot or robbed on holiday in many parts of America. Indeed, considering the extreme poverty so many people are forced to endure in Africa, it is surprising the crime levels are not far higher.

The first bit of standard advice to travellers is to use a money belt, but I would strongly advise against this. Muggers know that travellers routinely use these belts to put all their money, credit cards and documents in, and target them accordingly.

This belief was confirmed to me most forceably on one trip to Douala. My companion was mugged at knifepoint when five men descended upon him. The first thing they did was rip his shirt in search of a money belt. As there was none, they frisked him and left empty-handed. His money was stashed away in an elastic bandage around his lower leg. Strangely, the experience was not unduly alarming, because it was so slickly done and over in seconds, but it could have been a very different story if he had offered any resistance.

Obviously, it is wise not to flaunt any signs of wealth such as cash, jewellery or a camera, especially in urban areas where the threat of crime is greatest by far. Take taxis at night in the bigger towns and cities, rather than walk. Avoid going on the beaches alone. There should be no problems from fellow passengers or the driver when taking public transport, and the greatest worry here is instead the state of the roads and standards of driving.

In the unlikely event that you are mugged or carjacked, offer no resistance and hand over what is requested. Not only is there far more chance of escaping unhurt, but a wallet full of travellers' cheques is never worth as much as your life.

Don't expect miracles from the police if you are robbed: they may do little or nothing to help, or may request a payment, even to stamp an insurance form. In smaller communities or more rural areas it can be a good idea to offer a reward to entice locals to help.

WOMEN TRAVELLERS Sub-Saharan Africa is often seen by women travellers as a very safe place to visit, especially in rural areas. The exception to this – for all travellers, both male and female – is the cities, mainly at night. There may be a degree of flirting and even a direct proposition or two along the way, especially if you have a penchant for bars and nightclubs, but it is usually nothing a bit of humour or a firm refusal cannot diffuse. Women travelling alone may occasionally be asked the whereabouts of their husband, and it can sometimes be simplest to invent one and maybe flaunt a fake wedding ring. Carry photos of your family to haul out if need be.

Cameroonians tend to dress conservatively, and to minimise hassle women travellers should do so too, especially in northern Cameroon, which is largely Muslim. A long skirt or trousers are better than a pair of skimpy shorts and a revealing top. Sunglasses are useful for avoiding eye contact.

GOVERNMENT TRAVEL ADVICE Like many people, I used to think that the travel advice concerning developing countries dished out by Western countries was unnecessarily negative and alarmist – until I found out the hard way that instead it can be very accurate. Several of the potential problems that can occur in Cameroon highlighted in current government travel advice pages have recently either happened to me, my travelling companions or expatriates or residents of Cameroon I have met. This is said not to encourage paranoia – dwelling on these aspects does not really allow you to enjoy your trip – but the advice should be taken seriously. Fortunately most visitors to Cameroon have no such troubles and Cameroonians in general are very hospitable and friendly.

Current travel advice issued by the British, American and Australian governments notes that visitors should avoid the border areas with the Central African Republic, and Nigeria in the region of the Bakassi Peninsula as the demarcation of the disputed border is not yet settled. The border with the Republic of Congo is closed.

There are occasional reports of car hijackings and robberies, particularly in and around Douala, Yaoundé, Kribi and the three provinces of Adamaoua, the Northern, and the Extreme North. These are often armed. Four-wheel-drive vehicles are particular targets. Travel in convoy if possible and avoid travelling at night.

Most African crime, though, takes place in cities. You are far more likely to be robbed in bustling, downtown Douala or Yaoundé than when camping in the bush. In Yaoundé, isolated and poorer areas, particularly the Briquetterie, Mokolo and Mvog-Ada neighbourhoods, should be avoided. Robberies and muggings, often at knifepoint, are common after dark in Douala and Yaoundé so travel at such times should be by car. You should also not walk around Ngaoundéré or Bafoussam at night.

Consider recruiting a local guide to accompany you around potentially risky areas. Your hotel should be able to find someone reliable.

Petty theft, pickpocketing and bag snatching are quite common in busy areas like markets, buses and train stations. See page 81 for information on begging and bribery.

Identification (a certified copy of your passport) should be carried at all times as failure to do so can lead to detention by the police. It's a good idea to copy documents. Even better, take digital pictures of things like your ticket, passport and insurance and then email to an email account like Yahoo or Hotmail where you can retrieve them if required.

GREETINGS AND SOCIAL NORMS, PUBLIC ETIQUETTE AND CONDUCT A long drawn-out greeting made up of a handshake and various polite enquiries is common, even if you've just popped into a shop.

It is a good idea to try to lock into the local pace of life and thought patterns as soon as possible. Timekeeping is often far more relaxed in this part of the world, for instance, and it is best just to accept it. Just because the bus timetable is routinely ignored or a meeting occurs at 13.45 instead of the agreed 13.00 doesn't suggest an inferior way of life, simply a different one.

It is not unusual for men to hold hands with each other; for example, if you are male and ask directions and are then guided down the street by a stranger, he may do this.

Unlike in the West, beckoning with the palm upwards is considered obscene, so avoid this action. Beckon with your palm downwards instead.

To avoid the possibility of having to pay a bribe or even suffer arrest, if you hear the national anthem being played in public, or a flag being raised or lowered, stand still; never urinate in public; do not destroy any banknote; do not criticise the president or government in public where others could hear; remain stationary or leave the road if you see an official-looking convoy such as limousines and motorcycles approaching.

Public nudity, open displays of affection or anger and criticism of the country or government can all cause offence, especially the further north you go.

In non-touristy rural areas, if you wish to visit a settlement or tribal lands (which you may need to do to visit some of the crater lakes and mountains, for example) it is polite to ask permission by introducing yourself to the local chief, who is known as the *lamido* by the Fulani in the north of the country, and the *sultan* by the Bamoun and the *fon* by the Bamiléké in the west. It is often expected that you give a small present such as a bottle of whisky or the monetary equivalent.

Homosexuality is illegal in Cameroon as in many African countries – with jail sentences from six months to five years – and public displays of same sex affection, except the customary walking arm-in-arm or hand-in-hand, should be avoided.

According to some traditional beliefs, homosexual people are thought to be cursed or bewitched. There seems little chance of this changing in the near future; indeed, Cameroon was rocked by an anti-gay crusade in newspapers where more than 50 prominent figures including government ministers, newsreaders, popular singers and sports stars were accused of homosexuality.

Avoid political discussions in casual conversation with Cameroonian acquaintances. It is also generally impolite to enquire about a Cameroonian acquaintance's ethnic origins. Wait for them to bring the subject up. Do not point with a finger, as this is considered rude.

If you are ever in need of information or help, Cameroonians generally are very courteous in their willingness to assist. If they do not know the answer to your query, chances are they will find someone who does.

Hissing is a common way to attract a stranger's attention and is not an aggressive action.

Sometimes, when buying from a stall or visiting a shop, you may receive no courtesy, and this can be disconcerting. Yet there should be no assumption of offence and a simple smile and a '*Bonjour, madame*' at first and '*Merci*' as you leave can change things dramatically.

Likewise, occasionally you may experience some hard-looking man staring at you threateningly. Again, in most cases a simple '*Bonjour, monsieur*' will result in the most sincere smile and upturned palms in response. If not, run.

ISLAMIC CUSTOMS In the north, observe the following. If visiting a mosque, take off your shoes. Some mosques do not admit women, while others may have separate entrances for men and women.

Bear in mind that it is impolite to drink alcohol in a Muslim's presence unless he shows approval. If you're a woman, don't take offence if a Muslim man refuses to shake hands with you, as he is simply following the Koran.

If you have a taxi driver or guide for the day, he may have a prayer ritual, which occurs five times a day, including at midday, late afternoon and sunset. Drivers of public transport may also stop *en route* to carry out these rituals.

TIPPING Tipping is uncommon although Cameroonians often expect *cadeaux* (gifts) from foreign travellers, who tend to look rich to locals. Plan to tip 5–10% or so at better restaurants unless service has been included in the bill, which is likely at establishments geared to tourists or rich Cameroonians.

Drivers, guides, porters, hotel staff and taxis (not necessarily share taxis) will all greatly appreciate a small tip.

BEGGING With no social security system or welfare state, the giving of even the smallest coin will always be appreciated. (Indeed, one night in Douala a friend of mine was mugged while I was left alone, and I'm convinced that I was ignored because I had just given some coins to a small boy with a begging bowl.) If in doubt, give to the beggars the locals give to. One sad development in recent years in Cameroon is the rise in children begging. It is quite easy to distinguish the ones that are truly destitute, maybe supporting sick parents, from those that are simply trying their luck in places frequented by tourists.

For more lasting good, it is better to give a donation to a recognised local project like a school, charity, mission, aid agency or health centre than to indiscriminately hand out sweets, pens, toys and money to children, which further perpetuates the begging. See page 223 and *Appendix 2* for more information.

BRIBERY AND CORRUPTION Low and often overdue salaries help fuel the widespread system of bribery in this part of the world. It is common, for example, especially if you are a foreigner in a good car, to be stopped by the police at a roadblock where intimidating tactics may be used to extort a bribe. That said, most dealings with government employees should be trouble-free, and indeed many officials will go out of their way to help.

If you do encounter bribery, this shouldn't cause undue alarm, and instead it is better to approach the matter as if it is a game. Try to take the attitude of long-term residents, who are generally far more relaxed about the matter and see it simply as one of the inconveniences of day-to-day life.

Always remain polite, patient and in good humour if an official is clearly after a bribe, especially as tempers can fray alarmingly quickly if you instead become impatient or angry.

One long-term resident of the country gives the following advice: if the law the official is upholding has obviously been made up, you can enter into discussions about the matter in the hope that he will lose interest, or offer them a 'small gift' or 'special fee' of a 'dash' (don't use the word 'bribe'), maybe the equivalent of a couple of pounds or dollars, to help you on your way. If you suspect that you are indeed in breach of a law, you could suggest coming to an agreement or paying the fine (*amende* in French).

If the difficulty persists, take the names and numbers of the policemen or soldiers that they carry on their badges. If they are acting incorrectly they are likely to immediately try to hide their badges as you start writing the details down, but insist that they give the details to you.

Always ask for a receipt for the transgression. You cannot be fined without being issued one. Since the official is not able to issue a receipt if the charge is trumped up, you cannot pay. You might then suggest going to see the inspector at the police station, at which time the official will probably propose you a private settlement of say CFA5,000 (£5.35/US$9.45). In which case you give it to them as a gesture of goodwill and go on your way.

DRUGS Obviously, don't even think of contact with hard drugs. In this part of the world, long prison sentences in the grimmest conditions or the death penalty are more the norm. While discreet use of cannabis should not attract more than a fine, the fondness some members of the police have for extracting bribes means it might be pushing your luck to indulge in a marathon smoking session outside the Presidential Palace.

DRESS The dress code is rather conservative throughout the country but strictest in the Muslim north where women should cover up knees and shoulders. In many areas a Western man walking around bare-chested can cause offence or even anger. I was challenged to a fight once in Mora when I took my shirt off in the midday sun, as of course Englishmen are fond of doing.

Men with long hair, the wearing of tight trousers and shorts may not fare much better in some areas. Shorts are OK if you have a bike, are hiking or engaged in a sport. In general, the more conservative you dress, the better you will be received. So if you are making a visa application, it is better to turn up in smart clothes than a pair of jeans. Avoid wearing anything at all in a military style as you could be mistaken for a soldier.

GIVING SOMETHING BACK

Always attempt to minimise the negative impact of your travels: recycle as much as possible, favour locally owned businesses, spend as much as possible with local communities and support local sustainable development initiatives. Use and save energy, water and other resources efficiently and in keeping with local practices. Avoid places that use limited resources like water and electricity to the detriment of local people.

You can further minimise your impact on the environment by leaving no litter, using biodegradable soaps and detergents and conserving water. Campfires are inappropriate in areas where wood is scarce.

Walk and cycle when you can rather than opting for motorised transport. Not only is this more environmentally friendly, but you have far more chance to interact with locals and savour the country. Observe, but do not disturb, natural systems. Move cautiously and quietly in natural areas.

More information on the subject is available from Tourism Concern (*Stapleton Hse, 277–281 Holloway Rd, London N7 8HN, ☎ 020 7753 3330; www.tourismconcern.org.uk*). See *Appendix 2* for details on charities.

5

Health

With assistance from Dr Felicity Nicholson

Although there are a number of serious diseases that can be contracted in Cameroon, there is a lot you can do to greatly lessen the chance of trouble. With luck, the most you'll suffer from is a cold caught on the aeroplane, sunburn or short-term travellers' diarrhoea which is associated more with the change of environment than anything specific. That said, it is accidents that are most likely to carry you off. Road accidents are very common in many parts of Cameroon so be aware and do what you can to reduce risks: try to travel during daylight hours, always wear a seatbelt and refuse to be driven by anyone who has been drinking. Listen to local advice about areas where violent crime is rife too.

PREPARATIONS

HEALTH INSURANCE Ensure that you have adequate health insurance before setting off. Check that it covers such things as ambulances, emergency airlifts and flights home. See page 56 for more information.

PROTECTION FROM THE SUN Give some thought to packing suncream. The incidence of skin cancer is rocketing as Caucasians are travelling more and spending more time exposing themselves to the sun. Keep out of the sun during the middle of the day and, if you must be exposed to the sun, build up gradually from 20 minutes per day. Be especially careful of sun reflected off water and wear a T-shirt and lots of waterproof SPF15 suncream when swimming; snorkelling often leads to scorched backs of the thighs so wear Bermuda shorts. Sun exposure ages the skin and makes people prematurely wrinkly; cover up with long, loose clothes and wear a hat when you can. The glare and the dust can be hard on the eyes, too, so bring UV-protecting sunglasses and, perhaps, a soothing eyebath.

ASTHMA, SINUS AND RESPIRATORY PROBLEMS Dust and smoke can be a problem in the dry season, so take asthma and sinus medication if a sufferer.

VACCINATIONS Preparations to ensure a healthy trip to Cameroon require checks on your immunisation status: it is wise to be up to date on **tetanus, polio and diphtheria** (now given as an all-in-one vaccine, Revaxis, that lasts for ten years), and **hepatitis A**. Immunisations against meningococcus and rabies may also be recommended (see *Rabies* and *Meningitis* sections on pages 95 and 92 respectively). Proof of vaccination against **yellow fever** is mandatory for entry into Cameroon. The World Health Organization (WHO) recommends that this vaccine should be taken for Cameroon by those over nine months of age, although proof of entry is only officially required for those over one year of age. If the vaccine is not suitable for you then obtain an exemption certificate from your GP or a travel clinic. Immunisation against **cholera** is not usually required for Cameroon, unless you

LONG-HAUL FLIGHTS, CLOTS AND DVT

Long-haul air travel increases the risk of deep vein thrombosis. Although recent research has suggested that many of us develop clots when immobilised, most resolve without us ever having been aware of them. In certain susceptible individuals, though, clots form on clots and when large ones break away and lodge in the lungs this is dangerous. Fortunately this happens in a tiny minority of passengers.

Studies have shown that flights of over five-and-a-half hours are significant, and that people who take lots of shorter flights over a short space of time can also form clots. People at highest risk are:

- Those who have had a clot before – unless they are now taking warfarin
- People over 80 years of age
- Anyone who has recently undergone a major operation or surgery for varicose veins
- Someone who has had a hip or knee replacement in the last three months
- Cancer sufferers
- Those who have ever had a stroke
- People with heart disease
- Those with a close blood relative who has had a clot

Those with a slightly increased risk:

- People over 40
- Women who are pregnant or have had a baby in the last couple of weeks
- People taking female hormones, the combined contraceptive pill or other oestrogen therapy
- Heavy smokers
- Those who have very severe varicose veins
- The very obese
- People who are very tall (over 6ft/1.8m) or short (under 5ft/1.5m)

are staying for long periods of time or doing voluntary work in poorer areas. The oral vaccine Dukoral is about 75% effective against cholera and consists of two doses given at least one week apart and at least one week before entry for those aged six or over. For those under six, a three-dose regime is needed and therefore requires more time.

Hepatitis A vaccine (Havrix Monodose or Avaxim) comprises two injections given about a year apart. The course costs about £100, but may be available on the NHS, protects for 25 years and can be administered even close to the time of departure. **Hepatitis B** vaccination should be considered for longer trips (two months or more) or for those working with children or in situations where contact with blood is likely. Three injections are needed for the best protection and can be given over a three-week period for those aged 16 or over if time is short. Longer schedules give more sustained protection and are therefore preferred if time allows. Hepatitis A vaccine can also be given as a combination with hepatitis B as 'Twinrix' for those aged 16 or over, though two doses are needed at least seven days apart to be effective for the hepatitis A component, and three doses are needed for the hepatitis B.

The newer injectable **typhoid** vaccines (eg: Typhim Vi) last for three years and are about 85% effective. Oral capsules (Vivotif) are currently available in the US (and soon in the UK); if four capsules are taken over seven days it will last for five years. They should be encouraged unless the traveller is leaving within a few days

A deep vein thrombosis (DVT) is a blood clot that forms in the deep leg veins. This is very different from irritating but harmless superficial phlebitis. DVT causes swelling and redness of one leg, usually with heat and pain in one calf and sometimes the thigh. A DVT is only dangerous if a clot breaks away and travels to the lungs (pulmonary embolus). Symptoms of a pulmonary embolus (PE) include chest pain that is worse on breathing in deeply, shortness of breath, and sometimes coughing up small amounts of blood. The symptoms commonly start three to ten days after a long flight. Anyone who thinks that they might have a DVT needs to see a doctor immediately who will arrange a scan. Warfarin tablets (to thin the blood) are then taken for at least six months.

PREVENTION OF DVT Several conditions make the problem more likely. Immobility is the key, and factors like reduced oxygen in cabin air and dehydration may also contribute. To reduce the risk of thrombosis on a long journey:

- Exercise before and after the flight
- Keep mobile before and during the flight; move around every couple of hours
- Drink plenty of water or juices during the flight
- Avoid taking sleeping pills and excessive tea, coffee and alcohol
- Perform exercises that mimic walking and tense the calf muscles
- Consider wearing flight socks or support stockings (see www.legshealth.com)
- Ideally take a meal each week of oily fish (mackerel, trout, salmon, sardines, etc) ahead of your departure. This reduces the blood's ability to clot and thus DVT risk. It may even be worth just taking a meal of oily fish 24 hours before departure if this is more practical.

If you think you are at increased risk of a clot, ask your doctor if it is safe to travel.

for a trip of a week or less, when the vaccine would not be effective in time. **Meningitis** vaccine (ideally containing strains A, C, W and Y, but if this is not available then A+C vaccine is better than nothing) is recommended for all travellers, especially for trips of more than four weeks (see *Meningitis*, page 92). Vaccinations for **rabies** are ideally advised for everyone, but are especially important for travellers visiting more remote areas, especially if you are more than 24 hours from medical help and definitely if you will be working with animals (see *Rabies*, page 95).

Experts differ over whether a BCG vaccination against **tuberculosis** (TB) is useful in adults; discuss this with your travel clinic.

In addition to the various vaccinations recommended above, it is important that travellers should be properly protected against **malaria**. For detailed advice, see page 92.

Ideally you should visit your own doctor or a specialist travel clinic (see page 97) to discuss your requirements if possible at least eight weeks before you plan to travel.

MALARIA

Along with road accidents, malaria poses the single biggest serious threat to the health of travellers in most parts of tropical Africa, Cameroon included. It is unwise to travel in malarial parts of Africa whilst pregnant or with children: the risk of malaria in many parts is considerable and these travellers are likely to succumb rapidly to the disease. The risk of malaria over 1,800m above sea level is low.

The *Anopheles* mosquito that transmits the parasite is found throughout the whole country all year round.

PREVENTION There is not yet a vaccine against malaria that gives enough protection to be useful for travellers, but there are other ways to avoid it; since most of Africa is very high risk for malaria, travellers must plan their malaria protection properly. Seek current advice on the best antimalarials to take: usually mefloquine, Malarone or doxycycline. If mefloquine (Lariam) is suggested, start this two-and-a-half weeks (three doses) before departure to check that it suits you; stop it immediately if it seems to cause depression or anxiety, visual or hearing disturbances, severe headaches, fits or changes in heart rhythm. Side effects such as nightmares or dizziness are not medical reasons for stopping unless they are sufficiently debilitating or annoying. Anyone who has been treated for depression or psychiatric problems, has diabetes controlled by oral therapy or who is epileptic (or who has suffered fits in the past) or has a close blood relative who is epileptic, should probably avoid mefloquine.

In the past doctors were nervous about prescribing mefloquine to pregnant women, but experience has shown that it is relatively safe and certainly safer than the risk of malaria. That said, there are other issues, so if you are travelling to Cameroon whilst pregnant, seek expert advice before departure.

Malarone (proguanil and atovaquone) is as effective as mefloquine. It has the advantage of having few side effects and need only be continued for one week after returning. However, it is expensive and because of this tends to be reserved for shorter trips. Malarone may not be suitable for everybody, so advice should be taken from a doctor. The licence in the UK has been extended for at least three months' use and a paediatric form of tablet is also available, prescribed on a weight basis.

Another alternative is the antibiotic doxycycline (100mg daily). Like Malarone it can be started one day before arrival. Unlike mefloquine, it may also be used in travellers with epilepsy, although certain anti-epileptic medication may make it less effective. In perhaps 1–3% of people there is the possibility of allergic skin reactions developing in sunlight; the drug should be stopped if this happens. Women using the oral contraceptive should use an additional method of protection for the first four weeks when using doxycycline. It is also unsuitable in pregnancy or for children under 12 years.

Chloroquine and proguanil are no longer considered to be effective enough for Cameroon, but may be considered as a last resort if nothing else is deemed suitable.

All tablets should be taken with or after the evening meal, washed down with plenty of fluid and, with the exception of Malarone (see above), continued for four weeks after leaving.

Despite all these precautions, it is important to be aware that no anti-malarial drug is 100% protective, although those on prophylactics who are unlucky enough to catch malaria are less likely to get rapidly into serious trouble. In addition to taking anti-malarials, it is therefore important to avoid mosquito bites between dusk and dawn (see *Avoiding insect bites*, page 90).

There is unfortunately the occasional traveller who prefers to 'acquire resistance' to malaria rather than take preventive tablets, or who takes homoeopathic prophylactics, thinking these are effective against a killer disease. Homoeopathy theory dictates treating like with like so there is no place for prophylaxis or immunisation in a well person; bone fide homoeopathists do not advocate it. Travellers to Africa cannot acquire any effective resistance to malaria, and those who don't make use of prophylactic drugs risk their life in a manner that is both foolish and unnecessary.

DIAGNOSIS AND TREATMENT Even those who take their malaria tablets meticulously and do everything possible to avoid mosquito bites may contract a strain of malaria that is resistant to prophylactic drugs. Untreated malaria is likely to be fatal, but even strains resistant to prophylaxis respond well to prompt treatment. Because of this, your immediate priority upon displaying possible malaria symptoms – including a rapid rise in temperature (over 38°C), and any combination of a headache, flu-like aches and pains, a general sense of disorientation, and possibly even nausea and diarrhoea – is to establish whether you have malaria, ideally by visiting a clinic.

Diagnosing malaria is not easy, which is why consulting a doctor is sensible: there are other dangerous causes of fever in Africa, which require different treatments. Even if you test negative, it would be wise to stay within reach of a laboratory until the symptoms clear up, and to test again after a day or two if they don't. It's worth noting that if you have a fever and the malaria test is negative, you may have typhoid or paratyphoid, which should also receive immediate treatment.

Travellers to remote parts of Cameroon would be wise to carry a course of treatment to cure malaria, and a rapid test kit. With malaria, it is normal enough to go from feeling healthy to having a high fever in the space of a few hours (and it is possible to die from falciparum malaria within 24 hours of the first symptoms). In such circumstances, assume that you have malaria and act accordingly – whatever risks are attached to taking an unnecessary cure are outweighed by the dangers of untreated malaria. Experts differ on the costs and benefits of self-treatment, but agree that it leads to over-treatment and to many people taking drugs they do not need; yet treatment may save your life. There is also some division about the best treatment for malaria, but either Malarone or Coarthemeter are the current treatments of choice. Discuss your trip with a specialist either at home or in Cameroon.

OTHER INSECT-BORNE DISEASES

Malaria is by no means the only insect-borne disease to which the traveller may succumb. Others include sleeping sickness and river blindness (see box, *Avoiding insect bites*, page 90). Dengue fever is rare in Cameroon, but there are many other similar arboviruses. These mosquito-borne diseases may mimic malaria but there is no prophylactic medication against them. The mosquitoes that carry dengue fever viruses bite during the daytime, so it is worth applying repellent if you see any mosquitoes around. Symptoms include strong headaches, rashes and excruciating joint and muscle pains and high fever. Viral fevers usually last about a week or so and are not usually fatal. Complete rest and paracetamol are the usual treatment; plenty of fluids also help. Some patients are given an intravenous drip to keep them from dehydrating. It is especially important to protect yourself if you have had dengue fever before, since a second infection with a different strain can result in the potentially fatal dengue haemorrhagic fever.

FILARIASIS This infection is caused by a nematode, *Wuchereria bancrofti*, which normally resides in the lymphatic system of infected people. Infections can range from having no symptoms at all, through recurrent fever and lymphadenitis, to the chronic form where limbs can become grossly swollen. The disease may have a

As the sun is going down, don long clothes and apply repellent on any exposed flesh. Pack an insect repellent that contains around 50–55% DEET (roll-ons or stick are the least messy preparations for travelling). You also need either a permethrin-impregnated bednet or a permethrin spray so that you can 'treat' bednets in hotels. Permethrin treatment makes even very tatty nets protective and prevents mosquitoes from biting through the impregnated net when you roll against it; it also deters other biters. Otherwise retire to an air-conditioned room or burn mosquito coils or sleep under a fan. Coils and fans reduce rather than eliminate bites. Travel clinics usually sell a good range of nets, treatment kits and repellents.

Mosquitoes and many other insects are attracted to light. If you are camping, never put a lamp near the opening of your tent, or you will have a swarm of biters waiting to join you when you retire. In hotel rooms, be aware that the longer your light is on, the greater the number of insects will be sharing your accommodation.

Aside from avoiding mosquito bites between dusk and dawn, which will protect you from elephantiasis and a range of nasty insect-borne viruses, as well as malaria (see page 87), it is important to take precautions against other insect bites. During the day it is wise to wear long, loose (preferably 100% cotton) clothes if you are pushing through scrubby country; this will keep off ticks, tsetse and day-biting Aedes mosquitoes which may spread viral fevers, including yellow fever.

Tsetse flies hurt when they bite and it is said that they are attracted to the colour blue; locals will advise on where they are a problem and where they transmit sleeping sickness.

Minute pestilential biting blackflies spread river blindness in some parts of Africa between 190°N and 170°S; the disease is caught close to fast-flowing rivers since flies breed there and the larvae live in rapids. The flies bite during the day but long trousers tucked into socks will help keep them off. Citronella-based natural repellents (eg: Mosi-guard) do not work against them.

Tumbu flies or putsi, often called mango flies in Cameroon, are a problem where the climate is hot and humid. The adult fly lays her eggs on the soil or on drying laundry and when the eggs come into contact with human flesh (when you put on clothes or lie on a bed) they hatch and bury themselves under the skin. Here they form a crop of 'boils' each with a maggot inside. Smear a little Vaseline over the hole, and they will push their noses out to breathe. It may be possible to squeeze them out but it depends if they are ready to do so as the larvae have spines that help them to hold on.

In putsi areas either dry your clothes and sheets within a screened house, or dry them in direct sunshine until they are crisp, or iron them.

Jiggers or sandfleas are another flesh-feaster, which can be best avoided by wearing shoes. They latch on if you walk barefoot in contaminated places, and set up home under the skin of the foot, usually at the side of a toenail where they cause a painful, boil-like swelling. They need picking out by a local expert.

long incubation period of up to a year, but an acute allergic reaction may occur much earlier. It is spread by the bite of mosquitoes carrying infective larvae so make sure that you use mosquito repellents day and night (see box, *Avoiding insect bites* above). If you suspect that you have filariasis seek medical advice promptly as it can be treated.

TICKBITE FEVER African ticks are not the rampant disease transmitters they are in the Americas, but they may spread tickbite fever and a few dangerous rarities in

Cameroon. Tickbite fever is a flu-like illness that can easily be treated with doxycycline, but as there can be some serious complications it is important to visit a doctor.

Ticks should ideally be **removed** as soon as possible as leaving them on the body increases the chance of infection. They should be removed with special tick tweezers that can be bought in good travel shops. Failing that you can use your fingernails: grasp the tick as close to your body as possible and pull steadily and firmly away at right angles to your skin. The tick will then come away complete, as long as you do not jerk or twist. If possible douse the wound with alcohol (any spirit will do) or iodine. Irritants (eg: Olbas oil) or lit cigarettes are to be discouraged since they can cause the ticks to regurgitate and therefore increase the risk of disease. It is best to get a travelling companion to check you for ticks; if you are travelling with small children, remember to check their heads, and particularly behind the ears.

Spreading redness around the bite and/or fever and/or aching joints after a tick bite imply that you have an infection that requires antibiotic treatment, so seek advice.

BILHARZIA OR SCHISTOSOMIASIS

With thanks to Dr Vaughan Southgate of the Natural History Museum, London
Bilharzia or schistosomiasis is a disease that commonly afflicts the rural poor of the tropics. Two types exist in sub-Saharan Africa – *Schistosoma mansoni* and *Schistosoma haematobium*. It is an unpleasant problem that is worth avoiding, though can be treated if you do get it. This parasite is common in almost all water sources in Cameroon, even places advertised as 'bilharzia free'. The most risky shores will be close to places where infected people use water, wash clothes, etc.

It is easier to understand how to diagnose it, treat it and prevent it if you know a little about the life cycle. Contaminated faeces are washed into the lake, the eggs hatch and the larva infects certain species of snail. The snails then produce about 10,000 cercariae a day for the rest of their lives. The parasites can digest their way through your skin when you wade or bathe in infested fresh water.

Winds disperse the snails and cercariae. The snails in particular can drift a long way, especially on windblown weed, so nowhere is really safe. However, deep water and running water are safer, while shallow water presents the greatest risk. The cercariae penetrate intact skin, and find their way to the liver. There male and female meet and spend the rest of their lives in permanent copulation. No wonder you feel tired! Most finish up in the wall of the lower bowel, but others can get lost and can cause damage to many different organs. *Schistosoma haematobium* goes mostly to the bladder.

Although the adults do not cause any harm in themselves, after about four to six weeks they start to lay eggs, which cause an intense but usually ineffective immune reaction, including fever, cough, abdominal pain, and a fleeting, itching rash called 'safari itch'. The absence of early symptoms does not necessarily mean there is no infection. Later symptoms can be more localised and more severe, but the general symptoms settle down fairly quickly and eventually you are just tired. 'Tired all the time' is one of the most common symptoms among expats in Africa, and bilharzia, giardia, amoeba and intestinal yeast are the most common culprits.

Although bilharzia is difficult to diagnose, it can be tested at specialist travel clinics. Ideally tests need to be done at least six weeks after likely exposure and will determine whether you need treatment. Fortunately it is easy to treat at present.

AVOIDING BILHARZIA If you are bathing, swimming, paddling or wading in fresh water which you think may carry a bilharzia risk, try to get out of the water within ten minutes.

- Avoid bathing or paddling on shores within 200m of villages or places where people use the water a great deal, especially reedy shores or where there is lots of water weed
- Dry off thoroughly with a towel; rub vigorously
- If your bathing water comes from a risky source try to ensure that the water is taken from the lake in the early morning and stored snail-free, otherwise it should be filtered or Dettol or Cresol added
- Bathing early in the morning is safer than bathing in the last half of the day
- Cover yourself with DEET insect repellent before swimming: it may offer some protection

MENINGITIS

This is a particularly nasty disease as it can kill within hours of the first symptoms appearing. The telltale symptoms are a combination of a blinding headache (light sensitivity), a blotchy rash and a high fever. Immunisation protects against the most serious bacterial form of meningitis and the tetravalent vaccine ACWY is recommended for west and central Africa, but if this is not available then A+C vaccine is better than nothing. Other forms of meningitis exist (usually viral) but there are no vaccines for these. Local papers normally report localised outbreaks. A severe headache and fever should make you run to a doctor immediately. There are also other causes of headache and fever, one of which is typhoid, which can occur in travellers to Cameroon. Seek medical help if you are ill for more than a few days.

COMMON MEDICAL PROBLEMS AND RISKS

TRAVELLERS' DIARRHOEA Travelling in Cameroon carries a fairly high risk of getting a dose of travellers' diarrhoea; perhaps half of all visitors will suffer and the newer you are to exotic travel, the more likely you will be to suffer. By taking precautions against travellers' diarrhoea you will also avoid typhoid, paratyphoid, cholera, hepatitis, dysentery, worms, etc. Travellers' diarrhoea and the other faecal-oral diseases come from getting other peoples' faeces in your mouth. This most often happens from cooks not washing their hands after a trip to the toilet, but even if the restaurant cook does not understand basic hygiene you will be safe if your food has been properly cooked and arrives piping hot. The most important prevention strategy is to wash your hands before eating anything. You can pick up salmonella and shigella from toilet door handles and possibly bank notes. The maxim to remind you what you can safely eat is:

PEEL IT, BOIL IT, COOK IT OR FORGET IT.

This means that fruit you have washed and peeled yourself, and hot foods, should be safe but raw foods, cold cooked foods, salads, fruit salads which have been prepared by others, ice cream and ice are all risky, and foods kept lukewarm in hotel buffets are often dangerous. That said, plenty of travellers and expatriates enjoy fruit and vegetables, so do keep a sense of perspective: food served in a fairly decent hotel in a large town or a place regularly frequented by expatriates is likely to be safe. If you are struck, see box (opposite) for treatment.

INTESTINAL WORMS These parasites may enter through your skin (eg: hookworm) or be ingested in food such as undercooked meat (eg: tapeworm). Infestations may take a long time to show up and can cause later health problems, so it is worth considering being tested for parasites on your return home.

It is dehydration that makes you feel awful during a bout of diarrhoea and the most important part of treatment is drinking lots of clear fluids. Sachets of oral rehydration salts give the perfect biochemical mix to replace all that is pouring out of your bottom but other recipes taste nicer. Any dilute mixture of sugar and salt in water will do you good: try Coke or orange squash with a three-finger pinch of salt added to each glass (if you are salt-depleted you won't taste the salt). Otherwise make a solution of a four-finger scoop of sugar with a three-finger pinch of salt in a 500ml glass. Or add eight level teaspoons of sugar (18g) and one level teaspoon of salt (3g) to one litre (five cups) of safe water. A squeeze of lemon or orange juice improves the taste and adds potassium, which is also lost in diarrhoea. Drink two large glasses after every bowel action, and more if you are thirsty. These solutions are still absorbed well if you are vomiting, but you will need to take sips at a time. If you are not eating you need to drink three litres a day plus whatever is pouring into the toilet. If you feel like eating, take a bland, high carbohydrate diet. Heavy greasy foods will probably give you cramps.

If the diarrhoea is bad, or you are passing blood or slime, or you have a fever, you will probably need antibiotics in addition to fluid replacement. A dose of norfloxacin or ciprofloxacin repeated twice a day until better may be appropriate (if you are planning to take an antibiotic with you, note that both norfloxacin and ciprofloxacin are available only on prescription in the UK). If the diarrhoea is greasy and bulky and is accompanied by sulphurous (eggy) burps, one likely cause is giardia. This is best treated with tinidazole (four x 500mg in one dose, repeated seven days later if symptoms persist).

FOOD AND DRINK Much Cameroonian cooking involves a sauce or topping with fresh meat, chicken or fish or fresh vegetables, which have been thoroughly boiled or sautéed at a high heat. This is usually served over a carbohydrate like rice, millet, corn or a tuber which has been boiled.

While many seasoned travellers eat thoroughly cooked meat in this region without problems, think twice if you have any doubts concerning hygiene or preparation. Harmful bacteria is obviously much more likely to have been destroyed if the meat has been cooked in front of you rather than reheated after sitting around all day.

Avoid milk unless it has been pasteurised or boiled: it can harbour tuberculosis, brucellosis, typhoid and dysentery.

Water sterilisation It is much rarer to get sick from drinking contaminated water but it happens, so try to drink from safe sources.

Water should have been brought to the boil (even at altitude it only needs to be brought to the boil), or passed through a good bacteriological filter or purified with iodine; chlorine tablets (eg: Puritabs) are also adequate although less effective (they do not kill all parasites, such as gardia and amoebic cysts) and also they taste nastier. As a rule, mineral water is safer than contaminated tap water. Bottled water is readily available throughout the country: ensure the top is sealed. It is more expensive than beer, so try and buy it in a supermarket.

Tap water in Yaoundé and Douala is not considered safe to drink because although the water is chemically treated, the poor condition of water transport pipes and interruptions in service encourage contamination.

SKIN INFECTIONS Any mosquito bite or small nick in the skin gives an opportunity for bacteria to foil the body's usually excellent defences; it will surprise many

Health COMMON MEDICAL PROBLEMS AND RISKS

5

travellers how quickly skin infections start in warm humid climates and it is essential to clean and cover even the slightest wound. Creams are not as effective as a good drying antiseptic such as dilute iodine, potassium permanganate (a few crystals in half a cup of water), or crystal (or gentian) violet. One of these should be available in main towns. If the wound starts to throb, or becomes red and the redness starts to spread, or the wound oozes, and especially if you develop a fever, antibiotics will probably be needed: flucloxacillin (250mg four times a day) or Augmentin (250–500mg three times a day). For those allergic to penicillin, erythromycin (500mg twice a day) for five days should help. See a doctor if the symptoms do not start to improve in 48 hours.

Fungal infections also get a hold easily in hot moist climates so wear 100% cotton socks and underwear and shower frequently. An itchy rash in the groin or flaking between the toes is likely to be a fungal infection. This needs treatment with an antifungal cream such as Canesten (clotrimazole); if this is not available try Whitfield's ointment (compound benzoic acid ointment) or crystal violet (although this will turn you purple!).

EYE PROBLEMS Bacterial conjunctivitis (pink eye) is a common infection in Africa; people who wear contact lenses are most open to this irritating problem. The eyes feel sore and gritty and they will often be stuck together in the mornings. They will need treatment with antibiotic drops or ointment. Lesser eye irritation should settle with bathing in salt water and keeping the eyes shaded. If an insect flies into your eye, extract it with great care, ensuring you do not crush or damage it otherwise you may get a nastily inflamed eye from toxins secreted by the creature.

PRICKLY HEAT A fine pimply rash on the trunk is likely to be heat rash; cool showers, dabbing dry, and talc will help. Treat the problem by slowing down to a relaxed schedule, wearing only loose, baggy, 100% cotton clothes and sleeping naked under a fan; if it's bad you may need to check into an air-conditioned hotel room for a while.

HEATSTROKE Here the body temperature rises to dangerous, even fatal, levels (39°C/102°F–41°C/106°F). A feeling of being unwell is followed by little or no sweating, severe headaches, confusion and delirium. The patient needs to be fanned and taken away from the sun while their clothing is removed and replaced by a wet towel or sheet, and hospitalisation arranged.

HYPOTHERMIA Cameroon's mountains, especially, can become very cold at night. The symptoms of hypothermia, where the body temperature lowers to dangerous levels, include tiredness, numb skin, dizziness, shivering, slurred speech and irrationality. To avoid potentially fatal severe hypothermia, the patient needs to come out of the cold, have their clothes, if wet, replaced by warm, dry ones and be given high-energy food and hot drinks.

ALTITUDE SICKNESS Cameroon has a number of mountainous areas and a lack of oxygen at high altitudes (over 2,500m) can cause problems. It is worth remembering that while most people can travel up to 3,000m (9,843ft) in a short period, and can cope with 4,500m (14,764ft) after spending a night or two at 3,000m, going straight to 4,500m (little more than Mount Cameroon) can be dangerous. About half the people attempting this altitude can suffer headache, lethargy, loss of appetite and difficulty sleeping. Resting at the same altitude for a day or two should suffice, but if these symptoms persist then you should tell your guide and they will take you down at least 500m. More serious symptoms include turning blue, a dry cough leading to coughing up pink mucus, breathlessness, vomiting, drowsiness, confusion, and finally unconsciousness. This constitutes a medical emergency and immediate descent and other medical support is essential. Symptoms can appear within the first 24 hours but can take as much as three weeks.

Altitude difficulties can be discouraged by ascending slowly, using maximum sun-block, not over-exerting oneself, eating lightly, drinking plenty of fluids but avoiding alcohol, and keeping warm when the sun goes down. Consider taking an altimeter if you will be climbing in Cameroon.

SAFE SEX The risks of sexually transmitted infection are extremely high in Cameroon, whether you sleep with fellow travellers or locals. About 80% of HIV infections in British heterosexuals are acquired abroad. If you must indulge, use condoms or femidoms, which help reduce the risk of transmission. If you notice any genital ulcers or discharge, get treatment promptly since these increase the risk of acquiring HIV. If you do have unprotected sex, visit a clinic as soon as possible; this should be within 24 hours, or no later than 72 hours, for post-exposure prophylaxis.

RABIES Rabies is carried by all mammals (beware the village dogs and small monkeys that are used to being fed in the parks) and is passed on to man through a bite, scratch or a lick of an open wound. You must always assume any animal is rabid, and seek medical help as soon as possible. Meanwhile scrub the wound with soap under a running tap or while pouring water from a jug. Find a reasonably clear-looking source of water (but at this stage the quality of the water is not important), then pour on a strong iodine or alcohol solution of gin, whisky or rum. This helps stop the rabies virus entering the body and will guard against wound infections, including tetanus.

Pre-exposure vaccinations for rabies are ideally advised for everyone, but are particularly important if you intend to have contact with animals and/or are likely to be more than 24 hours away from medical help. Ideally three doses should be taken over a minimum of 21 days, though even taking one or two doses of vaccine is better than none at all. Contrary to popular belief these vaccinations are relatively painless.

If you are bitten, scratched or licked over an open wound by a sick animal, then post-exposure prophylaxis should be given as soon as possible, though it is never too late to seek help, as the incubation period for rabies can be very long. Those who have not been immunised will need a full course of injections. The vast majority of travel health advisors including WHO recommend rabies immunoglobulin (RIG), but this product is expensive (around US$800) and may be hard to come by – another reason why pre-exposure vaccination should be encouraged.

Tell the doctor if you have had pre-exposure vaccine, as this should change the treatment you receive. And remember that, if you do contract rabies, mortality is 100% and death from rabies is probably one of the worst ways to go.

MARINE DANGERS Before assuming a beach is safe for swimming, always ask local advice. It is always better to err on the side of caution if no sensible advice is forthcoming, since there is always a possibility of being swept away by strong currents or undertows that cannot be detected until you are actually in the water.

Snorkellers and divers should wear something on their feet to avoid treading on coral reefs, and should never touch the reefs with their bare hands – coral itself can give nasty cuts, and there is a danger of touching a venomous creature camouflaged against the reef. On beaches, never walk barefoot on exposed coral. Even on sandy beaches, people who walk barefoot risk getting coral or urchin spines in their soles or venomous fish spines in their feet.

If you do tread on a venomous fish, soak the foot in hot (but not scalding) water for some time after the pain subsides; this may be for 20–30 minutes in all. Take the foot out of the water to top up; otherwise you may scald it. If the pain returns, re-immerse the foot. Once the venom has been heat-inactivated, get a doctor to check and remove any bits of fish spine in the wound.

SNAKES Snakes rarely attack unless provoked, and bites in travellers are unusual. You are less likely to get bitten if you wear stout shoes and long trousers when in the bush. Most snakes are harmless and even venomous species will dispense venom in only about half of their bites. If bitten, then, you are unlikely to have received venom; keeping this fact in mind may help you to stay calm. Many so-called first-aid techniques do more harm than good: cutting into the wound is harmful; tourniquets are dangerous; suction and electrical inactivation devices do not work. The only treatment is antivenom. In case of a bite which you fear may have been from a venomous snake:

- Try to keep calm – it is likely that no venom has been dispensed
- Prevent movement of the bitten limb by applying a splint
- Keep the bitten limb BELOW heart height to slow the spread of any venom
- If you have a crepe bandage, wrap it around the whole limb (eg: all the way from the toes to the thigh), as tight as you would for a sprained ankle or a muscle pull
- Evacuate to a hospital that has anti-venom. At the time of writing this is only known to be available in Kampala. Many centres have an Indian anti-venom that does not include the most common biting snakes

And remember:

- NEVER give aspirin; you may offer paracetamol, which is safe
- NEVER cut or suck the wound
- DO NOT apply ice packs
- DO NOT apply potassium permanganate

If the offending snake can be captured without risk of someone else being bitten, take this to show the doctor – but beware since even a decapitated head is able to bite.

MEDICAL FACILITIES IN CAMEROON

Hospitals, clinics, surgeries, dentists and pharmacies are listed in the regional guide. The overwhelming majority are in Douala and Yaoundé. Unlike in the UK, pharmacies in Cameroon can dispense many drugs such as antibiotics and antimalarials without a prescription.

Commonly required medicines such as broad-spectrum antibiotics are widely available throughout the region, as are malaria cures and prophylactics. Malaria treatment packs, are best bought in advance – in fact it's advisable to carry all malaria-related tablets on you, and only rely on their availability locally if you need to restock your supplies.

Private clinics, hospitals and pharmacies can be found in most large towns. A high standard of dental treatment is available in both Douala and Yaoundé, and the best hospitals are in Yaoundé. Clinics elsewhere in the country, however, are often lacking in equipment and medicines and may have a low standard of cleanliness. The patient is generally expected to supply his or her own food and drink while in hospital. Treatment costs, consultation fees and laboratory tests are similar to those in most Western countries.

In all likelihood you will need to speak French with the doctors except in the anglophone west of the country.

If you are visiting the rainforest, the basic precautions for the whole country are even more vital, ie: ensure all immunisations and vaccinations are up to date, take precautions for malaria, use a mosquito net and insect repellent and carry a good first-aid kit. In the rainforest you will need clothing that covers your arms and legs, as well as high-topped boots because of the risk of snake bites. If a leech attaches itself to you, do not pull it off as the bite is more likely to become infected. Instead use salt or a lit cigarette to make it fall off.

If you are on any medication prior to departure, or you have specific needs relating to a known medical condition (for instance if you are allergic to bee stings or you are prone to attacks of asthma), then you are strongly advised to bring any related drugs and devices with you. It is a good idea to carry a prescription or letter from your doctor indicating that you can legally use the medication, to avoid potential problems from officials.

TRAVEL CLINICS AND HEALTH INFORMATION

A full list of current travel clinic websites worldwide is available on www.istm.org/. For other journey preparation information, consult ftp://ftp.shoreland.com/pub/shorecg.rtf or www.tripprep.com. Information about various medications may be found on www.emedicine.com/wild/topiclist.htm. The website www.malariahotspots.co.uk has information on malaria.

UK

Berkeley Travel Clinic 32 Berkeley St, London W1J 8EL (near Green Park tube station); ☎ 020 7629 6233

Cambridge Travel Clinic 48a Mill Rd, Cambridge CB1 2AS; ☎ 01223 367362; e enquiries@travelcliniccambridge.co.uk; www.travelcliniccambridge.co.uk; ⊕ 12.00–19.00 Tue–Fri, 10.00–16.00 Sat

Edinburgh Travel Clinic Regional Infectious Diseases Unit, Ward 41 OPD, Western General Hospital, Crewe Rd South, Edinburgh EH4 2UX; ☎ 0131 537 2822. Travel helpline ⊕ 09.00–12.00 w/days. Provides inoculations & anti-malarial prophylaxis & advises on travel-related health risks.

Fleet Street Travel Clinic 29 Fleet St, London EC4Y 1AA; ☎ 020 7353 5678; www.fleetstreet.com. Injections, travel products & latest advice.

Hospital for Tropical Diseases Travel Clinic Mortimer Market Centre, 2nd Floor, Capper St (off Tottenham Ct Rd), London WC1E 6AU; ☎ 020 7388 9600; www.thehtd.org. Offers consultations & advice, & is able to provide all necessary drugs & vaccines for travellers. Runs a healthline (☎ 09061 337733) for country-specific information & health hazards. Also

stocks nets, water purification equipment & personal protection measures.

Interhealth Worldwide Partnership Hse, 157 Waterloo Rd, London SE1 8US; ☎ 020 7902 9000; www.interhealth.org.uk. Competitively priced, one-stop travel health service. All profits go to their affiliated company, InterHealth, which provides health care for overseas workers on Christian projects.

Liverpool School of Medicine Pembroke Pl, Liverpool L3 5QA; ☎ 0151 708 9393; f 0151 705 3370; www.liv.ac.uk/lstm

MASTA (Medical Advisory Service for Travellers Abroad) Moorfield Rd, Yeadon, Leeds, West Yorks LS19 7BN; ☎ 0113 238 7500; www.masta-travel-health.com. Provides travel health advice, anti-malarials & vaccinations. There are over 25 MASTA pre-travel clinics in Britain; call or check online for the nearest. Clinics also sell mosquito nets, medical kits, insect protection & travel hygiene products.

NHS travel website www.fitfortravel.scot.nhs.uk. Provides country-by-country advice on immunisation & malaria, plus details of recent developments, & a list of relevant health organisations.

5

A kit could contain:

- A good drying antiseptic, eg: iodine or potassium permanganate (rather than an antiseptic cream)
- A few small wound dressings and plasters/Band-Aids
- Suncream
- Insect repellent; malaria tablets; impregnated bednet
- Aspirin or paracetamol (acetaminophen in the USA)
- Prochlorperazine or metachlopramide for nausea and vomiting
- Antihistamine for allergies, insect bites or stings and motion sickness
- Emergency dental repair kit
- Broad spectrum antibiotics if off the beaten track, for any unexpected infection
- Water purification tablets or iodine
- Calamine lotion, aloe vera or sting relief spray for insect bites, stings and sunburn
- Antifungal cream or powder (eg: Canesten)
- Diarrhoea treatment for mild cases (eg: Imodium/Loperamide or diphenoxylate) and ciprofloxacin or norfloxacin antibiotic, 500mg x 2 (or co-trimoxazole for children and pregnant women) for severe diarrhoea
- Tinidazole (500mg x 8) for giardia or amoebic dysentery (see page 93 for regime)
- Antibiotic eye drops, for sore, 'gritty', stuck-together eyes (conjunctivitis)
- Scissors and a pair of fine-pointed tweezers (to remove hairy caterpillar hairs, thorns, splinters, coral, etc)
- Sterile medical kit – a sealed medical kit with syringes, needles, etc
- Condoms or femidoms
- A malaria treatment kit if travelling off the beaten track
- Thermometer (although mercury thermometers are banned by airlines)
- A record of your blood group (and consider joining the Blood Care Foundation)

Nomad Travel Store/Clinic 3–4 Wellington Terr, Turnpike La, London N8 0PX; ☎ 020 8889 7014; travel-health line (office hours only) ☎ 0906 863 3414; e sales@nomadtravel.co.uk; www.nomadtravel.co.uk. Also at 40 Bernard St, London WC1N 1LJ; ☎ 020 7833 4114; 52 Grosvenor Gdns, London SW1W 0AG; ☎ 020 7823 5823; & 43 Queens Rd, Bristol BS8 1QH; ☎ 0117 922 6567. For health advice, equipment such as mosquito nets & other anti-bug devices, & an excellent range of adventure travel gear. Clinics also in Bristol & Southampton.

Trailfinders Travel Clinic 194 Kensington High St, London W8 7RG; ☎ 020 7938 3999; http://www.trailfinders.com/travelessentials/travelclinic.htm

Travelpharm The Travelpharm website, www.travelpharm.com, offers up-to-date guidance on travel-related health & has a range of medications available through their online mini-pharmacy.

IRISH REPUBLIC

Tropical Medical Bureau Grafton Street Medical Centre, Grafton Bldgs, 34 Grafton St, Dublin 2; ☎ 1 671 9200. Branches at Blanchardstown: Main St, Blanchardstown, Dublin 15; Dun Laoghaire: 5 Northumberland Av, Dun Laoghaire, County Dublin; Galway: 1st Floor, Ard Ri Hse, Lower Abbeygate St, Galway. The Bureau has a useful website specific to tropical destinations: www.tmb.ie.

USA

Centers for Disease Control 1600 Clifton Rd, Atlanta, GA 30333; ☎ 877 FYI TRIP; 800 311 3435; www.cdc.gov/travel. The central source of travel information in the USA. Each summer they publish the invaluable *Health Information for International Travel*, available from the Division of Quarantine at the above address.

Connaught Laboratories Pasteur Merieux Connaught, Route 611, PO Box 187, Swiftwater, PA 18370; ✎ 800 822 2463. They will send a free list of specialist tropical-medicine physicians in your state.
IAMAT (International Association for Medical Assistance to Travelers) 417 Center St, Lewiston, NY

CANADA
IAMAT Suite 1, 1287 St Clair Av W, Toronto, Ontario M6E 1B8; ✎ 416 652 0137; www.iamat.org

AUSTRALIA, NEW ZEALAND, THAILAND
IAMAT PO Box 5049, Christchurch 5, New Zealand; www.iamat.org
TMVC ✎ 1300 65 88 44; www.tmvc.com.au. Clinics in Australia, New Zealand & Singapore, including: *Auckland* Canterbury Arcade, 170 Queen St, Auckland; ✎ 9 373 3531

SOUTH AFRICA
SAA-Netcare Travel Clinics Sanlam Bldg, 19, Fredman Dr, Sandton, P Bag X34, Benmore, JHB, Gauteng, 2010; www.travelclinic.co.za. Clinics throughout South Africa.

SWITZERLAND
IAMAT 57 Voirets, 1212 Grand Lancy, Geneva; www.iamat.org

14092; ✎ 716 754 4883; e info@iamat.org; www.iamat.org. A non-profit organisation that provides lists of English-speaking doctors abroad.
International Medicine Center 915 Gessner Rd, Suite 525, Houston, TX 77024; ✎ 713 550 2000; www.traveldoc.com

TMVC Suite 314, 1030 W Georgia St, Vancouver BC V6E 2Y3; ✎ 1 888 288 8682; www.tmvc.com. Private clinic with several outlets in Canada.

Brisbane 75a Astor Terr, Spring Hill, QLD 4000; ✎ 7 3815 6900
Melbourne 393 Little Bourke St, 2nd Floor, Melbourne, VIC 3000; ✎ 3 9602 5788
Sydney Dymocks Bldg, 7th Floor, 428 George St, Sydney, NSW 2000; ✎ 2 9221 7133

TMVC NHC Health Centre, Cnr Beyers Naude & Waugh Northcliff, PO Box 48499, Roosevelt Pk, 2129 (Postal Address); ✎ 011 888 7488; www.tmvc.com.au. Consult website for details of other clinics in South Africa & Namibia.

Part Two

THE GUIDE

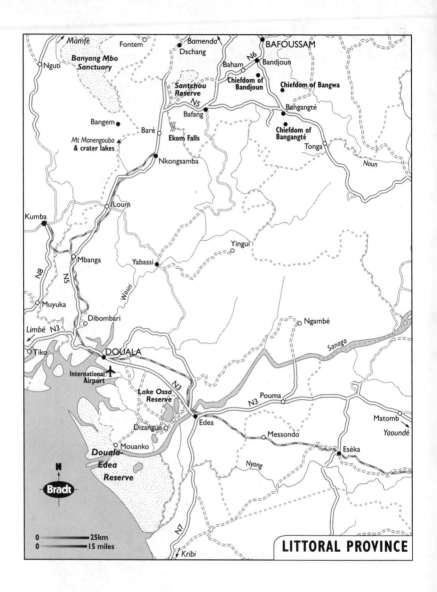

LITTORAL PROVINCE

0 ──── 25km
0 ──── 15 miles

6

Littoral Province

About a third of Cameroon's economic activity occurs in this province, not least because its biggest city is also the country's biggest city by far: Douala.

DOUALA *Telephone codes: 3342 (most common), 3344, 3340, 3343*

Yaoundé may be Cameroon's capital, but the considerably larger port city of Douala in Littoral Province is the economic centre of the country. Most visitors to Cameroon spend at least some time in this vibrant, colourful city with more than 1.8 million inhabitants (some estimates are well in excess of 2 million), especially as Douala is Cameroon's main hub for air travel. It has a sizeable foreign community, with particularly large numbers of Nigerian and French nationals as well as more than 200 Americans.

The sprawling city has come a long way from its origins, small fishing communities that the Portuguese, the first Europeans to set foot on Cameroon, encountered in the 15th century. This triggered the start of a long tradition of trading between coastal rulers and passing European ships.

You love or hate this city, often at the same time. Its pulsating atmosphere certainly excites, and it has a pleasant tropical ambience, with gradually decaying traditional colonial architecture (with verandas and louvred shutters) coexisting with modern buildings.

Yet the stifling humidity (it has often been dubbed the 'armpit of Africa') and its pushy inhabitants can be exhausting. A rapidly growing city, it is ageing rather ungracefully and the many pot-holed roads are appalling. Although it is guilty of having little traditional flavour and more than its fair share of dull architecture, as well as an alarming crime rate, considerable overpopulation, a woefully inadequate infrastructure and economic chaos, it is nevertheless a good base for some of Cameroon's most alluring destinations.

These include the white beaches of Kribi, the black-sand beaches of Limbé at the foot of Mount Cameroon, as well as the energetic town of Kumba near picturesque Lake Barombi Mbo, *en route* for Korup National Park and the Nigerian border. Continue eastwards from Kumba and you come to Mount Kupe and the twin crater lakes of Manengouba, which is excellent hiking country. All are within a few hours' travel from Douala.

Douala is great for nightlife, being packed with lively bars and restaurants and live music venues. The Bonapriso district south of the centre, and Akwa just north of it, are especially lively at night.

Yet you have to be on your guard, especially at night, as crime, including violent crime, has increased in recent years. The port area is especially to be avoided.

Dominated by Mount Cameroon (which you can see looking on from the port) Douala is located a few miles inland, 24km (15 miles) from the Atlantic coast on the southern shore of the Wouri River.

Douala also has its wealthy, extravagant side. Indeed, in the upmarket sections of the Boulevard de la Liberté, Douala's main street, you could almost be in Paris. Smartly dressed, glamorous-looking men and women smelling of expensive colognes talk animatedly in French, wave their hands and kiss each other theatrically and jump out of gleaming new cars into expensive restaurants.

But this does not disguise the largely characterless streets, concrete office blocks and overwhelming atmosphere of business. And the Parisian feel is fragile as poverty and dilapidation are never far away.

This being Africa, it is not a long walk from where the tarmac ends and the muddy streets begin, lined with haphazard shacks made of corrugated iron and scrap wood, for example the stretch from Avenue Ahmadou Ahido going into Boulevard de l'Unité, which becomes very pot-holed.

As the principal port, Douala handles almost all of Cameroon's maritime traffic and is the major entry point for imports to Cameroon, the Central African Republic, Chad, Equatorial Guinea and the Republic of Congo.

The city has few distinct sights or attractions as such, and is best enjoyed as an experience in itself, a slice of vibrant, shambolic Africa, rather than a city with a programme of museums, churches and galleries to tick off.

Central Douala is divided into distinct neighbourhoods, mainly named after the original ruling families. These include the upmarket residential quarter, Bonapriso, industrial Bonaberi and administrative sector Bonanjo. At the centre of the city is Akwa, the principal commercial district, where can be found lots of hotels, restaurants and shops. The main centre of activity here is the Boulevard de la Liberté.

GETTING THERE AND AWAY

By air Most international flights to Cameroon land at Douala's relatively small airport. Cameroon Airlines operates flights from Douala to the main cities, including Yaoundé, Maroua and Garoua. More details are in *Chapter 4, Travelling in Cameroon*, page 59.

By rail The station, the Gare de Bessengue, is northeast of the centre in the Bessengue neighbourhood. Trains go to Yaoundé (where you can get an onward train to Ngaoundéré), Nkongsamba and Kumba, although trains to the latter two are painfully slow. More details are in *Chapter 4, Travelling in Cameroon*, page 68.

By road

Yaoundé (for the north), Kribi and eastern destinations Most *agences de voyage* operate along Boulevard du Président Ahmadou Ahido, near the Place du Ahmadou Ahidjo, just east of the centre.

Centrale Voyages BP 2789; 1460 Bd Président Ahidjo, Akwa; ` 3342 03 16/3342 26 88. Currently offers a 07.00, noon & 16.00 luxury service to Yaoundé for CFA8,000, with a less salubrious CFA3,500 service at other times. They are super-efficient & the journey takes around 3hrs.

Garanti Express BP 3222; Bd Président Ahidjo, Akwa; ` 3342 61 91. Office is almost opposite Centrale Voyages. Offers a cheaper, less comfortable service to Yaoundé.

Also try Confort Voyages (` 9983 95 27) and Beauty Express (*Rue Congo Paraiso, Akwa;* ` 3342 83 96).

Bamenda, Bafoussam, Kumba, Limbé and the northwest Transport to Limbé, Bafoussam, Bamenda and other northern destinations is generally from the

Bonaberi *gare routière* (motor park), next to the concrete tower, about 6km northwest of the centre over the Wouri River Bridge. There are plenty of share taxis for various destinations operating from here.

Guaranti Express BP 3228; 5647 Gare Routière Nationale 3, Bonaberi; ☎ 3342 61 91
Binam Voyages BP 4293; Gare Routière Nationale 3, Bonaberi; ☎ 3344 57 17
Vatikan Express ☎ 7783 95 27

Tchatcho Voyages ☎ 3342 02 10. For Kumba & Mutengene, where you can obtain a share taxi for Limbé.
Linda Voyages 3340 39 57. For Nkongsamba.

Buses and share taxis for Buéa, Limbé and Nkongsamba also terminate and depart from the Rond-point Deido near Wouri Bridge, 2km north of the centre.

Ebolowa and southern destinations
Buca Voyages ☎ 3342 29 35

WHERE TO STAY Douala, along with Yaoundé, has the costliest accommodation in the country, but there are still plenty of inexpensive options to choose from. The area around the Wouri Cinema in the centre is a good starting point for finding some of the less expensive hotels, of which several are nearby.

🏠 **Hôtel Le Meridien** (144 rooms & 8 suites) BP 3232; 35 Av de Cocotiers; ☎ 3342 46 29/3342 50 00; www.lemeridien-hotels.com. One of Douala's most expensive hotels, in one of the city's most tranquil districts, it features attractive grounds overlooking the Wouri River, the harbour & a wooded park. It has good security, a pool (available to non-guests for a fee), gym, tennis courts, expensive book & gift shop, casino, travel agent & golf course. The clean rooms & suites have satellite TV, AC & internet access & start at about CFA110,000 but sometimes substantially less — it is worth asking. The poolside restaurant has a good menu, including fresh fish dishes. There is a free airport shuttle service, business centre & internet access in the lobby. Credit cards are accepted. A couple of recent visitors report problems with bad service, exhorbitant phone charges & the like, but others report friendly staff & excellent facilities. $$$$$

🏠 **Hôtel Akwa Palace** (60 rooms) & **Hôtel Akwa Palace II Pullman** (124 rooms) BP 4007; 52 Bd de la Liberté, Akwa; ☎ 3342 26 01/3342 07 49; e akwa-palace@camnet.cm. Located in the commercial heart of town a few hundred metres southeast of the shores of the Wouri River. The newer Pullman is ranked by the government as 4-star, while the original colonial Akwa Palace is a more modest 3-star. Most credit cards are accepted & travellers' cheques are cashed in most major currencies. Rooms start at CFA35,000 per night in the older section & otherwise start at CFA65,000 per night, which is good value considering the general

standards. The hotels feature a secluded garden area, a good restaurant (sandwiches CFA2100-2800), 3-course meal of the day (CFA12,000), a bar & nightclub, satellite TV in rooms & a 25m pool at the rear (CFA4,000 for non-guests). $$$$

🏠 **Hôtel Novotel Sawa** (291 rooms & 6 suites) BP 2345; 488 Av du Verdun, Bonanjo; ☎ 3342 08 66/3342 44 41; e hotelsawa@camnet.cm. Despite being described as international class, rooms & food are variable in quality & the water supply can be unreliable during the dry season although recent renovation may have cured this. The gardens are very pleasant, however. The good pool can also be used by non-guests, for a CFA3,000 fee. Most credit cards are accepted. The rooms & suites have satellite TV. $$$$

🏠 **Hôtel Arcade** (199 rooms) BP 12120; 731 Rue Tobie Kuoh, Bonanjo; ☎ 3343 33 23; e arcade_hotel@hotmail.com. A comfortable 3-star hotel (rooms for 1–4 people & the disabled) with a good restaurant, bar, nightclub, internet suite & swimming pool. Use of nearby tennis courts available. The hotel is next to a pleasant, inexpensive restaurant, Echo de Bonanjo. At the weekend room prices can be halved. Rooms are clean, have a bathroom & AC, but at the time of writing the stairways & corridors are grubby & the lifts are not operational. $$$

🏠 **Hôtel Ibis** (160 rooms) BP 12086; Rue Pierre Loti, off Av Charles de Gaulle, Bonanjo; ☎ 3342 5800/3342 5760; e hotel.ibis@camnet.cm; www.ibishotel.com. A reliable, secure, good-value but

6

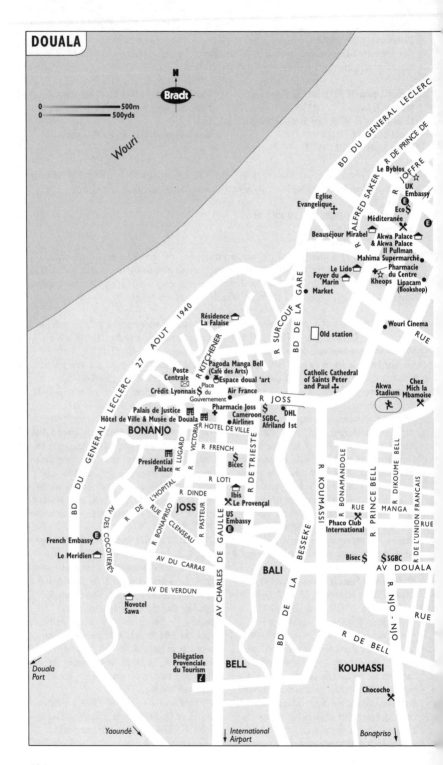

DOUALA

Wouri

0 ————— 500m
0 ————— 500yds

Bradt

BD DU GENERAL LECLERC

R DE PRINCE DE

R JOFFRE

Le Byblos

UK Embassy

Eco

Eglise Evangelique

ALFRED SAKER

Méditeranée

Beauséjour Mirabel

Akwa Palace & Akwa Palace II Pullman

Mahima Supermarché

Le Lido

Pharmacie du Centre

Foyer du Marin

Kheops

Lipacam (Bookshop)

Market

R SURCOUF

BD DE LA GARE

Old station

Wouri Cinema

RUE

Résidence La Falaise

R KITCHENER

Pagoda Manga Bell (Café des Arts)

Espace doual 'art

Catholic Cathedral of Saints Peter and Paul

Akwa Stadium

Chez Mich la Mbamoise

Poste Centrale

LECLERC 27 AOUT 1940

Place du Gouvernement

Air France

Crédit Lyonnais

R JOSS

Palais de Justice

Pharmacie Joss

Hôtel de Ville & Musée de Douala

Cameroon Airlines

SGBC, Afriland 1st

DHL

BONANJO

R HOTEL DE VILLE

R VICTORIA

R LUGARD

R FRENCH

R DE TRIESTE

R LOTI

Presidential Palace

Bicec

Ibis

Le Provençal

R KOUMASSI

R BONAMANDOLE

R PRINCE BELL

R DIKOUME BELL

R DE L'UNION FRANCAIS

JOSS

R DE L'HOPITAL

R DINDE

RUE CLENSEAU

R BONAPRISO

R PASTEUR

US Embassy

RUE

MANGA

Phaco Club International

BD DU GENERAL LECLERC

AV DES COCOTIERS

French Embassy

Le Meridien

AV DU CARRAS

R DE LA BESSEKE

BALI

Bisec

SGBC

AV DOUALA

R NJO-NJO

RUE

AV DE VERDUN

Novotel Sawa

AV CHARLES DE GAULLE

BD DE LA

R DE BELL

Douala Port

Délégation Provenciale du Tourism

BELL

KOUMASSI

Chococho

Yaoundé

International Airport

Bonapriso

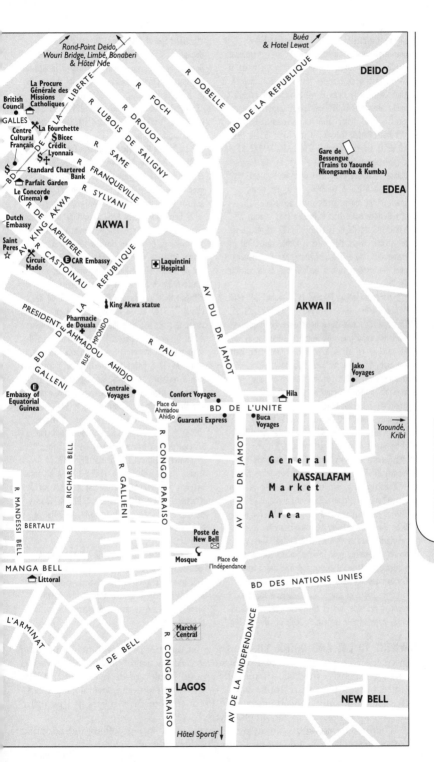

slightly characterless hotel with comfortable if unexciting rooms, ranked 3 star by the government. Popular with business people, being in the heart of the business area. Features restaurant, bar, shops & a pool. Consistently clean & well maintained. B/fast buffet around CFA7,000 pp. Free transport from the airport (7km). Major credit cards accepted. $$$

🏠 **Hôtel Parfait Garden** (78 rooms) BP 5350; 1010 Bd de la Liberté, Akwa; ☎ 3342 63 57/3342 83 98. A (government-ranked) 3-star hotel by the Akwa Palace in a very lively part of town; pleasant restaurant & bar & swimming pool. Has clean, spacious dbl rooms. Credit cards accepted. $$$

🏠 **Résidence Hôtelière la Falaise** (133 rooms) BP 5300; 503 Bd de la Liberté; ☎ 3342 46 46. Next to Jet Cam Tours, this hotel is rather smart but rather dull. There is a restaurant, bar & swimming pool. Most rooms have a bathroom & AC & satellite TV. $$$

🏠 **Hôtel Beauséjour Mirabel** (135 rooms) BP 5368; 337 Rue Joffre, Akwa; ☎ 3342 70 93/3342 38 85. This upmarket mid-range hotel on 6 floors just down the road from the Hôtel Lido has rooms with AC, satellite TV, bar & a restaurant next door. Staff are multi-lingual & car hire, a laundry & dry cleaning service & a business centre are also available. It has a swimming pool available to non-guests at a cost of CFA1,500. $$$

🏠 **Hôtel Lewat** (40 rooms) BP 12563; 2699 Bd de la République; ☎ 3340 00 24. A 2-star hotel with clean rooms & a good restaurant. $$

🏠 **German Seamen's Mission/Foyer du Marin** (18 rooms) BP 5194; Rue Galliéni, off Rue Joffre, Akwa; e douala@seemannsmission.org. A very good choice for its ambience, central location in the Akwa district, excellent standards & great value for money. Near the Hôtel Lido, it has very clean, recently refurbished rooms with AC & bathroom. There's an inviting swimming pool in immaculate attractive gardens, a restaurant with good food (such as German sausage with cabbage salad) & a bar. A favourite haunt of expats & travellers; a luggage room is available free of charge to guests. Because of its popularity it is best to book in advance. $$

🏠 **Hôtel Sportif** (30 rooms) Av des Palmiers, Bonapriso; ☎ 3343 76 40/3342 67 55. South of Bonanjo in Bonapriso. Rooms with shared facilities & fan start at CFA9,000, while an en-suite room with AC is CFA18,500. $$

🏠 **Hôtel le Nde** (50 rooms) BP 12990; 105 Bd de la Liberté; ☎ 3342 70 34. Good standard hotel with restaurant, bar & pool. $$

🏠 **La Procure Générale des Missions Catholiques** BP 5280; Rue Franqueville, Akwa; ☎ 3342 27 97; e progemis.douala@camnet.cm. This Mission is good value & very secure but is often full, being popular with missionaries, aid workers, teachers & other European visitors. Facilities include a swimming pool & spacious lounge. The restaurant is closed on Sun evenings. Rooms are clean & have AC & a shower room or shared facilities. It is opposite the British Council (1387 Rue Joffre), which can give advice & which has a fast internet service. $$

🏠 **Hila Hôtel** (22 rooms) BP 17497; 515 Bd de l'Unité; ☎ 3342 15 86. Although located on a busy street, this hotel is near the central market & buses & has friendly, accommodating staff. Rooms are self-contained with bathroom (not necessarily with hot water), AC, TV & phone & there is a bar, internet café & restaurant. A bakery, Boulangerie Akwa, is across the street & sells hamburgers, pizzas, etc. $$

🏠 **Hôtel de Lido** Rue Joffre, Akwa; ☎ 3342 40 86. Just around the corner from the Foyer du Marin, though far less inviting, with dbl rooms with fan or AC plus there is a more inviting restaurant/bar. $

🏠 **Hôtel du Littoral** (34 rooms) BP 1389; 38 Av Douala Manga Bell, Bali; ☎ 3342 58 05. A bit tatty but in a very central location. Bar & restaurant. $

🏠 **Hôtel Renom** (25 rooms) BP 17578; Av Charles de Gaulle; ☎ 3342 34 52. Formerly the Hôtel de l'Air, this hotel near the airport has en-suite rooms with AC. $

🏠 **Planet Hôtel** (52 rooms) BP 12985, Akwa. A spotless hotel in a good, central position in town with friendly English- & French-speaking staff. The rooms are en suite & have a TV & free internet connection. Bar & restaurant, & internet access in the lobby. $

✖ **WHERE TO EAT AND DRINK** There are a good number of restaurants at differing price levels, especially in the Bonapriso and Akwa neighbourhoods. Akwa has many inexpensive food stalls, especially around Boulevard de la Liberté and Rue Joffre, but few bars, apart from a couple by the Wouri Cinema, several basic shack-like establishments along Boulevard du Président, one or two bars in Rue Joffre and a few others scattered about elsewhere.

There are several Parisian-style cafés with good strong coffees and tempting pastries, especially in and around Boulevard de la Liberté.

✗ **Oriental Garden** 10 Rue Afcodi, Bonapriso; ☎ 3342 69 38. Pricey but good Chinese restaurant. **$$$$$**

✗ **Le Beaujolais** Rue Tokoto, Bonapriso; ☎ 3342 70 11. Rather pricey French food. **$$$$$**

✗ **La Fourchette** 317 Rue Franqueville, Akwa; ☎ 3343 26 11; m 42 14 88. Good value centrally located French restaurant. **$$$$$**

✗ **Le Tourne Broche** Hôtel Akwa Palace, Akwa; ☎ 3342 26 01. The best French cooking at the restaurant by the pool of the hotel. **$$$$$**

✗ **Le Provençal** 369 Av Charles de Gaulle, Bonanjo; ☎ 3342 70 17. French cuisine. **$$$$$**

✗ **Phaco Club International** BP 10063; 227 Rue Douala Mango Bell, near Rue Koumassi; ☎ 3342 68 81; m 9955 30 08. African dishes including a selection of exotic meats, with live music, dance & sometimes satirical comedy in the evening. **$$$$**

✗ **Chez Wou** 611 Av Charles de Gaulle, Bonanjo; ☎ 3342 33 10. Douala's oldest Chinese restaurant. **$$$$**

✗ **Méditerranée Restaurant** Bd de la Liberté, Akwa; ☎ 3342 30 69/3342 92 34. Good-value Greek food (tzatziki/taramarasalata) CFA2,000, salad CFA1,500, moussaka CFA3,500, white beans (vegetarian) CFA2,500, fillet steak CFA4,000, beer CFA1,000 at this outdoor restaurant opposite the Akwa Palace with a terrace looking out onto the busy street. A popular expat – & prostitute – hangout. **$$$**

✗ **Chez Mich la Mbamoise** Bd de la République, Bali; ☎ 3342 22 40. Al fresco eating with Cameroonian cuisine. **$$$**

✗ **White House Restaurant** Rue Pasteur Lottin Same; ☎ 3343 10 95; m 746 32 98/967 27 06; e whitehouserestaurant2000@yahoo.fr. An open-air restaurant with a tin roof & fans. A great choice of African food & some Western dishes, such as beef, lamb or pork chops in sauce with rice. Very popular with Douala Westerners & residents from the nearby Procure Générale des Missions Catholiques. **$$$**

✗ **La Coupole** 115 Av Charles de Gaulle, Bonapriso; ☎ 3342 29 60. Lebanese food & pizzas. **$$**

✗ **Le Dragon d'Or** 771 Bd de la Liberté, Akwa. Opposite the Akwa Palace Hôtel, this offers Chinese & Vietnamese cuisine. **$$**

✗ **Café des Arts** Pagoda Manga Bell, Pl du Gouvernement, Bonanjo; m 981 10 87. A clean, smart French restaurant with a pleasant little courtyard garden. Avocado vinaigrette CFA1,000, salad CFA1,500, beef fillet steak CFA4,000, mixed grill CFA7,000. **$$**

✗ **Circuit Mado** near Akwa Palace Hôtel, Akwa; ☎ 3342 99 69. Simple Cameroonian dishes, such as grilled fish or chicken in sauce. **$$**

✗ **Echo de Bonanjo** BP 11998; Rue de Trieste, Bonanjo; ☎ 3342 64 91. On the junction with Rue Joss, this pleasant, unpretentious restaurant has good yet inexpensive dishes including Cameroonian speciality ndole with meat or shrimps. Next to the Hôtel Arcade. **$$**

✗ **German Seamen's Mission/Foyer du Marin** Rue Galliéni, off Rue Joffre, Akwa; ☎ 3342 27 94; m 91 54 52. Brochette or German sausage, bread roll, sauerkraut & chips for CFA1,500, grilled meats from CFA3,000, omelettes from CFA800 & continental b/fast for CFA1,300 by the pool. **$$**

✗ **Le Glacier Modèrne** Bd de la Liberté, Akwa. Paris-style café for pastries, snacks & ice creams. **$$**

✗ **La Paillote** Bd de la Liberté, Akwa. Opposite the Hôtel Parfait Garden, this restaurant/club has snacks & a bar. **$$**

✗ **Ets Edere Café Restaurant** Bd de la Liberté, Akwa. Near the Pharmacie du Centre, this cheap & cheerful if a little dingy dive does a delicious roast chicken & plantain chips for CFA1,000 & steak & chips for CFA1,500. A big (0.65 litre) bottle of beer is CFA600. Where the locals eat. Take a taxi from here at night, even though it is centrally located. **$**

✗ **Le Regal du Plateau** Rue Joss, Bonanjo. By Rue de Trieste & several banks & airline offices, this simple, inexpensive snack bar has a small terrace for a drink after a typically lengthy banking transaction or flight booking. **$**

✗ **4ème Protocol Snack Bar and Piano Restaurant** Bd de la Liberté, Akwa. Inexpensive snacks by the Wouri Cinema, late-night opening. Next door is a 'pub' & a games room with slot machines, roulette, etc. **$**

✗ **King Akwa** In the Douala Bar area of Akwa. Unremarkable by day but takes off at night; head here for beer & roasted fish. The lively atmosphere, with plenty of tables & chairs outside, is augmented by street-sellers flogging anything from CDs to shoes. **$**

✗ **Chococho** Rue Njo-njo, Bonapriso. A good bakery with croissants, pizzas, sandwiches & a good range of breads. **$**

ENTERTAINMENT AND NIGHTLIFE Up the hill from Rond-point Deido, Rue de la Joie lives by night and is an absolute must as regards nightlife in Douala. Lively even on weeknights, an evening here begins with roasted fish & beer on the roadside, with nightclubs opening their doors from midnight until around 06.00.

To finish off things at sunrise, try a bowl of *bouillon*, a light broth, perfect for easing the oncoming hangover.

As for nightclubs elsewhere, admission and opening times vary greatly and names often change. They usually get going from around 23.00 and generally close anywhere between 02.00 and 06.00.

Nightclubs

☆ **Broadway** Rue Toyota, Bonapriso. Live performances enliven the dancing.

☆ **Le Club** 78 Rue Sylvani, Akwa. Swish, plays Western music & is popular with expats.

☆ **The Club** Rue Batibois, Bonapriso; www.bar-the-club.com. On the junction with Av Charles de Gaulle.

☆ **Le Byblos** Rue Joffre, opposite the Hôtel Beausejour, Akwa. Modern club, plays African & western music. Admission is CFA3,000.

☆ **Orange Metallic** Bonanjo; www.orange-mettalic.com. Popular with expats.

☆ **Saint Peres** Rue Castelnau, near Hôtel Parfait Garden. A popular expat haunt, playing a lot of Western music.

☆ **L'Elysee Nightclub** Near Marché Deido, north of the centre, is popular with locals; few expats or tourists visit.

☆ **Le Sunset** Av Charles de Gaulle, Bonanjo. Plays both Western & African music.

☆ **Kheops Nightclub** Bd du Président Ahmadou Ahidjo, Akwa (end of Bd de la Liberté). Plays Western & African tunes.

Cinema

◄ **Le Concorde** Av King Akwa, near Rue Boue Lapeyrère, Akwa

◄ **Le Wouri** Bd de la Liberté, Akwa; ✆ 3342 02 52. Occasionally has live theatre & music events too.

◄ **Cinema Rex** Bd du Président Ahmadou Ahidjo, Akwa

◄ **Bonapriso** Av de l'Indépendance, Bonapriso

Cultural centres

British Council BP 12801, 1387 Rue Joffre, Akwa; ✆ 3342 51 45/3343 49 66; e tc.douala@britishcouncil.cm; www.britishcouncil.org/cameroon. It has a cyber centre with fast internet access & BBC programmes are shown, & there are occasional events & language courses.

Centre Culturel Français Bd de la Liberté; ✆ 3342 69. 96. Occasional events like concerts, films, theatre, music & talks.

OTHER PRACTICALITIES
Air freight

DHL 224 Rue Joss, Bonanjo; ✆ 3342 98 82/3342 36 36

Arts and crafts

Ali Baba ✆ 3342 32 13

Coopérative des artisans et paysans Africains ✆ 3342 19 81

Banks There are several banks near the Akwa Palace Hôtel on Boulevard de la Liberté, including Standard Chartered Bank (*57 Bd de la Liberté, Akwa;* ✆ *3342 36 12*) and Ecobank (*Bd de la Liberté, Akwa;* ✆ *3343 8251*). Banks are also grouped together on Rue Joss in Bonanjo, just before Place du Gouvernement, and include Société Générale de Banques au Cameroun (SGBC) (*78 Rue Joss;* ✆ *3342 70 10*) which has an ATM; Société Commercial de Banque-Crédit Lyonnais (*Rue Joss;* ✆ *3342 65 01*); and Afriland First Bank. Banque Internationale du Cameroun Pour l'Epargne et le Crédit (Bicec) is at Avenue Charles de Gaulle (✆ *3342 84 31*). SCB-Crédit Lyonnais is at Rue Joss, Bonanjo (✆ *3342 65 02*).

Bookshops

Librairie Papétérie de Bonapriso 10 Rue Batibois, Bonapriso; ☎ 3342 63 67. Stocks English-language publications.
Lipacam 27 Av Ahidjo; ☎ 3342 04 69

Afrique Papyrus Bd de la Liberté, Akwa. Good for English & French publications.
Hôtel Le Meridien Bookshop 35 Av de Cocotiers; ☎ 3342 50 00

Internet access

@ **British Council** Bd de la Liberté, Akwa; ☎ 3342 51 45; e info.douala@britishcouncil.cm. It has a cyber centre with fast internet access.
@ **Cyberix** Bd de la Liberté, Akwa; ☎ 3343 75 50
@ **Cyber Bazaar** Av Charles de Gaulle, near Rue Pierre Loti, Bonanjo; ☎ 3342 60 36

@ **Cyberbao Internet Café** 1482 Bd de la Liberté, Akwa; ☎ 3342 29 16
@ **Dot.com** Bd de la Liberté, Akwa
@ **Square Net** Av Charles de Gaulle, on junction with Av de l'Indépendance, Bonapriso
@ **Global Net** ☎ 3341 02 72

Mail

✉ **Poste Centrale** (main post office) Place du Gouvernement, Bonanjo
✉ **Poste d'Akwa** Bd de la Liberté, Akwa

✉ **Poste de Deido** Rue Dibombe, Deido
✉ **Poste de New Bell** Av Douala Manga Bell, by Place de l' Indépendance, New Bell

Hospitals and clinics

✚ **Polyclinique de Bonanjo** Av Charles de Gaulle, Bonanjo; ☎ 3342 79 36/3342 17 80. A private medical clinic situated by the Hôtel Ibis, highly rated by expatriates. Most staff here speak English.

✚ **General Hospital** Bassa; ☎ 3337 01 44/3337 02 48/3337 08 48
✚ **Clinique Bel Air** 680 de la Rue Toyota (Rue no 1.239), Bonapriso; ☎ 3342 82 84/3342 89 13. A small clinic with 3 beds for in-patients.

Dentists

Dr Bernard Zipfel 2ème étage, Immeuble Neuilly II, Av Charles de Gaulle, Bonanjo; ☎ 3342 01 98/3343 37 12. Appointments for temporary residents/travellers average around CFA25,000–30,000.

Dr Caroline Eyidi 1871 Bd de la Liberté, Akwa; ☎ 3343 49 51. Appointments start at around CFA6,000.
Dr Claudette Nouni Panka Bonanjo; ☎ 342 22 03. Another centrally located dentist.

Pharmacies

✚ **Pharmacie Joss** Off Rue Joss, Bonanjo, next to Amity Bank & by Place du Gouvernement; ⊕ 24hrs
✚ **Pharmacie de Douala** 1017 Bd Président Ahidjo, Akwa; ☎ 3342 74 80; ⊕ 24 hrs
✚ **Pharmacie de l'Aeroport** 1934 Bd des Nations Unies, Bassa; ☎ 3342 28 76
✚ **Pharmacie de Bonapriso** Rue Tokoto, Bonapriso; ☎ 3343 48 61

✚ **Pharmacie de la Gare** 1079 Bd de la Réunification, Deido; ☎ 3340 18 70
✚ **Pharmacie du Plateau** 854 Rue Njo-Njo, Bonapriso; ☎ 3342 05 80; ⊕ 24 hrs
✚ **Pharmacie de la République** 668 Bd de la République, Akwa; ☎ 3342 09 98; ⊕ 24hrs

Photographic processing

Procolor Bd de la Liberté, Akwa. Developing & printing a 36-exposure colour negative film is CFA7,500.
Photo Logona BP 3271 By Résidence Hôtelière la Falaise, Akwa; ☎ 3343 92 34/3343 75 97

Laboratorie Photo Prunet 545 Rue Pau, Akwa; ☎ 3342 08 67

Fitness and sports

Centre de Pèche Sportive de Douala ☎ 3343 02 93
Association Equestre de Douala BP 1157; ☎ 3342 03 84; m 9981 94 15. Horseriding.

Golf Club de Likomba BP 156; Tiko, 40km from Douala. Golf club.

Club PAD (Port Autonome de Douala) Av Charles de Gaulle, Bonanjo; ☎ 3342 51 21. Tennis, swimming & basketball.
KSA Fitness Centre ☎ 3343 03 84
Atraf Fitness Clinic BP 84; ☎ 3343 70 23. Gym, aerobics, karate, kung fu, yoga, tae kwon do, table tennis, basketball, sauna.

Centre de Remise en Form BP 15453; Rue Copseco, Bonapriso; ☎ 3342 70 20. Gym, step, karate, judo, Tae Kwondo.
Swimming The Akwa Palace Hôtel & Le Meridien Hôtel have good swimming pools available to non-guests for a small fee.

Schools

American School of Douala BP 1909; 767 Av des Palmiers; ☎ 3342 14 37; m 791 65 89; e infor@asddouala.com; www.asddouala.com. An independent co-educational school offering an educational programme from pre-kindergarten through 12th grade/upper 6th for English-speaking students of all nationalities.

Supermarkets An extensive range including luxury – and pricey – foods imported from Europe are available south of the centre in Bonapriso from Unimarché on Rue Tokoto and from Score Supermarché nearby off Rue Tokoto. Cheaper options include Mahima Supermarché (*BP 15430;* ☎ *3343 44 87/3342 73 38*) on Boulevard Ahidjo and Onashi Supermarché (*BP 5527;* ☎ *3342 6182/3343 0190*) at 421 Rue Alfred Saker, both in the Akwa district.

Tourist office

ⓘ Délégation Provinciale du Tourisme Av Charles de Gaulle, Bonanjo; ☎ 3342 11 71/3342 14 22. Can provide some basic information about hotels, attractions & excursions.

WHAT TO SEE AND DO Northwards along the Boulevard de la Liberté is the **Akwa Palace**, an old colonial hotel. An expensive hotel, it is nevertheless a good spot to have a coffee or a beer on the terrace.. Northwards, at the junction with Rue Sylvani, is a Baptist church built by the Germans in 1899. Lovers of churches will find more than ten in the maze of streets of the New Bell neighbourhood southeast of Akwa. The Boulevard continues to the Deido district, which has a lively market. Cross the Wouri Bridge for the principally industrial Bonaberi neighbourhood.

Parallel with the Boulevard de la Liberté is **Rue Joffre**, which is worth walking down as you become immersed in the vibrancy of a bustling market street cluttered with stalls, curiously an inordinate number selling stationery, but others selling cheap watches, clothing, fruit, vegetables and kola nuts, the African beat always in the background.

Near here, just before the port, is the **Temple du Centenaire** or **Eglise Evangelique**. The first European settlers in Douala were English missionaries in the 19th century, the most well known of these being Alfred Saker, who in 1845 set up a missionary community at the site of this church, which is off, appropriately, Rue Alfred Saker. It was built to commemorate the 100th anniversary of his arrival.

The missionaries were soon followed by German trading companies who in 1884 signing treaties with the Douala chiefs which gave Germany legal rights under German law. The city was named Kamerunstadt and a German governor appointed. In 1907 Kamerunstadt was renamed Douala and became part of the French protectorate after World War I, when massive urban development and industrial growth set it on course to become the country's major economic centre that it is today.

Also near here, and also off the Boulevard de la Liberté, is the dusty, tree-lined **Boulevard du Président Ahmadou Ahidjo**, the main shopping street, with department stores and lots of stalls selling anything from football shirts to mattresses. Boutique Cicam (*BP 4089; 712 Bd Président Ahmadou Ahidjo;* \ *3342 61 81;* e *afric@camnet.cm*) has a great selection of African textiles for sale, with beautiful, vibrant 6m cotton prints starting at CFA5,000. More choice is available at Congo Market (Marché Congo) on Rue Congo Paraiso.

The Boulevard du Président Ahmadou Ahidjo becomes a heavily pot-holed mudbath, the Boulevard de l'Unité, where there is a sprawling **market** of seemingly endless stalls.

Move southwards along the wide, bustling Boulevard de la Liberté and you come to a neo-Romanesque 1930s-built, pale green and cream building, the city's **Catholic Cathedral of Saints Peter and Paul** (⊕ *06.15–18.30 daily & on Sun has an 06.30 choral mass, an 08.00 English mass, an 09.30 mass in the Douala language, an 11.00 mass in French and Latin and an 18.30 mass in French*). The interior consists of red brickwork, a wood-panelled ceiling and vivid stained glass. You can't miss it. Opposite the cathedral is a graveyard in the tropical style.

A little further on from here, as Rue Joss crosses a bridge over Boulevard de la Gare, there is a large expanse of lush greenery, a reminder of the huge amount of rainfall the city receives during the year.

Further southwards from the cathedral, the Boulevard de la Liberté leads into the Bonanjo district, the administrative sector of the city with a large square, the Place du Gouvernement, and various banks and offices.

The area around the **Place du Gouvernement** is like a sleepy provincial town when compared with Akwa, and the square itself is a sweet but rather tatty little scrap of a park. The main post office dominates the square and there is a World War II monument commemorating Général Leclerc. There is also a striking **pagoda**, once the home of Prince Rudolph Manga Bell, built in 1904, and now housing a restaurant. Next to it is a surprisingly swish gallery with small café housing modern African art, the **Espace doual'art** (\ *342 32 59*). Other art galleries in the city include Galerie Mam (\ *342 28 63*) and Les Galeries Continents (\ *342 14 07*).

Off the Place du Gouvernement is the **Musée de Douala** (⊕ *08.00–14.00 Mon–Fri, 08.00–noon Sat; CFA1,000*), located unobtrusively on the first floor of the Hôtel de Ville (the town hall). The museum is rather jumbled and erratic but is certainly worth a visit. Highlights include some clay Bamoun statues and a bronze cast, wooden Fang statues, colourful Douala *pirogue* decorations, a Fulani suit of mail with spears, Bamiléké thrones and Bamoun pictures.

Further south is the **Joss district**, which contains some German colonial buildings. Despite their general state of disrepair, UNESCO has classified the buildings as a World Heritage Site. Further west, towards the river, is the Presidential Palace, but this must not be photographed if you want to avoid trouble.

The open-air arts and crafts market, the **Centre Artisanal de Douala** or Artisanal Camerounais, has a good selection of artefacts and souvenirs and is situated at the Marché des Fleurs, 3km south of the centre off Avenue Charles de Gaulle in the Bonapriso district, a main residential area of Douala.

East of the centre, the bustling Lagos and Kassalafam neighbourhoods offer lively markets including Cameroon's biggest market, the **Marché Central** (or Marché de Lagos), south of Avenue Douala Manga Bell. Various ingredients for traditional African medicines are sold outside the mosque by the Place de l'Indépendence and the market becomes the fruit and vegetable market, Marché de Kassalafam.

Around Douala

Maka Castle North of Douala, about 8km from the town of Dibombari, is the German-built castle of Maka which features a 30m-high tower and a 300m-long tunnel under the Djouki River.

About 50km east of Douala on the main N3 road is the attractive town of Edea, home of the Bassa and Bakoko peoples. Edea has an impressive bridge spanning the Sanaga River, built by the Germans in 1903, which is 180m long. Edea has plenty of shops, banks, a post office, market and also a hydro-electric plant to admire.

WHERE TO STAY

Hostellerie La Sanaga (30 rooms) BP 54; 3346 49 62/3346 44 62. A comfortable hotel, with dbl rooms around CFA25,000. $$

Carrefour Hôtel (22 rooms) BP 56; 3346 48 18. Government-rated 1-star hotel with satellite TV, restaurant & bar. $

Hôtel Relais (18 rooms) BP 239. Simple, inexpensive hotel with satellite TV, a bar, restaurant & nightclub. $

AROUND EDEA

Lake Ossa Near Edea to the west, a few kilometres north of the town of Dizangue, is Lake Ossa, a lake created by tectonic movements occurring within the earth's crust. It is popular for fishing and various watersports and is surrounded by forest.

Douala-Edea Reserve Southwest of Edea and sandwiched between Douala and Kribi is the Douala-Edea Reserve, which features a wide variety of fauna and flora, as well as Lake Tissongo. Bordered on its northern edge by the Sanaga River and on its western edge by the Atlantic Ocean, it features a wide range of habitats.

Lying 135km and a two-hour drive from Douala, this sizeable town with a population of 110,000 is dominated by the 2,396m Mount Manengouba, which has two stunning crater lakes at its summit. Another local attraction is the Chutes d'Ekom, a magnificent waterfall.

WHERE TO STAY IN NKONGSAMBA AREA

Villa Luciole (7 rooms) BP 218; Melong Mungo; 7726 7155; m 9999 8991; e contact@ villa-luciole.com; www.villa-luciole.com. An old colonial house in stunning surroundings recently renovated by a French couple & 2 Cameroonian brothers. Surrounded by lush vegetation & with its own waterfall, this innovative hotel & restaurant is on the outskirts of the village of Mbouroukou, 15km from Nkongsamba. The villa has a family atmosphere where guests eat together at one table. The food is excellent & includes homegrown vegetables, & cheese production has recently started too. The rooms are impeccable & Luciole is an excellent base for outdoor activities like trekking & horseriding, with walks to the twin crater lakes, the Ekon Falls & Mount Manenguba, & overnight trips to the Bororo mountain villages. B/fast inc. $$$

Fere Hôtel (19 rooms) BP 368. A government-rated 1-star hotel with basic rooms, a bar & restaurant. $

Hôtel Le Parisien BP 182; 3349 33 48. Basic accommodation for CFA6,000. $

Hôtel du Moungo (42 rooms) BP 18; 3349 12 17/3349 14 57. Government-rated 1-star hotel with a bar & restaurant. $

Hôtel La Forêt (22 rooms) 3349 23 84. Small basic hotel. $

WHERE TO STAY IN BANGEM

Hôtel Prestige (10 rooms) BP 2697. On the outskirts of town. The area's best hotel. Small bar & dining area, & a small well-tended garden with a lawn & a replica of an old cooking hut. Clean dbl rooms, 6 opening out onto a courtyard at the back & 4 onto the gardens at the front. Each has a basic en-suite bathroom with cold running water & intermittent electricity — the area is prone to power cuts. No AC or TV. $

WHAT TO SEE

Chutes d'Ekom Some 30km down the road from Bafang are the impressive 80m-high Chutes d'Ekom on the Nkam River. To reach these you turn off the N5 road onto a track at a sign saying 'Chefferie de Bayong/Chutes'. The waterfall is another 12km or so from here and the last section is not accessible by car, and all of it may be impassable during the rainy season.

Manengouba Twin Crater Lakes These stunning sacred lakes, the smaller, algae-rich green 'Man Lake' and the bigger, deep blue 'Woman Lake', are situated within the large grass-covered volcanic depression at Manengouba, on the border with Southwest Province.

They are easily reached by walking from the pleasant town of Bangem, just over the provincial border in Southwest Province, which is about 40km north of Nyasoso (a three-hour drive on a good day) and home of the Bakossi people.

Visitors to the lakes are required to register and pay CFA1,000 at the police station next to the CPDM Party House (which provides simple accommodation) on the Melong Road in Bangem, leaving town. The lakes are a three-hour hilly walk. Start by leaving town on 2nd Street, staying on the main track which becomes more and more faint and gradually climbs to the steep edge of the crater to reach the 2,411m/7,910ft summit of Mount Manengouba. You should now be able to see the level floor of the depression. If you continue across the crater towards the mountain tops on the other side of the crater you come to the Woman Lake. Take a short climb up the little hill on the right to reach the Man Lake, which is surrounded by steep wooded slopes.

Camping, fishing and swimming are only allowed at the Woman Lake. This is an especially good region for hiking.

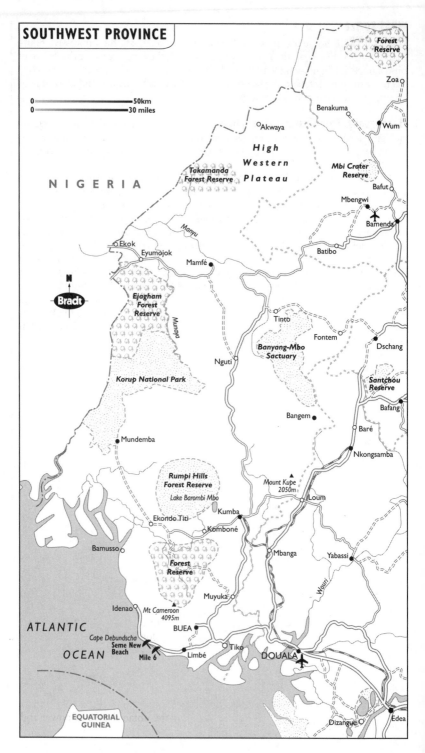

7

Southwest Province

This fertile region bordering Nigeria on its west side offers visitors Mount Cameroon to marvel at, and which is not too daunting a climb, beaches to relax upon at the old colonial town of Limbé, as well as beautiful crater lakes to explore and Korup National Park.

The eastern edge of Southwest Province roughly follows a volcanic mountain range that stretches from Mount Cameroon on the coast to the Bamenda Highlands. The mountain range continues northwards taking in the Adamawa Highlands, Atlantika Mountains and Mandara Mountains in the extreme north.

Inland, the region is often called the Grassfields. Popular crops here include the starchy root vegetable cassava, groundnuts (peanuts), cocoa and coffee. Bamenda and Bafoussam are prominent cities in this region.

LIMBE *Telephone code: 3333*

The pretty little port of Limbé, 74km (an hour's drive) from Douala, 31km from Buéa and 96km from Kumba, is situated on a bay of the Gulf of Guinea at the foot of Mount Cameroon. The bay is sandwiched between the huge Mount Cameroon on one side and Bioko (or Bioco) Island, which is part of Equatorial Guinea and is essentially another big volcano, rising out of the sea on the other. A memorable sight, to be sure.

This easy-going small-scale resort town with a population of about 50,000 is a welcome respite from overwhelming, chaotic Douala and boasts beautiful palm vistas, a lively, traditional market and British and German colonial architecture.

In 1858 Limbé (which was known as Victoria until 1982) was founded after the Baptist Missionary Society of London, needing a base, asked former naval engineer turned missionary Alfred Saker to buy land around Ambas Bay from King William of Bimbia, of the Isubu, which became the town.

The town was largely populated by Bimbia peoples and slaves from nearby countries like Liberia and Ghana who had been freed. The initial church influence in the town was soon overshadowed by growing English and German commerce, but Victoria remained the responsibility and ownership of the missionaries rather than Britain.

Presbyterian missionaries from Switzerland bought the land from the Baptists in 1887, by which time Cameroon was a German colony, Kamerun. Victoria was central to this colony both economically and politically, until it became part of the British protectorate in 1915.

Cocoa, palm, rubber and banana plantations around Victoria increased and expanded significantly after World War II and many remain today.

Limbé, in recent years, has been at the forefront of the anglophone opposition in the west of the country to what it sees as being the unfair degree of power and influence the francophone majority has over Cameroon.

The town today retains little of its former importance. The principal economic activity appears to be based around accommodating the weekend holidaymakers, especially expatriates from the nearby city of Douala, who flock here outside the rainy season.

The attractive beaches of Ambas Bay (well, attractive at least in the dry season) are a short drive out of town, and are a popular weekend getaway from Douala. Beware of the oil that sometimes builds up in the sea.

A canoe race is held, usually between December and March each year, in the Atlantic waters around Limbé. The event features traditional dances and music from the nearby coastal villages of Wovia, Botaland, Bimbia and Ideneau. There are also traditional Bakweri wrestling tournaments during the dry season throughout the region.

As for the layout of the town, moving eastwards along Idenao Road by the Limbé River you come to the main street containing an old Presbyterian church, various banks and the Presbook bookstore and Prescraft centre, which sells local art. Further east are a fish market, a government school of the German colonial era and Down Beach, where there is a monument built in 1858 in honour of Alfred Saker. Another historic item is the Cape Nightingale Light, a torch light built in 1903 to guide ships into the port.

Limbé is liveliest around Half Mile Junction, where Nambeke Street and Church Street intersect, at Limbé's only traffic light. The long-running nearby Bakassi border dispute with Nigeria has in recent years caused there to be a good number of sailors in the town, which can certainly liven things up at night.

Eastwards, along Church Street, are a number of bars and stalls selling street food. Most of the population of the town live away from the shoreline, in shanty town suburbs in valleys hidden from the resort by the clefts and spurs of the mountain.

GETTING THERE AND AWAY

By bus and taxi If you are coming to Limbé from Douala, be sure to tell your driver, otherwise you may end up in Kumba instead, which is further north.

Coming from Douala, typically you will be dropped off at a roundabout of sorts, the motor park at Mile 4, about 5km north of the centre on the Buéa road, where you await the next local bus for Limbé, which drops you outside the centre. A taxi to the centre costs around CFA500. Share taxis for Kumba, Buéa and Douala can also be picked up here.

The motor park has minibuses to Buéa (CFA400, 45mins, 30km), Douala (CFA1,000, 90mins – compared with CFA15,000 if you chartered a taxi, 75km) and Kumba (CFA1,500, 150mins, 100km). Departures are from Half Mile Junction in the centre of town all day.

Guaranti Express operates a service from Limbé at Mile 2 on the Buéa road to Douala, Yaoundé, Bamenda and Bafoussam, while Patience Express departs from the Buéa road about a kilometre from the centre, opposite the hospital. Yaoundé costs CFA5,000, while Bamenda and Bafoussam are CFA4,000.

Share taxis for the beaches at Mile 11 and Batoké go from Idenao Road, near the stadium.

By boat Weekly boats sail to Malabo, Equatorial Guinea. More details are available from Achouka, which is signposted on the Idenao road, a little under 2km after the botanical gardens.

Ferries regularly depart from Limbé port to Calabar/Oron in Nigeria, but as you will be passing the Bakassi Peninsula, subject of a long-standing Cameroon–Nigeria border dispute, check the situation locally before booking.

WHERE TO STAY

Savoy Palmz Hotel (150 rooms) BP 829; Sonara Rd; ✆ 3333 33 92; e guestservices@savoypalmz.com; www.savoypalmz.com. That rare thing in Cameroon, a luxury international-style hotel. This new hotel located in a secluded position yet near the bustling centre of town is convenient for the government ministries & commercial centre. It has extremely comfortable rooms, an impeccable indoor pool, cinema, fitness centre, 5 bars & 5 restaurants & wireless internet access. Live music on Fri evenings. It has an 18-hole golf course 20mins away in Tiko. $$$$

Atlantic Beach Hotel (49 rooms & 2 suites) BP 63; ✆ 3333 23 32/3333 26 89. Originally the botanic garden research laboratory, this was once Limbé's best hotel but is now distinctly shabby. There are rooms & suites with AC, although increasingly showers/lights & other fittings are broken. There is a swimming pool, an expensive bar (CFA700 for a small beer) & a good French/Cameroonian restaurant (king prawn & rice CFA4,000) overlooking the sea. With rooms facing the sea & gardens. Rates include a coffee & croissant b/fast. A more spacious garden apt is CFA50,000. Non-guests can use the swimming pool for CFA1,000. $$

The Bird Watchers' Club Seaside, Botanical Gdns; m 9968 07 64; e cameroonliaisons@yahoo.com. Follow the road through the botanical gardens towards the Hotel Miramar but instead of taking the right fork to the Miramar head left & follow the road for 200yds. The Bird Watchers' Club is the first building on the right. The club is an attractive, converted villa set in a tranquil location surrounded by the sea & its own gardens. It affords excellent views of the entire bay of Limbé & its islands. Rooms are fully AC with powershowers, baths & all modern facilities. You can dine on the roofed terraces or take a table by the sea. The menu includes both European & local dishes with BBQ'd seafood a speciality. The club can organise cultural & wildlife trips & 4x4 vehicle, motorcycle & bicycle hire are also available on site. By the way, there is no requirement to be a birdwatcher. The standard English b/fast is CFA1,500. $$

Holiday Inn Resort Hotel (22 rooms) BP 126; ✆ 3333 22 90. Northwards off Church St at the end of the road, this clean, comfortable hotel has AC rooms with bathroom, TV & a good-value restaurant, bar & beer garden. $$

Park Hotel Miramare (43 rooms) BP 63; Botanical Gdn Rd; ✆ 3332 23 32/3333 29 41. Run by the Atlantic Beach Hotel, this eternally popular hotel 2km west of the centre of town, is simple but clean & enjoys good views of Ambas Bay. Accommodation is in clean & affordable *boukarous* & some rooms have AC & there is a restaurant & pool. The staff are very welcoming & helpful. $$

South Atlantic Hotel (20 rooms) Mokundande St; m 7774 72 11. On the road to Sonara, rooms come with AC & cable TV. $$

Bay Hotel (23 rooms) BP 63; off Makangal St; ✆ 3333 23 32/3333 26 89; m 7773 36 09. A colonial building near Limbé's main roundabout enjoying a good view of the bay. Big en-suite rooms past their prime with fans or AC & a nearby restaurant. Co-owned by the Atlantic Beach Hotel, whose pool is available to guests. $$

Victoria Guest House Hotel (22 rooms) BP 358; ✆ 3333 24 46. Next to the Bay Hotel. Simple but clean lodgings, with most of the rooms AC or having a fan & a bathroom. There is a restaurant & bar. $$

Tabai Park Hotel (36 rooms) BP 10; ✆ 3333 26 22. Mid-range hotel with bar, restaurant & swimming pool. $$

King William Square Hotel (30 rooms) Makangal St; m 7774 72 11. Off the main roundabout, this hotel has basic but clean rooms with AC. The hotel can organise tours of the area. $

Botanic Garden Guest House (4 rooms) BP 437; ✆ 3333 26 20. This colonial building in pretty surroundings offers shared dorms & a **campsite**. CFA1,000 per person camping, CFA3,000 in the dorms. $

Tiko, outside Limbé on the Douala road, has a couple of inexpensive hotels, the Airport Hotel and the Park Hotel, with basic rooms.

For security reasons camping is not recommended on the beaches around Limbé.

WHERE TO EAT AND DRINK
There are lots of alternatives to the more expensive fare offered at the hotel restaurants. Each evening down the Bimbia road by the fish market at Down Beach, grilled fish with grilled plantain are on offer. Street food

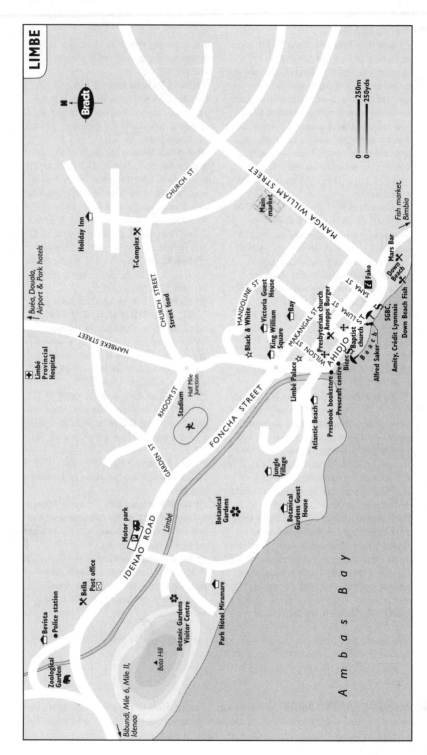

LIMBE

Bradt

Buéa, Douala,
Airport & Park hotels

Holiday Inn

T-Complex ✕

CHURCH ST

Main
market

MANGA WILLIAM STREET

Fish market,
Bimbia

Mars Bar

Down Beach Fish ✕   Down
Beach ✕

Fako ⛴

SAMA ST

Amity, Crédit Lyonnais $

SGBC, $

Baptist
church ✝

LUMA ST

Presbyterian church ✝

Anepps Burger ✕

Beach

Bieco ⚓
Prescraft centre ●

Alfred Saker ☆

AHIDJO ✝

WILSON ST

MAKANGAL ST

King William
Square ☆

Victoria Guest
House 🛏

Bay 🛏

Black & White ☆

MANDOLINE ST

Street food

CHURCH STREET

Limbé Palace 🛏

Presbook bookstore ●

Atlantic Beach 🛏

Limbé Provincial
Hospital ✚

NAMBEKE STREET

R'HOOM ST

Stadium

Half Mile
Junction

FONCHA STREET

Jungle
Village 🛏

Botanical
Gardens ✿

Botanical
Gardens Guest
House 🛏

Bibundi, Mile 6, Mile II,
Idenao

Bevista 🛏   ● Police station

✕ Bella   Post office ✉

IDENAO ROAD

Motor park 🅿

GARDEN ST

Limbé

Botanic Gardens
Visitor Centre ✿

Bota Hill ▲

Park Hotel Miramare 🛏

Zoological
Garden 🐾

A m b a s   B a y

N

0   250m
0   250yds

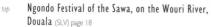

top Ngondo Festival of the Sawa, on the Wouri River, Douala (SLV) page 18

above Wood carving at the Museum of Babungo, Northwest Province (MB) page 161

right Ngoun Festival, Foumban (SLV) page 148

below Festival in Pouss, Extreme North Province (AA) page 215

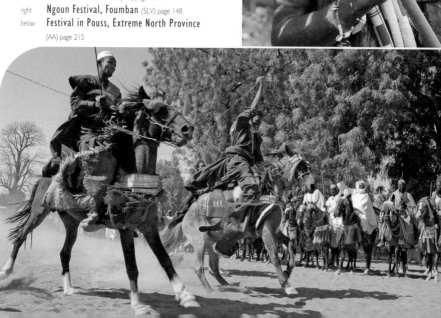

top	Sugarcane field, Bamessi, Northwest Province (SLV) page 161
above	Kola nuts are a popular snack (MB) page 71
left	Tea fields along the Ring Road (SLV) page 155
below	Traditional huts, Extreme North Province (SLV) page 201

top **Fishermen, Limbé, Southwest Province** (MB) page 117
above **Choa nomads, Extreme North Province** (SLV) page 17
right **Woman shelling groundnuts, Bandjoun, West Province** (MB) page 142
below **Mousgoum fisherman, Maga, Extreme North Province** (SLV) page 215

top **Ring Road, Northwest Province** (SLV) page 155
above **Beach at Limbé, Littoral Province** (SLV) page 117
left **Chutes de Tello, Adamawa Province** (RQ) page 200
below **Manengouba Crater Lakes, Littoral Province**
(SLV) page 115

top	Chari River, Kalamaloué National Reserve, Extreme North Province (SLV) page 217
above	Tea plantation below Mt Cameroon, Southwest Province (SLV) page 125
right	Bridge in Korup National Park, Southwest Province (RQ) page 133

above left **Pink frangipani**
(SLV)

above right **Red-headed agama lizard**
(SLV) page 35

right **Dwarf crocodile**
(RB) page 36

below left **Palm tree in Limbé's Botanical Garden**
(SLV) page 121

below right **Red hibiscus**
(SLV)

top left	Saddle-billed stork (SLV)
top right	African hoopoe (SLV)
above right	Abyssinian roller (SLV)
left	Violet turaco (KB)
below left	Helmeted guineafowl (SLV)
below right	Woodland kingfishers (SLV)

vendors appear around Half Mile Junction, Nambeke Street and Church Street in the evenings. Church Street also has a number of cheap restaurants and bars.

✘ **Bella Restaurant** Just off Idenao Rd west of the stadium; ☎ 3333 26 40. Offers both good Cameroonian & European food. $$

✘ **Mars Bar** Ahidjo Rd. A good spot for a sunset drink, chicken & chips or seafood. $$

✘ **Lady L Restaurant** Church St. Has a sign stating 'where beauty merges with class'. If beauty is a rutted car park, OK, but the menu is interesting, with gizzard stew & fufu, stockfish soup & bushmeat pepper steak & fufu. $$

✘ **Xplanade Bar** On the beach & near the Atlantic Beach Hotel & the old church. A great spot to watch the fishermen. Food stalls are either side of the bar. Grilled king prawns CFA1,000, sea bass with cassava or plantain are on offer. $

✘ **Anepps Burger** Off the road to Down Beach. For a fix of Western fast food, such as the omnipresent burger & chips. $

✘ **T-Complex Bar** Church St. A good spot for a drink & also offers burgers, chicken & chips & similar fare as well as more exotic choices such as bushmeat soup. $

NIGHTLIFE The Limbé Palace nightclub at Makangal St is one of the best in Limbé and plays both Western and Cameroonian music. Entrance is CFA2,000–5,000 and drinks typically CFA2,000.

The Black and White nightclub has similar prices but is slightly shabbier.

OTHER PRACTICALITIES

Banks Bicec, SGBC, Amity and Crédit Lyonnais are on the main road on the waterfront. Surprisingly for Cameroon outside Douala and Yaoundé, euros, dollars and sterling can usually be changed.

Hospital
✚ **Limbé Provincial Hospital** ☎ 3333 23 53

Internet access
🖳 **Bifunde Computer Centre** Bota Rd

🖳 **Web Centre** ☎ 3333 23 76

Mail The post office is on Idenao Road, past the entrance to the botanical garden, leaving the centre of town.

Tourist information
🛈 **Fako Tourist Office** Banley St; ☎ 3333 25 36/3333 28 61; e ftb@camnet.cm; ⏰ 07.30–17.00 Mon–Sat. Opposite the Crédit

Lyonnais Bank on the waterfront, this can organise local tours & boat trips to the nearby islands.

WHAT TO SEE AND DO

The islands The bay is dotted with fishing boats, numerous ships and a variety of small uninhabited islands, the Bota Islands, some of which have the remnants of buildings. They are still used for traditional ceremonies and the largest island has carved stone steps that can be climbéd. You can ask one of the fishermen to take you to the nearby islands (ask on the beach) or your hotel or the tourist office (details below) can fix up a trip. Either way the cost is around CFA20,000–30,000. *Pirogues* can also be hired for considerably less.

Limbé Botanical Gardens (*PO Box 437; Idenao Rd;* ☎ *3343 18 83/3343 18 72; e info@ mcbcclimbé.org; www.mcbcclimbé.org;* ⏰ *06.00–18.00 daily; admission CFA1,000*) Adjacent to the centre of town, just to the west, are the impressive Limbé Botanical Gardens founded a century ago by German horticulturists to introduce new economic and medicinal crops to Cameroon such as quinine, coffee, cocoa, rubber, tea and bananas. The shady gardens served as a training centre in agriculture, horticulture and forestry and is now an international research centre. The gardens were neglected for many years but recently they have been restored and are connected to the Mount Cameroon Project, which promotes ecological preservation. Guided tours of the gardens are available.

The gardens are ideal for a tranquil stroll and feature a so-called 'jungle village', with various cultural activities for visitors. There are various walks including a coastal trail, a biodiversity trail, and a riverside trail where many impressive trees, creepers and other plants can be seen, and the Bota adventure trail, which features some wild animals. The Hot Spot bar/restaurant overlooking the bay is ideally placed for a meal or a drink while visiting the gardens.

Limbé Zoological Garden (⊕ *09.00–17.00 daily; admission CFA1,000*) Connected to the Botanical Gardens (cross to the other side of Idenao Road) is one of the world's only (there are fewer than 20) primate sanctuaries. It has been established at the town's old and neglected zoo. The centre is internationally renowned and houses chimpanzees, gorillas, drills, mandrills, red-capped mangabeys, guenons, crocodiles, snakes and duikers and often houses the orphans of apes killed for bushmeat.

Boat trips Seagrams Voyages (✆ *3333 21 41*) on the seafront, arranges a number of tours from Limbé from CFA10,000 per person for a minimum of two people. These include four-hour boat trips up the Ndian River to Mundemba and Korup National Park, costing around CFA30,000. You're likely to see a good selection of wildlife, especially monkeys and birds, on this trip.

Ecotour Since 2003 the Bimbia Bonadikombo Natural Resource Management Council (BBNRMC) (*PO Box 414, Limbé;* m *6689 6022;* e *alegare1@sfu.ca*), a community-based non-governmental organisation located in Limbé, has been offering guided ecotours of the Bimbia Bonadikombo Community Forest, which it manages. Visitors to its Rainforest and Mangrove Nature Trail discover the natural wonders of the rainforest and the rich cultural heritage and history of the people of Bimbia. A typical trip costs a group of four visitors approximately CFA10,500 per person, which includes a local guide for the day, a traditional lunch, and transportation from Limbé to the trail and back. The guide meets visitors in Limbé where they usually leave at around 09.00. On the way to the trail visitors are first presented with some of the history of the local communities and observe slave artefacts near the village of Bimbia. They then begin the hike on the nature trail at approximately 10.30, leading through mangroves and later to a quiet beach for lunch, returning to Limbé at 15.00. While the trail is considered a short hike of easy to moderate difficulty that can be undertaken by visitors of all ages, access for persons with disabilities may be limited due to the rugged terrain.

AROUND LIMBE

THE BEACHES WEST OF LIMBE To the west of town, with Mount Cameroon towering above them, are a number of beautiful beaches bordered by tropical vegetation. Some of the beaches feature in the film *Chocolat*. Rarely for the region, the waters are generally suitable for bathing although the currents can at times be strong. The fine sand is dark brown, created from ancient lava flows from Mount Cameroon. The beaches offer great views of the islands.

Along the coastal road around the village of Bakingili you will notice lava flows from the 1999 Mount Cameroon eruption which formed a huge rock when it cooled down. You can follow this natural path of lava to see ferns and orchids that are just beginning to grow there. In the vicinity are the ruins of an old palm oil processing plant from the German colonial period.

To get to the beaches, taxis and share taxis are available from the Batoké motor park by the sports stadium near Half Mile Junction in Limbé.

At Mile 6 on the Idenao road there is a signpost to a popular public beach of dark chocolate volcanic sands, by an oil refinery, which costs CFA500 to enter. It is more pleasant than the rougher beach at Limbé. It has some monkeys who may pester you and a snack bar open during weekends.

At Mile 8 is Batoké fishing village with a beautiful beach bordered by mountains where lava flows from a few years ago can be seen on the mountain. It is usually free, but the nearby hotel, the Etisah, sometimes charges a small fee. You can get a good meal at the restaurant for around CFA6,500 ($$$).

Moving further west you come to the guarded remote tree-lined beach at Mile 11, also known as Seme New Beach, near the 1999 lava flows. A CFA1,000 fee is payable at the Seme New Beach Resort Hotel there. You are not allowed to bring your own food and drinks.

The metalled road to Idenao passes further good beaches and at Mile 17 it reaches Cape Debundscha, which is notable for being the second-wettest place on earth, with more than 10,000mm rainfall per year. The wettest place, according to the *Guinness World Records*, is currently Mawsynvan in Maghalaya State, India, with 11,873mm/467 inches annually.

Where to stay

🏠 **Seme New Beach Hotel** (88 rooms, 6 apts) BP 130, Mile 11, Rte Limbé-Idenao; ☏ 3333 27 69; e camrevtour@camnet.cm; www.semebeach.com. The comfortable AC rooms have either a shower or bathroom. There is a quite pricey but excellent restaurant & a small beer at the bar will set you back CFA1,200. There is a natural swimming/rock pool with ice-cold spring water from Mount Cameroon, a private beach, nightclub, secure parking & tennis courts. The hotel can organise a car with driver for excursions. $$$

🏠 **First International Inn** (18 rooms & bungalows) Sonara Rd; ☏ 3333 26 97; e dgi.pise@camnet.cm. Rooms from around CFA10,000–22,000 plus

bungalows, & a restaurant serving fish, African & European dishes. $$

🏠 **Coast Beach Hotel** (21 rooms) Sonara Rd, Bobende; ☏ 3333 29 27. The good-standard rooms at this hotel at Mile 6 have AC & bathroom & satellite TV for CFA20,000. $$

🏠 **Etisah Beach Hotel** (20 rooms) Batoké; m 9997 49 98/9998 32 39; e etisah.beach@yahoo.fr. Signposted from the main road at Mile 8, about 350km from the beach this hotel has simple rooms with fans or better ones with AC; there's a restaurant serving bushmeat & other meals from about CFA3,500. $$

WEST OF LIMBÉ

Cape Debundscha and the Bomana Falls
The visitors' centre at the Botanical Gardens in Limbé can provide a guide to take you to Cape Debundscha's crater lake, old German lighthouse and also the Bomana Falls. You can charter a taxi or take a share taxi the 48km to Idenao for the falls.

NORTH OF LIMBÉ

Engelbert Church
To the north of Limbé it is a pleasant uphill walk from the market of about 6km to Bonjongo where there is Engelbert Church, a splendid German Palatine Mission Church built in 1894. The hill, known as 'the Hill of Angels', boasts an impressive view of Ambas Bay.

Small Mount Cameroon (Mount Etinde)
From Bonjongo you can spend a day trekking up a sub-peak of Mount Cameroon, Mount Etinde (1,713m), which is

also known as Small Mount Cameroon. An extinct volcano, it can be reached on foot from Limbé, which makes for a very long day by the time you return (the climb, via Ekonjo, takes an afternoon or so). Alternatively take a share taxi to Batoké village and then a further taxi to one of the villages at the base of the mountain, Etome (also known as Etumba) or Ekonjo.

Guides for the trek (from CFA7,000 per day) are available from Cameroon Rev'Tours (342 10 05; e camrevtours@camnet.cm) based at the Seme Beach Hotel or from the Visitor Centre at the Limbé Botanical Gardens through the Mount Cameroon Ecotourism Project, which also has an office in Buéa. There is also a CFA3,000 fee per person plus a small fee for the local chief. Make sure you are clear about all fees beforehand, and whether you are providing food and drink for the guide on top, and ensure you have adequate food and drink for your party.

SOUTH OF LIMBE Southwards from Limbé, towards Mabeta, takes you past an army camp at Man O'War Bay after about 10km and then the village of Bimbia, where the missionaries first arrived in Cameroon in the 1840s. There's a Baptist church and some inexpensive bungalows bookable through the Saker Baptist Mission in Limbé (*BP29;* *3333 23 23*).

Another 2km further on from Bimbia is the Mabeta Moliwe Reserve, with lowland rainforest and mangrove, and a two- to three-hour nature trail that goes from Bimbia to Bonadikombo along a river towards the sea. Guides are obtainable at Bimbia or from the Botanical Gardens.

BUEA *Telephone code 3332*

Seventy kilometres and just an hour's drive northwest of Douala (and a regular *agences de voyage* route at just CFA1,000), Buéa (pronounced 'boyah') is the most popular gateway to an invigorating yet perfectly possible climb up Mount Cameroon – but little else.

Being more than 1,000m above the sea (and a half-hour drive from the coast), located on the lower slopes of the mountain amongst beautiful scenery, it is relatively cool, generally offering a refreshingly comfortable climate, especially during the dry season, from late November through February. Its trim tea gardens make it almost an African version of Darjeeling. After increasing cloud and rain in March and April, rain falls nearly every day from May onwards, and the town loses its charm somewhat.

Buéa was the German colonial capital from 1901, but only until 1909. During British rule, the town was under the authority of the Southern Provinces of Nigeria and the population reduced greatly. Soon after independence Buéa's importance increased again when it became the capital of the anglophone western Cameroon in 1961 but again this distinction was shortlived as 11 years later the post-independence federation became a republic and Buéa reverted to capital of Southwest Province only when Yaoundé was made the sole capital.

The sleepy town, now with around 60,000 inhabitants, many of them Bakweris, boasts some interesting German colonial architecture including a school, various administrative and commercial buildings and homes and a castle (*schloss*) built in 1900 for German colonial governor Jesco von Puttkamer. The building copies the architecture of a Wilhelminian hunting lodge in Brandenburg, Germany. It is now used by the president, so don't take photos. There is also the Bismarck Fountain built in 1904.

Buéa has various facilities including a post office and petrol station. The hospital (*3332 32 29*) is located near the Mermoz Hotel.

GETTING THERE AND AWAY The motor park for transport to Douala, Limbé and Kumba is about 5km from the centre of Buéa at Mile 17 along the Limbé road.

It is possible to walk to Limbé (around 22km) down the main roads going south from the Mermoz Hotel.

If you are thinking of moving on to Nigeria, Buéa has a Nigerian consulate (❐ *3332 25 28*), although it can be difficult for foreigners to obtain visas here and the consulate may require that you visit the high commission in Yaoundé for this.

If you are planning to visit Korup National Park, Buéa is 256km from Mamfé and 184km from Mundemba.

WHERE TO STAY

⌂ **Capitol Résidence** (30 rooms) BP 227; ❐ 3332 33 32. A new hotel with friendly staff & a good, if rather pricey, restaurant. Near the centre of Buéa, it has quite large, clean rooms. $$$

⌂ **Paramount Hotel** (25 rooms) Molyoko Rd; ❐ 3332 20 74. A hotel that has recently opened, with good, clean rooms from CFA8,000–16,000 & a bar & restaurant. $$

⌂ **Hotel Mermoz** BP 13, Long St; ❐ 3332 23 49. Although quite recently renovated, one resident of the hotel reports that the hotel was dirty & had 'a really bad vibe'. The slightly better rooms are on the 2nd floor. Both are with a shower & TV. There is a restaurant & bar. It's a bit noisy. $

⌂ **Parliamentarian Flats Hotel** (20 rooms) BP 20; Federal Quarters, Nigeria Consulate Rd; ❐ 3332 24 59. A short walk south of the police station

roundabout, this government-owned hotel has good, clean self-contained rooms, a restaurant, bar & good view of the mountain. $

⌂ **Presbyterian Mission** (6 rooms) BP 19; ❐ 3332 23 36. Past the police station roundabout & up the hill, about 800m southwest of Buéa market. Set in gardens with very clean rooms with shared or separate facilities. There is a communal kitchen for which there is a small charge. You can also **camp** on the grounds for CFA1,000 pp. $

⌂ **The Mount Cameroon Ecotourism Organisation** PO Box 66, Buéa, SWP; ❐ 3332 20 38; m 7758 45 93; e mountceo@yahoo.co.uk; www.mountcameroon.org. Offers guesthouses & B&Bs near their office. Just enquire in the office when you arrive or book in advance through email. $

MOUNT CAMEROON

Mount Cameroon, 180 miles west of the capital of Yaoundé, is one of the country's main tourist attractions. An occasionally active volcano, with its base directly at the ocean floor and summit nudging the clouds, it covers 800 square miles. At 13,500ft high (4,095m) it is the highest mountain in west Africa and the second-highest on the continent. In spite of its height, the mountain is relatively easy to climb, if somewhat arduous, and no particular climbing skills, climbing equipment or experience are needed, only a reasonable level of fitness and determination. The climb is much less strenuous than, say, Mount Kilimanjaro or Mount Kenya.

The mountainsides are coated in rainforest except for a few swathes of black rock formed by the cooling of recent lava flows. A series of fine beaches line the foot of the mountain, the sand a deep chocolate brown colour from the igneous rock. The lower sections of the mountain are a lush tropical wilderness extending right to the edge of the beach.

Its rugged peak, Great Cameroon, is the crown jewel of a succession of volcanic mountains that are strung like a giant necklace from the southwest to the extreme north of the country. A second distinct summit is the densely forested 5,820ft (1,713m) Little Cameroon. The entire massif is known locally as Mongo-mo-Ndemi, or Mountain of Greatness.

Mount Cameroon itself is known locally as Mount Fako or as Mongo-ma-Lobo, the Mountain of Thunder. It was described as long ago as 1472 by Portuguese navigator Fernando Po as the seat or the chariot of the gods. It has erupted seven times in the last 100 years, once during the filming of *Greystoke: The Legend of*

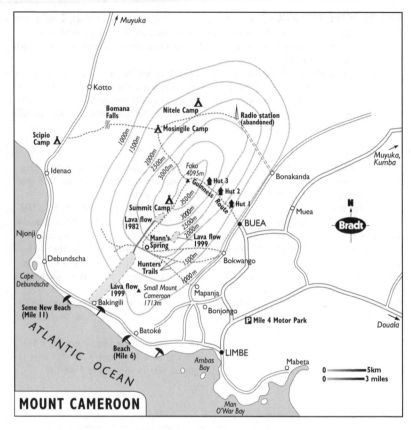

MOUNT CAMEROON

Tarzan, in 1982, in 1999 and most recently in the spring of 2000 when the eruption lasted about three weeks, causing no casualties. Locals of the Bakweiri ethnic group attribute the recent eruptions to the influences of ancestral spirits because of the recent death of Monono Otto, a Bakweri traditional chief.

Mount Cameroon is the closest African mountain to any sea coast. It rises from the waters of the Gulf of Guinea, which is a spectacular site when viewed from sea. The offshore island of Malabo, the capital of Equatorial Guinea, is south of the mountain. On this island, another volcano, Pico de Santa Isabel, rises to 9,868ft (3,008m).

Mount Cameroon was the site of one of the earliest recorded volcanic eruptions, in 5BC, which was observed by a Carthaginian ship while sailing down the Atlantic coast of Africa.

There are a number of local myths and legends about the mountain. For example, powerful ancestral spirits are said to inhabit the mountain's inner core. A mountain god called Epassa Moto (which when translated means 'half human') is considered the owner and protector of the mountain and permits people to live on and visit it as long as nothing is removed. It is believed that when he gets angry he shakes the ground and spits fire into the air.

Several aircraft on approach to Douala have crashed into the mountain, the last being in 1963: a DC6 hit the mountain resulting in 44 deaths.

Its very varied climatic conditions have given the mountain great biodiversity. Despite its equatorial latitude, snow, strong winds and freezing rain can often cover the summit.

THE ASCENT There are numerous trails and various route options are possible, passing through a variety of terrains including sub-alpine meadows and dense high-altitude tropical rainforest where no sun filters through, giant parasitic plants carpet the floor and trees are so big their roots are as thick as a tree you'd see in Europe. Typically a climb passes habitats of elephants, antelopes, primates and many tropical birds. Hiking here will uncover ever-changing vegetation – there are more than 42 plant species that are strictly endemic and another 50 species that are near-endemic to the mountain, for instance – as well as volcanic lava and even, at times, volcano smoke coming out of the stones under your feet.

To climb the mountain, a permit obtainable from the local tourist office and a guide are compulsory. Many of the guides and porters are ex-hunters.

For the trip the Mount Cameroon Ecotourism Organisation (details below) asks you to bring food for yourself, but you could ask your guide and porter to provide and cook food, which is recommended as long as you like Cameroonian food, since it's a lot easier than planning your own menu. Your guide and porter may expect you to have hired sleeping bags and tents on their behalf, especially since it can get very cold on the mountain – so check beforehand. These and other items like mats and raingear can be hired from the project office.

The round trip usually takes between one and six days depending on the trail chosen and your level of fitness. Apart from being gruelling, to do the trip in a day would be so rushed there's little time to appreciate the climb or the mountain.

It is possible to shorten some routes by arranging to have a vehicle collect you on the descent. However you do it, it is going to be easier than for intrepid Victorian explorer Mary Kingsley, whose famous ascent in 1895 was plagued by camps being washed away by the rains, a string of tropical disease casualties and attacks by swarms of bees.

New trails up the mountain have been introduced in recent years to complement the original, steep, direct, so-called Guinness Trail (see page 128) starting at Buéa, which has been neglected and therefore is not the best option. These newer trails are on the southeast face of the mountain because of the regular heavy rainfall and storms afflicting the other sides of the mountain. The southwestern side has an almost continuous rainy season with rainfall around 10,000mm per year, compared with around 2,000mm at the summit and 3,500mm as an average in the region.

The **Mount Cameroon Inter-Communal Ecotourism Board** (Mount CEO) (*PO Box 66, Buéa, SWP;* ↘ *3332 20 38;* m *7758 45 93;* e *info@mount-cameroon.org; www.mountcameroon.org*) supports the conservation of the biodiversity of the mountain. Its office is near the Mobil petrol station and the market, which taxi drivers are likely to know.

The MCEO is the only officially recognised organisation allowed to offer tours to Mount Cameroon. Numerous other organisations try to copy it, and clandestine guides wait along the road to pick up tourists by pretending to be members of the MCEO, with its flyer in their hands, in order to offer guiding services for low prices. Usually the service they offer is poor and there have even been cases of leaving tourists alone on the mountain and stealing from them.

A trip up Mount Cameroon through MCEO costs around CFA14,000 per person per day but can vary depending upon the size of the party and whether you are climbing to the summit. The costs are made up of fees per day of CFA6,000 for the guide, CFA5,000 for porters and a community fund per person of CFA3,000.

You can typically arrive at the office in Buéa, meet your guide and start your hike up the mountain the same morning although most people find the preparation for the climb entails an overnight stay in Buéa. There used to be a requirement to buy a bottle of whisky or to visit the chief of Bonakanda before going up the mountain but this is no longer necessary.

The best time to attempt the climb is during the drier months, between November and May. Be prepared for the extremes of temperature: while it can be over 20°C (68°F) at the foot of the mountain, it can be below freezing at the summit, so you will need warm waterproof clothes and a good sleeping bag if you are staying overnight. Humidity commonly reaches 96% in the summer. Although many climbers wear trainers, waterproof hiking boots with good ankle support are the ideal.

Further information is available from the tourist office (*Provincial Delegation of Tourism for the South West; BP20;* ☏ *3332 26 56/3332 25 34;* ⏲ *08.00–15.30 Mon–Fri*) on the main road in Buéa.

Guinness Trail On the Guinness Trail there are three very basic mountain huts *en route*, originally built by the Germans. The first is at 1,850m (about a two-hour walk). Another hour's walk gets you clear of the rainforest. Hut 2 is at an altitude of 2,800m (about three to four hours' walk from hut one) and hut 3 is at 3,600m, about three to four hours' walk from hut 2. From hut 3 to the summit at Fako Peak (4,100m) you can reckon on a further 90 minutes or so.

Apart from at hut 1 there are very few opportunities to get water on the mountain (which is surprising in one of the wettest regions on earth), so ensure you bring plenty. There may be rainwater collected at hut 2 (the climb from hut 1 to hut 2 is the toughest section), but don't count on it.

On a good day at hut 2 you can see Buéa, Small Cameroon, Douala, Limbé, the ocean, and even Bioko Island (Equatorial Guinea). From hut 2, climbing to the summit is relatively easy, but beware of repeatedly believing you are almost there as you will constantly see false summits.

Hunters' trails from Bokwango or Mapanja If instead you follow one of the old hunters' trails from Bokwango or Mapanja, which are south of Buéa, you go through savanna, montane forest and grasslands and pass lava flow from the 2000 eruption. Again there are good views of Small Cameroon, Bioko Island and the ocean on this route. There are two basic campsites on these routes at clearings in the forest, the first being Mann's Spring, where drinking water is available, and Summit Camp, where you're nearing the peak.

Radio station route Another newer route starts at the village of Bonakanda, where you follow a so-called 'radio station track' which leads from the village at around a height of 900m, rising up to about 2,600m then gradually descending to reach an abandoned radio station, now classified as an industrial monument, at 2,500m. The walk is about 15km, but it is not the easiest hike since you gain 1,700m in altitude fairly steeply from the village. The forest and scrub above Bonokanda vary but logging has resulted in there being little primary forest left.

Unfortunately, this is common on the mountain. The forests of the mountain are not currently protected under formal park status. On the eastern side of the mountain, for example, it has been estimated that as much as half of the forest cover has so far been lost.

From about 1,750m to the radio station is grassland. From the radio station you can descend down the northwest slope of the mountain to Nitele, a hunters' camp at an altitude of 1,870m, consisting of three small huts with straw beds. This is around another 7km from the radio station. Here there is some primary forest, starting as high as 2,300m, although much of the forest has been burnt, apparently as a result of fires spreading from the savanna above. Lower down, at about

2,000m, the trail passes through some tall, intact, primary montane forest, then emerges again into an open area of savanna just above Nitele.

The dense vegetation extends as far as the ocean and here there are an increasing number of coffee, rubber tree, oil palm and banana plantations where the forest has been cleared.

From Nitele, to reach the peak you follow the mountain around, via another basic campsite near Mosingile village.

DESCENT OF THE MOUNTAIN There are several options for descending the mountain, the quickest and most straightforward simply following the Guinness Trail, which can be done in about six hours, or following the hunters' trails via Mann's Spring. It is also possible to go down the west face of the mountain from Mosingile village to the village of Kotto, where you can join the road going to Idenao and Limbé. In good weather, in reverse this latter route acts as another alternative for ascending the mountain.

SHORTER TREKS Instead of tackling the summit, one-day treks going halfway to Mann's Spring are popular, and you can also take a short hike from Scipio Camp, 3km north of Idenao, which leads to the Bomana Waterfall.

THE RACE OF HOPE A tortuous 40km foot race or marathon up the mountain, also known as the Mount Cameroon Race and the Guinness Mountain Marathon, has been held on the mountain since 1973. Usually held on the last weekend in January or the first weekend in February, nearly 400 runners from all over the world are watched by more than 50,000 spectators.

The race starts from the stadium in Buéa, and the men's winner typically completes the ascent and descent of the steep and stony slopes in around four-and-a-half hours (meaning an average of a vertical 2,000ft/610m ascended or descended every hour) and the women's winner in little more, which are incredible feats, considering the rigorous climb, problems of altitude and heat, and fact that most people take a few days.

In 2002 athelete Ngeve Zache Etutu made history by completing the race despite losing a leg in 2000 in a motorcycle accident.

The feat took him 14 hours to get to the peak and another one hour and 43 minutes to descend. Other renowned champions include Amos Evambe, Walter Stifter, the late Timothy Lekunze, Tata Thomas and Sarah Etonge, known as Queen of the Mountain.

Further details of the race are available from the Fédération Camerounaise d'Athlétisme (*BP 353; Yaoundé;* ❧ *2222 47 44*) and the Provincial Delegation of Youth and Sports in Buéa (❧ *3322 21 52*).

KUMBA *Telephone code 3335*

Head for Kumba, the largest town of the Southwest Province (population about 125,000) 138km north of Douala and 160km south of Mamfé, to explore one of Cameroon's most beautiful regions, boasting among other things Barombi Mbo, a stunning crater lake with crystal-clear waters just a few minutes' drive away, and the tectonic Lake Dissoni.

Kumba is situated on the edge of the forest, and therefore many buildings are made from wood. The numerous elevated wooden verandas off these buildings coupled with the wide, dusty streets and badly pot-holed roads give the place the look and feel of the American Wild West.

Kumba doesn't really have a centre as such but to the east of the market (one of

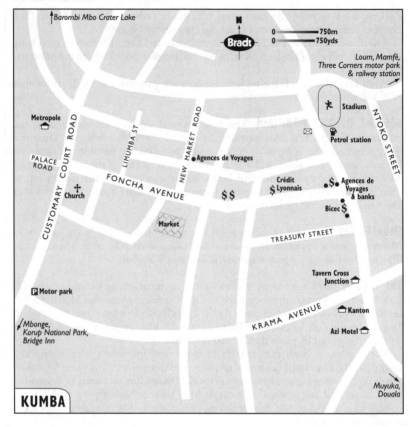

KUMBA

the country's biggest) is the principal motor park and further on are hotels, banks, the post office and *agence de voyage* offices for Douala and Mamfé. There is a general hospital (☎ *3335 41 39*).

Kumba has a sizeable Igbo (or Ibo) immigrant community from southeastern Nigeria. They are Nigeria's third-largest ethnic group and predominantly Christian. There is also a significant mix of Bassa, Ewondo, Hausa, Bamiléké and other ethnic groups.

GETTING THERE AND AWAY You can reach Kumba by train four times a day from both Douala and Nkongsamba via Mbanga.

The road to the train station, northeast of the stadium, also leads to the Three Corners motor park in Fiango on the northeastern edge of the town. This has share taxis for Bangem, Bafoussam, Tombel and Bamenda.

Southwest of the market on Ekondo Titi Road is the Mbanga motor park with share taxis to Mundemba (for Korup) and Ekondo Titi.

Share taxis for Buéa, Muyuka, Douala and Limbé are at the Buéa motor park on the Buéa road, southeast of town. As a guide to prices, Buéa is typically CFA1,000, while Limbé costs CFA1,200.

Agences de voyage for Douala, Bamenda, Bafoussam and Mamfé are in the centre of town in the vicinity of Foncha Avenue. They include Tonton Express, Symbol of Unity, Guaranti Express and Tchatcho Voyages. Bafoussam typically costs CFA1,200, while Bamenda costs CFA1,500.

WHERE TO STAY AND EAT

🏠 **Hotel Metropole** West of the market off Mundemba & Customary Court rds; ☎ 3335 40 64. This hotel is popular, with spacious rooms & en-suite facilities, fans or AC. There is a restaurant. $

🏠 **Azi Motel** (34 rooms) BP 304; Buéa Rd; ☎ 3335 42 91. Possibly Kumba's best hotel; good rooms with bathroom & AC. Facilities include a restaurant & bar. $

🏠 **Hotel Kanton** Buéa Rd; ☎ 3335 43 82. Restaurant & acceptable rooms for CFA5,000 upwards. $

🏠 **Tavern Cross Junction Hotel** Buéa Rd; ☎ 3335 43 39. Near Azi Motel & the centre, this has simple rooms with fans, & a bar & restaurant (probably the most popular in town) serving inexpensive Cameroonian food. $

🏠 **Bridge Inn** BP 385; Mundemba Rd. Basic rooms with fans or AC. **Camping** in the grounds is CFA2,000 pp. There is an inexpensive restaurant. $

WHAT TO SEE

Barombi Mbo Crater Lake Lake Barombi Mbo is about 5km north of Kumba, which is a CFA1,000 taxi ride or a walk of little more than an hour down Lake Road, northwest of the centre. Take the road going off to the left when you pass the Senior Divisional Officer's office little more than halfway. Entrance to the lake is CFA200.

Beautifully lush, thick, pristine rainforest with massive ancient tropical trees grows right inside the crater to the shore's edge. Measuring 2.5km across and over 100m deep, Barombi Mbo is one of the largest crater lakes in Cameroon. It is overwhelmingly peaceful.

The lake was designated on 8 October 2006 as being one of Cameroon's two Wetlands of International Importance. The other is the Waza Logone Floodplain in Extreme North Province. The site has a surface area of 415 hectares.

For hundreds of years the lake has provided all the needs of the Barombi people, who catch the cichlids (mouth-breeders) and catfish unique to the lake. The villagers continue to make their own basket traps by hand ensuring that only the larger fish are caught, so that the lake is not overfished.

If a fisherman is around he may take you around the lake or to Barombi village on the other side of the lake, at a price of about CFA800 (85p/$1.51). Dugout canoes are also available. There is a small, simple restaurant open during the dry season.

MOUNT KUPE

Mount Kupe (2,064m), northeast of Kumba, is one of a semicircle of mountains – the others being Mount Nlonako (1,825m) and the Manengouba Massif (2,411m) – combining to form a range which straddles the border between the Southwest and Littoral provinces and create the northern, southern and eastern borders of the Mamfé Depression, a region of low-lying, dense forest.

Mount Kupe, about 45km east of Kumba, is located at altitudes of between 450m and 2,064m above sea level and covers an area of about 30km^2 including 25km of primary montane forest. It dominates the town of Tombel (or Toumbel).

Along with the Ijim and Kilum forests at Mount Oku, near Kumbo, and the forests at Mount Cameroon, the forest of Mount Kupe represents a chain of montane forest with an exceptional degree of endemism. Mount Kupe is an area of great importance biologically as it has a number of endemic species of bird, reptile, amphibian, plant, insect and mammal, and a very rich montane flora.

To give an indication of the exceptional diversity, in 2005 more than 2,300 plant species were surveyed by scientists from Kew's Royal Botanic Gardens in the UK, and many were newly discovered.

There is an exceptional range of birdlife, with more than 320 species recorded, and the mountain is also home to chimpanzees and some species of rare primates, spectacular chameleons, pygmy crocodiles, golden cats, huge frogs and others.

These include *Pentaphlebia stahli*, a large forest- and stream-dwelling damselfly occurring commonly on Mount Kupe. The genus is found only in montane forest in central Africa and its nearest relatives occur in a similar habitat in Venezuela, South America.

Mount Kupe is also of great importance to the dense local human population of around 150,000 who consider it home to their ancestral and forest spirits and the source of all wealth. The mountain has great subsistence value to these peoples, who are distributed within 16 villages and towns on both sides of the mountain. The population is English-speaking on the western side of the mountain, and is mainly made up of Bakossi (Akosse) peoples, while on the eastern side the population is composed of Bafun, Bakaka and Manehas and a high proportion of non-natives.

For hundreds of years the mountain has provided wood for building, carving and fuel, as well as bushmeat, plants and seeds for food, plants for medicines, and cane for baskets.

GETTING TO THE MOUNTAIN To approach the mountain, head for the Bakossi village of Nyasoso, situated on the mountain slopes and surrounded by farmbush. It is around 12km north of Tombel (about a CFA15,000 taxi ride, and share taxis are regularly available from Kumba. Nyasoso takes around six hours from Douala by share taxi via Loum and Tombel and it takes around four hours by car, and a 4x4 vehicle is recommended if you are travelling between June and October. The road is paved to Loum, but from Loum to Nyasoso it deteriorates rapidly. If you're stuck in Tombel, there is basic **accommodation** available at Alison's Guesthouse.

CLIMBING THE MOUNTAIN BirdLife International established a conservation project on the mountain in 1991 and the Mount Kupe Forest Project (MKFP), which is part of the World Wide Fund for Nature, manages the area. The WWF have an office in Nyasoso overseeing various conservation projects. It has no telephone, and communication is by radio, but you can contact WWF Cameroon's headquarters in Yaoundé (\ *2221 62 67*) in advance.

Strictly speaking, according to the WWF, a permit from the Ministry of Environment, and, if you plan to take photos, a permit from the Ministry of Information, both in Yaoundé, are required, although in practice this may not be the case.

The project office in Nyasoso can provide good information on the ecology of the mountain as well as a list of mountain bird species, and a guide to its nature trail, a short loop of under a mile which passes through some fields into forest near the village. It begins at the southern end of the school grounds.

To climb the mountain, there is a mandatory community forest fee of CFA2,000 per person per day spent in the forest and a mandatory guide at CFA3,500 per day plus optional porters at CFA2,500 per day, and an allowance for meals per day for you, your guide and porter/s is also required. The guides are generally very good, and the best ones will recognise the various wildlife calls and know the best places to spot them.

Camping is permitted on the mountain. If you plan to camp, you need to provide a tent for your guide. You don't need to provide cooking supplies, but can bring your own food. Alternatively, you can arrange for a porter to bring up food each day if you plan to stay a few days. You need some way of keeping your gear dry, as there can be heavy rains, even in the dry season.

The climb to the awesome view (on clear days) at the summit is steep but can be completed in around six to eight hours. The trails, marked with altitude markers, Max's Trail and the Shrike Trail, pass through beautiful forest with striking flowers, fruits and epiphytes. Both are steep and can be difficult to locate, which is why a guide is required.

Shrike Trail The Shrike Trail is very steep. It starts at the right-hand side of the pink building at the far end of the school grounds, behind the dam. This trail soon reaches primary forest and provides the best chance of seeing the rarest and most endangered bird on the mountain, the Mount Kupe bush shrike, first observed in 1952, then assumed extinct until spotted again in 1989 (see page 37). There is a campsite on the trail.

Max's Trail Max's Trail begins at the WWF project leader's cottage next to the school, about 1.5km from the village, through bush and secondary forest. It has a campsite at 1,500m (Nyasoso is at an altitude of about 800m) after a steep climb up primary forest, but is much easier going above the campsite.

WHERE TO STAY IN NYASOSO There are several guesthouses with basic accommodation including Thekla's Guest House, Mrs Ekwoge's Guest House and the Women's Centre, with rooms costing about CFA6,000 per night. Lucy's Guest House provides good, basic meals and a pleasant guest's sitting room. Bathrooms are shared.

The WWF's guesthouse has closed down, but the WWF office in the town may be able to suggest guesthouses or accommodation in private homes at CFA3,000 per person per night.

BAKOSSI MOUNTAINS

Head for the little explored Bakossi Mountains, an area of lower montane forest northwest of Mount Kupe, if you want to experience real remoteness and endless dense forest. Access is quite difficult and facilities non-existent, but guides may be found in Nyasoso or in the villages of Ngomboko, 10km north of Nyasoso, or Edib, about 7km north of Baseng.

One route into the mountain forests goes from Ngomboko then 4km west to Bangem. You then ford a river and walk northwards to Edib village (6km). Two kilometres west of here is Lake Edib, and from there you can proceed to Masaka or Nyali, each about 6km from the lake. The route is completed by reaching Nyandung village, 3–4km from Masaka, which is near the Mamfé–Kumba road, accessible by a track road from Masaka village.

KORUP NATIONAL PARK

Korup is Africa's oldest remaining rainforest. Scientists estimate that this living museum is more than 60 million years old. An area of extensive primary lowland tropical rainforest on the border of Nigeria, it is the most accessible forest of its type in Cameroon. The park was officially created in 1986 and is joined to Nigeria's Cross River National Park.

With a surface area of 1,260km^2 (126,000ha), Korup featured in the British television screening of *Korup: The Story of an African Rainforest* which did much to cause awareness of the plight of rainforests worldwide.

Korup's dense primary tropical rainforest has the highest number of species and natural genetic richness recorded so far in Africa. Isolated by the surrounding river systems; logging and agriculture are not permitted and the forest is home to more than 1,000 known species, with 60 occurring nowhere else and 170 considered endangered or vulnerable. One of these is the Cross River gorilla, which in 2000 the International Union for the Conservation of Nature (IUCN) put on the critically endangered list, ie: close to extinction, as there are thought to be only 150–200 remaining.

There are more than 600 tree and shrub varieties and more than 400 bird species as well as more than 100 species of mammal. In addition there are 950 butterfly species, 174 species of reptile and amphibian and 140 varieties of fish, with new discoveries being made yearly. Korup is home to a quarter of Africa's primate species.

There are populations of forest elephant, buffalo, drill, antelope, sitatunga, leopard and chimpanzee, and more specifically, the collared mangabey, russet-eared guenon, red-capped mangabey, preuss's red colobus and the putty-nosed monkey.

Its rich flora and fauna result from Korup surviving the Ice Age. More than 90 plants in Korup are and have been used for medicinal purposes and one creeper (*Ancistrocladus korupensis*) is believed to have constituents useful in the cure of some forms of cancer and HIV.

If you visit the park, you are likely to see few animals although you would be unlucky not to at least encounter monkeys leaping through the trees. Animals or not, the experience will still be fascinating. There is a gigantic variety of plants and trees and a similar variety of birds creating a cacophony overhead. The forest floor is typically rather dark, shaded by the many different levels of growth overhead, from huge trees to tiny saplings, all competing for light.

Brightly coloured, exotic fruits and flowers hang from the trees and the smell of fermenting fruit is strong. When you come to a clearing, where a tree has fallen, the sunlight on the forest floor causes lush green undergrowth, flowers, and butterflies to appear.

KORUP NATIONAL PARK PROJECT The WWF's Korup National Park Project is one of the organisation's largest integrated conservation and development projects. The WWF has two offices in the Korup region, one at Mundemba in the south and another at Nguti in the north.

Designed to protect and manage the national park and integrate it into the local economy and regional development plans, the project links park development, environmental education, scientific research, rural and tourism development, sustainable natural resources utilisation and use of non-timber forest products. The Korup Project has undertaken a number of conservation and poverty alleviation initiatives including the building of bridges, access roads, community halls and schools, and supported income-generating activities like cassava grinding mills, palm oil presses, cocoa driers and sprayers, natural resource plantations, and goat, pig and cattle farming.

GETTING TO THE PARK Access to the park can be a bit of a struggle due to the poor roads but the park itself is especially rewarding as there are more than 100km of marked trails and good anglophone guides.

It takes a full day's travelling from Douala to reach Mundemba, which is near where the main entrance to the park is located. It is far easier to reach in the dry season, as the road from Kumba to Mundemba is untarred and the 150km (93 miles) stretch can turn into a mudbath during the rainy season. Regular share taxis travel from Douala to Mundemba, via Kumba and Ekondo Titi.

You can either walk the 8km to the park entrance or the Korup Information Centre at Mundemba (details below) can provide a park vehicle accommodating eight at CFA8,000 per return trip.

You can also enter the park further north at Baro, via Nguti on the road from Mamfé to Kumba. There are few share taxis for the last stretch, the 35km from

Nguti to Baro, although you may be able to hitch a lift at Nguti with WWF staff. At Baro you enter the forest by crossing the Bake River. There are fewer facilities and infrastructure geared to this northern region of the park.

You can also reach Korup by boat, along the Mana River as far south as Idenao, although it is not cheap at around CFA250,000 for a boat holding six, one way. This can be arranged by the Korup Tourist Information Centre. You can also charter a boat to visit nearby Pelican Island and the mangrove swamps, which costs CFA125,000 or so.

Boats also sail from Limbé through the Rio del Rey into the Ndian River to Mundemba, or, if you are approaching from Nigeria, by boat via the creeks from Calabar and Ikang, down the River Ndian to Bula Beach near Mundemba, which takes around three hours. If you plan to sail from Nigeria, check the situation concerning the Bakassi Peninsula border dispute with Nigeria.

WHERE TO STAY AND EAT IN MUNDEMBA Vista Palace is the cheapest option: simple rooms with separate or shared facilities for CFA3,000 shared, CFA4,500 with bathroom. It has a good, inexpensive restaurant, and the **Chez Controleur Tourist Café** opposite also does good-value meals.

Korup Park Hotel, near the post office, has en-suite rooms with fans for CFA5,000–7,500 as well as a restaurant and bar.

Hotel Bosema, on the edge of the village, is said to have rooms in good condition for around CFA15,000 a night. Breakfast and lunch are available at an additional cost.

WHERE TO STAY IN NGUTI Safariland Hotel, the **Green Castle** and, less centrally, the **Samba Inn** have basic accommodation at under CFA5,000.

THE PARK Arrangements for entering the park are through the Korup Information Centre (*in the centre of Mundemba;* m *7710 91 75;* e *korup@wwf.cm;* ⊕ *Nov–May 07.00–17.00 daily; Jun–Oct 08.00–15.30 Mon–Fri, 07.30–08.30 & 16.30–17.30 w/ends*). There is a CFA5,000 park entrance fee payable per day plus CFA4,000 per day and CFA1,000 per night for a compulsory guide (most of whom are very enthusiastic and knowledgeable) and CFA2,000 per day and CFA1,000 per night for a porter (optional). The centre also hires out sleeping bags and camping equipment. You can arrange this, and accommodation, in advance by contacting the WWF headquarters in Yaoundé (↘ *2221 62 67;* e *www.wwfcameroon.org*) or by email, see above for details.

If you want to make an early start to the park, it is important to arrive before 16.30 the previous day to make arrangements in Mundemba.

Don't forget to take insect repellent for the multitude of mites including driver ants, bees and blackflies, the last attracted by the water if you have a swim in the rivers. You should dress for the extreme wet, to cope with the 100% humidity and the fording of waist-high pools.

At the approach to Korup, you pass regimented oil palm plantations as the huge forest trees rise up in front of you, sounds of strange cries of birds and the hum of insects getting louder and louder. You cross the Mana River, which borders the forest, on an awe-inspiring 120m-long wooden suspension bridge (built in 1989 to allow all-year access; this has recently been out of action and if this is still the case you will have to boat or walk across) spanning the river, and the forest then closes around you.

If time is short, and you can only visit for the day, follow the marked nature trail, which features information posts explaining points of interest such as the varied fauna and flora.

Further information on the park is available from the WWF Cameroon headquarters in Bastos, Yaoundé (see previous page for details).

WHERE TO STAY IN THE PARK Day trips are worthwhile but there are three basic campsites with beds, insect-screened huts, drinking and bathing water, latrine toilets and simple kitchens with firewood. Mattresses and cooking equipment can be hired from the Korup Information Centre.

The basic **Iribe Irene Camp** is 1.7km from the park entrance on the nature trail.

Rengo Rock Camp is 8km in, past the Mana River Waterfall to the south and near some caves that are well worth exploring, and which lead to Mount Yuhan (1,079m). Rengo Rock Camp is situated next to a forest stream. There are four quite spacious wooden huts (two with bunk beds).

There is also the larger **Chimpanzee Camp**, 10km from the entrance, where you may hear or see chimpanzees.

WHAT TO SEE

Rumpi Hills Forest Reserve If you head in the opposite direction, ie: eastwards out of the park to Rumpi Hills Forest Reserve (which extends to 45,843ha or 458km²), you come to the Meta Waterfall (a good four-hour hike from Mundemba) and, 20km south of this, the Iyombo Waterfall. On the eastern border of the reserve, just west of Dikome Balue, is Mount Rata (1,770m).

Forest reserves In the Korup region are several forest reserves in addition to Rumpi Hills: Mawne River and Nta-ali (35,000ha or 350km²) east and southeast of Mamfé, Ejagham (74,851ha or 749km²), a continuation of Korup, as well as the Banyang Mbo Wildlife Sanctuary near Nguti. Many small villages are scattered around this region, mainly belonging to the five main tribes of the region, namely Oroko, Ejagham, Balong, Korup and Isangele.

Komboné This village near Kumba has a typical small coffee and cocoa farm where, if it is in use, it is possible to visit the drying house where the beans are prepared for shipment.

MAMFE Telephone code: 3334

Anglophone Mamfé, north of the Korup National Park, is the last sizeable town before the Nigerian border at Ekok and therefore the main southern entry point into Nigeria. The road to Mamfé can be very difficult in the rainy season, when it is generally better to enter Nigeria from the north of the country. Yet the road enjoys some marvellous landscapes as it plunges through rainforest and around the mountains.

This rather unremarkable, remote town is somewhat livened up by the travellers and traders who perpetually descend upon the place, many of whom are selling goods smuggled from Nigeria. It is also known for the witchcraft practised in the area. Mamfé has a good spread of shops, a bank, hospital and petrol station.

GETTING THERE AND AWAY The motor park just southwest of the centre of the town has regular share taxis to Kumba and Ekok (65km) on the Nigerian border, and sometimes into Nigeria.

There are also share taxis to Bamenda (145km) and Dschang, but bear in mind that the admittedly beautiful mountain roads for these destinations are often quite treacherous and often impassable during the rainy season. Going south to Kumba and then on to Bamenda (180km and then 250km) is a more time-consuming route but significantly safer.

Agences de voyages Ali Baba, Tchatcho Voyages, Guaranti Express and Tonton Express have regular services to Kumba, which average under CFA2,000 in the dry season and CFA4,000 when the rains make the roads very difficult.

For Korup National Park, take a share taxi on the N8 road to Nguti for the northern entrance or the far longer journey to Mundemba, via Kumba, for the southern, main entrance.

WHERE TO STAY

Data Club Hotel (20 rooms) BP29; just under a mile's walk northwest of the centre; ✎ 3334 13 99. Has a good restaurant & good views of the Cross River. Clean AC en-suite rooms. $

Heritage Hotel Nguti Rd. Opposite the school, this has a variety of simple rooms. $

Great Aim Hotel BP 69; north of & near the motor park. Has a bar & restaurant & rooms for under CFA5,000 with fans & shared facilities. $

Abunwa Lodge (8 rooms) ✎ 3334 12 47. Basic accommodation. $

WHAT TO SEE

Ekok The 60km road from Mamfé to Ekok gets so bad during the rainy season that it is usually best to take a motorised *pirogue*. These ply the Cross River from Mamfé to Ekok, setting off from the old German bridge at Mamfé. In the dry season the journey can usually be covered easily in an afternoon.

The Nigerian border is continually open, but there are a few very basic hotels and guesthouses in Ekok, which in the evening can also offer rows of lively stalls and plenty of loud music.

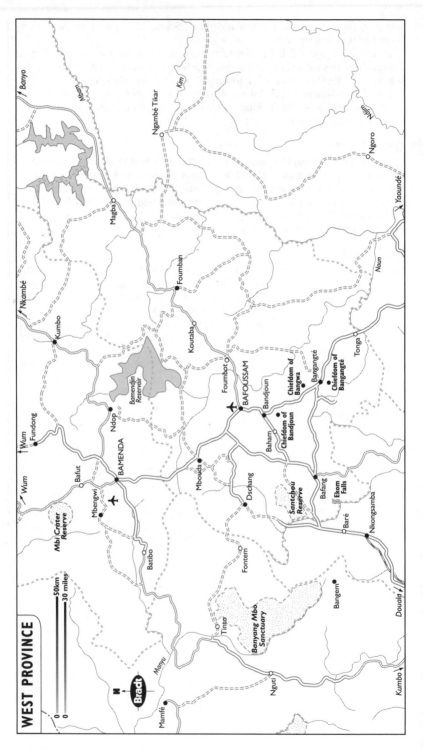

WEST PROVINCE

0   50km
0   30 miles

8

West Province

The northern sector of western Cameroon – the Central Highlands – provides a visitor with a stunning succession of landscapes including volcanic crater lakes surrounded by dense vegetation, rolling hills and spectacular waterfalls. This region is also crammed with cultural distractions, and is rich in fascinating ancient chiefdoms.

This area is relatively easy to explore as paved roads and a good selection of transport options connect the main towns.

Rich volcanic soils in the west have encouraged much higher rural population densities than elsewhere in the country. Coffee and cocoa are widely cultivated in the region.

The Bamiléké dominate francophone West Province, notably in the large town of Bafoussam. The Bamiléké originated from the north and probably settled in this region around the start of the 17th century. Bamiléké country also extends to towns such as Bandjoun, with its historic chiefdom, and the German colonial mountain resort town of Dschang.

The Cameroon Highlands are also populated to a lesser extent by other semi-Bantu peoples like the Tikar and Bamoun. The east of the province is home to the latter, who are centred around Foumban, which has a number of sights for visitors including a splendid palace.

BAFOUSSAM *Telephone code: 3344*

Rapidly enlarging, with a population of more than 200,000, this dusty, lively and loud regional commercial centre, a 285km drive from Douala, is strongly dominated by the Bamiléké. The administrative capital of the West Province, its francophone nature contrasts strongly with neighouring anglophone Bamenda.

There is a *chefferie*, or chief's compound, southeast of the centre off the road that goes to Bandjoun and Douala. The entrance fee is CFA2,000 and there is a further charge of CFA1,500 for photography. A better example of a traditional chefferie can be seen in Bandjoun, just under 20km further on down the road.

The Bamiléké built up Bafoussam through trading coffee, which is widely grown in the nearby fertile hills, and latterly, through industry. It is also a major cocoa-producing area.

The town is split into an administrative quarter, the Tamdja district, and the commercial neighbourhoods Famla and Djeleng, in the middle of which is held the market on a small hill, every four days. The market is very dark and claustrophobic so beware of pickpockets.

The main drag, Avenue Wanko, is where you will find several banks as well as major shops. Crafts such as carved wooden sculptures and furniture can be bought at the market and also at the workshops along Rue Nguetti Michel.

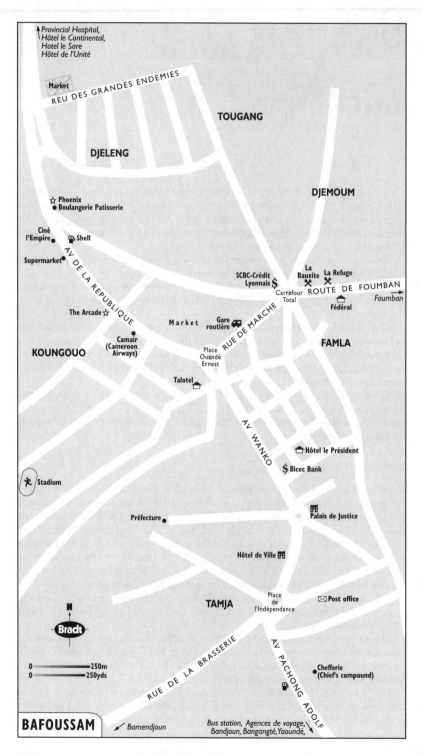

Provincial Hospital,
Hôtel le Continental,
Hôtel le Sare
Hôtel de l'Unité

Market

REU DES GRANDES ENDEMIES

TOUGANG

DJELENG

DJEMOUM

☆ Phoenix
● Boulangerie Patisserie

Ciné
l'Empire ●   🅿 Shell

Supermarket ●

AV DE LA REPUBLIQUE

La
Bauxite La Refuge
SCBC-Crédit   ✕ ✕
Lyonnais $
Carrefour   ROUTE DE FOUMBAN
Total   Fouman →
🏛
Fédéral

The Arcade ☆   Market   Gare
routière 🚐

FAMLA

Camair
(Cameroon
Airways)

KOUNGOUO

Place
Ouandé
Ernest

Talotel 🏠

RUE DE MARCHE

AV WANKO

🏠 Hôtel le Président

$ Bicec Bank

🏃 Stadium

Préfecture ●

🏛
Palais de Justice

Hôtel de Ville 🏛

Place
de
l'Indépendance   ✉ Post office

TAMJA

N

Bradt

0 ————— 250m
0 ————— 250yds

RUE DE LA BRASSERIE

AV PACHONG ADOLF

Chefferie
● (Chief's compound)
🅿

BAFOUSSAM   ↙ Bamendjoun   Bus station, Agences de voyage,
Bandjoun, Bangangté, Yaoundé, ↓

GETTING THERE AND AWAY The main *gare routière* by the market has share taxis to destinations south of the town, such as Bandjoun, Bafang and Kumba, as well as minibuses to Foumbot and Foumban.

Share taxis to Foumban and Foumbot can be found at the Foumban *gare routière* opposite Crédit Lyonnais on the Carrefour Total roundabout.

Share taxis to Dschang and Bamenda leave from near the Shell station northwest of the centre. There are *agences de voyage* offices in this sector. Operators include Jeannot Express and Unity Express.

Agences de voyage offices, such as Binam, with services to Yaoundé (CFA2,000), Douala (CFA1,000) and Dschang are located along the Rue du Marché by the market and near the chefferie in the south of the town. For Bamenda (typically CFA800, one hour), *agences de voyage* offices, such as Jeannot Express and Savannah Enterprises, are on Avenue République near the Hôtel Continental, 1km north of the centre. Other *agences de voyage* include Mayo-Banyo, Tonton Express, Paradise Travel and Vallance and go to destinations including Ngaoundéré.

There is no direct transport to Limbé from Bafoússam and therefore for Limbé go to Douala first.

WHERE TO STAY

🏠 **Hôtel Talotel** BP 110; Pl Ouande Ernest; e hoteltalotel@camnet.cm. Off Av Wanko & by Le Ritz Palace nightclub, this very comfortable central hotel has well decorated & furnished en-suite rooms with satellite TV. Family rooms & apts available. There is a good restaurant & bar. On the downside, one recent visitor found cockroaches in his room. $$$

🏠 **Le Manoir** (22 rooms) South of the centre opposite the Douala *gare routière*; ✆ 3344 49 09. One of Bafoussam's top hotels, with good, clean rooms with bathrooms. Prices can often be negotiated. There is also a restaurant. $$$

🏠 **Hôtel Le Saré** (35 rooms) BP 731; Rte de Bamenda; ✆ 3344 25 99; m 7722 18 98; e hotellesare@yahoo.fr. A quite upmarket hotel situated in spacious gardens. Clean chalets with AC, & a good restaurant offering French cuisine & a bar. Spacious, comfortable rooms with bathroom (best rooms in the north wing). $$$

🏠 **Hôtel Le Continental** (25 rooms) BP 136; Av de la République; ✆ 3344 14 58. On the noisy main road, this government-rated 1-star hotel has self-contained rooms with balcony & TV, a European restaurant of average standard (dishes CFA1,500–3,000) & an extraordinary bar with eclectic décor that's worth seeing. $

🏠 **Hôtel Fédéral** BP 136; Rte de Foumban; ✆ 3344 13 09. Recently renovated & close to the centre, clean rooms with shower/bathroom, balcony & TV & there is a good restaurant & a bar. There are slightly cheaper rooms at the front but these are noisier. $

🏠 **Hôtel Le Président** (56 rooms) BP 78; 1er Rue Famla 1; ✆ 3344 11 36. Rather faded hotel yet the AC rooms, some with TV, are good value. $

🏠 **Hôtel de l'Unité** (30 rooms) BP 99; ✆ 3344 15 16. Basic rooms, bar & restaurant. $

🏠 **Airport Hotel** (16 rooms) BP 565; ✆ 3344 37 95. Government-graded 2-star hotel with plain rooms, a bar & restaurant. $

WHERE TO EAT AND DRINK There are numerous bars around the Avenue de la République while around the Rou Joumou and the Foumban *gare routière* are some good, inexpensive eateries including **La Bauxite** for snacks and **La Refuge** for Cameroonian dishes. There are one or two patisseries in the centre, including **Boulangerie Patisserie** near the Hôtel Le Continental, which has a large selection of cakes, pastries, croissants and French breads for CFA200–400. There are various UCCAO (Union Centrale des Sociétés Cooperatives Agricoles de l'Ouest) **coffee stalls** that do a good coffee. The one set well above street level in Avenue Wanko, is a great place to watch the world go by. Boys passing by selling cakes and doughnuts on the street below will happily climb the numerous stairs to sell you one. Heading west along the Bamenda Road, turn right after the Shell petrol station for a number of cheap food stalls. **Le Bonne Table de l'Ouest** on the Bandjoun/Douala road south of the centre is a popular, good eaterie with both Cameroonian and European cuisines.

ENTERTAINMENT AND NIGHTLIFE The **Phoenix Nightclub** on Rue de République boasts a live DJ on Saturdays (entrance CFA1,000) and is recommended. **Le Ritz Palace** at the Talotel Hotel, and **The Arcade**, off Avenue de la République are further options.

The Cine l'Empire on Avenue de la République shows recent films in French and occasionally in English, four showings afternoon and evening, CFA800–1,200.

OTHER PRACTICALITIES
Banks
$ **Bicec** Av Wanko

$ **SBC-Crédit Lyonnais** Foumban Rd

Hospitals
✚ **Provincial Hospital** ☏ 3344 12 11
✚ **Dispensaire Urbain** ☏ 3344 13 46

✚ **Hôpital de Mbo** ☏ 3344 23 26

Internet
🄴 **Cyber Espace Maflo** ☏ 3344 60 70

🄴 **Cyber Café Premier** ☏ 3344 41 66

Pharmacies
✚ **Pharmacie Binam** ☏ 3344 25 55
✚ **Pharmacie du Benin SARL** ☏ 3344 15 57
✚ **Pharmacie Madelon** ☏ 3344 62 62
✚ **Pharmacie de l'Amitie** ☏ 3344 18 33

✚ **Pharmacie du Marché** ☏ 3344 66 11
✚ **Pharmacie des Montagnes** ☏ 3344 42 18
✚ **Pharmacie du Secours** ☏ 3344 13 27

Tourist information, tour operators and travel agents
🆔 **Tourist office** Near the Palais de Justice; ☏ 3344 11 89/3344 77 82
Tandel Voyages BP 994; ☏ 3344 65 81/3344 64 58

West Camtour BP 731; ☏ 3344 25 99
MTA ☏ 3344 49 210

WHAT TO SEE Within the rough triangle created by the Bamboutous Mountains to the west and the Noun River to the northeast there are a number of **chiefdoms**, which could have populations ranging anything from under 100 to over 25,000. There are also a number of **crater lakes**, including Lake Monoun, 3km east of the River Noun. The water depth of the lake remains a constant 96m, despite the season. Crater lakes are at risk of expelling poisonous gases (the most well-known one being at Lake Nyos in 1986, covered in the next chapter) and indeed poisonous gases at Lake Monoun asphyxiated 37 people on 16 August 1984.

Baleng In the Baleng region, just north of Bafoussam, there is the crater lake of Baleng as well as the chefferie or chiefdom of Baleng. The area is dotted with mud huts with tall 'witches' hat' roofs often made from corrugated iron. Other crater lakes in the area include ones at Banefo and Doupe, and near the town is the Metchie Falls.

Baleng also boasts a forestry reserve, created in 1935. Unfortunately, the reserve has suffered from a great deal of logging in recent years, triggered somewhat by economic crisis in 1986.

BANDJOUN _Telephone code 3344_

This is the biggest of the Bamiléké chiefdoms and contains one of the most impressive traditionally built palaces in west and central Africa.

Nearly 20km south of Bafoussam, Bandjoun is rich in the distinctive Bamiléké architecture, which typically consists of a square-shaped room made of mud and bamboo or palm leaves, with a thatched (although increasingly corrugated iron) conical roof and an exterior augmented by carved wooden panels.

The chief's palace is about 3km, a 15-minute walk, south of the centre on the Route de Bangangté, near the Yaoundé intersection. Such compounds typically have a huge thatched reception hall which traditionally would have been used as a court and for assemblies, a market square and various huts for the chief and his wives. This one features tall, thin totem-pole-like columns, bamboo walls decorated with geometric designs and elaborately carved doorways.

Under the chief, the judicial and religious leader and owner of all land in the chiefdom, was a hierarchy of notables, freemen and slaves. Although this rigid social organisation has all but gone, various associations and secret societies relating to the chiefdom still remain. Today, the chief lives in a modern palace, located opposite the colonial-style treasury.

WHERE TO STAY

🏠 **Centre Climatique de Bandoun** (20 rooms) 🦅 3344 67 50. Outside town on the road to Bafoussam, this hotel has a restaurant & comfortable rooms with bathrooms & TV. $$$

🏠 **Hôtel de Bandjoun** Near the *gare routière*, simple rooms. $

WHERE TO EAT AND DRINK, AND NIGHTLIFE The **Concorde Restaurant**, near the market, offers good-value food and there are various food stalls around the market, with music and dance bars around the main square.

WHAT TO SEE

Museum of Bandjoun (*BP 141;* m *7731 1777/9920 8660;* e *bandjoun@museumcam.org; www.museumcam.org; admission CFA2,000 plus CFA2,000 for photography*) Housed in the treasury, this smart museum has more than 100 major and significant objects of the cultural and artistic heritage of Bandjoun. There are rare pieces, including some masterpieces of African art. They celebrate the pomp of the court of the kings of Bandjoun, the grandeur and the power of these monarchs and their retainers, and the solidity of the institutions. They also materialise universal themes such as death, life, defeat, love, victory, power, prestige and occult forces. Objects include royal thrones, magnificent masks and beaded objects, wooden carved panels, richly decorated architectonic elements, fabrics with enigmatic patterns, statues and furniture, musical instruments and various cultural objects. This is one of four stunning museums in the highlands of the west and northwest of Cameroon. The other three are at Baham, Babungo and Mankon.

Baham Museum (*BP 73;* m *7712 6652/7753 9766* e *baham@museumcam.org; www.museumcam.org; admission CFA2,000 plus CFA2,000 for photography*) The village of Baham, southwest of Bandjoun, has one of the stunning museums mentioned above. The collection here covers history, secret societies and religion, kings and dignitaries, maternity, fertility, war and architecture, and includes costumes, textiles, art and musical instruments.

BAFANG *Telephone code: 3348*

Bafang itself is nothing special, but the scenery around it is beautiful. There are various waterfalls, including the Chutes de la Mouenkeu, signposted from the Nkongsamba road a short walk out of town.

Another 30km down this road are the more impressive 80m-high Chutes d'Ekom on the Nkam River. Details of how to reach these are in *Chapter 6, Littoral Province*, page 115.

The town has various *agences de voyage* going to Yaoundé, Douala, Kumba and Bamenda.

WHERE TO STAY

Hôtel la Falaise (48 rooms) BP 143; 3348 63 11/3348 63 13. Opposite the Palais de Justice, this 3-star hotel has AC rooms, a restaurant & bar. $$

Grand Lux (35 rooms) Hotel BP 396; 3348 61 58. By the Palais de Justice, clean rooms with bathrooms & balconies There is a good café/bar. $

Hôtel le Samaritain BP 155; 3348 71 55. Has very basic rooms. $

Hôtel Le Calypso (22 rooms) BP 211; 3348 62 11. A government-graded 2-star hotel with basic but comfortable rooms, bar & restaurant. $

BANGANGTE *Telephone code: 3348*

The pleasant town of Bangangté, a short drive south from Bandjoun, has a renovated traditional chefferie. Another, the Chefferie de Bana, is located off the road from Bangangté to Bafang, a route rich in spectacular scenery, not least the Col de Bana, or Bana Pass, where the elevation rises to 1,736m. Just north of Bangangté is another chiefdom, at Bangwa (or Bangoua).

WHERE TO STAY

Hôtel Cristal (30 rooms) BP143; 3348 91 16. West of the motor park, very comfortable clean self-contained rooms plus restaurant & bar. $$$

Hôtel Le Bazar (18 rooms) BP 35; 3348 44 38. A couple of hundred metres east of the motor park along the main road, is better than it looks with clean en-suite rooms. $

Hôtel Le Paysan (22 rooms) BP 13; 3348 41 88. By the motor park, the hotel has rooms with bathrooms as well as an inexpensive restaurant. $

Jenyf Hotel (30 rooms & 6 apts) BP 143. Comfortable rooms & apartments, a bar & inexpensive restaurant. $

DSCHANG *Telephone code: 3345*

Established by the Germans in 1903, Dschang is a mountain resort, an old colonial and university town situated at an altitude of 1,400m (4,600ft), which makes the temperature pleasantly cool. Principally Bamiléké, it has a population of approximately 140,000.

Apart from accommodation, there is not too much to distract in the town: a lively market, a municipal lake surrounded by banana, mango and pear trees, and a number of crafts shops.

In 1942 Europeans in the area created the Centre Climatique as a holiday centre as, it being World War II, they were unable to go abroad for their holidays. The centre is still open today (see *Where to stay* below).

GETTING THERE AND AWAY Dschang can be reached by taking the paved road by share taxi from Bafoussam, (48km, which takes under an hour), the Bamenda road passing the Bamboutous Mountains which peak at 2,740m, and the paved road from Mbouda. The attractive but slow minor route through coffee and cocoa plantations from Melong, southwest of Bafang, was not possible at the time of writing because of bridges that have collapsed.

There are minibuses and *agences de voyage* for destinations that include Yaoundé, Douala, Bafoussam and Bamenda.

WHERE TO STAY

🏠 **Centre Climatique** (50 rooms) BP 40; 📞 3345 10 58. This holiday complex has bungalows in a range of price categories, from basic with shared facilities to the luxurious with a spacious balcony. There are landscaped gardens, an expensive but good restaurant, bars, a swimming pool (available to non-guests for a small fee), horseriding & tennis courts. Car hire can be arranged for exploring the region. $$$

🏠 **Teclaire Palace Hotel** (45 rooms) BP 238; 📞 3345 11 75; e info@tph-dschang.net; www.tph-dschang.net. A comfortable hotel with a bar & restaurant. $$

🏠 **Hôtel Constellation** (40 rooms) BP 22; 📞 3345 10 61. Centrally located near the *gare routière*. There is a bar & restaurant. $$

🏠 **Hôtel Menoua Palace** (20 rooms) 📞 3345 16 93. Simple rooms. $

WHERE TO EAT AND DRINK, AND NIGHTLIFE The **Phoenix Restaurant** has interesting Cameroonian dishes, and prices vary from around CFA1,000–4,500. Popular bar **La Maison Combatant de la Menoua** features traditional Cameroonian dancing and local dishes that include bushmeat. If you've the energy to stay up late, there's **Conclusion** nightclub.

OTHER PRACTICALITIES Facilities in Dschang include a **hospital** (📞 *345 13 66*) and **tourist office** (📞 *345 21 25*).

WHAT TO SEE AND DO An excursion takes in two waterfalls: leave Dschang on the road from the Place de l'Indépendence heading for Fongo-Tongo; the pretty hills and valleys lead to a signpost for a waterfall, the Cascade de Lingam, after about 10km. The same distance again leads you to another, bigger waterfall, the Chute de la Mamy Wata, accessible from a side road.

Around 24km north of the town is Dsjutitsa, a beautiful, restful tea plantation with a lodge with rooms for under CFA5,000.

FOUMBAN Telephone code: 3348

About 250km northwest of Yaoundé and 72km northeast of Bafoussam, the town of Foumban (or Fumban) is particularly history- and culture-rich. It is predominantly Muslim and the seat of the Sultan of the Bamoun people. At 1,200m above sea level and located on the northeast edge of a mountain range, it sits by a vast plain. It is a bit touristy and you won't be short of children approaching you, asking to be your guide.

The Bamoun Kingdom was founded here at the start of the 15th century by Nchare Yen, and therefore Foumban represents one of the oldest towns in Cameroon.

Considered one of the art capitals of Africa, Foumban has a number of attractions, not least the outstanding Royal Palace of the Sultan, which the town is organised around. If you are lucky, you may be able to meet him. There are two good museums, a colourful market in the centre with art objects, textiles, foodstuffs, etc (market days are Saturday and Wednesday) and plenty of opportunities to buy arts and crafts at a variety of shops and stalls. Foumban also has a number of buildings dating from its period of German colonisation.

On the west side of town is the administrative quarter, with government offices, a hospital, the town hall and post office, while touristic sites are generally clustered around the Royal Palace at the centre.

GETTING THERE AND AWAY The motor park is by the market and has transport to Foumbot, Kumbo, Bamenda, Bafoussam and Nkongsamba. Bafoussam, for example, is typically CFA1,000 and takes an hour on the good roads.

Agences de voyage for Yaoundé, Douala (seven hours) and Bafoussam are generally west of the town.

Road conditions to the north are very bad and there is no direct transport so allow at least a couple of days to reach Ngaoundéré. It can take even more, and may be impossible in the rainy season. If you take this route, you can take a taxi to Banyo (see page 201), staying overnight at the simple Auberge Pasada (CFA2,500) or Auberge le Sare (under CFA5,000) near the market and then getting transport to Tibati (a four-hour trip). From here you can take the crowded afternoon bus to Ngaoundéré, arriving around midnight, or alternatively a taxi to Ngaoundal (under two hours) and then catching the train to Ngaoundéré. This should arrive in Ngaoundal at around 03.00 but can be delayed for some hours.

WHERE TO STAY

Hôtel Le Chalet Down a side road off the road to Bafoussam; ☎ 3348 62 67/348 24 12.This hotel has good, quiet rooms, but is significantly west (3km) of the centre. $

Hôtel le Zenith BP 122; off the Bafoussam road; ☎ 3348 24 25. Modern hotel with clean rooms with en-suite facilities & some with TV. $

Résidence Palace Baba BP 10; ☎ 3348 27 48. Away from the centre. $

Hôtel Beau Regarde BP 29; Rue de l'Hôtel Beau Regarde; ☎ 3348 21 82/3348 21 83. Well past its heyday as a smart hotel, it now has basic,

acceptable rooms, some with bathrooms. In the centre, with a decent bar. $

Hôtel Le Prunier Rouge BP 13; off the Bafoussam road; ☎ 3348 23 52. Simple rooms, pretty views & a restaurant. $

Catholic Mission Hotel Rd. In the centre near the church, has an attractive garden & very basic rooms with dormitory beds costing CFA2,500. $

Relax des Princes Basic rooms behind the bar, but don't count on a restful night. It is to the left of where the Banyo bus stops. $

WHERE TO EAT AND DRINK
Street food is available just east of the *gare routière*. **Relax des Princes** is a very lively bar in the centre (see above) augmented by full-blast television. The barbecues outside the bar can bring grilled fish, plantain, rice and cassava to your table for CFA250. To the left of Relax des Princes a five-minute walk up the hill brings you to a square of sorts on the left, with numerous bars and food stalls and a great atmosphere.

Royal Café, Route de Bamenda, near the market, has Cameroonian/Western food from CFA2,000. **Restaurant de la Maturité**, opposite the *gare routière*, serves meals for around CFA500.

OTHER PRACTICALITIES There are no banks in Foumban but the local hospitals are the District Hospital (☎ 3348 21 23) and the Hôpital du Palais (☎ 3348 24 47).

WHAT TO SEE AND DO
The Royal Palace and the Sultan's Museum
(☎ 3348 22 27; *grounds free, palace CFA2,000; CFA1,500 for photography*; ⊕ *08.30–18.00 daily*) The Bamoun can trace the lineage of their sultan back to 1394. Of the 17 kings in the present dynasty, the first, Nshare Yen, the son of a Tikar chief, proclaimed himself king with Foumban as his capital (then called Mfomben) after leading a group of rebels from the Tikar homelands. Another, Mbuembue, allegedly had a speaking voice that carried over a mile.

The old palace (the new one houses the present sultan) was completed in 1917 and designed by the king at that time, Ibrahim Njoya, inventor of the Bamoun alphabet. He converted to Islam and became a sultan.

The palace is architecturally unique and to an extent resembles a medieval chateau with German Baroque and Romanesque styles thrown in. It was more recently restored by UNESCO. Approached via a huge palm-fringed courtyard,

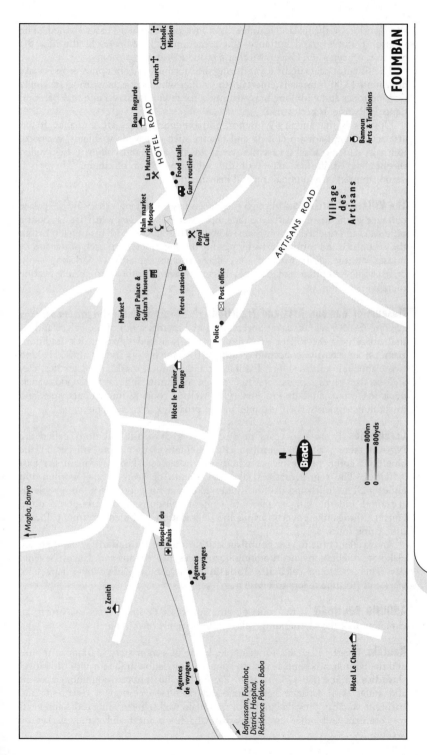

FOUMBAN

8

147

the exterior of the palace features balconies of elaborately carved wood. The interior features grand entrance and reception halls, a room of thrones, the Sultan's, Queen's and Queen Mother's résidences and an armoury.

The sultan appears in the foyer during the morning, and after prayers on Fridays at around 13.00 musicians entertain the sultan while subjects wearing strikingly flowing robes and with long brass trumpets meet with him. A traditional Bamoun dance, Mbansie, is performed.

Upstairs is the Sultan's Museum, and bilingual guides are available. It has artefacts of the Bamoun culture and history such as jewellery, shields, weapons, journals, dancing masks, carvings, royal gowns, arms and colourful bejewelled thrones carved in the shapes of the sultans who sat on them. There is a demonstration of traditional musical instruments.

The Village of Artisans Although there are a few art and craft shops by the palace entrance in the main square, the far more extensive Village of Artisans is about a mile away and reached by going west down the Bafoussam road, turning left before the post office and turning left after passing the sports stadium. Each of the row of houses on the short road to the village square contains a workshop, with craftspeople sculpting and carving, basket weaving, embroidering and beating metals.

Museum of Bamoun Arts and Traditions (✎ *348 25 86; admission free but donation expected;* ⏲ *09.00–17.00 daily*) Several hundred metres south of the palace and on the square near the Village of Artisans is this Musée des Arts et des Traditions Bamoun, an extensive collection relating to Bamoun history and art housed behind two elaborately carved doors. Exhibits include statues, masks, dyed textiles, clay and bronze pipes, spears, charms, carved furniture and carved wood panels depicting events in Bamoun history as well as cooking implements, jugs and musical instruments, such as gongs and an ornately carved xylophone.

Ceremonies Every two years in December a colourful ceremony called the **Ngoun** takes place in Foumban. Representatives of all the villages in the chiefdom come to the palace where the sultan is asked to explain his past activities. The representatives take care not to be seen by any women and children. The following day the sultan addresses his people at noon, problems are aired and the king is asked to suggest solutions. Problems posed often concern things like poverty, crime and degradation of the environment. Plenty of feasting follows.

An excellent time to visit Foumban is at the **end of Ramadam**, when there are elaborate celebrations incorporating horse races, processions and dances. Seventy days later the town celebrates **Tabaski** extravagantly, marked by a parade of *marabouts* (fortune tellers and wise men).

AROUND FOUMBAN If the touristic atmosphere of Foumban gets too much, an exploration of the surrounding villages can be richly rewarding.

Koutaba Nearby Koutaba, for example, home of a monastery of Trappist monks and the Foumban Nkounja Airport, has accommodation in the form of the **Hôtel Paradise Palace** (*BP 116;* ✎ *230 67 85;* $). The hotel has air-conditioned rooms and suites with separate bathrooms and satellite television, a restaurant and barbecue, and can provide guides for mountain walks, horseriding tours and visits to Foumban and other local sites. Koutaba has a meat and cattle market on Wednesdays.

Foumbot On Sundays and Thursdays the nearby village of Foumbot holds a market known for its pottery, as well as for vegetables, fruit, meat and other foods. Accommodation is available at the basic 16-room **Hôtel de Stade** (*BP 257;* ☏ *344 21 55;* $), which has a bar.

Magba This village northeast of Foumban holds a market on Sundays specialising in fresh and smoked fish.

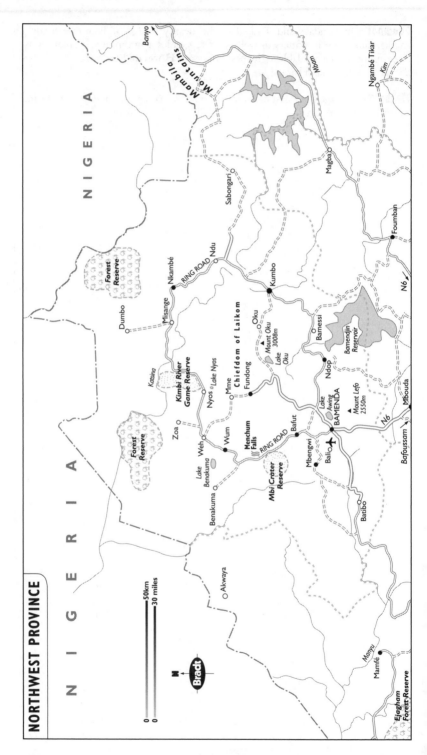

NORTHWEST PROVINCE

9

Northwest Province

This anglophone region has beautiful hilly scenery and enjoys a cool, comfortable climate. As with the West Province, the rich volcanic soils in the area have permitted much higher rural population densities than elsewhere in the country and coffee and cocoa are widely grown here.

Of most interest to travellers is probably the Ring Road, a beautiful red-earthed route which navigates the mountainous Grassfields and various Fulani settlements and Tikar chiefdoms. Bamenda, the capital of the Northwest Province, is a good springboard for this.

BAMENDA *Telephone code: 3336*

Capital of Northwest Province, anglophone Bamenda is about four or five hours by car from Douala along a horribly pot-holed road with lots of speed bumps to further make the journey somewhat resemble a fairground ride. It can be quite a contrast to francophone Bafoussam. This is the heart of the English-speaking opposition movement against the French-speaking dominance within the country, and in recent years there have been various demonstrations and riots, although unrest has calmed down somewhat. An indication of the discord is present in many of the town's streets which have both an official name given by the government and the established name used locally.

Gateway to the Fondom of Bali and Awing Crater Lake, the town, with a population of around 220,000, is located around pretty mountain scenery and has a pleasant climate, being at an altitude of more than 1,000m.

Resplendent in pine and banana trees, Bamenda has a museum and a craft market. Its administrative and commercial sectors are geographically separated by a steep drop.

Climb the snake-like road from Nkwen motor park and at 300m you come to one of the most prestigious neighbourhoods, Upper Station (or Upstation), which has a suburban flavour and contains government offices and much of the best residential property. Far more lively is the downtown area centred around the almost 2km-long Commercial Avenue. Noisy and bustling, here is where all the businesses and shops are, with lots of opportunities to buy local crafts.

For example, such local crafts are available from the market behind the Ideal Park Hotel; the Prescraft Centre, by the British Council Library on Commercial Street; and the Handicraft Cooperative, east of town on the road climbing to Upper Station.

It is possible to hire a helicopter for an air tour of the town. Contact Hellimission (\ *3336 13 89*) for more details.

GETTING THERE AND AWAY Nkwen motor park, at the foot of Upper Station, has transport to Bamessi and Kumbo, while Bali motor park, about 1km southeast of the centre, is for Bali, Batibo and Mamfé. Ntarikon motor park, just northwest of the centre, has vehicles going to Bafut and Wum.

There are numerous *agences de voyage* in Bamenda, especially on the Sonac road and near Hospital Roundabout. Between them they go to a number of destinations including Douala, Yaoundé, Wum, Kumbo, Kumba, Buéa, Bafoussam and Dschang. It's best to ask around.

WHERE TO STAY

Ayaba Hotel (100 rooms) BP 315; Hotel Rd; 3336 13 92/3336 13 56; e ayabahotel@refinedct.net. Located near the Bamenda Handicraft Cooperative Society. Once one of Bamenda's best hotels, it has certainly seen better days. Graded by the government as a 3-star hotel, there is a good restaurant with African & European dishes & Sun lunch buffet, a snack bar, bar, internet access, conference rooms, w/end disco & swimming pool that can be used by non-guests at CFA1,500 per day. Self-contained rooms (with AC installed but which a recent visitor notes did not work in all the ones he & his companions saw), aged, uncomfortable beds, satellite TV & radio. Walk into town rather than pay CFA3,500 for the b/fast buffet, which at the time of writing consisted of boiled egg, croissant, white bread, yoghurt, pineapple & watermelon. $$

International Hotel (40 rooms) BP 124; International St; 3336 25 27. Acceptable spacious en-suite rooms in the centre of town. There is an inexpensive restaurant. $$

Hôtel Mondial (35 rooms) BP 9; off Sonac St & Hotel Rd; 3336 18 32. This good hotel has clean rooms with bathrooms & balconies overlooking town. There is a nightclub, bar, good restaurant & a path in the grounds leading to Upper Station. $$

Ideal Park Hotel (16 rooms) BP 5; off Commercial Av; 3336 11 66. Right in the middle of the market area & therefore lively. Bamenda's oldest hotel, this is very good value, with a bar, nightclub of sorts & good restaurant with very low prices & a bar. Clean, spacious rooms with bathrooms $

Presbyterian Church Centre (20 rooms) Off Longla Rd; 3336 40 70. Signposted 1km north of the centre, has clean but basic rooms: 7 sgls, 5 dbls, 2 with 4 beds & 6 with 3 beds. **Camping** CFA2,000 per tent. Meals & drinks can be provided on request. $

Tip Top Savannah Hotel (55 rooms) BP 227; off the southern end of Commercial Av; 3336 12 76. Simple rooms, some with bathrooms, but noisy. $

Baptist Mission Resthouse (20 rooms) BP 1; at the start of the road leading to Upper Station, near the motor park; 3336 12 85. Clean rooms with shared facilities. $

Holiday Hotel (22 rooms) BP 7; 3336 13 82. Clean rooms, acceptable restaurant. $

Hôtel le Bien (26 rooms) BP 69; 3336 12 06. Basic hotel with a bar & inexpensive restaurant. $

South of Bamenda, at Mbouda, is the **Hôtel le Bamboutos** (*BP 110; 3345 10 55;* $) with 49 basic rooms, a bar and restaurant.

WHERE TO EAT AND DRINK

There are plenty of choices of places to eat in Bamenda, from the numerous roadside stalls and cheap eateries around Commercial Avenue, to better European and African cuisine at the more expensive hotels.

The **Handicraft Cooperative Restaurant** on Station Road, *en route* for Upper Station, offers good snacks, both European and Cameroonian ($). **Gracey's Cafeteria and Restaurant**, next to the Prescraft Centre on Commercial Avenue, has inexpensive European dishes including good omelettes and steak and chips ($). **Mustard Seed**, nearby, has a terrace on the street ($).

Sister Rose An established Bamenda institution which tends to move a lot so ask around for its latest whereabouts. Last seen on Wum Rd it had a choice of fish dishes & huge helpings of chicken with plantains. $$

Lisbon Snack Bar By the Holiday Hotel; 3336 13 82. Offers various grills & pepper soup. A whole chicken for 2 will set you back around CFA5,000. $$

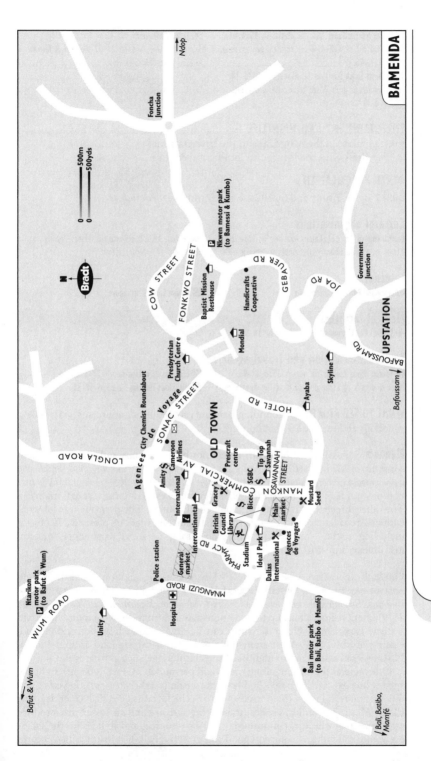

✗ **Dallas International** Quartier Metta; ✆ 3336 41 88. Grilled fish & half & whole chicken, pepper soup, from CFA2,000. $

✗ **St Denis Snack Bar** Cow St, Nkwen; ✆ 3336 14 84. Hamburgers, grills & ice cream. Meals average CFA2,000. $

✗ **Tower Restaurant** 4th Floor, Fru Ndi Bldg, Commercial Av; ✆ 3336 21 02. Western & African cuisine from CFA1,500. $

ENTERTAINMENT AND NIGHTLIFE For nightlife, opt for the bigger hotels, such as the nightclubs at the **Mondial** and the **International**.

The **Roxi Cinema** is just off Commercial Avenue.

OTHER PRACTICALITIES

Banks Bicec, Amity and SGBC are on Commercial Avenue.

Cultural organisations
British Council BP 622; Commercial Av; ✆ 3336 20 11; e bc-bamenda.library@camnet.cm. Library with more than 10,000 publications, videos, facility to show BBC TV, internet access.

Internet
e **Maryland Café** Commercial Av

e **British Council**, as above

Medical facilities
✚ **Mezam Polyclinique** Bali Rd; ✆ 3336 14 32

Tourist information and travel agencies
🛈 **Tourist office** Commercial Av; ✆ 3336 13 95. Maps & details of excursions, such as the Ring Road.

🛈 **ECO Travels & Tourism** ✆ 3336 16 16
🛈 **Highlands Tourism** ✆ 3336 18 35

WHAT TO SEE AND DO Surrounding Bamenda are beautiful mountains, crater lakes, waterfalls and traditional chiefdoms.

Mankom The village of Mankom is just north of Bamenda and has the excellent Museum of Mankom (*BP 1092;* m *7721 9547/7782 5776* e *mankom@museumcam.org; www.museumcam.org; admission CFA2,000 plus CFA2,000 for photography*). This is one of four stunning museums in the highlands of the west and northwest of Cameroon. The other three are at Baham, Bandjoun and Babungo. The permanent exhibition, entitled Arts, Heritage and Culture from the Mankon Kingdom, presents 179 objects including statues, masks, furniture, costumes, personal ornaments, musical instruments and arms.

Pinyin In the village of Pinyin, near Mankom, an organisation called the Pinyin Sustainable Farming System (PISUFAS) (*PO Box 218, Former British College Building, Swamp Quarter, New Food Market, Mankom, Bamenda;* m *7768 4868/7768 4879*) offers visitors a hike up to its demonstration farm to enjoy fabulous views and a rustic experience. Other activities can be arranged, such as horseriding and visiting nearby caves. Apart from these activities at the site and around Pinyin, PISUFAS can assist visits to traditional and cultural sites such as palaces and shrines.

One night at the site including meals and personnel is CFA17,000, hiking at the site for one day is CFA15,000, and both horseriding at the site or visiting caves and other features in Pinyin (on horseback or by vehicle) costs CFA20,000 per day. The PISUFAS project builds, creates, transforms and sustains processes that produce environmentally healthy communities sharing resources and abilities for the socio-economic and cultural common good and growth of all. It initiates joint-ventures and partnership development for projects, products and services that provide income, sustainability and development.

Lake Awing and Bafut-Nguemba Forest Reserve This is easily reached from Bamenda, by driving south on the N6 main road and taking a left turn onto a dirt road after about 18km, just before you reach the town of Santa. A radio mast is on the right just before the turn. If you go by taxi from Bamenda, ask the driver to take you to Lake Awing. Walk from the two metal poles about 3km along the dirt track from the main road. Lake Awing, a peaceful crater lake, surrounded by hills, is another 3km or so.

The reserve, which has been substantially destroyed, is mainly made up of eucalyptus plantations rather than forest and is rich in birdlife.

Mount Lefo Although 2,550m (8,364ft) high, this mountain can be climbéd from Lake Awing in a day, although it is strenuous towards the summit. You are rewarded with fabulous views of various crater lakes and the Bamenda Plateau. The Fon (chieftan) of Awing (several kilometres down the road towards Mbouda) can provide a guide.

Bali Bali, situated amongst stunning scenery 20km west of Bamenda, is one of the principal chiefdoms in the area. It is an ideal day excursion from Bamenda.

Founded in around 1825, it has had numerous conflicts, not least with the neighbouring Bafut chiefdom. Its background is Chamba, which originate in the Adamawa region to the east.

Although the **Fon's Palace** is modern, it can provide information on local excursions. These include a cave containing the skulls of enemies of Bali. The palace can also provide guides and if you are fortunate, you may be able to meet the fon himself. If so, you will be taken to his audience chamber where there are ancient thrones which are beaded all over or decorated with cowrie shells. Stylised handclapping begins, before the fon enters, dressed typically in embroidered robes and a fez-like cap.

The town has a German church built in 1903 and a Prescraft artisan centre, and its craftspeople can be seen working during the week.

Also in the area can be seen Forthung's Tower of Babel, a 70-room building that was never completed.

Bali has an end-of-year three-day festival, the Leya, towards the end of December, though not every year.

Where to stay

🏠 **Bali Safari Lodge** (32 rooms) BP 19; book through the Atlantic Beach Hotel, Limbé, ☏ 3336 23 32. Outside town on the Bamenda road, comfortable en-suite rooms. $$$

🏠 **Mission House** Rooms are bookable at Bamenda's Prescraft Centre (☏ 3336 12 81). $

Batibo Batibo, some 40km from Bamenda, is the unofficial palm wine capital of Cameroon. The villages in the region produce 7,000–10,000 litres of the highly alcoholic drink daily for sale across the country, and there are numerous palm wine markets in the area.

THE BAMENDA HIGHLANDS RING ROAD

The 360km Ring Road passes through some wonderful scenery, the pasturelands of the Grassfields area of west Cameroon. There are terraced fields in the mountains, forests and meadows, with nomadic Fulani herders grazing cattle.

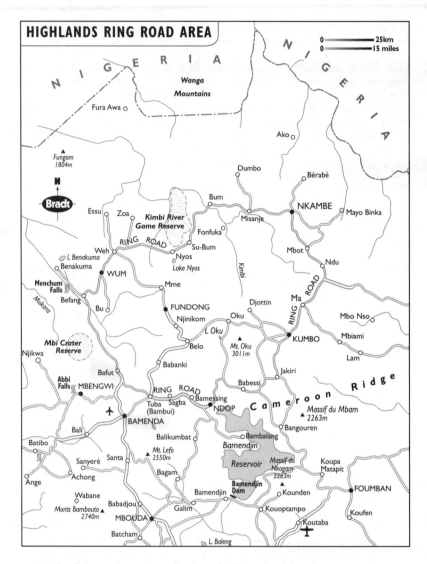

HIGHLANDS RING ROAD AREA

0 ———— 25km
0 ———— 15 miles

NIGERIA

NIGERIA

Wanga Mountains

Fura Awa

Fungom 1804m

N

Bradt

Ako

Dumbo

Bérabé

Bum

Essu   Zoa   Kimbi River Game Reserve   Misanje   NKAMBE   Mayo Binka

Fonfuka

Weh   Su-Bum

L Benakuma   Nyos

Benakuma   Lake Nyos   Mbot   Ndu

WUM   Kimbi

Menchum Falls   Mme

Befang   Djottin   Ma

Bu   FUNDONG   Oku   Mbo Nso

Njinikom   RING   Mbiami

Mbi Crater Reserve   L Oku   KUMBO   Lam

Njikwa   Belo   Mt. Oku 3011m

Babanki   Jakiri

Abbi Falls   Bafut   Babessi   Cameroon   Ridge

MBENGWI   RING   ROAD   Bamessing   Massif du Mbam 2263m

Mukara   Tuba   Sagba   NDOP

(Bambui)   Bangouren

BAMENDA   Bambalang

Bali   Balikumbat   Bamendjin

Batibo   Santa   Reservoir   Massif du Nkogam 2263m   Koupa Matapit

Sanyerè   Mt. Lefo 2550m   FOUMBAN

Ange   Achong   Bagam   Bamendjin Dam

Wabane   Babadjou   Bamendjin   Kounden   Koufen

Monts Bambouto 2740m   Galim   Kouoptampo

MBOUDA   Koutaba

Batcham   L Baleng

Much of the road consists of red-earth dirt track, although some sections are paved. In the region are over 35 volcanic crater lakes, several volcanic mountains, including the 2,900m-high Mount Oku, rolling hills, and waterfalls such as the impressive Menchum Falls.

The Ring Road encompasses many small villages located between the towns of Nkambé, Kumbo, Wum and Bamenda on the road. If time is scarce, there is the option of a shorter route, via Bamenda, Wum, Weh, Fundong, Belo and Bambui. An eventful trip is mentioned in Dervla Murphy's travelogue *Cameroon with Egbert*.

You can reach all the main towns on the routes by public transport, but having access to a car here (ideally a 4x4) is ideal as it allows you to reach many more interesting sites along the way, many of which are off the main road.

The condition of the road varies greatly from season to season and year to year and recently the section between Nkambé and Wum could not be completed by vehicles because of collapsed bridges near Nyos and at Weh (or We), so check locally before setting off, for example at the tourist office in Bamenda.

When the road is in good condition, the longer Ring Road can be done by car comfortably in a couple of days. It's also an ideal route for trekking and, in the dry season, mountain biking, which takes about a week.

All the towns on the two routes have at least simple accommodation, and the region is ideal for camping too, but obtain permission first from the village chief if you are camping in a village compound.

Going clockwise from Bamenda, the first principal place of interest you come to on the route is Bafut, 18km from Bamenda.

BAFUT Telephone code: 3336

This traditional Tikar chiefdom was somewhat put on the map by a 1950s book by naturalist Gerald Durrell, *The Bafut Beagles*. An established 700-year-old kingdom (or *fondom*), the town has a large fon's palace (*admission to the compound CFA1,000, museum admission CFA2,500 , plus CFA1,500 to take photographs or video*), a complex of traditional buildings and courtyards, including houses for the fon's numerous wives and children. The Achum, the palace of the last fon and featuring a striking, characteristic pyramidal thatched roof, is the most sacred of these buildings and cannot be viewed. Traditional dances to the rhythms of drums and other local instruments can be performed at a cost of CFA10,000–15,000 per group, although this is negotiable.

The Fon's wives guide visitors and the tour includes viewing the 'Nighaa Ni Bifh', a huge 300-year-old talking drum used to send messages around the Bafut Fondom, as well as ancient stones where prisoners of war and disloyal subjects were put to death. The palace features carvings of animals, which are special protectors of the fon.

There are various colourful festivals in this region. Richly embroidered robes are usually worn for such ceremonial occasions which include funeral ceremonies (known as 'cry dies') as well as the festivals of the various fons. There is much music and dancing, and visitors are often welcome.

There is an annual grass-cutting festival, featured in *The Bafut Beagles* which entails the village venturing to the grassfields in April to collect bundles of grass for thatching buildings, followed by a feast in the company of the fon. A similar ceremony occurs just before Christmas most years, with four days of costumes and masks, dancing and music.

Bafut also has a market every eight days. One of Durrell's characters, Peter Shu, the King of the Snakes, puts on a show (CFA1,000 plus CFA2,500 for photography) where he handles dangerous snakes such as pythons, vipers, cobras and mambas. It is well worth seeing if he is performing. It is best to telephone him in advance, on ☏ 3336 38 15.

Getting there and away There are regular share taxis to and from Bamenda every day, with more on market day.

Where to stay You can stay in a century-old **guesthouse** which was Gerald Durrell's home when he wrote the book. It overlooks, and is bookable through, the Fon's Palace (m *7796 83 05/3336 38 18*). Simple rooms with shared facilities are CFA4,000 and meals are available.

🏠 **Savannah Botanic Gardens** (9 rooms) BP 2153; ☏ 3336 38 70. 5km out of the town on the Bamenda road, there are rooms with bathrooms (which work intermittently), a good restaurant & camping is permitted. $

MENCHUM FALLS Moving northwards from Bafut on the west side of the Ring Road, the vegetation becomes thicker as the road gets worse. It can become impassable during the rainy season and taking the shorter route (details follow) to reach Wum, via Fundong and Weh, can be a better option.

The dramatic Menchum Falls, around 20km south of Wum and 30km north of Bafut, are away from the road on the west side, so listen out for the crashing sound of the water. The road may be churned up from tyre marks leading to the falls from the road. Beware of the safety rails – people have fallen to their deaths from them.

LAKE BENAKUMA An optional detour is the track road to Benakuma from Belifang, which leads to the crater lake Benakuma.

WUM *Telephone code: 3336*
There is almost no public transport available beyond Wum, located 60km from Bamenda, and the recent collapse of bridges at Weh and Nyos has made moving onto Nkambé along the road – or rutted track, to be more precise – almost impossible, although the present situation may be improved. Hitching a lift in a lorry is not cheap: around CFA45,000 to Nkambé. Wum has a few basic guesthouses.

A couple of miles northwest of the town centre in the hills is Lake Wum, another beautiful crater lake. It is possible to swim in the deep waters, but bear in mind what happened at Lake Nyos (details below) – there is some local as well as international concern about the safety of the crater lakes.

There are several basic guesthouses here.

SHORTENING THE ROUTE Northeast of Wum you have two choices when you get to Weh: either to continue along the main ring road, or take the right turning going south back to Bamenda via Fundong, which constitutes a far shorter round trip. There is little public transport along this route.

After passing the village of Mme, you come to the Chimney Waterfalls at the peaceful, relaxing, friendly town of Fundong. As an optional trek in this hilly area of lush vegetation, a track road here to the village of Lara leads to Mount Oku (2,900m/9,864ft).

At Fundong you can stay at the **Tourist Home Hotel** where simple but clean rooms cost under CFA4,000.

From Fundong this shorter route continues to the Chiefdom of Laikom to the left of the road and then to the village of Belo (or Befo), where there are a few cheap hotels and guesthouses and where you can begin a morning's trek eastwards into the Ijim Forest, heading towards Mount Oku, Lake Oku and the Kilum Forest.

WUM TO NKAMBE: CONTINUING ON THE RING ROAD If you do not deviate from the main ring road at Weh and instead continue east, you come to a collapsed bridge, which, until it is mended, stops you in your tracks unless you are prepared to hike. The region becomes much wilder, with beautiful landscapes and Fulani herders grazing their cattle, and a far thinner population generally.

Lake Nyos Travelling further along the ring road, and around 30km from Weh, you come to Nyos, site of a huge natural tragedy and now a dead village. It holds the dubious world record as the lake with the highest number of deaths, drowning excluded. On 21 August 1986 at Lake Nyos, in the throat of an old volcano in the Oku volcanic field and which is a couple of kilometres south of the village, there was a mysterious natural gas eruption with a massive cloud of suffocating carbon dioxide and other gases expelled by the lake, with such velocity that vegetation and some trees were levelled.

The cloud travelled northeast towards Su-bum, now the only substantial settlement in the area, up to 25km from the site, and an estimated 1,800 people, possibly more, and countless animals lost their lives. Survivors were rehoused in infertile areas in grim concrete two-roomed huts with tin roofs and mudbrick cooking huts. Their sense of being misplaced and forgotten about has been high.

Lake Nyos is one of only three lakes in the world known to be saturated with carbon dioxide. The others are Lake Monoun, also in Cameroon, and Lake Kivu on Rwanda's border with Democratic Republic of Congo.

Scientists disagree about the source of the tragedy. Because the lake lies in the crater of a volcano, some believe that the gas was volcanic in origin. Other scientists believe that the decomposition of organic material at the base of the lake caused gases to naturally build up and temperature changes at the surface of the lake, where there were warm waters, reacted with cold gas-saturated deep waters, triggering the gas to be released. If either of these theories is true, presumably the same thing could happen again at any of the deep lakes in the area. Many locals are suspicious that the catastrophe was caused by Western scientific research. The lake is the subject of ongoing research.

Kimbi River Game Reserve Around 50km along the road from Wum is the Kimbi River Game Reserve. There is very basic accommodation available in the reserve (further details from the Bamenda Tourist Office) and you will need a vehicle to explore – which will be tricky while the bridges are in disrepair.

Misanje – for hiking into Nigeria Another 25km from the Kimbi River Game Reserve along the road eastwards (and 20km from Nkambé) is the village of Misanje with barely acceptable rooms available for under CFA5,000.

From here you can head north for 18km on the track to Dumbo, for a fantastic two-day trek to Bissaula (or Bissuala) in Nigeria. The walk starts with a mild climb, a level section and then a steep descent into Nigeria takes in farmland, forest and rocky escarpments with fantastic views at their summits.

The hike is quite tough and it is also easy to get lost as the footpaths can be very faint in places, and therefore it is a good idea to obtain a guide at Masanje, at Bamenda Tourist Office or failing that at Dumbo, which is also where immigration and customs formalities are processed. Or you could hire a Fulani herdsman in the vicinity.

There is a basic hotel (under CFA5,000) at Dumbo. Nigerian immigration and customs are at Bissaula, which has no accommodation.

NKAMBE *Telephone code: 3336*
This sparsely populated, almost infrastructure-free section of the Grassfields abruptly ends at the town of Nkambé, which has bars and restaurants, medical facilities, a post office, petrol stations and accommodation including the **Divisional Hotel** (✆ *3336 13 24, rooms under CFA5,000*). Here you could try to cadge a lift or take a share taxi for the 35km to Abonshie on the Nigerian border, via Ako.

NKAMBE TO KUMBO The Ring Road continues south towards Kumbo passing the chiefdom of Mbot and its Fon's Palace, very near Ndu. Ndu has guesthouses with basic rooms for under CFA5,000.

At Ndu you have the other option of taking a track road going eastwards to the village of Sabongari, and then the Mambila Mountains into Nigeria.

KUMBO By Grassfields standards, Kumbo (or Banso, being home to the Banso people of the Nso linguistic group) is a large town and has a good range of restaurants, bars, banks and shops, petrol stations and a post office, a cathedral as well as two good hospitals: Banso Baptist Hospital and Shisong Catholic Hospital. It is at an altitude of over 2,000m, giving it a pleasant, cool climate. A large market is regularly held, and one section is devoted to traditional medicine.

Getting there and away Transport is available to Nkambé, Elak (or Oku-Elak or Oku), Bamenda and, except in the rainy season, Foumban.

🏠 Where to stay
🏠 **Fomo '92 Hotel** (18 rooms) BP 46; 📞 3348 16
16. North of the centre with good value clean
rooms with bathrooms. $

What to see and do About 500m east of the town centre is a **cave containing ancient skulls**. Ask around for a guide to show you.

As part of **Nso Cultural Week**, Guinness sponsors an annual horse race at Tobin Stadium, and horses also race through the streets. This is usually held in mid-November. Fulani and Banso riders compete in the exciting competition. Further details are available from the Bamenda Tourist Office or Guinness's headquarters in Kumbo (📞 *348 12 23*).

Kumbo is the seat of a powerful chiefdom, and the **Fon's Palace** can be visited (admission free but donation expected). Colonial times were particularly troubling for the Banso, who resisted the Germans and were defeated by them in 1906, at which time their fon was executed.

Another place worth visiting is the **Musa Heritage Gallery** (Mus'Art) (*PO Box 21;* e *musartgallery@yahoo.com; www.musartgalllery.info.ms*), a museum named in memory of Cameroonian artists Daniel and son John Musa. This started as a family museum preserving the works of the departed artists and later on diversified to cover the arts and crafts of Cameroon's western Grassfields. With a collection of over 400 varied objects mainly from the last three decades of the 20th century, it continues to acquire contemporary Cameroonian art and craft objects and is setting up a music information centre for folk and contemporary music from Cameroon as well as music from other countries.

Oku and Mount Oku From Kumbo you can take a track road heading west that deviates from the Ring Road and leads to the village of Oku (marked Elak on some maps) on the northern slopes of Mount Oku. At 2,900m (9,879ft), Mount Oku is the second-highest mountain in west Africa, after Mount Cameroon.

Oku is the settlement of the Oku Fondom. The Oku have a rich history and are known for their great knowledge of traditional medicines and practice of witchcraft. Each April for a week various spectacles, such as masked dancing, can be seen, held at the Fon's Palace at the far end of town. There is basic accommodation in the village, including rooms at the **Elak Guesthouse**, and the **Touristic Hotel**, by the market.

If you want to climb the mountain or see its lake, take a gift of a bottle of whisky or something similar to the Fon's Palace. The palace can provide a guide, which should cost in the region of CFA4,000 but may be as much as CFA6,000.

Climbing the mountain takes about seven hours as a round trip. The climb is not particularly strenuous or challenging, and passes steep farmland which gives way to a large area of montane and riverine forest before becoming sub-alpine grassland. This forest, the Kilum Forest, adjoins the Ijim Forest, accessible from the smaller ring road at Belo (or Befo). The forest is rich in birdlife, including some Cameroon endemics. The Kilum Mountain Forest Project (✆ 336 32 93) in Elak, run by BirdLife International, can provide more information on these forests.

A trail begins on the opposite side of the road to the project headquarters, starting with farmland (a walk of about 40 minutes) and then the forest, at an altitude of about 2,200m/7,218ft. The trail splits into two branches soon after the school, into the less steep, less challenging KA trail on the right, and the steeper KD trail to the left.

At 2,200m on the western slopes of Mount Oku is the beautiful rich green volcanic crater lake, Lake Oku, which is surrounded by dense forest. Like most of the crater lakes in the region, it is sacred and therefore swimming and fishing are forbidden by locals.

KUMBO TO BAMENDA This region is the most densely populated on the Ring Road. Moving south towards Jakiri and its nearby superb range of hills, there are great views of the Ndop Plains, a bed for the waters of the huge reservoir there, Bamendjing Lake. There is basic accommodation in Jakiri.

From Jakiri you can either continue south towards Foumban or continue on the Ring Road heading west past excellent landscapes, the village of Bamessi (or Bamessing) and the town of Ndop. It is especially beautiful between Ndop and Bambui and well worth visiting if you have not got time to explore the Ring Road.

At Babungo, east of Bamessi and north of Ndop, you can visit the **Museum of Babungo** (*BP 8; Ndop;* e *babungo@museumcam.org; www.museumcam.org; admission CFA2,000 plus CFA2,000 for photography*). This is one of four stunning museums in the highlands of the west and northwest of Cameroon. The other three are at Baham, Bandjoun and Mankon. The museum presents a sample of significant objects from the rich cultural and artistic heritage of Babungo, which was formerly the most important iron-work centre in Cameroon. It includes statues and furniture, musical instruments, masks, costumes and personal adornments.

BAMESSI, SAGBA AND NDOP Bamessi, about 25km east of Bamenda, has an artisans centre and a handicrafts training centre, where craftspeople can be seen at work and items like masks and pottery can be purchased. The village of Sabga can also be visited, 4km west on the Bamenda road, where there is a hill half a kilometre after the village, which is very easy to climb, for views of the surrounding landscapes.

Further west towards Bamenda is Ndop, which has some facilities including filling stations and basic accommodation including the **Green Valley Resort** (✆ *3336 34 00*) with a restaurant and simple rooms for CFA4,000.

At Ndop a branch road leads east to Bambalang, by Bamendjing Lake, otherwise you can complete the Ring Road, returning to Bamenda.

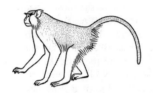

10

Centre Province

Of most interest to the majority of visitors to this province is the lush, climatically pleasant capital, Yaoundé, which has enough distractions alone to warrant a visit.

Virtually no roads penetrate the northern half of this province, and apart from a few exceptions, such as the impressive Nachtigal Falls near Ntui, north of Yaoundé, and the Sanaga Beaches around Monatélé, most people enter this region to reach Yaoundé, *en route* for the chiefdoms and mountains of the west, the beaches of Kribi or Limbé, or, occasionally, the rainforests of the east. Yaoundé is also the departure point for the train to the north of the country, where further spectacular scenery and exotic villages await to be discovered.

YAOUNDE Telephone codes: 2220, 2221, 2222, 2223

Yaoundé, the capital and home of the government, is the political epicentre of Cameroon. Located in the southwestern corner of the country, Yaoundé is about 200km (124 miles) from both the Atlantic Ocean and the southern border.

Yaoundé comes from the word *Ewondo*, the name of the ethnic group that had settled in the region during the German era. Commercial activity started here early in the last century and after World War I the French established Yaoundé as the capital of its new territory, with its British counterpart choosing Buéa as its capital.

Known as the city of seven hills, it expanded onto many other hills some years ago. Sprawled over these undulating hills, Yaoundé lacks a coherent street pattern and most streets are snake-like. It is characterised by a heady mixture of modern architecture and shanty towns.

Being at an altitude of about 700–1,000m (2,000–3,000ft), climatically it is much cooler than one would expect in a city only 5°N of the Equator, and certainly it is far more comfortable than Douala. Its sleepy reputation is gradually being lost with more and more modern buildings sprouting up, especially in the administrative quarter.

Despite being the capital of the country, Yaoundé's population, at around 1.2 million, is considerably behind Douala's. Many visitors see it as a far friendlier, better-kept town than Douala.

One of the first things to strike many people driving from the airport, Nsimalen, is the greenery. Yaoundé, which stretches over an area of about 9km by 6km, is very fertile and large trees abound throughout the city. The attractive range of peaks around the capital, such as Mont Fébé, add to the attraction of the place.

The River Mfoundi runs through the city, but along with the Municipal, Biyemassi and Ngoa-Ekelle city lakes, is suffering somewhat with pollution from metals, household refuse and industrial waste. As a result, aquatic life has dwindled greatly.

For a capital city, Yaoundé does not have a great number of specific attractions geared to the visitor and it is better to simply soak up the atmosphere, people-watching at a café perhaps.

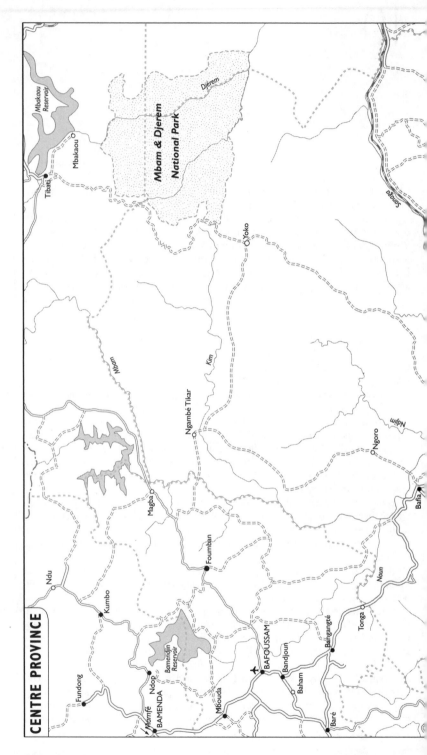

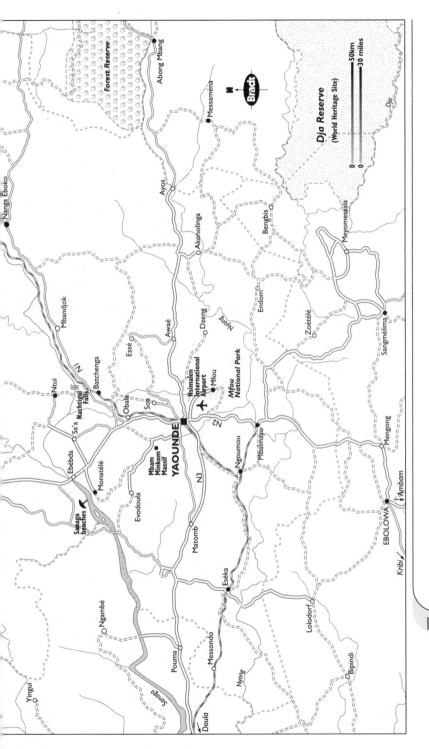

THE CENTRE Yaoundé's centre is focused upon the streets leading from the Place Ahmadou Ahidjo, a square which has a striking 1950s building with a large sloping roof, the Cathedral of Notre Dame. The cathedral is on Avenue Monseigneur Vogt, where a number of banks are located.

Also off the Place Ahmadou Ahidjo, and branching off from Avenue Président Ahidjo, is Avenue John Kennedy, the main commercial corridor with upmarket shops and terraced cafés and an unmistakably French air. At its northern end is another square, the Place Kennedy, upon which is the **Centre d'Artisanat**, containing Cameroonian and regional arts and crafts, which are available to buy.

Also leading off the Place Ahmadou Ahidjo is the Avenue Président Ahidjo and halfway up this is the busy *marché central* (central market), a massive market somewhat resembling a car-boot sale in a multi-storey car park.

QUARTIER DU LAC AND MELEN NEIGHBOURHOODS The tranquil Lake Quarter, roughly to the west of Place Ahidjo between Boulevard du 20 Mai and Yaoundé's polluted and stagnant lake, contains many administrative offices and some interesting examples of modern building design.

MESSA, MOKOLO AND BRIQUETERIE NEIGHBOURHOODS The lively residential districts of Messa, Mokolo and Briqueterie, poor districts northwest of the centre, are hidden away in the hills. They all have numerous unlicensed chicken houses, which serve excellent grilled chicken and Messa has a bustling market, the **Marché Mokolo**, with foods, fabrics and clothes. Briqueterie houses Yaoundé's grand mosque.

BASTOS AND OTHER NEIGHOURHOODS This tranquil neighbourhood in the extreme north of the town has the most exclusive residential properties, top restaurants as well as the president's palace and various embassies. Weekly English-language services are held at the Bastos Presbyterian Church.

Other neighbourhoods include the residential quarters of Nkoldongo, Obili, Biyem Assi and Ngoa-Ekele south of the centre, and Nkolmesseng, Mimboman and Djoungolo to the east. Djoungolo features a temple entirely constructed with stones in 1937 by American William Caldell Johnston.

GETTING THERE AND AWAY

By air The international airport, Nsimalen, is appproximately 19km and a 40-minute drive south of Yaoundé's main square, Place Ahmadou Ahidjo, and is off Ebolowa Road. Taxis vary between around CFA2,000 during the day and CFA3,000 at night.

By train The train station, Gare Voyageurs (*2223 40 03/2223 50 03*) is by Place Elig Essono, which is a kilometre north of Place Ahmadou Ahidjo. The train to Ngaoundéré leaves at around 18.00 each day, and the Douala service at 07.40 and 13.30 daily.

By road Many of the buses/*agences de voyage* are located on Boulevard de l'OCAM, about 3km south of the centre towards Quartier Mvan. Companies change frequently. A ticket to Douala (239km) typically costs from around CFA2,000 to CFA3,000 in a minibus to CFA8,000 to CFA10,000 for a non-stop express service in a first-class bus.

Alliance Voyages Goes to Batouri & Bertoua (CFA6,000, 8hrs).
Jeannot Express Goes to Buéa & Bamenda.

Guaranti Express opposite Nsam Shell petrol station; 2230 28 83; m 7708 41 08. Goes to Douala, Buéa, Bamenda, Limbé & Bafoussam.

Bucca Voyages Goes to Mbalmayo & Ebolowa.
Ocean Voyages Goes to Kribi.
Centrale Voyages BP 2789; south of centre in Rue André Amougou, Mvog-Mbi; ☎ 2230 39 94/2230 39 04/770 19 94. A good 3hr service to Douala, for CFA3,500 or CFA8,000 for a sleek luxury AC bus with waitress service. Central also goes to Bafoussam.

Confort Voyages BP 5029; ☎ 2221 57 16. For Bafoussam & Foumban, departing from *gare routière* d'Etoudi, 5km north of the centre.
Binam Voyages BP 4293; ☎ 2220 93 92. Bafoussam (CFA3,000, 5hrs), again departing from *gare routière* d'Etoudi.

🏠 WHERE TO STAY

🏠 **Yaoundé Hilton** (257 rooms) BP 11852; Bd du 20 Mai; ☎ 2223 36 46; e info_yaoundé@ hilton.com; www.yaoundé.hilton.com. Located in the heart of the Government district & Yaoundé's top hotel, the 5-star Hilton's restaurants, coffee shop & bars (inc a panoramic bar with a good view of downtown Yaoundé) are expensive & the AC rooms on 11 storeys with internet access including 14 suites start at CFA88,000 although may be negotiable. Rooms are clean with modern bathrooms, satellite TV, safe, minibar. A steel band plays in the foyer every afternoon & there's live entertainment on Fri & Sat evenings. There is a health club, 2 floodlit tennis courts & a squash court. Other facilities include car hire, a casino, currency exchange, a business centre, hairdresser, shuttle bus to town, laundry service, internet in the lobby, playground, 24-hr room service, but of course you pay through the nose for all this. For example, a beer is CFA2,000, where you would pay CFA500 in a bar on the street. Credit cards are accepted, which is just as well. A recent visitor reports a coterie of rather clingy prostitutes in the bars. $$$$$
🏠 **Djuega Palace** (72 rooms) BP 2659, Av Narvick; ☎ 2222 64 69/2222 46 46; e sales@djuega.com; www.djeuga.com. This good-value 4-star hotel with attractive décor opened in 2002 & has spacious rooms, 2 restaurants, a pool, gym & spa. Other features include a business centre, a casino & nightclub. Ask for a room on an upper floor for a quieter night. There is a free airport shuttle service & car hire can be arranged. $$$$$
🏠 **Hôtel Mont Fébé** (218 rooms) BP 711; ☎ 2221 40 02. Away from the city centre in the tranquil Presidential Palace district situated on the upper slopes of the Fébé Mountain, this 4-star rated hotel enjoys magnificent views over Yaoundé. However, at the time of writing, the Foreign Office advises caution if venturing to this area because of a spate of muggings, robberies & violent attacks. Once part of the Sofitel chain, the hotel is now owned by the government & standards have dropped significantly. The rooms have satellite TV & phone. Facilities include a faded 18-hole golf course, 2 tennis courts,

a swimming pool (*CFA2,000 to non-residents*), a formal, expensive restaurant, an open-air buffet restaurant by the pool & a snack bar. There is also a bar, casino & 'Le Balafon' nightclub. $$$$$
🏠 **Hotel Azur** (66 rooms) BP 2169; Bastos; ☎ 2221 16 39. A smart 3-star hotel. Restaurant, bar, internet access, secure parking. $$$$
🏠 **Merina Hotel** (98 rooms) BP 14304; Av Président Ahidjo; ☎ 2222 21 31; www.accorhotels.com. A comfortable hotel in the centre of the city with rooms (40 non-smoking) averaging around CFA45,000, a bar, restaurant, terrace, function room, & tennis courts. Built in 2000, it is 1km from the Convention Centre. Offering secure parking, it provides an airport shuttle service. $$$$
🏠 **Hôtel Des Députés** (145 rooms/suites) BP 24; Quartier du Lac; ☎ 2223 15 55; e hotel.deputes@iccnet.cm. This government-rated 3-star hotel is located in the centre of the Government district, away from the centre. Basic but comfortable, rear rooms have a pleasant view over a lake with the Prime Minister's résidence & other exclusive homes in the background. There is a large restaurant, nightclub & lounge bar area. There is a swimming pool & 2 tennis courts, all of which can be used by non-residents for a small fee. The rooms & suites have satellite TV & AC although some equipment may be faulty. Security is good. The mini-suites at CFA40,000 are good value. $$$
🏠 **Laginaque Hotel** (10 rooms) BP 1611; Carrefour Bastos; ☎ 2221 05 54. Just off the main drag, includes comfortable rooms with AC & separate bathroom. No restaurant, but there is room service. $$$
🏠 **El Panaden** (36 rooms) BP 8457; Pl de l'Hôtel de Ville, Rue de l'Indépendance; ☎ 2222 27 65; e elpanaden@yahoo.fr. In the commercial district; there's a garden restaurant (La Terrasse) & the clean rooms have AC, TV & room service, but the en-suite shower rooms can be very basic & do not always have hot water. Most have a balcony. $$$
🏠 **Meumi Palace Hotel** (110 rooms) BP 1225; Bastos; ☎ 2221 16 07/2220 28 37. A 2-star hotel

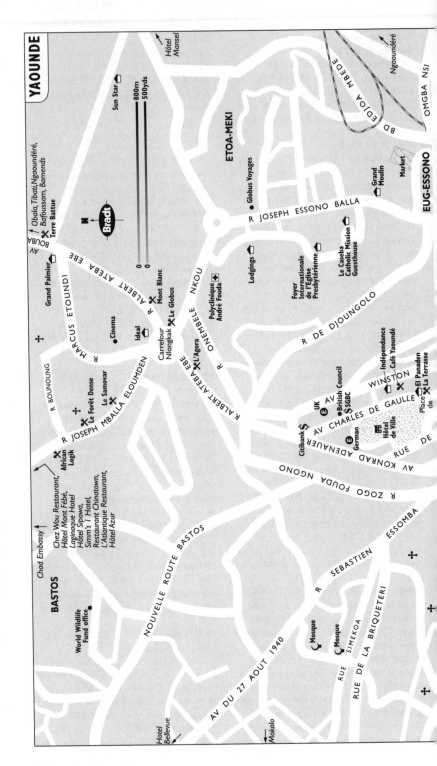

YAOUNDE

Sun Star

↑ Obala, Tibati, Ngaoundéré,
Bafoussam, Bamenda
✗ Terre Battue

AV BOUBA

Grand Palmier

✝

R BOUNOUNG

R MARCUS ETOUNDI

AV ALBERT ATEBA EBE

Hôtel Mansel ↗

800m
500yds

0
0

N Bradt

Mont Blanc
✗ Le Globus

R ALBERT ATEBA EBE

Cinema

Ideal

Carrefour
Nlongkak ✗ L'Agora

R ONEMBELE NKOU

Polyclinique
André Fouda ✚

ETOA-MEKI

● Globus Voyages

R JOSEPH ESSONO BALLA

Grand
Moulin

Market

EUG-ESSONO

OMGBA NSI

Ngaoundéré ↗

BD EDJOA MBEDE

Lodgings

Foyer
Internationale
de l'Eglise
Presbytérienne

Le Caseba
Catholic Mission
Guesthouse

R DE DJOUNGOLO

Le Forêt Dense ●
✗ Le Samovar
✝

R JOSEPH MBALLA ELOUMDEN

✗ African
Logik

Chez Wou Restaurant, ✗
Hôtel Mont Fébé,
Laginaque Hotel
Hôtel Sipowa,
Restaurant Chinatown,
Simm's I Hotel,
L'Atlantique Restaurant,
Hôtel Azur

Chad Embassy ↗

BASTOS

World Wildlife
Fund office ●

NOUVELLE ROUTE BASTOS

R ALBERT ATEBA EBE

Indépendance
Café Yaoundé
WINSTON ✗
El Panaden
✗ La Terrasse
Place
de

UK
⒝ AV British Council
$ SGBC
AV CHARLES DE GAULLE

Citibank $

German ⒝

Hôtel
de Ville

AV KONRAD ADENAUER

RUE DE

R ZOGO FOUDA NGONO

SEBASTIEN

ESSOMBA

✝

R SIMEKOA

Mosque ☾
Mosque ☾

RUE DE LA BRIQUETERI

✝

✝

AV DU 27 AOUT 1940

Hôtel
Bellevue

Mokolo ↓

AV MARCEL MBOU...

Cablys

R MANFORD OTTO FOUDA

R ANTOINE ESOMBA MANY

Nsimalen Airport

R ZE MENDOUGA

R ZE MENDOUGA

MVOG-ADA

Railway station

La Maison Blanche

R JOSEPH

R GRAFFIN

R ABESSOLO

RUE MANY EWONDO

Auberge de la Paix

Freicheur Hôtel, Mvan, southeast

Place Etoa-Meki

AV MVOG-FOUDA ADA

R MENGUE

SOGO

AV MONSEIGNEUR VOGT

SGBC & Crédit Lyonnais

Jolly Voyages

Lodgings

Centre d' Artisanat

Le Challenge

Goethe Institut

Bicec

Crédit Lyonnais

BD DE L'OCAM

Douala

Bus station/Gare Central des Autobus

Prestige

Place Kennedy

AVENUE JOHN KENNEDY

MARIE GOKER

Cathédrale Notre Dame

Place Ahmadou Ahidjo

CHARLES ATANGANA

CHURCHILL

Royal Oxygen

Canadian

AV DE L'INDEPENDANCE

Central post office

Charles Atanaga

Central

Musée Afhemi, Douala

T'Independance

CERCLE

MUNICIPAL

R DE NACHTIGAL

NARVICK

Marché Central

AV PRESIDENT AHIDJO

R DU 20 MAI

Katios

Centre Culturel Français

US Embassy & cultural centre

RUE

DE

FOCH

Le Marseillais

Arizona

BD Hilton

AV DES MINISTERES

Le Capitole (cinema)

AV

L'Abbia (cinema)

Place du 20 Mai

AV DES MINISTERES

Douala, Nigeria

R HENRI DUNANT

Central Hospital

Hôtel Des Députés

Musée National

Monument de la Réunification

BD RUDOLPH MANGA BELL

R PAUL MARTIN SAMBA

Lac Municipal

QUARTIER DU LAC

MELEN

Kribi

BD DE LA REUNIFICATION

169

with rooms with satellite TV. Restaurant, café, internet access, minibus service. Beware, there have recently been negative reports of grimy rooms & broken facilities. $$$

🏠 **Hôtel Sipowa** (78 rooms) 450m northwest of Carrefour Bastos, opposite the Saudi Embassy on the main road in the Bastos neighbourhood; ✆ 2221 95 71; e contact@sipowahotel.com. In a pleasant area, this has friendly staff & clean en-suite rooms with TV & AC; pay more for bigger rooms. Continental b/fast extra. The food in the hotel is acceptable but rather expensive, & a better option would probably be to visit one of the street vendors, restaurants, bars, supermarkets or boulangeries in the nearby Bastos neighbourhood. The hotel is within easy walking distance of the Palais de Congrès, & therefore convenient for conference participants & business travellers. $$

🏠 **Central Hotel** (25 rooms) BP 06; off Rue Jezoiun; ✆ 2222 65 98. A no-frills hotel in the Lake Quarter, ranked by the government as a 3-star. Continental b/fast, included. Better-quality suites with fridge & separate lounge room. There is a good restaurant. Ideal if you have a vehicle, but few taxis visit. $$

🏠 **Hôtel Mansel** (80 rooms & 2 suites) BP 2060; Quartier Fouda; ✆ 2220 73 44/2220 24 62. A government-rated 2-star hotel in a quite noisy location, but the rooms & suites are comfortable & there is a restaurant & bar. $$

🏠 **Royal Hotel** (42 rooms) BP 446; ✆ 2222 44 28. A basic hotel with a restaurant, bar & nightclub. Located in the central business district. $$

🏠 **Hôtel Indépendance** (40 rooms) BP 474; Av Winston Churchill; ✆ 2223 47 71. Now rather faded, the hotel has comfortable rooms with bathrooms, AC & satellite TV. There's a bar & nightclub. $$

🏠 **Cablys Hotel** (28 rooms) BP 6478; ✆ 2222 61 09. A government-rated 2-star hotel in the centre with a bar & restaurant. $$

🏠 **Hôtel Kaelly** (22 rooms) BP 4336; ✆ 2221 90 96. Near the Omnisport sports stadium about a mile northeast of Carrefour Nlongkak, this hotel has a bar & clean rooms with AC. $$

🏠 **Simm's I Hotel** (24 rooms) BP 4293; Carrefour Bastos, off Rue Joseph Mballa Eloumden; ✆ 2220 53 75. Bar, restaurant & clean but faded rooms. $$

🏠 **Hôtel Grand Moulin** (58 rooms/suites/apts) BP 43 36; Rue Joseph Essono Balla; ✆ 2220 68 19. En-suite rooms, suites & apts. There is a restaurant & bar. $$

🏠 **Hôtel Prestige** (32 rooms & 2 apts) BP 2697; Av Charles Atangana; ✆ 2222 60 55/2222 60 39/2231 82 52. Dbl rooms & apts with balconies overlooking the centre of town. Rooms (cash only) have bathrooms, AC, TV & phone. There is a snack bar, bar & restaurant serving both European & Cameroonian dishes. Although in a noisy location it is such good value it is often booked out. $$

🏠 **Freicheur Hotel** (30 rooms) BP 4707; off the Bd de l'OCAM south of the bus station, between Boulangerie Acropole & Mvog-Mbi junction; ✆ 2222 86 05. This centrally located hotel offers great value for money & has friendly staff & a restaurant & rooftop bar offering a good view of the city & Mount Fébé. Clean AC rooms with bathrooms. $$

🏠 **Foyer Internationale de l'Eglise Presbytérienne (the Presbyterian Mission)** (8 rooms) Off Rue Joseph Essono Balla; m 9985 23 76. Reached via the hill behind the 4 big concrete water towers on the hill above Carrefour Nlongkak. This popular, basic, quiet guesthouse has clean rooms & dormitories with beds with shared facilities at CFA3,000, sgls/twins with shared bathroom from CFA5,000 & tents for CFA2,000. There is also a shared kitchen. $

🏠 **Ideal Hôtel** (28 rooms) Rond-point Nlongkak; ✆ 2220 98 52. In a rather noisy – but convenient – neighbourhood; basic rooms with fans, bathrooms & sometimes a balcony. It is behind a 6-storey building. $

🏠 **Hôtel Grand Palmier** (16 rooms) BP 976; Rue Albert Ateba Ebe, Bastos; ✆ 2220 45 93. Has spacious if tatty rooms & a bar. Take a taxi during night-time in this lively neighbourhood, which is north of the centre. $

🏠 **Hôtel Le Faubourg** (41 rooms) BP 1207; ✆ 2222 39 30. A government-rated 1-star hotel with plain rooms, bar & restaurant. $

✖ **WHERE TO EAT AND DRINK** There are lots of cheap restaurants and stalls on the streets selling cheap snacks, especially around Carrefours Nlongkak and Bastos, and on Rue Onembele and Rue Albert Ateba Ebe, and to a lesser extent the Quartier du Lac during working hours. Carrefours Nlongkak and Bastos are also good for a choice of bars. The Mvog-Ada neighbourhood is full of simple fish bars, and fish stalls are also on Place d'Indépendance. Rue Joseph Essono Balla (the main road in Bastos) has a good selection of mid-range and more expensive establishments.

The cheapest cafés and restaurants are outside the centre, notably in the poorer suburbs like Briqueterie and Messa.

✕ **Restaurant Chinatown** Rue Joseph Mballa Eloumden; ☎ 2221 45 14. Another Chinese restaurant in Bastos, but with cheaper fare. Around CFA9,000 per head. $$$

✕ **Le Forêt Dense** Rue Joseph Mballa Eloumden; ☎ 2220 53 08. Exotic Cameroonian dishes generally ranging from CFA5,000 to CFA8,000 & simpler staples like ndole & chicken with plantains. $$$

✕ **L'Agora** Rue Ateba Ebe, off Rond-point Nlongkak; ☎ 2222 35 96. Quite expensive but good Cameroonian food such as ndole, with fish on the menu. $$$

✕ **Terre Battue** Rue Albert Ateba Ebe, off Rte de Obala. Good-value Cameroonian menu & excellent live music. Around CFA5,000 per head. $$$

✕ **Le Samovar** Rue Joseph Mballa Eloumden, Carrefour Bastos, adjacent to Le Forêt Dense & Le Gastrot; ☎ 2222 55 28. Popular with expats; French & Russian meals from about CFA5,000. $$$

✕ **Café Yaoundé** Av Winston Churchill; ☎ 2222 85 94. An Italian-style restaurant resembling a Roman villa, perched on a hillside & surrounded by lush gardens. A live monkey guards the entrance. $$$

✕ **L'Atlantique** Rue Joseph Mballa Eloumden, Bastos, east of Carrefour Bastos; ☎ 2221 43 44. European dishes such as good pizza & grills in a pretty courtyard setting. Meals from CFA4,000 upwards. $$

✕ **La Terrasse** Pl de l'Indépendance, adjacent to El Panaden Hotel; ☎ 2222 12 62. A popular hangout, live music in the evenings. Cameroonian & Italian cuisine with pizzas around CFA3,500. Excellent steak with plantain chips CFA3,000. $$

✕ **Bar Sintra** Av Kennedy. This upmarket brasserie for 'business-types' with mobiles is good for people-watching. There is a French-based menu with dishes like steak, beef in red wine sauce & coq au vin for CFA2,500–5,000, with a '33'/Castel beer CFA400 & CFA700 for a large Guinness. $$

✕ **Chez Wou** Rue Joseph Mballa Eloumden; ☎ 2220 46 79. Good Chinese food from CFA4,000. $$

✕ **Le Challenge Restaurant** Av Kennedy; ☎ 2223 96 60. Going south down the Av de l'Indépendance & turning right you come to this self-service café purporting to be vegetarian; it instead offers many good-value meat & fish dishes such as fricasseed chicken, porc rôti, fish provençale with rice & various stews for CFA2,500–3,500, beers CFA400. $$

✕ **Mont Blanc** Rue Ateba Ebe, off Rond-point Nlongkak. Cameroonian & European cuisine from around CFA2,500 & a good bar. $$

✕ **Le Globus** Rond-point Nlongkak. Meals are not too pricey (CFA2,500) & it's a good place for watching the city with a cold beer in this lively spot from the terrace. $$

✕ **African Logik** Rue Joseph Mballa Eloumden. Great atmosphere, grilled fish, chicken & chips & similar from about CFA2,000, with live music 19.00–22.00 some nights. $$

✕ **La Maison Blanche** Rue Rudolphe Abessolo. Wakes up at night, & a good place for grilled chicken, fish & plantain dishes. From CFA2,000. $$

✕ **Resto Thifany** Rue Joseph Mballa Eloumden, Bastos. B/fast from CFA1,000 & inexpensive European/Cameroonian dishes from around CFA2,000. $$

▭ **Boulangerie Patisserie** Av de l'Indépendance. About halfway down the avenue, this excellent patisserie sells fresh-baked baguettes, pastries & probably one of the best croque-monsieurs you will ever taste. Prices hover around CFA400–600. $

▭ **Boulangerie Calfatas** Rue Nachtigal, opposite American Embassy. Excellent cakes, pastries & croissants. $

✕ **La Marseillais** Av Foch & Rue Nachtigal; ☎ 2223 46 88. Central restaurant with good-value fare. $

♀ **Campero Bar** Corner of John F Kennedy Av. A rather rough & raucous bar with a video blaring in the corner. Lively & popular with the militia – so watch your step. Interestingly, the beer (CFA400 for Castel, CFA700 for Guinness) is served from behind a wire cage. $

ENTERTAINMENT AND NIGHTLIFE Compared with Douala, Yaoundé has a very subdued nightlife scene. The more expensive hotels such as the Hilton and Mont Fébé have discos and nightclubs and some restaurants and cafés also offer live music, and there are a handful of nightclubs and discos. The simple grilled fish bars around Mvog-Ada often feature traditional music and dance. Because of the increased security risk in recent years, use taxis to get about.

☆ **Le Caveau** South of Pl Ahidjo, Pres de la Gare, Mvog-Ada. Pulsating with African or Western music, there is sometimes live bikutsi music, the local speciality.

☆ **Bar Safari** Near Pl de l'Indépendance. Popular with expats, this club, run by a Scotsman, attracts a young crowd & boasts a disco (loud Western music after 23.00), has video screens & a couple of pool tables. A beer is CFA1,500 rising to CFA2,000 after 23.00.
☆ **Katios** Av Président Ahidjo by Rue Goker; ☎ 223 14 91. Expensive but a good, lively nightspot.
☆ **Club Parallel** Rue Ebe. Cameroonian & Western music plus good menu.

☆ **La Paloma** Mvog-Ada. For Assiko traditional dancing.
☆ **Super Paquita** East of Pl Ahidjo, Mvog-Ada Quarter. Dance music & some live bands away from the centre.
☆ **Oxygen** Off Av de l'Indépendance, by Royal Hotel; ☎ 2223 42 80. Disco with both African & Western music, popular with expats.
♀ **Arizona** Bd du 20 Mai, opposite Hilton. Bar with live music.

Cinemas
◾ **L'Abbia** Rue Nachtigal; ☎ 2222 31 66. Mainly shows American films dubbed into French & costs around CFA2,500. It also holds occasional live concerts.

◾ **Le Capitole** Av Foch; ☎ 2222 49 77

Also see *Cultural centres* below.

OTHER PRACTICALITIES
Airfreight
DHL ☎ 2223 13 58

Banks
$ **Amity** Bd du 20 Mai, near the Hilton Hotel
$ **Citibank** Av Charles de Gaulle
$ **Bicec** BP 5; just north of Pl Ahmadou Ahidjo; ☎ 2223 41 30
$ **Crédit Lyonnais** BP 700; near Pl Ahmadou Ahidjo; ☎ 2223 40 05

$ **SGBC** BP 244; Av Charles de Gaulle, by the British Council; ☎ 2223 10 60 (it has an ATM)
$ **SGBC** Av Monseigneur Vogt; ☎ 2223 10 60 (ATM also)
$ **Standard Chartered** Av de l'Indépendance; ☎ 2222 38 80
$ **Union Bank of Cameroon** Pl Ahmadou Ahidjo

Books Place Ahmadou Ahidjo has a number of street stalls selling books.

Cultural centres These have programmes of events like concerts, films, talks, etc.

American Cultural Center Rue Narvick; ☎ 2223 16 33/2223 14 37. Regular exhibitions & library. Americans can also get in touch with a sizeable community of fellow nationals at the American School of Yaoundé in the Quartier du Lac (☎ 2222 9465/2223 0421).
British Council BP 818; Av Charles de Gaulle; ☎ 2221 16 96/2220 31 72; e bc-yaoundé@

britishcouncil.cm. Library, video club, cyber centre, BBC TV showings, English-language teaching.
Centre Culturel Français Av Président Ahidjo; ☎ 2222 09 44. Films are regularly shown in its new auditorium.
Goethe Institut BP 1067; Av Kennedy; ☎ 2221 44 09/2222 35 77

Dentists
Polyclinic André Fouda Rte de Ngousso; ☎ 2222 66 12/2222 93 67

Clinique Dentaire Adventiste Rte de Ngousso, Elig-Essono, near railway; ☎ 2222 11 10. Near the American Embassy & Adventist Church & operated by the Seventh-Day Adventists.

Internet Internet access costs around CFA500 per hour.

🌐 **ADT** Rue de Narvik, Bastos
🌐 **Espresso Hse** Carrefour Bastos
🌐 **Sidenet** Av de l'Indépendance; ☎ 2222 35 74

🌐 **Ureds Cyber Café** Rue 1271, Essos; ☎ 2222 22 76; e ureds@camnet.cm

Medical services

✚ **L'Hôpital Général de Yaoundé** ☎ 2220 11 22/2220 22 44. 24-hr on-call emergency service & has medical & surgical specialists with US & European training although the hospital is underfunded & has inadequate medical supplies.

✚ **Polyclinique André Fouda** Rte de Ngousso, in Elig-Essono, to the southeast of Carrefour Nlongkak; ☎ 2222 66 12/2222 93 67

✚ **Le Médecin Chef du Centre Médico-Social,**

✚ **Coopérant Française** ☎ 2223 01 39/2223 01 37
✚ **Central Hospital** ☎ 2223 40 20/2222 20 86
✚ **Cabinet Medical International** ☎ 2223 98 51
✚ **Polyclinique de la Grace** Rue Nachtigal, near the Abbia Cinema; ☎ 2222 45 23
✚ **Hôpital Jamot** ☎ 2220 43 90
✚ **Fondation Chantal Biya: Centre Mère et Enfant** ☎ 2222 20 00

Pharmacies

✚ **Pharmacie de l'Intendence** 190 Pl J F Kennedy, Centre Ville; ☎ 2222 46 94
✚ **Pharmacie Française** Av J F Kennedy; ☎ 2222 14 76
✚ **Pharmacie Bastos** 1290 Rue Joseph Mballa Elounden, Bastos; ☎ 2220 6555

✚ **Pharmacie des Nations** 437 Rue Albert Ateba Ebe, Nlongkak; ☎ 2220 93 56
✚ **Pharmacie Provinciale** Av Adenauer; ☎ 2220 94 93
✚ **Pharmacie du Soleil** 682 Av El Hadj Amadou Ahidjo, Centre Ville; ☎ 2222 14 23

Post office The main post office is on Place Ahmadou Ahidjo (⊕ 07.30–15.30 Mon–Fri, 07.30–noon Sat/Sun). International telephone and fax, and post restante service.

Schools

American School of Yaoundé BP 7475; ☎ 2223 0421/2222 9465; ℮ school@asoy.org; www.asoy.org. A independent co-educational school offering an educational programme from pre-kindergarten through upper 6th/12th grade for English-speaking students of all nationalities.

Rain Forest International School BP 1299; ☎ 2230 56 21; ℮ webmaster@rfis.org; www.rfis.org. Provides an international secondary education permeated with a Christian world view, using English as the medium of instruction.

Sport and fitness

Golf Club de Yaoundé BP 59; ☎ 2220 75 83. Located at the foot of Mont Fébé, this 18-hole golf course is one of the most spectacular in west Africa. There are sand greens, a practice range, & a clubhouse. Daily & w/end rates are available.

Hôtel Des Députés and the Mount Fébé Hotel both have tennis courts and swimming pools available to non-members.

Supermarkets **Tigre**, Rue Joseph Essono Balla, north of the centre, is the biggest; **Score**, Place Ahmadou Ahidjo; **Niki** has branches in Mvog-Mbi, Nlongkak and Messa.

WHAT TO SEE AND DO

Musée d'Art Camerounais (*Quartier Fébé;* ☎ *2221 49 43;* ⊕ *15.00–18.00 Thu, Sat, Sun & by arrangement; admission free, but donation expected*) The Cameroon Art Museum is near the foot of cool, lush green Mount Fébé, 5km and a CFA2,000 taxi ride from the centre of town. Housed in a Benedictine monastery (which holds a weekly English-language mass) there are steps leading to the museum from the main road that goes to Hôtel Mont Fébé. Although it is small, this is one of the region's best museums and has a very impressive collection, much from the west of the country, including carved wooden panels, ivory, terracotta, bronze and wooden pipes, various masks, bowls and other artefacts, all displayed against a plain white backdrop. The monastery's **chapel**, underneath the main church (*mass 11.00 Sun*), is decorated with an array of local textiles and crafts. There is a guidebook in English and French at the entrance to the museum. Mount Fébé rises to an altitude of 1,000m (3,280ft) and you can wander up for great views of the city.

Musée National (*Av Marchand;* ☎ *2222 23 11;* ✆ *09.00–16.00 Mon–Sat; admission CFA1,000*) Off the Avenue des Ministères and southeast of the lake, in a former ministerial résidence on the road leading to the Yaoundé Central Hospital close to the Ministry of Public Service and National Education. The small National Museum has thrones, masks, sculptures and tools, and has information on a range of aspects of Cameroonian tradition and culture including art and rituals.

Monument de la Réunification (*Bd de la Réunification*) This spiral memorial is in recognition of the uniting of the francophone and anglophone sectors of the country.

Musée Afhemi (*Quartier Nsimeyong;* ☎ *2231 54 16/2231 90 38;* m *994 4656;* ✆ *09.00–20.00 Tues–Fri, 10.00–20.00 Sat/Sun, also by appointment & entrance can be*

THE MBAM MINKOM MASSIF

Colin Workman

Located approximately 40km northwest of Yaoundé is the Mbam Minkom Massif, a region of lowland mountain rainforest. Despite its proximity to the capital, the area, which has a population of around 3,000, is still farmed by the local people in the traditional way: clearing the forest to make an area to grow the staple diet of plantains, bananas and *manioc* (cassava) as well as other crops. The protein element of the diet has primarily been provided through hunting and trapping.

The area has a rich diversity of plant and animal life including many endangered and unique species endemic to the region which have adapted to their mountain environment and which are now in effect trapped, as the area is surrounded by lower, flatter terrain. It is this unique environment which makes the area so interesting for the nature lover; it is also an area of interest to science with a number of studies taking place here, some of which are being funded by the British Foreign Office.

The birdlife is particularly diverse with species such as the grey-necked picathartes (*Picathartes oreas*) a beautiful ground-dwelling bird that is only found in this type of mountainous rainforest, as well as long-crested and Cassin's hawk eagles, African harrier hawks, turacos and parrots to name just a few. The area also has a variety of primate species and the villagers have stated that there are also gorillas in the region.

The mountains are very steep and precipitous with a high point of 1,295m. Although the whole of the area has been allocated to the local people, there is still primary rainforest, as well as secondary forest, farmland and abandoned farms. The crop rotation cycle allows for two or three years of farming, followed by seven years fallow.

The villagers are very interested in using their forest in non-destructive ways with cash crops such as cacao being introduced in a small way, and they are hoping to start a bee-keeping collective and to encourage ecotourism. There is also the possibility of profiting from the medicinal properties of the many unique plants in the area.

Facilities for tourism are limited at present with no accommodation, shops or restaurants. It is, however, possible to camp and buy produce off the locals, but this would need to be negotiated. Walking in the mountains, birdwatching and village life are the main attractions of the area.

combined with lunch if booked in advance; admission CFA3,000) Tours in English also bookable in advance. 6km southeast of the centre of the city, this varied and extensive collection of regional art includes textiles, carvings and pictures.

Mvog-Betsi Zoo *(Mvog-Betsi; ⊕ 09.00–18.00 daily; admission CFA2,000, photography CFA5,00).* Jointly run by MINEF (the Ministry for the Environment and Forests) and CWAF (Cameroon Wildlife Aid Fund: *www.cwaf.org*), a UK-registered charity based at Bristol Zoological Gardens, this once-neglected zoo has been transformed in recent years into an impressive centre concerned with primate protection and conservation and includes animals saved from the bushmeat trade. The zoo is about a kilometre from Melen market and inhabitants include lions, a hyena, snakes, rodents, amphibians and reptiles, birds of prey and other forms of native fauna as well as a collection of primates such as chimpanzees, gorillas, baboons, mandrills, mangabeys, guenons and drills, the last a highly endangered species.

Paroisse de N'Djong Melen Catholic Church *(Quartier N'Djong Melen)* This church holds a fabulous, energetic mass each Sunday from 09.30 to noon. The open-air mass (inside the church during the rainy season) is spoken in Ewondo

For walking trips in the forest it is necessary to arrange a guide (approximately CFA3,000 per day), not only for direction through the forest, but also to ensure that the correct etiquette is kept with the local villagers and their leaders.

A trip to the region is hugely rewarding. To fully appreciate the area and the local community it is essential to speak French if travelling independently as there are currently no English-speakers in the villages.

I travelled with a trip organised through Earthwatch (*www.earthwatch.org*) an environmental charity that originated in the US but also has offices in the UK. They are supporting a project run by the Cameroon Biodiversity Conservation Society (CBCS), investigating the habitat of the grey-necked picathartes and using this as an indicator species for the environment as a whole. I was part of a group of approximately 20 people, four Westerners through Earthwatch, with the others being Cameroonian students, researchers and CBCS support staff.

The project was hugely rewarding and enlightening, with the opportunity to contribute to the environment and giving a real chance to meet, befriend and work with the local people and be a part of their team rather than just a spectator passing through. The CBCS have been working closely with the local people for a number of years and organised transport, guides, provision of water and the accommodation (tents, the campsite was made in a clearing behind the village, with basic facilities: pit toilet, bucket shower, kitchen and a covered communal area).

The time the CBCS have invested in the area made it possible for us to understand the village etiquette, allowing us to have a better interaction with locals. When we arrived there was a welcome from the village chiefs with dancing and drums and before we left the locals put on a banquet of local foods and palm wine.

The local villagers have had very little interaction with Westerners/white people. One of the village leaders was discussing the project with us before we left and he commented how pleased he felt our project had gone, as the villagers had been unsure how to treat us as we were the first to come and stay with them. The only other Westerners coming to the region, which is on average around two per month, tend to be either scientists or diplomats on a day away from Yaoundé.

and blends Western and African cultures. It is popular with tourists as it features drumming, singing and dancing, and everyone dresses up.

LUNA PARK

Two kilometres from Obala, a 45-minute drive from Yaoundé on the N2 Bamenda road, Luna Park is a sort of weekend holiday resort about 30km from Yaoundé. It features a large swimming pool, volleyball court, accommodation in *boukarous*, a restaurant and greenery beside a river. The facilities can be enjoyed for free as long as you eat at the restaurant (around CFA2,500 per meal). Luna Park used to keep monkeys and gorillas, until its animals were confiscated by the International Primate Protection League, In Defense of Animals, Yaoundé Zoo and Limbé Wildlife Centre in recent years due to inadequate care. Chimpanzees and other primates had been chained for many years with insufficient food and water.

MFOU NATIONAL PARK

This park, at Mfou, southeast of Yaoundé, is run by Mvog-Betsi Zoo in Yaoundé (↘ 2220 75 79), MINEF (the Ministry for the Environment and Forests) and CWAF (Cameroon Wildlife Aid Fund: *www.cwaf.org*), a UK-registered charity based at Bristol Zoological Gardens, concerned with primate protection and conservation. The park contains rescued primates such as monkeys and gorillas. For further details, call ↘ 2221 90 44 or m 9969 01 81.

NACHTIGAL FALLS AND NANGA EBOKO

A two-hour drive from Yaoundé on the N2 and then N1 roads leads you to this waterfall on the Sanaga River, northeast of Obala. It is about 20km further on from the small town of Batchenga. Guided tours of the Sanaga tobacco plantation in Batchenga are sometimes possible. Even further east along the N1 is the town of Nanga Eboko which has a crafts centre and basic accommodation in the form of the **Etoile d'Or de Nanga** (under CFA5,000) although sometimes damaged bridges along this route make it impassable.

MBALMAYO *Telephone code: 2228*

The good N2 road south from Yaoundé to Gabon passes forest and coffee and cocoa plantations and after about 40km reaches the humid and hot town of Mbalmayo, a handy base with a good range of shops, a bank, post office, petrol station and a divisional hospital (↘ 2228 15 79).

Founded by the Germans and largely populated by the Ewondo, Mbalmayo stretches along both banks of the River Nyong. Timber extraction is a principal industry here. An excellent view of the town can be seen from the top of Vimli Rock, 7km from the town.

There are regular minibuses and share taxis from Yaoundé to Mbalmayo as well as a service offered by *agence de voyage* Beauty Express. The rail network also has a branch line, although this is a slower option than by road.

Also in this area is the village of Akono, which has one of the few Catholic cathedrals in black francophone Africa.

⌂ WHERE TO STAY
⌂ **Jardin des Tropics** (28 rooms) ↘ 2228 16 10.
En-suite rooms with AC. $$

WHAT TO SEE AND DO One very worthwhile diversion here is the **Centre Art d'Appliqué de Mbalmayo** (*BP 50;* m *9931 29 81/9992 75 08;* e *caambyo@yahoo.fr; www.caambyo.com*). It has some outstanding ceramic art for sale.

From here it is possible also to visit the **Mbalmayo Forest Reserve**, about 10km out of town on the Ebolowa road. **Accommodation** is available at the Ebogo (or Eboko) Tourist Site (CFA5,000–8,000). This eco-tourist destination is situated by the Nyong River and trips can be taken on a *pirogue* from Mbalmayo down the river. Fishing is available; there are a large variety of bird species in the area, and the locality is rich in several varieties of butterfly. There is a simple restaurant on the riverbank and Ebogo village has traditional huts made from local forest materials. The 640km River Nyong is the second-biggest river in the country and noted for its dark appearance which is characteristic of alluvials deposits.

AYOS

If you are heading into East Province, this sleepy village is a convenient, if unexciting, stop-off point in what becomes a very sparsely populated area (the population within a 7km radius from Ayos is only around 600). Ayos is halfway between Yaoundé and Bertoua and around 75km north of the Dja Reserve.

WHERE TO STAY
⌂ **Auberge de Moins Coin** A very basic hotel with intermittent electricity & water supply. $

PRACTICALITIES
Hôpital de District de Ayos (Ayos District Hospital)
BP36; m 7754 53 77

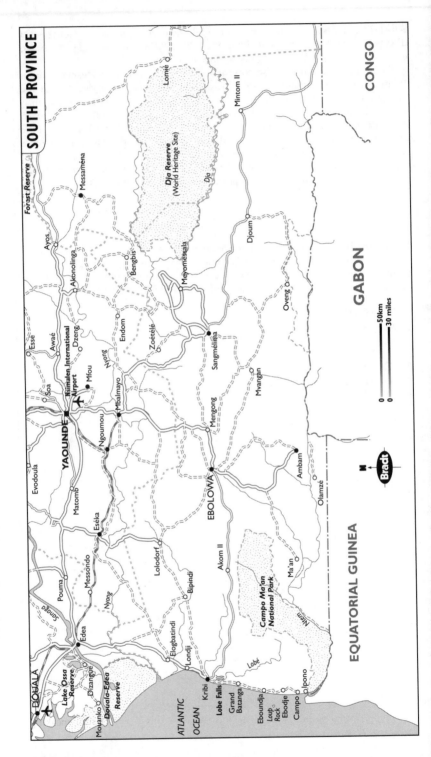

SOUTH PROVINCE

CONGO

GABON

EQUATORIAL GUINEA

ATLANTIC
OCEAN

Forest Reserve

Dja Reserve
(World Heritage Site)

Campo Ma'an
National Park

Douala-Edea
Reserve

Lake Ossa
Reserve

YAOUNDÉ

EBOLOWA

Nsimalen International
Airport

Lobé Falls

DOUALA

Edéa

Sanaga

Nyong

Nyong

Nyong

Dja

Ntem

Lobé

Messaména

Ayos

Akonolinga

Lomié

Dzeng

Awaé

Essé

Soa

Mfou

Ngoumou

Mbalmayo

Bengbis

Endom

Zoétélé

Meyomessala

Djoum

Mintom II

Sangmélima

Mengong

Mvangan

Overg

Ambam

Olamzé

Akom II

Ma'an

Bipindi

Lolodorf

Eséka

Matomb

Evodoula

Messondo

Pouma

Molyanko

Dizangue

MOUANKO

Kribi

Grand
Batanga

Eboundja

Loup
Rock

Ebodjé

Campo

Ipono

Elogbatindi

Londji

178

50km

30 miles

N

Bradt

South Province

This area offers lush vegetation and 'Pygmy' villages nestled in the rainforest, but most visitors come here for the superb beaches.

Along the Atlantic coast, between the fishing village of Londji and the town of Campo on the border of Equatorial Guinea, there is a whole range of spectacular beaches, with Kribi in between, Cameroon's second port and a beach resort surrounded by gorgeous white beaches. It is the first choice for weekenders like government officials and expatriates from Yaoundé and Douala to head for a holiday.

Much of the interior of the south of the country is thick rainforest and the forest in the southwestern section, the Province du Sud, extends into Equatorial Guinea and Gabon. Much of this region, apart from along the coast, has few good roads and very little public transport or tourist facilities and therefore is a challenge to explore.

So-called 'Pygmies', Cameroon's oldest peoples, used to dominate in this region, but now those from the Bantu-language groups like the Bakoko and Batanga dominate, although some 'Pygmies' remain.

THE COAST

KRIBI *Telephone code: 3346*
Its superb beaches – wide, white and sandy and virtually deserted for much of the year – and a good range of accommodation and good road access combine to make Kribi the country's top beach resort. It is a drive of around two hours from Douala and four from Yaoundé.

Kribi is Cameroon's second port (after Douala) although the shallow waters prevent larger vessels from entering the German-built harbour.

Kribi has recently been transformed by the influx of industry and attention brought by the building of a controversial US$3.7 billion, 1,070km Chad–Cameroon oil pipeline to develop landlocked Chad's southern oilfields. This ends up at Kribi despite pressure from environmental groups who say that the project threatens the Pygmy and other populations along the pipeline route.

The environmentalists also believe that construction of the pipeline has worsened deforestation and risks spillage and other damage to plants and animals. Indeed, in January 2007, with the pipeline in full operation, the World Bank was in discussions with the Cameroon Oil Transportation Company, operator of the pipeline in Cameroon, because of an accidental oil spill at the marine terminal that month.

To make things worse, ExxonMobil, which constructed the pipeline, has admitted building stretches of the pipeline across three archaeological sites rather than bypassing them.

The name Kribi is derived from the word *kiridi*, which translates as 'small men', the 'Pygmies' who were the original inhabitants of this region. Bantu-speaking groups are the main inhabitants of Kribi today.

An attractive town though no longer the quiet backwater it once was, Kribi is located at the southernmost bridge over the Sanaga River, 177km from Douala and 112km from Edea. Kribi has numerous hotels, shops, a bank, hospital, a post office and a market.

Among Kribi's low-key sights are a colonial cathedral upon the nearby hillside and some German administrative buildings along the northern beachfront. But Kribi's principal attraction is the gorgeous palm-fringed white beaches, a dramatic contrast to the volcanic, sometimes rocky, black ones of Limbé.

During the day the locals on the beach are very friendly and may offer to catch you fish and shrimps, scale the trees for coconuts and avocados or let you try out their dugout canoes they make on the beach. They often prefer to be paid in cigarettes rather than hard currency.

Check locally before swimming as currents can sometimes be strong, there may be an undertow and riptide. Also, don't walk along the beaches alone, especially at night. Kribi is best avoided during the heavy rains, from around June to mid-November, and is best from mid-November to February.

Getting there and away From Douala, the journey time on the relatively new, well-surfaced road is under three hours. The quickest route from Yaoundé is via Edea, but you can also go on tracks through the forests, passing the odd waterfall and 'Pygmy' villages, at least in the dry season. If you take this far slower option, head for Ebolowa and then for Lolodorf and Bipindi, or Akom II.

The *agences de voyage* have offices on or near Rue du Marché in the centre, which is also where the main *gare routière* is, where non-agency vehicles and share taxis depart from.

Central Voyages and La Kribienne go regularly each day to and from Yaoundé (CFA3,500) and Douala (CFA2,300) in under three hours. Other operators include Bon Pied la Route, Syd Voyage to Ebolowa and Transcam, which goes to Campo (CFA1,500).

Where to stay There is a good range of hotels in Kribi, but they tend to fill up quickly on weekends during the dry season months, especially in December and January. It is becoming possible to stay at people's homes, so ask around. Camping on campsites along the beach is popular, although it is increasingly not considered safe anymore, unfortunately.

🏠 **Hotel Ilomba** (40 rooms) BP 305; Quartier Bwambe; m 9991 29 23. Currently the most popular hotel in Kribi. A very comfortable, secure hotel accessed down a dirt track overlooking a gorgeous beach, & with a good restaurant. The Swiss owner speaks both English & French. High-standard rooms. $$$

🏠 **Palm Beach Plus Hotel** (70 rooms) BP 351; Rte de Campo; ☎ 3346 14 47; e hotelpb@iccnet.cm; www.hotelpalmbeachplus.net. On a paved side road off the road going to Campo, this 3-star hotel has a good bar & restaurant & comfortable rooms including 5 suites by the sea. $$$

🏠 **Résidence Jully** (40 rooms, 3 suites, 2 apts) BP 195; north of the centre by the beach about 3km off the Douala road; ☎ 3346 19 62. This 3-star hotel has very good-quality rooms, suites & apts with bathroom, TV & AC & a popular beachfront restaurant. $$$

🏠 **Hôtel Coco Beach** (20 rooms) Just southwest of the bridge on the beach; ☎ 3346 15 84. This small, popular, long-established hotel with a good restaurant has a few very good AC rooms. $$$

🏠 **Hôtel de l'Océan** (18 rooms) Near Hotel Coco Beach; ☎ 3346 16 35; m 9990 0169. This beachside hotel with a good restaurant has chalet rooms. $$$

🏠 **Hôtel Le Paradis** (53 rooms/suites/apts) BP 232; signposted north of the centre; ☎ 3346 19 93; e hotelleparadis-kribi@yahoo.com. This hotel opened in 2001 & has comfortable rooms, suites & apts with en-suite facilities, AC, phone & satellite TV plus a good restaurant specialising in seafood (*dishes average CFA5,000*), a bar, BBQ & swimming pool.

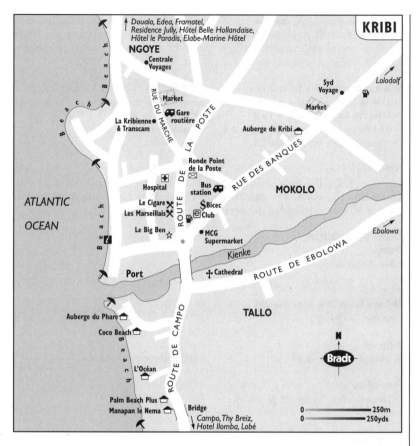

Douala, Edea, Framotel,
Residence Jully, Hôtel Belle Hollandaise,
Hôtel le Paradis, Elabe-Marine Hôtel

NGOYE

Centrale
Voyages

Syd
Voyage

Lolodolf

RUE DU MARCHE

Market

Gare
routière

La Kribienne
& Transcam

Market

ROUTE DE LA POSTE

Auberge de Kribi

Beach

Ronde Point
de la Poste

RUE DES BANQUES

ATLANTIC

OCEAN

Hospital

Bus
station

MOKOLO

Le Cigare
Les Marseillais

Bicec
Club

Le Big Ben

ROUTE DE CAMPO

MCG
Supermarket

Ebolowa

Kienke

Port

Cathedral

ROUTE DE EBOLOWA

TALLO

Auberge du Phare

Beach

N

Coco Beach

Bradt

L'Océan

Palm Beach Plus

Manapan le Nema

Bridge

Campo, Thy Breiz,
Hotel Ilomba, Lobé

0 ———————— 250m
0 ———————— 250yds

Just 100ft from the ocean, it has pleasant gardens.
$$$

🏠 **Elabé-Marine Hotel** (10 rooms) North of the city
beside the Résidence Jully; m 9990 77 84.
Relaxing, unpretentious beachside hotel with excellent
restaurant. $$$

🏠 **Les Polygones d'Alice** (17 rooms) BP 97; Rte de
Campo; ✆ 3346 15 64. This 3-star hotel has
comfortable rooms with en-suite bathroom & satellite
TV, a bar & restaurant. $$$

🏠 **Hôtel Belle Hollandaise** (48 rooms) BP 128,
Kribi; ✆ 3346 17 13. Large AC rooms with satellite
TV, a large pool, garden, nightclub, mini golf & jet-
ski hire. $$$

🏠 **Framotel** (24 rooms) BP 355; off Edea Rd;
✆ 3346 16 40. North of the centre, this
government-rated 3-star hotel has a restaurant, bar,

pool, playground, gardens & a private beach nearby.
$$

🏠 **Auberge du Phare** (40 rooms) BP 319; south of
the cathedral off Rte de Campo; ✆ 3346 11 06;
m 7564 04 64. With a pleasant setting overlooking
the ocean; there is a good restaurant & good-value
rooms with bathrooms & with or without AC. $$

🏠 **Auberge Tara Plage** (10 rooms) BP 103; some
3km south of the centre, signposted & 500m off the
main road; ✆ 3346 20 83/3346 20 38. On the
beach, it is in an attractive setting, has a restaurant
& AC en-suite rooms. **Camping** is CFA3,000 per tent.
$$

🏠 **Auberge de Kribi** (12 rooms) BP 355; Lolodorf
Rd; ✆ 3346 15 41. This is about 500m east of the
gare routière & has simple but good-value rooms
with fans & shared facilities for around CFA5,000. $

✗ **Where to eat and drink** A rather expensive but very attractive option for dining
is at the beachfront restaurants, which, unsurprisingly, specialise in seafood. The
hotels by the beach have restaurants, which tend to get busy at weekends. A much

cheaper (around CFA1,000) yet excellent option is to visit the food stalls selling freshly grilled and barbecued fish, such as at Carrefour Kingue and on the beach south of the Hotel Framotel Grill, prepared by a group of women in daylight hours. Cheaper restaurants are near the market on the Rue du Marché.

✕ **Restaurant les Marseillais** Rte de la Poste; ☎ 3346 18 63. Good seafood at a price. $$$$
✕ **Le Forestier Restaurant** At Hôtel Le Paradis; ☎ 3346 19 93. Well-rated hotel restaurant signposted north of the centre, with dishes from about CFA5,000. $$$

✕ **Fleur Marine** ☎ 3346 20 11. French seafood restaurant near the school. $$
✕ **Le Cigare** Rte de Poste; ☎ 3346 19 28. Good seafood menu. $$

Nightlife There are various late bars and nightclubs including the most established, **Le Big Ben** on the roundabout near the bridge (☎ *3346 19 28*), **Geraldine** (☎ *3346 82 29*), and the **Palm Beach Plus Hotel's upmarket club** playing African and Western sounds (see page 180 for contact details).

Other practicalities
Bank
$ **Bicec** Lolodorf Rd

Hospital
✚ **Central Hospital** West of the post office roundabout; ☎ 3346 11 31

Internet
🖥 **Cyber@ljo** Rte de la Poste

🖥 **Club Internet** Rue des Banques

Post office
✉ **Route de la Poste** Southwest of the post office roundabout

Supermarket
MCG Supermarket Rue des Banques

Tourist information
Tourist office ☎ 3346 10 80

THE COAST NORTH OF KRIBI

Beautiful white-sand beaches extend as far as the small fishing village of Londji, which is 24km north of Kribi on the way to Edea. It is a particularly picturesque section of coastline and passes Mpalla village, and after 15km Cocotier Plage, a very attractive beach with very basic accommodation available. There is also quite a good beach 12km from Kribi, at Costa Blanca.

LONDJI *Telephone code: 3346*
Londji is quite a sleepy, relaxing, but rather isolated place; it's a 24km taxi ride from Kribi (about CFA3,000) and share taxis also visit during the day.

Londji's beach is spread around a huge coconut tree and palm-fringed bay with calm waters. It tends to get an influx of expats at weekends but is very quiet during the week.

The village fishermen take their canoes out on the bay after midnight and may take you for a small charge.

If your budget doesn't stretch to the seafood restaurant at the Auberge Jardinère, grilled fish and rice and similar dishes are available in the village, and there are one or two basic bars.

Where to stay

🏠 **Auberge Jardinière** (12 rooms) BP 250; ☎ 3346 11 27; m 9991 72 69. On the beach, this is the most comfortable accommodation option for around CFA10,000. $$

There are also *boukarous* on the beach at around CFA5,000, and **camping** on the beach is possible, with a small fee payable to the village chief.

ELOGBATINDI Continuing along the main road to Douala, away from the coast you come to the village of Elogbatindi, which has a number of 'Pygmy' camps.

THE COAST SOUTH OF KRIBI

Further beautiful white beaches extend as far as the town of Campo by the border with Equatorial Guinea.

LOBE FALLS About 7km south of Kribi, just before reaching the village of Grand Batanga, are the signposted Lobé Falls (Chutes de la Lobé), one of only a few waterfalls in the world that fall directly into the sea. The River Lobé empties its waters into the ocean through a series of waterfalls more than 30m high, the force of the rapids producing a brown foam in the bay.

The nearby beaches are clean and good for swimming but the area is a bit touristy. Grilled-fish dishes are available at a small restaurant at the foot of the falls. There may be guides for hiking around the falls available and you may be offered a half-day canoe trip (about CFA2,500 per hour) up the river to see 'Pygmy' villages. The villages are unconvincing but the boat trip is worthwhile.

A taxi from Kribi is around CFA2,000 but it is a good idea to pay extra for the driver to wait, as transport back to Kribi can be very infrequent.

An ideal place to stay is the **Hotel Ilomba**, listed in the Kribi accommodation section (see page 180) and located about 500m from the falls in an idyllic beachside setting.

GRAND BATANGA AND EBOUNDJA The village of Grand Batanga is 12km south of Kribi and has a good restaurant about 1km south of the centre, **Auberge Mimado** (m *9997 79 17*), although no accommodation as yet. There are also good, deserted beaches around the village.

Another 8km south is the fishing village of Eboundja where you can **camp** on the beach. It is virtually an expat-free zone and has no tourist infrastructure. It is ideal for chilling out with some grilled fish, a beer or palm wine with the locals.

LOUP ROCK A few kilometres further south reveals Loup Rock (Rocher du Loup), a supposedly wolf-like, dramatic rocky land formation rising from the ocean.

EBODJE Ebodje is another fishing village situated on the Atlantic shore before reaching Campo. Daily minibuses stop *en route* for Campo and Kribi. The beaches around here are beautiful, and sea turtles usually come to the beaches from November–January to lay eggs. Excursions by canoe to the sea or the Likodo River are offered locally.

Ebodje was recently chosen as a site for the protection of sea turtles by a very effective regional project organised jointly by the Cameroonian government and the Netherlands Development Organisation (SNV).

11

Andrew Pape-Salmon

Campo-Ma'an National Park and the surrounding region provide a glimpse of the African wilds within easy access of Kribi. The park appears to offer something for all visitors, regardless of their adventure quotient: ranging from day trips to the three 'Chutes de Menve ele' outside of the eastern boundary of the park, to multi-day adventures hiking within the park and seeing a unique ecosystem with significant biodiversity.

Be warned that it is a relatively new tourist destination and there are still some bugs to iron out – all the more reason for the adventurous types to go now.

The hilly national park has several ecological zones with varied tree species including some rare ones, over 100 elephants, some large primates, lots of other mammals (we saw boars and white-nose monkeys), and numerous exotic birds. Its southern border is marked by the powerful Ntem River, which forms a biologically rich (and fish- and shrimp-filled) estuary at Campo entering into the Atlantic Ocean. The southwest corner of the park between the Ntem and Bongola rivers is fabled to have an old German settlement that has not yet been 'discovered'.

Ebodje is a gorgeous community on the road between Kribi and Campo that has declared itself as an 'eco-tourism' village. You can easily spend three days there and enjoy a number of their organised activities through arrangements with the tourism office, currently managed by Alain Ngomi. In our one day in the community, arriving from Campo by boat, we enjoyed a traditional couscous (*fufu*) and peanut sauce lunch at Marie's clean beachside facilities (which includes lodging for CFA2,000 per night) and had a guided tour of the village to learn about its culture and history. The community was one of the most relaxing we experienced on our trip – and yet it was also stimulating to learn about how things work in rural Cameroon.

Ebojde is famous for its sea turtles which appear at night to lay their eggs. Tobie Mediko is managing the turtle project which includes viewing opportunities at night,

The co-ordinator of the project based at WWF's Yaoundé office (☏ *2221 62 67/2221 70 83/2221 70 84*) can provide further information.

Accommodation is available in local homes for a nominal fee, and meals are CFA2,000.

CAMPO You are likely to come across customs and immigration checks at the border town of Campo which has a large beach extending to the mouth of the Ntem River, the border with Equatorial Guinea.

Campo-Ma'an National Park (⊕ *08.00–18.00 daily*) Campo is home to this 2,640km² reserve, the Parc National de Campo Ma'an, consisting of dense unmanaged rainforest of extremely rich biodiversity.

The park contains more than 1,500 species of plants and over 300 species of birds and a variety of rainforest vegetation including coastal forest and sub-mountainous forest at an altitude of up to 800m.

It contains a wide range of wildlife including buffalo, lion, leopard, hippo, mandrill, gorilla and forest elephants. There are more than 70 monkey species including the red-capped mangabey, as well as pangolin, duiker and python. In the Ntem River region there are crocodiles and sea turtles.

The park is not particularly geared to visitors – there is only very basic accommodation and no public transport to it – but the infrastructure is slowly being improved, and a track road cuts eastwards through the reserve from Campo to Ma'an, passing near to the Menve (or Menve ele) Falls halfway.

tagging, and sponsorship opportunities. The tourism office can arrange a cultural evening, hikes in the forest, and *pirogue* trips up the Likido River.

We began our trip by making contact with the co-ordinator of the Campo-Ma'an Project at WWF's Yaoundé office. Their approach to wilderness conservation is to facilitate a source of income for nearby populations through tourism – essentially converting (poacher) hunters into wilderness guides and creating economies around the lodging, feeding and entertaining of visitors. WWF also works co-operatively with neighbouring communities, forestry companies that harvest trees outside of the park and maintain the road within the park, and the agricultural operations (palm oil) on the west side of the park.

In 2004, WWF is constructing facilities for researchers, tourists and dignitaries near Chutes de Menve ele, including lodging. WWF is also mapping the whole region. They can put visitors in touch with reliable guides in the area.

Although we were limited to one day in the park, we learned a lot from our guide named 'Innocent' who lives in the community of Nko'élon west of the park. We stayed at the WWF/MINEF house for a week on Campo Beach (facing Equitorial Guinea) and enjoyed many evening conversations with the WWF co-ordinator, Bertin Tchikangwa Nkanje, and the Park Ranger (Conservateur), Djogo Toumouksala, during our stay. They share an office in front of the power plant, about 1km east of the centre of Campo town. You can telephone the ranger if you have no luck with WWF (m 9955 01 03/7745 41 69; ℡ 3346 12 84).

You can contact Ebojde through their Kribi agent (m 9977 32 36/9959 10 16). The government of the Netherlands helped establish these operations through the 'Project Campo Man'an' initiative that was wound down in late 2002.

For me, the best things about Kribi include eating fresh barbecued fish on the beach; staying and eating at the beachside Elabé-Marine Hotel; heading downtown on Saturday night for some electric guitar in classic Cameroon style with mysterious Bassa dancers providing a visual spectacle; and walking for many kilometres along the beach.

The forestry office (*poste forestier*) in Campo and Kribi's tourist office can both help with providing an obligatory guide (CFA3,000) and the location of tracks in the forest. There is a CFA5,000 entry fee, payable to the forestry office in Campo. Obtain a receipt to show at the entrance.

At the entrance to the park, the village of Nko'elon has guides who can take you to caves containing bats as well as on a variety of forest walks.

Accommodation in Campo consists of the **Auberge Bon Course** (basic clean rooms for CFA5,000), at Bon Course supermarket at the main road junction. Daily minibuses go to and from Kribi to Campo.

IPONO Another 10km south of Campo, at this small village you can take a *pirogue* the 10km journey up the Ntem River to Yengue in Equatorial Guinea where you get your passport stamped. A track leads to the road to the town of Bata. In Ipono there is simple accommodation for under CFA5,000.

THE INTERIOR

GETTING TO KRIBI VIA LOLODORF
If you are going the long, slow way from Yaoundé to Kribi, 75km on from Ebolowa, you reach Lolodorf (the name, 'Lolo's village', originates from the German phase of Cameroon's history) where there is some basic accommodation. The 120km stretch from here to Kribi is slow, due to the condition of the forest tracks, which pass various 'Pygmy' villages. At the village of Bidjoka, 35km on, just to the east are the Bidjoka Falls and a further

10km is the village of Bipindi, which has a rudimentary clinic as well as more 'Pygmy' encampments.

EBOLOWA *Telephone code: 2228*
Ebolowa is the provincial capital, with a population of around 50,000, mainly made up of the Bulu peoples. Located in a valley surrounded by lush green hills, the town is 170km from Yaoundé and 120km from both Mbalmayo and Sangmélima.

It has an artificial lake and few specific attractions (other than, of all things, a dentist's chair used by Albert Schweitzer at the Hôpital Enongal) but facilities that include a bank, shops, supermarket, large market and a post office. It boasts two hospitals, the Provincial Hospital (\ *2228 32 20/228 33 33*) as well as the Enongal (\ *2228 33 23*). It is a cocoa-producing town and most of the population works in this sector.

Getting there and away The main *gare routière* has regular share taxis to Yaoundé, approximately a three-hour journey, and some to Kribi, depending on the state of the roads. There are also *agences de voyage* on the road to Yaoundé, including Buca Voyages and Jet Voyages.

Transport for Ebibiyin (Equatorial Guinea) and Bitam (Gabon) is available from Ambam, further south on the N2, which on the map looks like a primary road but soon becomes unsurfaced when you leave Ebolowa. The visa for Equatorial Guinea is currently CFA36,000 and for Gabon is CFA37,000.

Where to stay
Hôtel Le Ranch (25 rooms) BP 690; \ 2228 40 37/2228 35 32. By Mount Ebolowa, just southwest of the centre, this government-graded 2-star hotel has clean rooms with bathrooms. There is a bar & restaurant. $$

Hôtel Porte Jaune (36 rooms) BP 817; \ 2228 39 29. One of Ebolowa's better hotels. Rooms have bathrooms & either AC or a fan. $$

Mvila Hotel (16 rooms) BP 896; \ 2228 43 34; m 943 91 72. This acceptable but basic hotel has suites with AC. $

Hôtel Ane Rouge (20 rooms) BP 315; \ 2228 34 38. Near the main roundabout in town, this has simple, clean shared & self-contained rooms. $

What to see Ten kilometres east of the town is a natural tunnel, known as Phantoms Cave or Mbil Bekon ('hole of ghosts'), and 40km south on the road to Ambam are the magnificent Ako'akas Rocks.

SANGMELINA *Telephone code: 2228*
Sangmélima is southeast of Mbalmayo (Mbalmayo is covered in *Chapter 10, Centre Province*, page 176) on the N9 branch road. It has a hospital, bank, petrol stations and a post office. Sangmélima is a good base if you are tackling a visit of the rather remote East Province.

Where to stay
Jardin des Tropiques BP 537; Rte de Mbalmayo; \ 2228 86 91. *Boukarous* right next to the rainforest. $$

Hôtel Afamba BP 423; \ 2228 84 27. Quite comfortable rooms with AC. $$

Hôtel Bel Air (18 rooms) BP 499; \ 2228 81 42. A bar/restaurant & basic en-suite rooms. $

Hôtel Kono Refuge BP 654; Ndonkol; \ 2223 09 43. Restaurant, small gym & AC rooms, 35km from Sangmélima. $

AMBAM Thick forest gives way to this transit town with basic accommodation at several auberges and Hôtel La Couronne. To reach it take the track next to the Police and Affaires Sociales office and continue bearing left.

Getting there and away The motor park opposite the post office has share taxis to Equatorial Guinea, which go via a ferry over the Ntem River and stop just before the border town of Ebebiyin. To reach Gabon, share taxis depart from the market in the town, stopping for the market on Saturdays at Aban Minkoo.

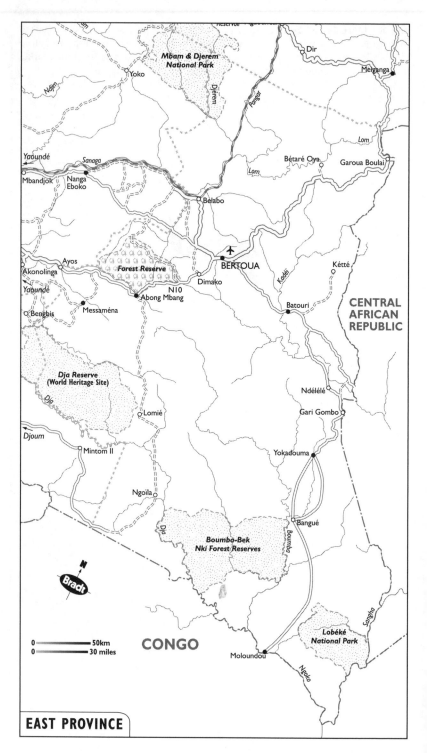

12

East Province

The eastern region of southern Cameroon is part of the central African belt of rainforest, the Congo Basin, which constitutes the largest stretch of unbroken forest in the world after the Amazon. This region has vast forests that continue into the Central African Republic, Gabon, Republic of Congo and Equatorial Guinea.

This area has changed dramatically in recent years due to poaching, metal/mineral prospecting and widespread, almost unrestricted logging, yet much is still untouched wilderness with extensive populations of wildlife including forest elephants, gorillas and chimpanzees and an unparalleled biodiversity that remains largely unexplored. One-hundred-foot mahogany trees sit side by side with Baka 'Pygmies' still maintaining their traditional lifestyle.

EXPLORING THE REGION

This is the most difficult area of Cameroon to explore. There is a poor road network (the logging companies 'maintain' many of the roads that head east from Yaoundé and these are often damaged by their heavy trucks) and there is a considerable lack of facilities, but if you are adventurous and have the time and determination there is much to experience in the rainforest.

At the time of publication the Foreign Office advises against all travel around the area bordering the Central African Republic because armed banditry is common there. Check the security situation locally if you plan to head near the border.

BERTOUA *Telephone code: 2224*

Bertoua, the capital of East Province and 338km east of Yaoundé, borders savanna and rainforest. Logging and other commercial activities have caused the population to rapidly grow to over 100,000, bringing a wide range of facilities so that it now has numerous hotels, cafés, bars and restaurants, shops, a post office, hospital (✆ 2224 18 29), bank, cinema and airstrip.

Botanists may note that the town of Nguelemendouka, southwest of Bertoua, is notable for having a two-headed palm tree.

GETTING THERE AND AWAY Bertoua is reached via the N1 road following the railway track and Sanaga River (where one can view the Nachtigal Falls on the Sanaga, about 20km further on from the small town of Batchenga) via Nanga Eboko (which has a crafts centre and basic accommodation in the form of the **Etoile d'Or de Nanga**, under CFA4,000) although sometimes damaged bridges and road surfaces along this route can make it impassable. An alternative route follows the Nyong River taking the N10 road via Abong Mbang, and which is surfaced as far as Ayos in Central Province, 150km from Yaoundé. Abong Mbang has several examples of architecture of the German period, including a fortress, now the central prison.

About 18km south of Abong Mbang are the caves of Ntimbe: ask around Abong Mbang for a guide if you want to see them. The route also passes through the town of Doume, which was previously the capital of the eastern sector. It contains some interesting colonial buildings including a fortress built during the German period.

Transport for most destinations is available from the main *gare routière* in the centre of Bertoua near the market. There are *agences de voyage* for destinations that include Yaoundé (CFA5,000, around eight hours), Garoua-Boulai, Batouri, and Belabo (the last for joining the Yaoundé–Ngaoundéré train). By road Ngaoundéré typically costs CFA8,000 and takes around 12 hours.

Cameroon Airlines flies from Bertoua to Douala and Yaoundé.

 WHERE TO STAY

⌂ **Hôtel Mansa** (48 rooms) BP 285; ☎ 2224 16 50/2224 13 33. By an artificial lake, this newish single-storey motel is the best in town yet you should still save a bucket of water during the dry season as the town supply is poor. Good rooms with AC & satellite TV. There is a restaurant, bar, swimming pool (available to non-guests for a small fee) & tennis. $$$

⌂ **Phoenix Hotel** (20 rooms) BP 215; ☎ 2224 27 29. Near the motor park, with a good restaurant. Clean rooms with bathrooms. $$

⌂ **Hôtel de l'Est** (21 rooms) Poste Central Rond-point; ☎ 2224 23 42. Rooms with AC & either shared or self-contained facilities. $

✗ **WHERE TO EAT AND DRINK, AND NIGHTLIFE** As well as hotel restaurants such as Mansa's, the **Café Moderne** at the *gare routière* has dishes from under CFA1,000 and others include the **Savannah** (☎ *2224 12 85*) and **Grill la Ménagère** (☎ *2224 16 82*). Nightclubs include **Kristal** and **Espace Nkam Palace** in the centre.

BELABO

Tourists usually only head for Belabo, about 80km northwest of Bertoua, to catch the daily southbound train heading for Yaoundé and the northbound train for Ngaoundéré.

The trains stop at Belabo station usually anytime between 10.30 and 13.00 in either direction. If you have a first-class ticket you can wait in the first-class lounge rather than on the platform or street. Security can be bad here and therefore take a taxi or *moto* (motorbike taxi) to take you to your hotel. There isn't much choice – the Cajat and La Giraffe are probably the best, although the appointed three stars they both possess is rather overdoing it – most recent reports suggest that rooms are very dirty. There are several basic hotels in town. Rooms average around £2.

About 23km west of Belabo on the Nanga Eboko road (take a taxi or *moto*) is the Sanaga Yong Chimpanzee Rescue Centre, which looks after 15–20 chimps.

GAROUA-BOULAI

Garoua-Boulai is little more than a rough and ready border town, and its highly transient population has contributed to its alarming rate of HIV/AIDS, which apparently half the population had in some sections of the local population at one point. For accommodation the town has a Catholic mission and inexpensive though not too pleasant auberges.

Garoua-Boulai is on the border with the Central African Republic. The border is by Garoua-Boulai's motor park, and there is a customs point at Beloko on the other side. At the time of writing the Foreign Office advises against all travel around the area bordering the Central African Republic because of the threat of armed banditry, so check the security situation before venturing here.

The motor park has share taxis and buses to Ngaoundéré via Meiganga. At Meiganga you can also take a share taxi west to Ngaoundal to join the Yaoundé–Ngaoundéré train.

Southwest of Garoua-Boulai is a gold mine at Betare-Oya, and just south of this, 7km from Ndokayo, are the Mali Waterfalls.

The route from Bertoua to Garoua-Boulai has been much improved recently, and around the village of Ndokayo there are splendid mountain landscapes.

BATOURI _Telephone code: 2226_

Batouri is a good base for exploring Mount Niong (or Nyong, 778m) and Mount Pandi, and also, in this gold prospecting area, a mining village a couple of miles away.

GETTING THERE AND AWAY The 90km of road leading from Bertoua to Batouri is generally in poor condition. The landscape changes from forest to savanna and a network of rivers including the Kadei and Koubou.

There is daily transport to Yaoundé, Bertoua, Yokadouma and Kenzou, just west of Gamboula, the latter for the Central African Republic, 100km away.

If you are heading for the Central African Republic, the route is along difficult roads and tracks. Share taxis usually leave for the border town of Kenzou around 04.30 from the _gare routière_. Once inside the Central African Republic, share taxis are usually available to take you the 100km to the town of Berberati. Ask about the current condition of the roads before setting off.

WHERE TO STAY

🏠 **Hôtel Mont Pandi** ✆ 2226 25 77. Attractively located with en-suite rooms & there is a restaurant. $$

🏠 **Hôtel Belle Etoile** ✆ 2226 25 18. Clean simple rooms for under CFA10,000 plus restaurant. $

🏠 **Auberge Cooperant** ✆ 2226 23 00. Acceptable rooms in the town centre for under CFA5,000. $

DJA RESERVE

The Reserve du Dja is an extensive area of primary rainforest, part of the Congo rainforest, 243km southeast of Yaoundé, at an altitude of between 400m and 800m.

This faunal reserve covers a surface area of 5,260km² (526,000ha) and the Dja River almost completely encircles it, forming its natural boundary, except to the southwest. The reserve is remote and has few facilities for tourists. Only consider visiting Dja if you have ample time, patience and endurance.

The Dja comprises one of the largest and best-protected forests in Africa, and is noted for its biodiversity and wide variety of primates. Around 90% of its area has been left undisturbed. It is reported to have received some protection as early as 1932, with further laws protecting it in 1950 and 1973. It was internationally recognised by the United Nations Educational, Scientific and Cultural Organisation as a UNESCO Biosphere Reserve in 1981 and declared since 1987 a World Heritage Site for its outstanding natural significance.

Except in the southeast, the reserve is fairly flat and is made up of a series of round-topped hills. Cliffs run along the course of the river in the south for 60km, and a section features rapids and waterfalls.

More than 1,500 plant species have been identified here including 43 species of tree forming the canopy of the forest. The shrub layer alone contains over 53 species. Other main vegetation types are swamp vegetation and secondary forest around old villages which were abandoned in the late 1940s, and recently abandoned cocoa and coffee plantations.

Although the reserve has been little surveyed, it is known to have 107 mammal species, notably forest elephants and chimpanzees. Dja also has western lowland gorillas and indeed is one of the few remaining gorilla sanctuaries in the world. Primate species include greater white-nosed guenon, moustached guenon, crowned guenon, talapoin, red-capped mangabey, white-cheeked mangabey, agile mangabey, drill, mandrill, potto, Demidorff's galago and black and white colobus monkey.

Other mammals include bongo, sitatunga, buffalo, leopard, warthog, giant forest hog, and pangolin. Reptiles include python, lizard and several species of crocodile.

Widespread hunting and the nature of the forest, which is so dense you can generally only see a short distance in front of you, means that many animals are difficult to see easily. Birdwatching, on the other hand, is far easier and there are 320 bird species including hornbills.

Baka 'Pygmies' live within the eastern part of the reserve in small sporadic encampments, maintaining an essentially traditional lifestyle, although increasingly succumbing to a more modern one.

The reserve has an equatorial climate, with constant rain from August to November, rainfall peaking in May and September, and temperatures similar throughout the year, at around 23°C. August is the coolest month, and April the hottest. The best time to visit is between December and early March.

ACCESSING THE RESERVE Ecosystem Forestier d'Afrique Centrale (ECOFAC) (*Av Adenuer, Yaoundé;* \ *2222 42 71;* e *ecofac@camnet.cm; www.ecofac.org*) is in charge of conservation and tourism in the reserve and should be contacted before a visit.

ECOFAC can provide information as well as compulsory guides for Dja at CFA3,000 per day and porters at CFA2,000 per day as well as basic accommodation at CFA5,000 at its training centre at Samalomo (or Somalomo) village on the northern border of the reserve. Samalomo also has a choice of simple accommodation.

Buses go to Samalomo from Mvog-Ada in Yaoundé and if you go independently the best route is Yaoundé–Mbama–Messamena–Samalomo. The 250km journey takes a full day to travel from Yaoundé to Samalomo. Public transport is available to Samalomo on Mondays, Tuesdays and Fridays and back to Yaoundé on Tuesdays, Wednesdays and Saturdays.

Samalomo is not the only access point to the park but is probably the best. From Samalomo you can trek for a day or so to Bouamir (around 35km) and camp at a disused research centre maintained as a tourist camp, and then go further into the endless primary forest. From Samalomo it is also possible to arrange trips along the River Dja.

Another alternative is to enter Dja from the east at Lomié, where guides are also available. Lomié has changed in recent years from an isolated, quiet town into a busy base for commercial forest activity. It is a good place to base yourself for exploration of the reserve, and Baka 'Pygmy' guides are available via ECOFAC for trekking into the forest and staying at their forest villages around the eastern boundary of the reserve.

In Lomié **accommodation** is available at the Auberge de Raffia, a mile out of the village, which has basic but clean rooms for CFA5,000 ($).

A third option is to approach the reserve from Djoum, southeast of Sangmelina, although facilities here are patchy.

Further information on the reserve is available from the International Union for Conservation of Nature and Natural Resources (IUCN) (*Rte de Mont Fébé, Bastos, Yaoundé, near the home of the Nigerian High Commissioner;* ✆ *2220 88 88*); and the Coordinateur du Programme Dja, Ministère de l'Environment et des Forêts, Yaoundé (✆ *2223 92 32*).

YOKADOUMA Telephone code: 2224

Along with towns like Moloundou and Salapombe, Yokadouma has been transformed by the logging companies from an isolated village in the midst of untouched forest into a bustling hub of commercial activity with all the bars, brothels and boarding houses that go with it. Apart from logging, other intensive human activity that has grown up around it in recent years includes sport hunting, environmental development, gold prospecting and even missionary work, with religious relocation programmes aimed at settling Baka 'Pygmies' in permanent roadside settlements with their objective of bringing God's words nearer to the people.

Bushmeat is a thriving business, with about a dozen vendors most days at the market selling wild animal carcasses, such as skinned antelope, chimpanzee, gorilla and elephant meat, chopped into big cubes. Dead monkeys, their tails tied around their necks as handles, hang for sale along all the roads around the town.

The WWF have an office here, and can assist with arranging a visit to nearby Nki and Boumba-Bek forest reserves and Lobéké National Park.

Further information on the protected areas in the region and help with visiting the reserves are available from the WWF in the town north of the centre or at the Cameroon headquarters at Bastos in Yaoundé (✆ *2221 62 67; www.wwfcameroon.org*).

GETTING THERE AND AWAY During the dry season at least, there are daily services to Moloundou, Batouri (195km) and Bertoua (279km). These can be quite torturous, especially as roads become very rutted and traffic jams are common. Check at the motor park about the condition of the roads before setting off.

WHERE TO STAY
L'Elephant ✆ 2224 20 77. Good rooms with AC. $$

La Cachette ✆ 2224 28 63. Acceptable rooms in the centre with bathrooms. There is a bar/restaurant. $

MOLOUNDOU Telephone code: 2224

This border town is about an eight-hour drive/bus journey from Yokadouma is *en route* for Ouesso in the Congo and the Nki Reserve.

WHERE TO STAY
Jardin du Rose Simple rooms. $

La Forestière A small hotel with basic rooms. $

NKI & BOUMBA BEK FOREST RESERVES & LOBEKE NATIONAL PARK

The southeastern corner of Cameroon is part of the thick Congo Basin rainforest, and extends into the nearby Central African Republic, the Congo and Gabon.

From Yokadouma the track road to the frontier town of Moloundou leads to the Lobéké National Park and Boumba Bek and Nki reserves. Lobéké and Boumba Bek are accessible by 4x4 vehicle, but the Nki has to be approached by boat up the River Dja.

12

Reaching the three areas involves a lot of time and patience. Travel from Yaoundé takes a long two days at the very least each way in the dry season, so you will need to allow for a week in total as a bare minimum.

The region is rich in wildlife yet the dense vegetation makes the wildlife here very difficult to spot. The best time to visit is when the region is driest, between December and early March.

These protected areas have suffered from logging and poaching, disturbing the lives of the Baka 'Pygmies', other traditional local groups and wildlife. Because the region is well known for its rich biodiversity in various forest wildlife species and commercial timber trees, it has attracted many fortune seekers who over the last three decades have greatly exploited natural resources especially destined for European markets.

More than 283 bird species are recorded in the region and include the rare Dja warbler, the Nkulengu rail and Bate's nightjar. More than 300 fish species are recorded, with at least three species recently new to science. The Nki Falls harbour significant populations of the Nile crocodile.

The two main ethnic groups in this region are Bantus and Baka 'Pygmies'. The Bantus in the region comprise more than 70% (20,000 inhabitants) of the population and sub-divide into nine tribal groups including the Mbimo, Movongmvong, Konabembe, Djem-Dzimou, Bakwele and Bangandos.

Around a fifth of the population are Baka (5,000 inhabitants) and the rest (10%, or 3,000) are outsiders such as Muslim traders and people from other west African countries.

The Bantus in this area are principally farmers and forest gatherers, their main cash crops being cocoa. Their hunting is mainly meant for domestic consumption although they increasingly sell bushmeat.

The Baka remain more attached to traditional hunting and forest gathering and many still hunt using primitive methods such as poisoned arrows and pit holes for larger game. In the forest they also harvest things like mangoes, honey and yams.

To the Baka the forest is mother, father and guardian, and they have a forest god, Jengi. The WWF, in the course of carrying out their conservation programme in the area (also called Jengi) found unexpected resistance from the Baka despite their efforts to help them. For example, one old Baka woman was against the formation of a protected area because she claimed the tomb of her forefathers was situated within it and it would prevent her from carrying out her ritual rites. And an eight-year-old girl went on hunger strike because her teeth had not been chiselled. She said that not only did chiselling her teeth make her more beautiful, but it also better adapted her to eat meat.

Conservation interest was manifested more than 20 years ago when the first exploration missions of Boumba Bek and Nki strongly highlighted the biological diversity of the area. By the mid-1980s, IUCN had classified the area as a critical site for conservation and since 1994 the WWF has been actively present and working in the region in collaboration with other conservation agencies and organisations including the Ministry of Environment and Forests (MINEF) (✆ 2224 28 99) to protect the forest and develop an ecotourist initiative which would provide local people with alternatives to the bushmeat and forestry industries. There are research camps in the three reserves, which can provide basic accommodation. More details are available from the WWF.

NKI AND BOUMBA BEK FOREST RESERVES Boumba Bek Forest Reserve is reached by heading westwards by vehicle and then on foot from Ngola, which is north of Mambele on the main Yokadouma road.

To reach Nki from Moloundou you take a boat westwards down the Dja River and then proceed on foot into the forest. The WWF project staff can help with obtaining a boat which is likely to cost in the region of CFA30,000 per person for five people.

The Nki Reserve on the River Dja in particular offers an opportunity to observe one of the most remote and relatively untouched parts of the Congo Basin forest. It is hilly and devoid of human habitation. Unlike Lobéké and to some extent Boumba Bek, it remains substantially intact and comparatively untouched by the chainsaws of the logging companies, its protection from logging imposed by nature rather than anything else. Developing the necessary infrastructure such as roads for logging operations, especially in the southern part of Nki, would be very costly.

The Nki is a last true wilderness, much of it still unexplored with new discoveries still being made. It gives the opportunity to view nature in its true and primitive form, and the wide variety of species in the region still goes through the basic rudimentary evolutionary processes not influenced by man's alteration of habitats to meet his overwhelming needs.

Studies indicate the high biological diversity in the area of the reserves. The 600,000ha Boumba Bek and Nki forest block harbours more than 5,000 elephants. Other important species of conservation significance include gorillas, chimpanzee, buffalo, bongo and host of other forest antelopes. Various diurnal primate species, notably the highly threatened crested monkey, De Brazza monkey and the black colobus are found in the Nki Forest.

LOBÉKÉ NATIONAL PARK Lobéké is the most accessible of the three areas and can be a fantastically rewarding – if strenuous – experience. It contains some of the highest densities of forest elephants and western lowland gorillas in all of Africa, as well as large numbers of chimpanzees and other primates, leopards, and ten species of forest ungulates. There are a few viewing platforms for observing the wildlife.

Except for the large concentrations of people around Moloundou (approximately 5,000), the Lobéké region is sparsely populated, with fewer than one person per square kilometre in most areas. These groups live almost exclusively along the main road running north–south from Yokadouma to Moloundou.

One recent study in the Lobéké found that the buffalo in this area feed in the night while the sitatunga (large antelope) feed in the same place during the day. It is interesting that these two animals feed at the same spot but each of them know to do so at set different times.

To visit Lobéké, first call in at the WWF office in Yokadouma to obtain information. A CFA5,000 entry fee per day and CFA3,000 guide fee per day are payable at the adjacent Ministry of Finance office, for which you should get a receipt. You will need to charter transport into the park.

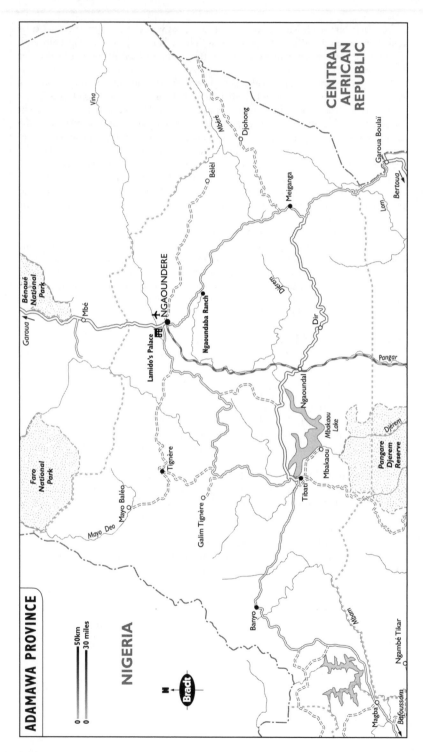

13

Adamawa Province

Much of Adamawa (or Adamaoua) Province is made up of a huge area of savanna and forest the size of Scotland which neatly separates northern and southern Cameroon. This region is very thinly populated and very hard to navigate as there are only a handful of very poor roads and the Yaoundé–Ngaoundéré railway line running through it. Travel through this region is far quicker by train, around 12 hours from Yaoundé, compared with around three days or so on the poor roads.

Adamawa Province is cattle-raising country, thanks to the many water sources including beautiful lakes and waterfalls, and pastures. Its peoples include Fulani, Mousgoum, Mboum and Mambila.

NGAOUNDERE *Telephone code: 2225*

When you arrive from the south, Ngaoundéré, capital of Adamawa Province, is the first sizeable town you come to in northern Cameroon. The town, the terminus of the solitary railway line from the south, is attractive, with tree-lined streets and a pleasingly mild climate due to its 1,300m elevation.

The town's first settlers, the Mboum, were defeated by the Muslim Fulani in the 1830s. The Fulani influence remains strong, from the architecture of the mosques and other buildings, to the flowing robes of the people. The town changed little until the railway line was extended to Ngaoundéré in 1974, helping to trigger a boom in population from under 20,000 to over 150,000 now, and rising rapidly.

The commercial centre with banks, post office and various restaurants and shops, is focused around Rue Adhijo and the Rue du Petit Marché. Rather confusingly, the town's *petit marché* on this latter street has become the principal market, rather than the town's walled *grand marché* on the Rue de la Grande Mosquée.

This latter market, down from the huge and magnificently gaudy grand mosque, sells bric-a-brac like plastic buckets and vegetables past their best. Some stalls are more useful: if you have any clothes needing repair, or want to have a shirt, dress or trousers made from some African fabric you may have picked up, there is an excellent tailor who will do such things for under CFA4,000. At last sighting you could find him by entering the market on the west side, turning left and heading straight into the corner.

Outside the market is a raised oval of ground with a few hawkers but also several Muslim barbers who will massage your face with oil and then meticulously and gently shave it with a cut-throat razor. A marvellous, soporific experience – well, for a man, anyway.

GETTING THERE AND AWAY Most visitors to Ngaoundéré arrive by train and upon arrival, after admiring the striking architecture of the station, taxi drivers are likely to descend and attempt to take your baggage, to secure your custom. They will most probably demand CFA1,000 to take you into town but will almost certainly accept under CFA400.

Roads heading south are bad, so travel in that direction is best done by train, although there are some minibuses to Garoua-Boulai and Bertoua. The Yaoundé train departs from Ngaoundéré station (✆ 2225 12 71/2225 13 77) at around 18.00 daily to arrive around 07.00 the following morning, although notable delays are common.

For northern destinations, *agences de voyage* Woila Voyages (*BP 630;* ✆ *2225 25 08;* m *9985 54 87*), Joli Voyages (✆ *2225 14 19*) and Touristique Express (✆ *2225 19 73*) have services covering the 300km route to Garoua (about five hours) and even further to Maroua (CFA6,000, eight hours).

For eastern Cameroon and the Central African Republic again take the train as far as Belabo and then take a taxi or minibus to Bertoua.

At the *gare routière* next to the central market share taxis and minibuses are available going west to Tibati *en route* for Foumban. The road to Tibati is basically a dirt track and the torturous journey from Ngaoundéré takes around eight hours – in the dry season.

Cameroon Airlines (✆ *2225 12 95*) operates flights to Yaoundé, Douala, Garoua and Maroua from Ngaoundéré's airport (✆ *2225 12 84*) 4km west of the centre.

🏠 WHERE TO STAY

🏠 **Hôtel Transcam** (43 rooms) BP 179; off Rte de Garoua-Boulai; ✆ 2225 12 52/2225 13 32. Located 1km or so southwest of the centre, this is the most comfortable option in Ngaoundéré. A government-rated 3-star hotel with a bar, good restaurant, nightclub, tennis courts, swimming pool & good AC rooms with bathroom & satellite TV. $$$

🏠 **Hôtel du Rail** (18 rooms) BP 319; Rte de Garoua; ✆ 2225 10 13. A few mins' walk from the train station, this long-established hotel has good rooms, a bar & a restaurant, which does a good meat stew. Also a bar & nightclub. $$

🏠 **Hôtel Relais** (34 rooms) BP 47; near the junction with Rue du Petit Marché & Rue de Grande Mosquée; ✆ 2225 11 38. This hotel enjoys a perfect position in the centre of town & has friendly, helpful staff. The rooms are clean & have a TV but have very basic bathrooms, with missing fixtures & no hot water. There's a rather sad little bar & although there is no restaurant, b/fast is available (*omelette, bread & coffee for CFA1,500*). $$

🏠 **Hôtel les Alizes** (11 rooms) BP 405; Plateau Mandock; ✆ 2225 16 89. Away from the centre, this pleasant option has an attractive garden, a good restaurant & bar, & balconied rooms with bathrooms. $

🏠 **Auberge de la Gare** (18 rooms) BP 203; ✆ 2225 22 17. Up the hill from the train station. A small hotel of an acceptable standard with a good-value restaurant & comfortable rooms with bathrooms. $

Further out

🏠 **Ngaoundaba Ranch** (32 rooms) BP 3; ✆ 2225 24 69/2225 19 05; ⊕ Nov–May. Along the Meiganga road before the village of Bandal, 35km southeast of Ngaoundéré, is this mountain lodge, open Nov–May, that is straight out of colonial Africa. A few kilometres from the main road, at a privately owned cattle ranch, it is nestled in the mountains 1,360m above sea level next to a beautiful volcanic crater lake. Here you can birdwatch, fish, swim & take a boat on the lake. The stone dining room is lined with animal trophies from hunting safaris of the past & accommodation is in *boukarous*. B/fast & dinner are CFA6,000. Bookable through the Alissar supermarket in Ngaoundéré. $$

✗ WHERE TO EAT AND DRINK
The cheapest eateries are in the vicinity of the Rue de la Gare and the Rue de la Grande Mosquée and there are street stalls around the train station.

✗ **Adamaoua Losirs** Rue Ahidjo. One of the best bars & has inexpensive simple meals as well as a procession of hawkers selling anything from kebabs, nuts, belts & shoes. $

✗ **Marhaba** Near the cathedral. This has a disco at w/ends & serves several fish & meat dishes. $

✗ **Restaurant Au Feu de Bois** Rue de la Grande Mosquée. Has Cameroonian options like *ndole* as well as Western fast food. Prices start at under CFA1,500. $

✗ **Le Délice** Rue de la Grande Mosquée. Good meals for under CFA2,000. $

✗ **Santana Express** Rue de la Grande Mosquée. Good-value food. $

✗ **Bar Laitier** Near the cathedral. For coffees, pastries & *dakkere*, local yoghurt with rice. $

✗ **L'Egi d'Or** Near the cathedral on the main street. In the busy part of town, so great for people-watching. Reasonable prices, a good atmosphere, popular with expats at night. Draught '33' lager & excellent *chawarmas* (a Lebanese dish of grilled lamb slices served in pitta bread with a chickpea sauce) as well as good coffee, cakes & croissants, pizzas & burgers. $

✗ **La Plazza** Rue de la Grande Mosquée. Opposite Au Feu de Bois, this has a wide range of good dishes as well as live music. $

OTHER PRACTICALITIES

Banks Bicec and Crédit Lyonnais are off Rue Ahidjo.

Groceries

Commerce General Supermarket Behind Hôtel le Relais

Alissar Ailmentation Near Au Feu de Bois restaurant

Hospital

✚ **Norwegian Protestant Mission Hospital** BP 6; southeast of the centre; ☎ 2225 11 95

Internet

🅴 **Complexe Lin** Rue de la Grande Mosquée

🅴 **Globalisation** Rue du Petite Marché

Moped hire

Outside Hôtel le Relais.

Tourist information and travel agents

🇮 **Tourist office** BP 527; Av Ahidjo; ☎ 2225 11 38/2225 24 63/2225 25 89. They can advise on accommodation, restaurants & bars & travel in the region.

Alto By the Grand Marché; ☎ 2225 15 24/2225 11 29. Various local excursions including on horseback.

WHAT TO SEE AND DO

Lamido's Palace (*Near the grand marché. Admission CFA2,000; French-speaking guide CFA1,000; photography CFA1,000*) The old town is dominated by the Palais du Lamido. where the *lamido* (chief) lives with his wives. The palace and its courtyards, homes and public rooms are surrounded by a wall, in which people are buried. The palace is, in the Hausa language, a type of building known as a *sare* with huts topped with large cone-shaped thatched roofs that nearly reach the ground and which were used to hide children in times of war. You can see things like the *lamido*'s ancient telephone installed next to his throne; you are whisked around in about ten minutes.

There is a colourful Friday prayer service with the *lamido* leading a procession of notables, decked out in bright orange and red, to the mosque. There are also similar events on Saturdays and Sundays.

You can enter the complex by booking at the tourist office on Rue Ahidjo or alternatively at the *lamido*'s secretariat office, the new concrete building by the entrance. Don't used the touts.

Around Ngaoundéré This region is dotted with mud huts with tall 'witches' hat' thatched roofs which almost seem to have simply grown out of the earth without the involvement of man. On the outskirts of Ngaoundéré is some beautiful forest with numerous types of conifer.

Lakes

Dang Lake Just north of the city by the main road to Garoua and near to the university, is a large, shallow lake that is a haven for birdlife and wildlife, including moorhens, geese and ducks.

Lake Tison (also Lake Tyson or Tizon) A circular volcanic crater lake 9km from Ngaoundéré, reached by taking the Garoua-Boulai–Meiganga road southwards for 5km where there is a signpost for the lake, which is about 2km eastwards from here, through the woods. Above the lake is a wooden chalet with a bar where visitors can camp.

Lake Mbalang An irregular-shaped crater lake, 1km long with a little wooded islet in the middle. It is about 21km east of Ngaoundéré.

Lake Myam A lake of about 800ha surrounded by forest and home to hippos and crocodiles.

Waterfalls

Beni Falls An impressive tabular waterfall at Mbang Mboum, 20km or so northeast of Ngaoundéré.

Vina Falls The impressive **Vina Falls** are on the Garoua-Boulai–Meiganga road, soon after Wakwa village, 15km from Ngaoundéré. The water drops about 30m from a rocky table, and vast meadows form an impressive backdrop.

Lancrennon Falls The equally impressive Lancrennon Falls, with a drop of around 100m, are situated in the extreme east of the country by the border with the Central African Republic, about 80km from Djohong.

Tello Falls Les Chutes de Tello (or Telo), are on the Addi road eastwards from Ngaoundéré, before the village of Tourningal, , another notable group of waterfalls in the region and about 50km from the town. Endless streams of water tumble 50m down a great canyon into an emerald-green pool. There is a beach by a large red rock. A smaller waterfall sits beside the main one, perfect for a shower. There are caves to explore behind both waterfalls. It is an isolated spot especially popular with expat families at weekends.

Nyem Nyem Caves The refuge of the Nyem Nyem peoples when they resisted the Germans, these caves are situated west of Ngaoundéré on the top of Mount Djim, about halfway between Tignere and Tibati, near Galim, about 65km from Tignere. Traditional festivities are held each January here.

TIBATI Telephone code: 2225

Tibati, 280km westwards by challenging road from Ngaoundéré, is a sleepy village with a slightly Wild West air, by Mbakaou Lake and a good base for the Pangare Djerem Reserve. It is essentially a junction, with five roads intersecting with the main one.

WHERE TO STAY AND EAT The centrally located **Auberge Kautang** has a lively, loud bar and the very basic rooms (behind the bar) are CFA2,000–3,000.

Alternatively take a *moto* to the **Auberge le Djrem**, an informal, family-run auberge with a public room with a blaring television, and another, the far quieter

Brian Cruickshank

The drive through east–central Cameroon from Ngaoundéré along the twisting D22 road is rough, and is sometimes paved, sometimes not. It is very sparsely populated, save for the very small villages that occur every so often.

The scenery on the route is otherworldly. Few trees, and lots of small, mushroom-like ant-hills dot the roadside. The condition of the road can go from decent to bad rather quickly, so be prepared to swerve to miss giant holes in the road, or more likely, dried-up water channels where the rainy season waters have carved deep ruts across the track. The D22 road continues through Djohong and stops at the Central African Republic.

The village of Djohong is populated mostly by civil service workers, government officials, policemen, teachers and farmers. Others earn their living as labourers, builders, merchants, craft persons, tailors, farmers and cattle herders. There are smaller communities situated around Djohong, with populations of around 30 inhabitants. The nearest place for medical treatment is a Norwegian hospital at Belel, near the end of the D21 road.

The indigenous tribes of the area include the Gbaya and Mbéré. There are also, and have been for years, many Foulbé people in Djohong, and more recently, many Mbororo. A range of religions is represented through the diverse cultures in this area. Often the local religion is a mixture of animism along with other widely practised religions such as Islam and Christianity.

The region around Djohong is a savanna, with gently rolling terrain. It is mostly grassland with lots of small trees. Small wild animals are common, including monkeys and gazelle. Long-horn cattle also graze on the plateau, but during the dry season the semi-nomadic farmers take them to areas near the Ngou or Mbéré rivers to graze.

Rains are hard and roads sometimes become temporary rivers during the summer months and into September. By the end of the rainy season, the grasses can grow as tall as a man, and certain varieties can then be used for thatching roofs, weaving fences or making mats, baskets and ropes. The dry season, from October to March, is dusty and windy and temperatures are generally cooler, going as low as 12°C/53°F. During December the Harmattan can be very strong here, making the area a dusty place indeed.

'Buffalo Room', named after the buffalo head on top of the now-defunct 1950s television. The auberge offers dishes like meat stew (CFA700) and very basic rooms with a hole-in-the-floor loo and shower for CFA2,500–3,000.

BANYO

Minibuses from Tibati to sleepy Banyo (CFA3,800) take around five hours by virtue of the abysmal roads.

The bus for Foumban (CFA4,500, five hours) can easily take two or three hours to fill up, but sweet tea is available opposite the bus station for a handsome CFA25 while you wait.

WHERE TO STAY Banyo has two basic auberges, the **Auberge le Sare** ($) and the better **Auberge Posada** ($). Turn right out of the bus station and walk until you hit the left fork at the Elf petrol station. Rooms are around CFA3,000.

WHERE TO EAT AND DRINK The liveliest road here is Rue Djouda, which has several bars including the **Spot Bar** and the **Club de Dandys**, and the **Restaurant de Pasta**, which has basic European meals for CFA1,500–3,000. Further down the road **Restaurant du Temps** serves couscous, liver, tripe, *bouillon* and plantain chips for CFA600 and a good omelette breakfast for the same price.

14

North Province

A trip to northern Cameroon offers a great change of scenery, climate and culture. Its scantly vegetated savanna terrain, blistering, harsh temperatures, Islamic culture and archaic, primitive villages are a big contrast to the cooler, lushly vegetated more developed, more densely populated, Christian, southern parts of the country.

The north's principally Islamic culture is most noticeable in the larger towns, Maroua and Garoua, where flowing Islamic robes are often in abundance, in contrast to the omnipresent jeans and T-shirts typically worn in the south of Cameroon.

The southern border of Northern Province roughly follows the Adamawa Mountains cutting across the centre of the country from east to west.

Whereas the south has been in contact with Europe for more than 500 years, until the 20th century the north was part of a series of quasi-feudal Muslim Fulani (or Foulbé) kingdoms based in Nigeria.

Resistance to change and outside influence has meant that Western-style development has generally been small. Despite this, this is one of the easiest regions of Cameroon to travel through, not least because there are good sealed roads stretching from Ngaoundéré all the way to Kousseri on the Chadian border.

GAROUA *Telephone code: 2227*

Most people's first impression of Garoua, the capital of the Northern Province and principal economic and administrative centre of the north, isn't too inspiring: a tatty motor park with stalls selling anything from breakfasts of rice and beans, dodgy aspirins and toothpastes and *brochettes* of meat doused in hot chilli sauce. Look around and there are dreary modern office blocks and wooden and cement homes with tin roofs.

Garoua is 296km from Ngaoundéré, and 212km from Maroua. Its population has grown steadily in recent years and now exceeds 290,000, with many being Choa, Foulbé, Fali and Mandang. Its population is heavily Nigerian and Chadian as well as Cameroonian.

Garoua evolved in the 18th century after the first peoples began to settle in the area, including Bata and Fali. Then came nomadic Fulani herders in the 1800s, who built defences around the town to dispel invaders. Then other Muslim peoples settled at Garoua including Hausa and Shua Arabs.

The town was colonised by the Germans in 1901 and they established a port, which helped forge links with Nigeria and Chad. This was the birthplace of former president Ahidjo, who invested heavily in the town and it now has a thriving range of industries.

Despite being located well into the interior of Cameroon, Garoua has a large port, third to Douala and Kribi, on the wide Bénoué River, although it is far less busy than in the past. It can only operate during the rainy season. A large bridge crosses the river.

Garoua has very few sights as such apart from the huge Grande Mosquée on Route de Maroua. Non-Muslims are not admitted. There is a good range of

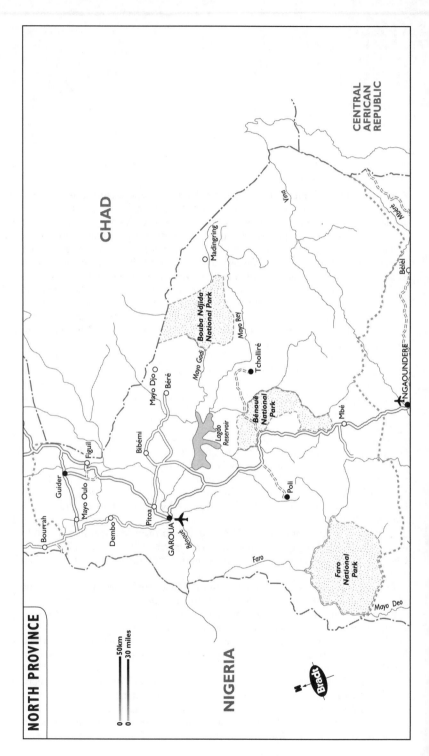

NORTH PROVINCE

CHAD

CENTRAL AFRICAN REPUBLIC

NIGERIA

Madingring

Bouba Ndjida National Park

Mayo Rey

Mayo Godi

Tchollire

Bénoué National Park

Mbé

NGAOUNDÉRÉ

Bélél

Vina

Mbéré

Mayo Dio
Béré

Logdo Reservoir

Bibémi

Poli

Figuil

Guider

Mayo Oulo

Bourrah

Dembo

Pitoa

GAROUA

Bénoué

Faro

Faro National Park

Mayo Deo

0 ___ 50km
0 ___ 30 miles

Bradt

facilities including banks, two hospitals, a post office, petrol stations, an airport and a number of hotels.

The central market is a lively destination, busiest at weekends, and there is a *petit marché* just southwest of the centre, near plenty of bars and simple restaurants. For purchasing arts and crafts, head for the group of traders under the neem trees just north of the market.

GETTING THERE AND AWAY Most *agences de voyage* are near the central market around Rue des Banques and Rue du Pont and go to Maroua (three hours) and Ngaoundéré (five hours) and include Lux Voyages (✆ 2227 52 98), Super Voyages (✆ 2227 12 03), Amy Voyages (✆ 2227 33 05), Narral Voyages (✆ 2227 11 16), Woila Voyages (✆ 2227 30 82) and Star Voyages (✆ 2227 14 85).

There are share taxis for Nigeria at the *gare routière*, 5km north of the centre on the Maroua road.

Cameroon Airlines (✆ 2227 10 55; airport: ✆ 2227 14 81) flies to Yaoundé, Douala, Maroua, and N'Djamena in Chad. The airport is 5km north of the centre.

WHERE TO STAY

🏠 **Relais Saint Hubert** (45 rooms) BP 445; Rue du Novotel; ✆ 2227 22 34/2227 30 33. This has an expensive bar, a restaurant serving Cameroonian & European fare (*CFA3,500–4,500 for main dishes*) & a reasonably extensive but expensive wine list (*CFA5,000–15,000*) as well as a pool & gardens & good, clean, comfortable AC rooms with TV, room service & en-suite facilities. The price varies according to room size. Guides are likely to approach you for tours in the locality, such as Rhumsiki. $$$

🏠 **Tourist Motel** (52 rooms) BP 1169; Rue de la Gendarmerie; ✆ 2227 32 44; m 997 92 41. Under 2km northwest of the centre this comfortable hotel has a swimming pool (non-guests can use for a small fee) & rooms with TV, AC & phone. $$$

🏠 **Hôtel la Bénoué** (52 rooms) BP 291; Rue du Mgr Yves Plumey; ✆ 2227 15 58. This upmarket hotel has a good restaurant, a nightclub, swimming pool, tennis court & good rooms with shower/bathrooms & AC. $$

🏠 **Auberge Hiala Village** (35 rooms) BP 354; Rue Boumare; ✆ 2227 24 07. Good-value simple rooms with bathrooms plus good restaurant & bar, located near the port. $

🏠 **Auberge Centrale** (15 rooms) BP 33; Rue Adamou Amar; ✆ 2227 33 49. Near the central market, this newer option has AC rooms, some with bathrooms. $

🏠 **Auberge le Salam** (10 rooms) BP 496; ✆ 2227 24 26. Near the central market, there are basic rooms with fans & shared facilities around a courtyard. $

✗ WHERE TO EAT AND DRINK, AND NIGHTLIFE Some inexpensive eateries are on Route de Maroua and around the *petit marché*.

Super Restaurant, opposite Star Voyages on Route de Maroua, offers reasonable prices, delicious fresh fruit drinks, a good avocado salad and various Sudanese dishes. It is in the busy section of the city and therefore great for people-watching.

In the northern section of town off Rue de la Gendarmerie in the Roumde Adjia neighbourhood are several bars, cafés and simple restaurants (eg: **Chez Marie Bamiléké** ($) and **Chez Lyna** ($)) with cheap Cameroonian dishes. An expensive option, for French cuisine, would be **Le Nautic** ($$$), off Route Périphérique, southwest of the centre. Other options include **Le Baoba** ($) and **Restaurant d'Afrique** ($).

Head for the Yelwa district just southwest of the centre for plenty of bars, cafés and cheap restaurants. **Hotel la Bénoué** on Rue du Mgr Yves Plumey has a pricey nightclub attached.

OTHER PRACTICALITIES

Banks Several banks are located on or around Rue des Banques (also known as Rue Centrale) including Bicec, Crédit Lyonnais and SGBC, which has an ATM.

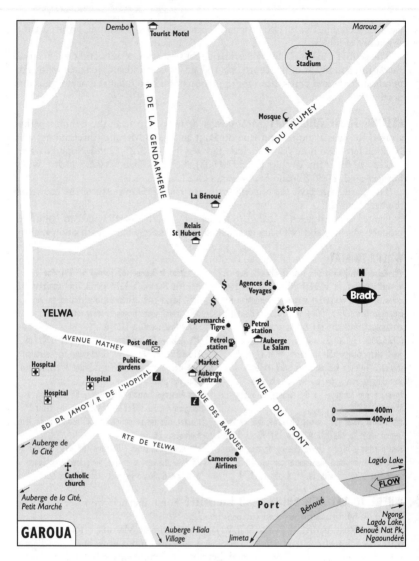

GAROUA

Bookshops
Librarie Nouvelle Moderne Rue des Banques

Groceries
Supermarché Tigre Rue du Pont

Hospitals
✚ **Provincial Hospital** ✎ 2227 14 14
✚ **Southia Clinic** ✎ 2227 21 33
✚ **Centre Medico Social** ✎ 2227 16 08

Internet
@ **Ets Bao** ✎ 2227 13 97

Pharmacies

+ **Pharmacie du Grand Marché** ☎ 2227 20 95   + **Pharmacie du Nord** ☎ 2227 13 79

Photography

Photo FM ☎ 2227 29 23

Tourist information

🗎 **Tourist office** Off Rue des Banques; ☎ 2227 22 90

THE NATIONAL PARKS AND RESERVE

This region still has large mammal populations big enough to be considered of international importance but among these are some of the world's most threatened species. The WWF has been involved in conservation projects here since the early 1990s, notably working on the dwindling rhino population and inventory and management-related work on elephants.

The three parks in this region, Faro, Bénoué and Bouba Ndjida, are most popular for hunting and Waza, further north, is a better bet for observing wildlife. All the parks are off the fast, good-quality paved Ngaoundéré–Garoua road. You need to fix your own transport, hiring a vehicle at Ngaoundéré, Garoua or Maroua. Accommodation in the *campements* in the parks can be reserved through the Garoua tourist office (*BP 50; Garoua;* ☎ *2227 22 90*). Accommodation tends to fill up quickly at weekends.

FARO RESERVE The 500,000-acre Reserve de Faro consisting of forested savanna, hills and mountains extends to the border with Nigeria but has been badly affected by poaching in recent years so Bénoué and Bouba Ndjida national parks are a far better bet for wildlife-watching. There are small populations of such animals as rhinoceros, buffalo, elephant and harnessed guib, and the Atlantika Mountains – which the Cameroon–Nigeria border slices through the middle of – are to the north. **Accommodation** is available at the exclusive, very pricey Faro West camp above the Faro River, principally used by hunters. The luxury air-conditioned boukarous feature a living room, dining room, bar, balcony with panoramic view and kitchen.

BÉNOUÉ NATIONAL PARK (*Entry is at the small towns of Mayo Alim or Banda;* ☉ *Dec–May; admission CFA5,000, vehicle charge CFA2,000 per day, guide obligatory at CFA3,000 per day. These fees are not always collected*) The Parc National de la Bénoué, with the wettest climate of the three, is situated on the Bénoué Plains halfway between Garoua and Ngaoundéré in the northern Guinea savanna belt. It covers 180,000ha, much being Guinea woodlands. It features a wide frontage to the Bénoué River. Inhabitants include lion, giraffe, hyena, panther, Nile crocodile, giant eland, antelope including kob, hartebeest and waterbuck, as well as topi, black and white colobus, guereza colobus, red-fronted (Thomson's) gazelle, green sun-squirrel, baboon and warthog as well as several hippopotamus colonies and elephant and buffalo herds. It is popular with anglers.

🏠 Where to stay

🏠 **Campement de Buffle Noir** (18 rooms) BP 50; Garoua; ☎ 2227 22 90. Situated inside the park on the banks of the Bénoué River, this lodge is in a great setting. A bit rundown, it has a restaurant (meals CFA6,000–9,000) & rondavels with comfortable rooms with separate bathrooms sleeping 4 at CFA21,000. **Camping** is possible. The campement is supposed to be accessible from tracks leading from the entrances at both towns, Banda & Mayo Alim, yet at time of going to press only the most direct route to the *campement*, leaving the main road at Banda, is negotiable & even this is not in the best of shape. Allow 90mins or so to drive the 27km from the main road to the *campement*. $$$

Campement Grand Capitaine On the main road from Tchollire to Guidjiba; ☎ 2227 22 90. This has comfortable *boukarou* rooms at around. $$

BOUBA NDIJDA NATIONAL PARK (*Main entrance at Koum, about 45km east of Tchollire; ⏰ Nov–May; admission CFA5,000, obligatory guide CFA3,000 per day, payable to the conservator of Bouba Ndjida in Tchollire*) The Parc National de Bouba Ndjida is a rugged reserve on the banks of the Mayo Lidi River and on the border with Chad. It covers around 220,000ha and is particularly remote and beautiful, with open wooded and bush savanna including elements of the landscape of the Sahelian zone. It contains most of Cameroon's population of the almost extinct west African black rhinoceros as well as the rare Derby eland, the biggest antelope in the world.

A recent study by WWF found a population of between 1,000 to 3,500 Derby eland and that the total area of distribution of the species has drastically reduced over the years from human pressure and habitat fragmentation. A 1990 IUCN report considers the Derby eland as a species threatened by extinction.

There are also buffalo, elephant, lion, leopard, wild dog and antelope, and dinosaur fossils are also located in the park. Game can be difficult to see because of the size of the park and the more than 430km of tracks.

Where to stay

Campement de Boubandjida (16 rooms) BP 50, Garoua; ☎ 2227 22 90. Situated 42km within the park by the River Mayo Lidi, this has comfortable en-suite rooms. There is a bar & good restaurant. $$$

WHAT TO SEE

Rey Bouba The village of Rey Bouba, sandwiched between the Bouba Ndjida and Bénoué Parks, is a traditional Fulani *lamidat* (or principality), but the palace rarely receives visitors. There is a traditional, very basic resthouse.

Lagdo Lake It is possible to stay at an excellent retreat right on this huge lake about 30km southeast of Garoua. Lagon Bleu at Lagdo, near Ngong (m *9946 89 83/9985 53 53*) offers ten rooms of comfortable self-contained *boukarous* accommodation with fans or air-conditioning all overlooking the lake. Rooms with a double and single bed are CFA20,000 and two-room suites sleeping four are CFA30,000. There is a good restaurant, pretty garden and lakeside beach. A boat and *pirogue* are available for exploring the lake and its islands.

15

Extreme North Province

Along with the Western Highlands, the hot, dry north is certainly one of the most fascinating areas to visit in Cameroon. As well as containing the striking and spectacular Harmattan-battered Mandara Mountains, exotic villages and Cameroon's best national park, Waza, it has a whole hotchpotch of peoples including Choa, Moundang, Toupouri, Mafa, Kapsiki and Mousgoum. The Fulani (or Foulbé) dominate and have strong traditional leadership structures. There is a high rate of immigration into the area from the Sahel.

North of here the country joins up with Lake Chad, which varies from floods from the Chari and Logone rivers during the brief rains each year, to dryness at other times.

MAROUA *Telephone code: 2229*

At 812km (503 miles) northwest of Yaoundé and 210km north of Garoua, Maroua, capital of the Extreme North Province, is Cameroon's second-biggest northern city (latest estimates suggest a population of over 200,000) and was one of the few cities that existed before colonial times.

It retains a traditional air, and the Mayo Kaliao River (which dries up during the dry season) cuts through its centre, separating its north and south as the Thames does London. Neem trees line and shade its sleepy streets.

Located at the border of Sahelian Africa, Maroua is particularly ethnically diverse and is where the dominant Muslim peoples of the plains, particularly the Fulani and Mandara (or Wandala), meet the Kirdi (or mountain peoples) who live in perched villages in the highlands.

In the 18th century Maroua was controlled by a powerful Fulani leader, Sokoto Caliphate, until the Germans came along in 1902. It was then occupied by the French in September 1914, after which it became part of French Cameroon, remaining so until Cameroonian independence in 1960.

There is a large and lively daily market, busiest on Mondays when Kirdi peoples come from the mountains to trade. Anything from fruit, meat and vegetables to textiles, traditional medicines and Japanese electronic goods is sold. The city is a centre for traditional crafts and is known for its jewellery, leatherwork, silverwork, baskets, swords, bangles, painted ostrich eggs, dyes and perfumes. It has a big handicrafts centre, Centre Artisanal, close by.

Its location, in the foothills of the eastern edge of the Mandara Mountains, make it popular with travellers as a base for trips to these as well as Waza National Park (125km away) and nearby pictureque villages like Mora (60km away) and (75km distant).

Places worth visiting include the little-attended **Diamaré Museum** (⏰ *08.00–13.30 & 14.30–18.00 Mon–Sat; admission free, but CFA500 donation expected*). It contains articles from the Sao civilisation, the Toupouri, Massa and Mousgoum peoples as well as the Fulani culture. There are musical instruments,

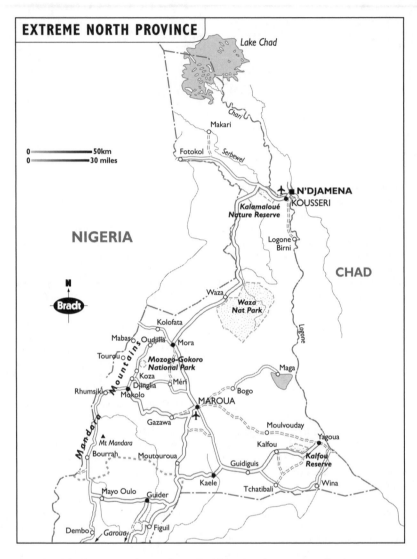

Lake Chad

Chari

Makari

Fotokol

Serbewel

N'DJAMENA

KOUSSERI

Kalamaloué Nature Reserve

Logone Birni

NIGERIA

CHAD

Waza

Waza Nat Park

Kolofata

Logone

Mabas   Oudjilla

Touro   Mora

Mozogo-Gokoro National Park

Maga

Koza

Rhumsiki   Djinglia   Méri

Mokolo   Bogo

MAROUA

Gazawa

Moulvouday

Yagoua

Mt Mandara

Kalfou

Bourrah   Moutouroua

Kalfou Reserve

Guidiguis

Mayo Oulo   Kaele   Wina

Guider   Tchatibali

Dembo   Garoua   Figuil

carved calabashes, pottery, jewellery, shields, a *lamido*'s gown and other treasures dating back as far as the 1100s.

The building also contains a craft market selling such things as jewellery, hand-woven cloth and leather goods, some made locally, others from further afield in Africa.

GETTING THERE AND AWAY

By road Regular transport for Kousseri and other destinations in the extreme north is available at the *gare routière* east of the centre.

For Garoua and Ngaoundéré, there are various *agences de voyage* on Boulevard de Diarenga and around the *marché central*, including Amy Voyages (↘ *2229 16 99*), Jolis Voyages (↘ *2229 31 31*) and Woila Voyages (↘ *2229 17 57*).

Star Voyages on Boulevard de la Renouveau (↘ *2229 25 22*) goes to Mokolo, and Yagua and Kaele on the Chadian border.

Non-agency transport to Rhumsiki, Mokolo and destinations south leave from Carrefour Parrah, about 3km southwest of the centre.

By air Cameroon Airlines (↘ *2229 19 49/2229 15 15/2229 20 19*) flies to Yaoundé, Douala, Garoua, Ngaoundéré and N'Djamena (Chad) from Maroua's chaotic airport (↘ *2229 10 21*) located south of the centre, about 20km down the Garoua road.

⌂ WHERE TO STAY

⌂ **Hôtel Mizao** (53 rooms) BP 381, Quartier Sonel; ↘ 2229 13 00. Comfortable but rather dull international-standard hotel with facilities like a swimming pool (*CFA1,500 to non-guests*), tennis courts, a nightclub & restaurant (*CFA5,000*). The hotel also offers car hire. $$$

⌂ **Motel le Saré** (25 rooms) BP 11; ↘ 2229 12 94. Good-value upmarket 3-star graded hotel set in pleasant gardens with swimming pool, tennis, good restaurant & bar. There are 3 apts available. Clean, comfortable rooms with AC. $$$

⌂ **Maroua Palace** (50 rooms) BP 381; ↘ 2229 32 52/2229 31 64. In the centre, this very comfortable hotel has a good restaurant, bars, tennis & swimming pool (*CFA1,500*). The smart rooms have TV, phone & bathroom. Also offers car hire & credit cards are accepted. $$$

⌂ **Hôtel Le Sahel** (28 rooms) BP 853; Bd de Diarenga; ↘ 2229 29 60. Acceptable rooms, restaurant. $$

⌂ **Le Relais de la Porte Mayo** (22 rooms) BP 112; ↘ 2229 33 56/2229 26 92. Very-good value hotel with AC self-contained *boukarous*, a courtyard restaurant & bar with pleasant terrace that is popular with Europeans & a craft shop. The hotel has a chauffeur, 4x4 transport & guide available. $$

⌂ **Fety Hotel** (28 rooms) Bd de Diarenga; ↘ 2229 29 13. Relatively new, this small hotel near most of the *agences de voyage* has a restaurant, bar, clean rooms with AC & bathrooms. $

⌂ **Relais Ferngo** (14 rooms) BP 112; off Bd de Diarenga ↘ 2229 21 53. Basic *boukarous* with AC/fans & bathrooms. Also **camping** at CFA1,000 pp. Restaurant. Near the bus stops. $

✕ WHERE TO EAT AND DRINK
There are numerous options, from cheap street food upwards. There are a number of clubs and bars along Boulevard de la Renouveau and some cheaper bars serving simple dishes like grilled fish on a street off this road, L'Avion Me Laisse.

✕ **Chez Emmanuel (Bimarva Snack Bar)** Just east of the market; ↘ 2229 19 95. A variety of dishes from CFA2,000, outdoor seating & satellite TV. $$

✕ **Le Baobab Restaurant** ↘ 2229 19 03. This *boukarous* located east of the market serves good-value Cameroonian cuisine. There are outdoor tables & meals cost from CFA2,000. $$

✕ **Chez Moussa** East of the market, with inexpensive fare from *brochettes* for CFA100 to substantial meals for over CFA3,000. $$

✕ **Restaurant de l'Artisanat** Opposite the market entrance, this has filling Cameroonian dishes from around CFA900. $

OTHER PRACTICALITIES

Banks Several are near the market including Bicec, SGBC and Crédit Lyonnais.

Cinema The Diamare is by the Cameroon Airlines office.

Groceries Both CGD Supermarché and Nziko are east of the market.

Hospitals
✚ **Hôpital Meskine** Southwest of the centre off the Garoua road; ↘ 2229 25 79

✚ **Provincial Hospital** About 500m west of the *lamido*'s palace; ↘ 2229 11 75

Internet Marouanet is on Rue Mobil.

Pharmacy
✚ **Pharmacie du Centre** ☎ 2229 12 09/2229 31 20

Post office Located at west end of Avenue du Kakataré.

Tourist information
📋 **Provincial Delegation of Tourism Far North** BP 675; ☎ 2229 22 98

Safari Kirdi e yadjedabala@yahoo.fr. The owner of this company offering tours, Mr Dabala, is very reliable & speaks French, English & German.

WHAT TO SEE
The Maroua region As well as its ethnic diversity – with a hotchpotch of Shua Arabs, Choa, Fulani, Kirdi and others – the Mandara Plateau is also one of the most environmentally and agriculturally diverse regions of west Africa. Its forests, savannas, mountains and rivers contain many species, from colourful geckos to large mammals, although these are increasingly threatened by overgrazing and burning.

Mindif La Dent de Mindif (Mindif's tooth) juts up from nowhere 25km (16 miles) southeast of Maroua near the town of Mindif. It is one of the most challenging peaks to climb in Africa. Also on the road to Mindif is a tannery, which is also worth a visit. Admission is CFA1,000.

VILLAGES AROUND THE MANDARA MOUNTAINS
The scenery of this region is stunning, at turns both beautiful and desolate, with the volcanic plugs of the Mandara Mountains rising up strikingly to the west of Maroua.

The most popular towns and villages visited by travellers include the rather touristy Rhumsiki and Oudjilla, which has a traditional chief's compound and a surrounding wall that is reputedly over three centuries old. Mokolo is a charming, sleepy village and Mora has a great market. Other villages include pretty Djingliya, Mabas and Koza, Tourou, Maga, Bogo and Mogode, north of Rhumsiki.

The region has limited facilities for travellers: no banks, few shops, cafés and restaurants and most hotels are of a basic standard. Make sure you have adequate food and water as opportunities for these can be infrequent. Petrol is sold in Maroua and Mokolo and is commonly also sold on the road.

MOKOLO *Telephone code: 2229*
About 75km west of Maroua, the small, sleepy town of Mokolo situated in a rugged rocky setting, is the capital of the Mafa mountain peoples. It has grown quite significantly in the last 20 years or so from little more than some round stone houses with thatched roofs and a motor park, and sadly is considerably less attractive now. But it is perfect as a base for excursions into the mountains and has a huge lively market on Wednesdays and a small museum near the motor park which has a collection of local crafts.

Getting there and away If you are taking a minibus from Garoua to Mokolo, ensure you tell the driver your destination. You will usually be deposited at a crossroads at Carrefour Gakle (CFA3,800, four hours) where another minibus should take you the further stretch to Mokolo (CFA1,000, two hours).

The departure point for most destinations, including Maroua and Koza, is the market in the centre. Transport for Roumsiki usually leaves before 08.00, west of the centre where the covered road ends. Transport is busiest on market day, Wednesday.

⌂ **Where to stay** For the cheapest option, ask around to see if anyone will put you up in their home. They are used to this.

⌂ **Campement de Flamboyant** (22 rooms) BP 22; ☏ 2229 51 16/2229 55 85. Comfortable AC rooms with bathrooms, some AC. The restaurant's menu is extensive but in reality steak, chicken or kebab & chips for CFA2,500 is generally all that is on offer. There is also a bar. $$$

Bar Metcheme (see below) has several small, reasonably clean and comfortable rooms with fans and a cold shower for CFA3,000.

✗ **Where to eat and drink** As well as the **Flamboyant** ($), another option is **Café Fait-Tous** ($), with dishes starting at around CFA1,000.

Around the corner from the Campement de Flamboyant is the **Bar Metcheme** ($), a rather grubby, loud and entertaining bar run by the convivial Mr Francis. Barbecues near the bar will happily bring you a plateful of fish, liver, beef, chicken or tripe and plantain for CFA1,000–2,500.

What to see and do

Try the local brew If you are the adventurous sort and want to sample the local millet-based brew, *bili-bili*, go to the water tower to the left of Mokolo's market a quarter of the way in and go through the double iron green doors with 'La Maison de Commandant' painted upon them. The CFA100 brew is served by several women in an earthenware jug and you are given a wooden bowl to drink out of.

Trekking in the mountains The Mandara Mountains are just southwest of Mokolo and offer great opportunities for trekking. Ask around for a guide, who typically costs from around CFA3,500–6,000 per day. You can also organise a donkey for your luggage, or a horse if you wish to ride in the surrounding countryside.

DJINGLIA This pretty village located on a hill 15km north of Mokolo on the way to Koza has basic accommodation from CFA3,000 at the Société Cooperative Artisanale de Djingliya (*BP 94; Mokolo*) which also has local crafts for sale, a restaurant and bar.

KOZA This pleasant hillside village located 20km from Mokolo and 30km from Mora at an altitude of 1,100m/3,600ft has a few basic places to eat but no accommodation unless you can find a villager to put you up. Market day is Sunday and there are daily vehicles to and from Mokolo.

RHUMSIKI (OR ROUMSIKI) Approximately 55km (34 miles) from Mokolo and 120km from Maroua, nestling deep in the mountains, is the small village of Rhumsiki. It is the most touristic place in northern Cameroon, but since the country has so little tourism, that should not put you off. Although a rather nondescript village itself, it is set in a spectacular, almost lunar landscape of extraordinary volcanic plugs and basalt outcrops surrounded by a series of imposing peaks, the highest being Kapsiki Mountain or Peak. André Gide found the area so attractive he considered it to be 'one of the most beautiful landscapes in the world'.

15

The mountains are dotted with little stone thatched houses huddling against the rocks and that look almost as if they have simply grown rather than been constructed.

You are likely to be mobbed by village children urging you to follow their tour of sights of the village. These include the *féticheur*, or crab sorcerer (a fortune teller who tells your future by watching the moves of a crab), traditional dancers, and crafts- and tradespeople like potters and blacksmiths.

Hikes can be taken in the surrounding mountains (accompanied, these vary between under a day to several days and start at around CFA10,000 per day including camping with your own tent, staying in a local home, and food) or climb a hill at dawn or dusk to gaze over the beautiful landscape. You can cross into Nigeria from here, which is under two miles away, but be sure to be accompanied by a local guide. Tours are offered by most hotels.

This whole region is a genuine crossroads of races, tribes and religions, and their customs, clothes, hairstyles and physical characteristics are fascinating to compare.

Getting there and away There is regular transport to Mokolo and Maroua, with the most choice on market day (Sunday in Rhoumsiki, Monday in Maroua and Wednesday in Mokolo).

Where to stay and eat The cheapest option is to stay in a village home. Ask around. Most other options are along the main road and can arrange trekking.

La Maison de l'Amitie (12 rooms) ☎ 2229 21 13. Good *boukarous* accommodation, a restaurant, & trekking arranged. $

Campement de Rhumsiki (23 rooms) BP 27 Mokolo; ☎ 2229 16 46. Attractive *boukarous* facing the mountains with AC rooms. There are tennis courts & a restaurant with meals for under CFA5,000. $$

Auberge Le Kapsiki (18 rooms) ☎ 2229 33 56. A bar & restaurant & basic *boukarous* with fans & shared facilities. Trekking & horse trekking arranged. $

✗ **Bar le Baobab** An excellent restaurant near the centre, & its owner, Jules Keka, speaks both French & English & is a perfect guide. $$

MORA *Telephone code: 2229*

Capital of the Wandala (or Mandara) people, like Mokolo, the little village of Mora has lost its attractiveness somewhat in recent years. Located 60km from Maroua, it has one of the best markets in Cameroon, held each Sunday. Share taxis take a 67km route from Mokolo via Koza to Mora on this day, which is prettier than the alternative route via Maroua. It is 30km or 19 miles from the Nigerian border. Minibuses from Ngaoundéré take the better part of a day.

The market attracts a curious mixture, with Muslim Fulani women covered from head to foot as well as the bare-breasted Kirdi mountain women, the Podoko and Mofou, as well as the Wandala, Shua Arabs all coming from Chad and Nigeria as well as Cameroon.

Foodstuffs, like grains, vegetables, fruit and slaughtered animals, cauldrons of maizemeal gruel, roasted corn and rice are typically sold as well as bright, colourful textiles, intricate carvings, painted gourds, leather goods, jewellery and *gris-gris* (necklace charms). There are open-air barber shops, blacksmiths with hand bellows, and local doctors selling traditional medicines, and a separate section for trading animals, particularly donkeys, goats and cattle. There are few of the garish cheap plastic goods so often seen in the south.

Getting there and away There is daily bus transport to and from Maroua.

Where to stay

Auberge Mora Massif Some 400m west of the main junction/2 blocks east of the motor park. Has a bar/restaurant & simple, clean rooms & *boukarous*. **Camping** is CFA1,000 pp. $

Auberge le Podoko Off the main road to Maroua. Has *boukarous* with fans & separate bathrooms, & a good restaurant. $

TOUROU This is another village in the area set in pretty countryside, which gives an excellent insight into the authentic, ancient animist culture of the region. The women of this Kirdi mountain village wear distinctive red decorated wooden calabashes on their heads that look rather like army helmets and which indicate things like their marital status and number of children they have. There is little public transport available but market day is Thursday, for the best choice, although recently the Rhumsiki–Mabas–Tourou road has been impassable at times.

OUDJILLA A popular destination for tourists in this region (although there is no accommodation), the Podoko hilltop village of Oudjilla is about 12km from Mora. The mountain road to Oudjilla is only really suitable for vehicles like motorcycles, 4x4s and heavy landcruisers rather than cars. It is a hard walk by foot up the mountain. The distinctive round thatched mud huts you see from the road are a striking sight.

Parts of the village, which provides glorious views of the region, date back 400 years. You can visit the chief's walled compound (*sare*) (CFA1,000) which is an excellent example of the vernacular architecture. Here you can meet the chief, who lives here in his palace with more than 50 wives and many children. Each wife has a hut and a kitchen and the compound includes other buildings such as a courthouse, huts with the tombs of the chief's father and grandfather and a prayer hall. The walls are made from earth and the roofs of woven straw. A dance may be performed when you visit at a cost of around CFA10,000 per group of visitors. The colourful market is usually held on Wednesdays and Sundays. At a ceremony in April, the Podokwo feast, a sacred bull is sacrificed.

MAGA This picturesque village on the Logon River has excellent white beaches.

It has domed homes that have been made completely from clay. Basic accommodation is available. There is no direct road from Mora to Maga and therefore access is via Maroua, 90km away.

POUSS Located around 10km northeast from Maga, there is a market here on Tuesdays. Pouss has a magnificent Mousgoum vernacular architectural heritage and an excellent museum about it. A highlight here is the sight of locals sailing to Chad over the Logon River.

MABAS This small Kirdi village very near the border with Nigeria is notable for its *chefferie* that enjoys uninterrupted breathtaking views across the large Bornou Plains of Nigeria and where one can still see primitive blast furnaces.

AMSA At Amsa village blacksmiths can be seen at work, making vases and statuettes.

MOZOGO-GOKORO NATIONAL PARK

This relatively small (1,400ha) protected area south of Waza has only 10km of paths and is not open to the public, although this policy may change. It has not suffered from burning of the vegetation for over four decades and therefore it has become thickly forested. Warthog, bushbuck, grey duiker, python, vervet monkey, patas monkey and olive baboon have all been recorded here in recent years.

WAZA NATIONAL PARK

(Main entrance, marked by 2 huts, is just outside the village of Waza; ⊕ 15 Nov–15 Jun 16.00–18.00 daily; admission CFA5,000 plus CFA2,000 per vehicle, CFA2,000 for photography & obligatory guide per vehicle CFA3,000 per day. Walking in the park is not permitted) The Parc National du Waza is located in the flat plains of the far north of the country 334km north of Garoua, 122km north of Maroua and nudging the borders of both Chad and Nigeria. Not only is this Cameroon's most accessible, well-known and visited national park, but it contains some of west and central Africa's most impressive wildlife. It can be visited on a day trip from Maroua provided you start out early in the day.

Covering more than 170,000ha (1,700km²), Waza is home to the 'big five' animals of Africa. The large expanses of flat acacia savanna, seasonal marshes and grassland make viewing of game, especially herds of elephant and giraffe, hippos and antelopes, relatively easy. The variety of landscapes, including forested areas and a huge expanse of grassland dotted with inselbergs and seasonal marshes, supports a wide range of wildlife. The waters of the rainy season bring endless waterbirds, usually peaking in September.

Although the flat scrubland does not make a striking landscape, one major attraction is the hundreds of elephants that gather at the Mare aux Eléphants, the main watering hole. Huge numbers of elephants can also be seen at other watering holes in the park, especially in the dry season. It is not unusual to see herds of over 100. The Mare aux Eléphants takes three or four hours to reach from the northwest entrance of the park. You also have a good chance of spotting lion, many species of antelope, hippo, warthog, cheetah, water buck, topi, red-fronted gazelle, sable roan, domilesque, hartebeest, kob, baboon, monkey, giraffe (these tend to be near the entrance) and buffalo.

Birdlife at the park is prolific and includes eagle, hornbill, black-crowned crane, maribous, pelican, duck, goose, ostrich, heron, stork and guineafowl.

Waza is Cameroon's wildlife park most geared to visitors by far. Camping is not permitted in the park, but you can camp at the entrance and accommodation is available. The best time of year to see animals is from late March to early May, which unfortunately is also the hottest season. When the rains come, from May to October, not all areas of the park are accessible.

Further information on the park is available from the International Union for Conservation of Nature and Natural Resources (IUCN) (*Rte de Mont Fébé, Bastos, Yaoundé;* \ *2220 88 88, Maroua: 2229 22 68*), near the home of the Nigerian High Commissioner.

GETTING THERE AND AWAY The entrance to the park is signposted around 500m from the main road. There are no vehicles for hire at the park, but buses run from Maroua and you can also hire vehicles in Maroua. Some roads around the park can be impassable during the rainy season.

 WHERE TO STAY

⌂ **Campement de Waza** (40 rooms) BP 13; Maroua; \ (Maroua) 2229 16 46/2229 10 07, (Waza) m 7765 77 17/7765 75 58; e reservation@ campement.parcdewaza.com; www.parcdewaza.com. On a hill 600m from the park entrance, this, although the most comfortable option & therefore tending to get booked up, is rather faded & rundown now. Boukarous with AC, clean rooms & private bathrooms are built around a swimming pool (CFA1,000 for non-residents). The restaurant (meals are expensive,

216

with dinner averaging CFA6,000 for soup, main course & fruit, but French fries & omelettes are a cheaper option) has great views of the park. $$

🏠 **Centre d'Accueil de Waza** (15 rooms) Near the main entrance to the park; 📞 2229 22 07. *Boukarous* for 2 with fans & shared facilities. There

is a kitchen available to residents & meals can also be provided, costing about CFA2,000. **Camping** per tent is CFA2,500. $

🏠 **GIC-FAC Café Restaurant du Ilme Millenaire** On the access road to the park just off the main road. Basic accommodation. $

KOUSSERI AND AROUND *Telephone code: 2229*

The paved road (currently particularly damaged between Maroua and Mora) continues northwards from Waza as far as the port town of Kousseri, at the confluence of the Chari and Logone rivers. It sits next to the capital of Chad, Ndjamena, which is reached by either crossing a bridge over the border or taking a boat or *pirogue*. Kousseri has a market on Thursdays.

WHERE TO STAY

🏠 **Auberge Le Confort** 📞 2229 46 36. A restaurant, bar & clean rooms. $

🏠 **Campement du Relais de Logone** 📞 2229 41 57. Outside the centre, with clean rooms. $

NORTH OF KOUSSERI Apart from at the Kalamaloué National Reserve there is no accommodation north of Kousseri on the way to huge Lake Chad. Check the current local security situation in this region before setting out as it has suffered from a number of incidents involving armed bandits in recent years.

Lake Chad To reach Lake Chad take a share taxi the picturesque route to Makari and then another to Blangoua by the river. When the river is not dry motorised *pirogues* can take you to the lake from here for around CFA5,000.

Within the Lake Chad basin is the **Waza Logone Floodplain** of the lower Logone River in the extreme north of the country. It was designated on 20 March 2006 as being one of Cameroon's two Wetlands of International Importance. The other is the Barombi Mbo Crater Lake in Southwest Province (see page 131).

Kalamaloué National Reserve Just northwest of Kousseri is the relatively small (4,500ha) Kalamaloué National Reserve. Created to protect animals crossing to and from Nigeria and Chad, it offers opportunities for viewing wildlife including antelope, giraffe, monkey and warthog, although animal populations have greatly declined. There are also guided walks to view hippo and crocodile in the Chari River. Basic accommodation may be available at the Campement de Kalamaloué, although this was closed at the time of writing.

Moving on to Chad From Kousseri take a taxi across the bridge to Ndjamena.

Moving on to Nigeria Head for Fotokol to cross the border to Gambouru in Nigeria.

Moving on to Niger You can cross Lake Chad to reach Nguigmi in Niger, but it is better to make the journey from Ndjamena rather than from the northern extremities of Cameroon, where there may not be any border facilities.

Appendix I

LANGUAGE

FRENCH AND CAMEROONIAN FRENCH, AND COMMON CAMEROONIAN TERMS
The basics

excuse me	*pardon*	OK	*d'accord*
goodbye	*au revoir*	please	*s'il vous plaît*
hello	*bonjour*	thank you	*merci*
I don't understand	*je ne comprends pas*	What is your name?	*Comment vous appelez-vous?*
I understand	*je comprends*		
no	*non*	My name is	*je m'appelle ...*
yes	*oui*		

Questions

at what time?	*à quelle heure*	when?	*quand?*
Do you speak English?	*parlez-vous anglais?*	where?	*où?*
		why?	*pourquoi?*
how?	*comment?*		

Getting around

aeroplane	*avion*
boat	*bateau*
bus	*autobus*
bus (large)	*car*
bush taxi	*taxi brousse* (also *cinq-cent quatre/brake/sept-place* for Peugeot 504) or *bâché*, a covered pick-up
bus/taxi station/bush taxi park/motor park/lorry park	*gare routière/autogare/garage/gare voiture*
car	*voiture*
car breakdown service	*dépannage*
canoe (dug-out or larger narrow fishing boat)	*pirogue*
dugout canoe	*pirogue*
estate car	*break*
fine or penalty	*amende*
four-wheel-drive (4x4)	*quatre-quatre*
go straight ahead	*continuez tout droit*
I'd like a one-way ticket	*je voudrais un billet aller simple*
I'd like a return ticket	*je voudrais un billet aller retour*
kerosene	*pétrole*
lorry/truck	*camion*
minibus	*petit car*
moped	*mobylette*

motor park	*stationnement*		
petrol/gas	*essence*		
pick-up truck or van	*bâché*		
railway station	*gare*		
road block or barrier	*barrage*		
roundabout	*rond-point*		
saloon car	*berline*		
shared taxi	*taxi-course*		
surfaced road	*route bitumée/goudronée*		
ticket office	*vente de billets/la billeterie*		
track or dirt road	*piste*		
When does it arrive?	*il arrive à quelle heure?*		
When does it leave?	*il part à quelle heure?*		
Where can I rent a bicycle?	*où est-ce que je peux louer un velo?*		
Where is the airport?	*où est l'aéroport?*		

Directions

after	*après*	next to	*à côte de*
before	*avant*	right	*à droite*
behind	*derrière*	road map	*carte routière*
far	*loin*	straight on	*tout droit*
here	*ici*	there	*là*
I am looking for…	*je cherche…*	turn left	*tournez à gauche*
in front of	*devant*	turn right	*tournez à droite*
later	*plus tard*	under	*sous*
left	*à gauche*	where is the…?	*où est…?*
near	*près/pas loin*		

Accommodation

air conditioning	*climatisé*	inn or boarding house	*gîte*
bed	*lit*		
campsite	*camping*	key	*clef*
Do you have rooms available?	*avez-vous des chambres libres?*	May I see the room?	*puis-je voir la chambre?*
hotel-cum-brothel	*maison de passage*	room (with a fan)	*chambre (ventilée)*
hotel (inexpensive)	*auberge*	rural guesthouse	*campement*
hotel (hut with thatched roof)	*boukarou*	shower	*douche*
		small hotel or guesthouse	*auberge*

Eating and drinking

breakfast	*petit-déjeuner*	lunch	*déjeuner*
dinner	*dîner*	refreshments stall	*buvette*
drink	*boire*	street food stall	*chantier/circuit*
eat	*manger*		

Money

bribe, tip	*cadeau, dash*	sterling (pounds)	*livres sterling*
currency or money	*devises, fric, sous, l'argent*	travellers' cheques	*des chèques de voyage*
I want to change money	*je voudrais changer de l'argent*		

Shopping

charm or amulet	*gri-gri*	how many/much	*combien*
closed	*fermé*	inexpensive	*bon marché*
entrance	*entrée*	open	*ouvert*
expensive	*cher*	shop	*magazin*
food shop/grocery	*alimentation*	supermarket	*supermarché*
exit	*sortie*		

Places and people of interest

bakery	*boulangerie*	market	*marché*
bank	*banque*	post office	*la poste/PTT/bureau*
beach	*plage*	town hall	*mairie/hôtel de ville*
bridge	*pont*	traditional	*griot*
BP	*Boîte Postale* (post office box)	entertainer (eg: musician, storyteller)	
countryside, the bush	*brousse*		
crossroads or meeting place	*carrefour*	witch doctor or magic man	*féticheur*
hut	*case*		

Health

chemist	*pharmacie*	pain	*douleur*
doctor	*médecin*	stomach ache	*mal à l'estomac*
headache	*j'ai mal à la tête*	water suitable for drinking	*eau potable*
malaria	*palu/paludisme*		
medicines/medical supplies	*médicaments*	Where is the hospital?	*où est l'hopital?*
mosquito net	*moustiquaire*		

Red tape

checkpoint	*contrôle*	document	*fiche*
chief or boss	*chef* or *patron*	identity card	*carte d'identité*
chief or king (northern Cameroon)	*lamido*	identity papers	*pièces*
		policeman	*flic*
		police station	*préfecture*
chief or king (western Cameroon)	*fon*	prohibited	*interdit*
		required or demanded	*exigé*
details or information	*renseignements*		

Time

in the afternoon	*après-midi*	today	*aujourd'hui*
in the evening	*soir*	tomorrow	*demain*
in the morning	*matin*	two o'clock	*à deux heures*
midday	*à midi*	week	*semaine*
month	*mois*	year	*an*
now	*maintenant*	yesterday	*hier*

Other

a lot	*beaucoup*	biro	*bic*
bad	*mauvais*	cold	*froid*
big	*grand*	discuss	*discuter*

enjoyable	*intéressant*	more	*plus*
festival	*fête*	out of order	*en panne*
go away	*va t'en*	rainy season	*hivernage*
good	*bon*	slum	*bidonville*
hot	*chaud*	small	*petit*
less	*moins*	with	*avec*
little	*un peu*	without	*sans*
man	*homme*	woman	*femme*

THE USE OF TU AND VOUS

- Adults use *tu* to children
- Children use *vous* to all adults
- Adults use *vous* to other adults whether they are business or social contacts
- Cameroonian acquaintances, office employees, workers, etc should be given the *vous* greeting
- Women should use *vous* when talking to Cameroonian men. If a friendship develops, a Cameroonian will sense when to shift to *tu*, and you can follow.

Appendix 2

CHARITABLE ORGANISATIONS WORKING IN CAMEROON

Bushmeat Crisis Taskforce 8403 Coleville Rd, Suite 710, Silver Spring, MD 20910-3314, USA; e info@bushmeat.org; www.bushmeat.org. The Bushmeat Crisis Task Force is a consortium of conservation organisations & professionals working throughout Africa, including Cameroon, & is dedicated to the conservation of wildlife populations threatened by illegal, commercial hunting of wildlife for sale as meat.

Cameroon Biodiversity Conservation Society BP 3055; Messa, Yaoundé; 2221 16 58; m 772 66 08; e cbcs@iccnet.cm. This organisation, an affiliate of BirdLife International, works in the field of rural development & poverty alleviation, encouraging the conservation of Cameroon's biological diversity through the protection of natural habitats, as well as the promotion of study & enjoyment of wildlife for the benefit of people. It implements research, conservation, awareness-raising & education projects, as well as community-based natural resource management projects. One of its recent projects concerned beekeeping in the Mbam-Minkom region near Yaoundé, encouraging villagers to create alternative income sources to allow them to benefit from their forest without the destructive effects of clearing for farming or timber. Colin Workman writes about this in *Chapter 10, Centre Province*, page 174.

Cameroon Education Corporation Suite A, 333 Cedarcreek Dr, Nashville, TN 37211; 615 833 1740; e mlantum@excite.com. The Children's Reading Corner Remedial Nursery & Primary School in Buéa was formed by The Cameroon Education Corporation, a recognised non-profit organisation. It provides pre-nursery, nursery, & primary remedial education to over 180 children aged 3–14.

Cameroon Wildlife Aid Fund www.cwaf.org. This British wildlife charity works in Cameroon on projects such as educational programmes aimed at encouraging schoolchildren to stop eating the meat of endangered species. The charity began work at Yaoundé Mvog-Betsi Zoo in the late 1990s as an initiative to look after primates orphaned as a result of the bushmeat trade. A UK-registered charity based at Bristol Zoological Gardens, it also operates from the forest of Mefou National Park on the outskirts of Yaoundé, where young gorillas & chimpanzees are looked after in spacious enclosures, rescued from threats such as poachers wanting them for bushmeat. It offers 3-month placements for volunteers.

Centre pour l'Environment et le Développement (CED) BP 3430; Yaoundé; 2222 38 57; www.cedcameroun.org. The centre researches potential threats to the environment such as illegal timber extraction.

Childhealth Advocacy International (CAI) Conway Chambers, 83 Derby Rd, Nottingham NG1 5BB, UK; 0115 950 6662; e office@caiuk.org; www.caiuk.orgi. This s a small international charity which runs projects to do with maternal & child health, including some projects based in Bamenda Provincial Hospital.

Earthwatch Institute (UK) 01865 318 838, (US & Canada) 1-800 776 0188, (Australia) 03 9682 6828; www.uk.earthwatch.org. Earthwatch Institute is a non-profit organisation matching members of the public with scientists all over the world. Cameroon is one of the countries with projects where volunteers can participate. There are 3 current projects. One is helping to save the rockfowl, a threatened species, where volunteers join ornithologists to assess the population status & determine ecological requirements of the bird. It involves camping in the forest & trekking long distances & the share of costs is £895. Another project involves documenting endemic plants in the rainforest, & the last measures the impact of public health efforts on intestinal parasites in remote Cameroonian villages. There are also occasional fellowships for students & teachers available. The website www.volunteerabroad.com has details of Earthwatch & other expeditions.

ECOsystèmes Forestiers d'Afrique Centrale (ECOFAC) 2222 42 71/2220 94 72; e ecofac@camnet.cm; www.ecofac.org. ECOFAC is the European Union's organisation set up to help protect central Africa's forest ecosystems & the forest-dwelling peoples. Cameroon is one of the 6 countries covered by the programme (the others being Congo, the Central African Republic, Equatorial Guinea, Gabon & São Tomé & Príncipe, all with a combined population of 20 million, which is growing

A2

223

by 3.2% yearly). Tropical rainforest stretches over about 670,000km² of these countries' territory but is being lost at a rate of almost 1% each year.

Elephants of Cameroon www.nczooeletrack.org. Cameroon's elephant population stands at around 20,000 & faces considerable threats. A research team from the North Carolina Zoological Park, Cameroon's Ministry of Environment & Forests, & the Cameroon office of the WWF are studying elephant migration patterns by placing satellite tracking collars on animals & then analysing their movements over many months. The conservation research programme has produced maps that detail elephant locations, help predict where herds will be at specific times & highlight travel corridors that the herds use to move between territories. The programme's website provides the opportunity to interact with project researchers & post questions, read field diaries, see elephant location data & participate in online discussion forums.

Emicam 4, High Swinton, Masham, North Yorks HG4 4JH, UK; ☎ 01322 8666577; e info@emicam.org.uk; www.eagleheights.co.uk. British charity aiming to help conserve wildlife, specifically birds of prey.

Forests Monitor 69a Lensfield Rd, Cambridge CB2 1EN, UK; ☎ 01223 360975; www.forestsmonitor.org. Monitors activities like illegal logging.

Global Witness PO Box 6042, London N19 5WP; ☎ 020 7272 6731; www.globalwitness.org. Global Witness was launched in 1995 & works on forest issues, especially illegal logging & the problems intensive logging causes. It does this at an international policy level. In Cameroon it is the official independent monitor of the sector.

Greenpeace International Keizersgracht 176, 1016 DW, Amsterdam, The Netherlands; ☎ 20 626 1877; www.greenpeace.org. Among its activities in Cameroon is the investigation of illegal timber extraction. For example, in 2002 Greenpeace released information about the illegal logging activities in southeast Cameroon of Dutch logging & timber-trading company Wijma.

In Defense of Animals – Africa (IDA-A) 700 SW 126th Av, Beaverton, OR 97005, USA; ☎ 503 643 8302; ida-africa.org. Supporting Africa's chimpanzees, this joint project of In Defense of Animals & a non-governmental organisation in Cameroon provides a sanctuary for captive chimpanzees in Cameroon & wages a conservation campaign aimed at saving the country's remaining wild chimpanzees. The sanctuary, the Sanaga-Yong Chimpanzee Rescue Center (SYCRC), was founded in August 1999 in a forest within the Centre Province of Cameroon. This primate care facility is dedicated to the rescue & rehabilitation of threatened adult chimpanzees, occupies over 2km², & is currently home to around 24 chimpanzees. The sanctuary accepts animals that are commonly rejected at other facilities due to their overpowering size, strength & level of psychological damage.

International Fund for Animal Welfare (IFAW) 87–90 Albert Embankment, London SE1 9UD; ☎ 020 7587 6700; e info@ifaw.org; www.ifaw.org. IFAW works towards improving the welfare of wild & domestic animals throughout the world by reducing commercial exploitation of animals, protecting wildlife habitats & assisting animals in distress. They seek to promote animal welfare & conservation policies that advance the well-being of both animals & people. Founded in 1969, IFAW has grown to become one of the largest international animal welfare organisations in the world.

International Primate Protection League (IPPL) PO Box 766, Summerville, SC 29484, USA; ☎ 843 871 2280; e info@ippl.org; www.ippl.org. IPPL has field representatives in Cameroon working towards creating & preserving national parks & sanctuaries, strictly controlling primate hunting, trapping & sale.

International Union for the Conservation of Nature (IUCN) Rue Mauverney 28, Gland, 1196, Switzerland; ☎ 999 0000; in Cameroon BP 5506; Yaoundé; ☎ 2221 6496; www.iucn.org. IUCN works in Cameroon to prevent the bushmeat trade.

Peace Corps ☎ 1 800 424 8580; www.peacecorps.gov. Peace corps volunteers have done 2-year fieldwork stints in Cameroon for many years. Applicants have to be US citizens aged over 18.

People's Trust for Endangered Species 15 Cloisters Hse, 8 Battersea Pk Rd, London SW8 4BG; ☎ 020 7498 4533. Works to preserve & raise awareness for endangered species.

Rainforest Action Network (RAN) Suite 500, 221 Pine St, San Francisco, CA 94104, USA; ☎ 415 398 4404; www.ran.org. RAN works in Cameroon & other countries in Africa, helping communities to protect their land by allowing their voices to be heard in the power institutions to which these local people have no access. RAN focuses on institutions & companies based in industrialised countries that profit from Africa's riches, often adversely. It has confronted the World Bank & its role in creating an economic framework that perpetuates exploitation of the land at the expense of sustainable development.

Rainforest Foundation Suite A5, City Cloisters, 196 Old St, London EC1V 9FR; ☎ 020 7251 6345; www.rainforestfoundationuk.org. This charity was set up by rock star Sting in 1989 to support the indigenous people & traditional habitats of several countries including Cameroon. In Cameroon it is encouraging greater autonomy for Baka people, & protection of some of the undamaged rainforest that remains in the south & east.

Stuff Your Rucksack See page 82 for details.

Survival International 6 Charterhouse Bldgs, London EC1M 7ET; ☎ 020 7687 8700; e info@survival-international.org; www.survival-international.org. Survival International is currently lobbying the Cameroonian government to recognise the rights of the 'Pygmy' peoples, who see their rainforest homes threatened by logging, & are driven out by settlers. In some places they have been evicted & their land has been designated as national parks. In Cameroon, the life of the Bagyeli has been disrupted by the World Bank-sponsored Chad–Cameroon oil pipeline. Survival opposed the building of the pipeline, & lobbied governments, oil companies & the World Bank to that end.

The Jane Goodall Institute 8700 Georgia Av, Suite 500, Silver Spring, MD 20910-3605, USA; ☎ 301 565 0086; e info@janegoodall.org; www.janegoodall.org. The Jane Goodall Institute promotes primate habitat conservation, non-invasive research programmes on chimpanzees & other primates, activities ensuring the well-being of chimpanzees, other primates & animal welfare activities in general. In Cameroon the institute is focusing on the commercial bushmeat trade.

The Bushmeat Project www.bushmeat.net. The Bushmeat Project develops & supports community-based partnerships to benefit local people & develop alternatives to unsustainable bushmeat commerce. The programme works to provide economic & social incentive to people to protect endangered wildlife.

Voluntary Services Overseas (VSO) ☎ 020 8780 7200; www.vso.org.uk. A long-established charity that sends teachers, health workers & other qualified people to projects in developing countries, including Cameroon.

Wildlife Conservation Society 2300 Southern Bd, Bronx, New York 10460, USA; ☎ 718 220 5100; www.wcs.org. The Wildlife Conservation Society has headquarters at the Bronx Zoo in America & works towards saving wildlife & wild lands throughout the world. In Cameroon it is currently working on a conservation & community participation programme in Banyang-Mbo Forest Reserve, is looking into crop raiding & the economic losses faced by local communities, as well as compiling a biological inventory of the Banyang-Mbo Forest Reserve.

World Parrot Trust www.worldparrottrust.org. The World Parrot Trust works towards the survival of parrot species in the wild & the welfare of captive birds everywhere. They restore & protect populations of wild parrots & their native habitats, promote awareness of the threats to all parrots, captive & wild, oppose the trade in wild-caught parrots, educate the public on high standards for the care & breeding of parrots & encourage links between conservation & aviculture. In Cameroon the Trust supports the protection of land that includes clearings which attract tens of thousands of African grey parrots.

World Wide Fund for Nature (WWF) ☎ 2221 62 67; www.wwfcameroon.org. WWF's Cameroon's headquarters are in Yaoundé behind the BAT factory in the Bastos district. They have numerous current projects around the country & protect various sites.

Appendix 3

BIRDING SITE GUIDE Keith Barnes

KORUP NATIONAL PARK (see page 133) Korup supports 425 bird species. Many lowland forest birds are found at Korup, but the greatest prize is the grey-necked rockfowl. Other delights include black guineafowl and both black-eared and grey ground-thrush. Although the bushmeat market has taken its toll, many mammal populations are recovering here and the forests are home to forest elephant, buffalo, sitatunga, leopard, chimpanzee and the magnificent drill as well as collared mangabey, greater white-nosed guenon, Preuss's red colobus, russet-eared guenon and the bizarre water chevrotain.

Birding Mundemba Heading to Mundemba at Korup from Kumba, some 30km before Mundemba there is some excellent forest that is worth birding. The secondary growth offers black-and-white-casqued and yellow-casqued wattled hornbill as well as flocks of noisy grey parrots. At Mundemba itself one must arrange permits and a compulsory guide and porters at the WWF office. The Hotel Iyaz, where one can stay, is 1km beyond the WWF offices, the rare Bates's swift has been recorded over the now closed hotel. The scrub around the hotel may produce western bluebill, Levaillant's cuckoo, chattering cisticola, white-breasted nigrita and olive-bellied sunbird. In the secondary growth around Mundemba both black bee-eater and black-bellied seed-cracker are possible. After passing through Mundemba (*en route* to the park) check the roadside pools and lakes for Hartlaub's duck. As you approach the park, about 10km from Mundemba, one crosses the Mana River and its famous suspension bridge. This area is well worth birding, rock pratincole are regularly seen on exposed rocks in the river, and the surrounding trees are good for hornbills. Be there first thing in the morning to maximise your chances of both black and yellow-casqued wattled hornbills.

To find Picathartes Knoll you will certainly need a guide, which is compulsory to enter the park anyway. Near the entrance to the park there are a number of well-maintained foot trails (120km) and four camps with shelters and latrines. To see the rockfowl, one will need to walk the 8km to the basic Rengo Camp and spend at least one night (more for determined rockfowlers). It is best to be at Picathartes Knoll before 15.30, where you take up a position in or near the cave (follow the advice of your Korup NP guide) and wait patiently for the birds. The birds frequently come to roost at the knoll, which is about 1.5km from Rengo Camp and 180m north of Hunters' Trail. Sometimes the birds do not return to the knoll at all, and one needs several nights there to improve the chances of meeting these scarce creatures. Also, follow the advice in the box to *Finding grey-necked rockfowl*, page 38.

The trails right near Rengo Camp are excellent and red-billed dwarf hornbill (fairly common), bare-cheeked trogon, blue-headed bee-eater, Latham's forest francolin, Nkulengu rail, grey-throated rail, vermiculated fishing owl, Sjostjedt's owlet and black guineafowl were all seen very near the camp in April 2003. The trails to and from Rengo Camp hold 11 different species of greenbul, white-crested and piping hornbill, buff-spotted woodpecker, blue-headed crested flycatcher, chestnut and white-spotted wattle-eye, red-tailed and white-tailed ant-thrush, fire-crested and brown-chested alethe, black-eared ground-thrush, forest flycatcher, black-capped and brown illadopsis and Gray's and Rachel's malimbés. Rengo

Rock is reasonably reliable for Cassin's and Sabine's spinetails, chocolate-backed kingfisher, tit hylia and blue cuckooshrike. Between Ibene Irene Camp and the suspension bridge it is possible to encounter black-casqued wattled hornbill, rufous flycatcher-thrush, white-browed forest-flycatcher, spotted, Sjostedt's, Xavier's and icterine greenbul, yellow and grey longbill and little green sunbird. At Ibene Irene camp listen and look for rufous-sided broadbill, blue cuckoo-shrike, green hylia, red-vented malimbé and spot-breasted Ibis particularly in the early mornings.

Birding Nguti From Nguti, the road to the radio mast supports blue cuckooshrike and many-coloured bushshrike. To the west of Nguti, the village of Baro (30km), has barely been birded, but has already turned up some excellent birds including black spinetail, chocolate-backed kingfisher, blue-headed bee-eater and Willcock's honeyguide. Once at Baro, bird the access road for long-tailed hawk and golden-crowned woodpecker. The track to Korup, reached by heading towards the church, and following the track to the right after 1km, leads to a rope bridge over the river, which is good for blue-headed crested flycatcher and Kemp's longbill, and on to some good forest. The WWF may now have facilities in the park worth exploring.

Other bird species at Korup Palm-nut vulture, Congo serpent-eagle, African green-pigeon, grey parrot, yellow-billed turaco, great blue turaco, Levaillant's and red-chested cuckoo, African emerald cuckoo, yellowbill, little swift, African pygmy and woodland kingfisher, white-throated bee-eater, blue-throated and broad-billed roller, African pied piping, white-crested hornbill, speckled tinkerbird, yellow-spotted barbet, fire-bellied woodpecker, buff-spotted and golden-crowned woodpecker, forest woodhoopoe, black-headed paradise-flycatcher, square-tailed and shining drongo, common wattle-eye, forest robin, little, grey, Ansorge's, plain, slender-billed, simple, eastern bearded, yellow-whiskered, red-tailed and white-bearded greenbul, leaf-love, common and green-tailed bristlebill, yellow-spotted nicator, wood warbler, white-breasted and pale-fronted nigrita, black-headed waxbill, yellow and African pied wagtail, Vieillot's black weaver, Gray's malimbé, green, collared and olive sunbird.

Also present, but a lot less common are white-crested tiger-bittern, afep pigeon, brown nightjar, white-bellied kingfisher, spotted and Willcock's honeyguide, olivaceous flycatcher, white-throated blue swallow, lemon-bellied crombec, maxwell's black weaver, crested malimbé and Johanna's sunbird.

BAMENDA HIGHLANDS: BAFUT-NGUEMBA FOREST RESERVE (see page 155) This area comprises a mosaic of disjunct remnant montane and riverine forest within the Cameroon Mountains EBA. It is undoubtedly the best site to see two highly localised endemics: Bannerman's turaco and banded wattle-eye and the near-endemic Bannerman's weaver. The best area for these birds is right next to Lake Awing. Other specialities that can be seen here include yellow-breasted and mountain boubou, brown-backed cisticola, bangwa scrub warbler, mountain robin chat, forest swallow, Cameroon mountain greenbul, green longtail and cameroon sunbird, little grey flycatcher, grey-chested illadopsis, black-collared apalis, Congo serpent-eagle and a mystery nightjar which was seen here in 2003. It is best to spend a night in Bamenda at the Skyline Hotel where both white-crowned cliff chat and Neumann's starling can be seen in the garden.

Birding Bafut-Nguemba Leaving Bamenda, it is worthwhile checking the grounds of the Bali Safari Lodge, where Bamenda apalis has been recorded, particularly on the stretch of road towards Bamenda; check the first 500m. To get to Bafut-Nguemba, turn east off the N6 18km south of Bamenda, or 33km north of Mbouda, and drive a further 3km before reaching forested gullies amongst eucalyptus plantations. Although all the specials have been seen here, if you can, head straight up to Lake Awing, where most of the target birds are easy.

Bannerman's turaco, banded wattle-eye and Bannerman's weaver are all seen here with relative ease. Other excellent species one might notch up in this seemingly unimpressive forest patch include Cassin's hawk-eagle, yellow-breasted boubou, mountain boubou, forest swallow, Petit's sawwing, Cameroon mountain greenbul, Cameroon olive greenbul, Cameroon sunbird, oriole finch, purple-throated cuckooshrike, Ruwenzori hill-babbler, Elliot's woodpecker, brown-capped weaver and Johanna's sunbird.

Birding Mount Oku For Mount Oku head to Kumbo (aka Banso) from Bamenda and the village of Elak, where BirdLife International's Kilum Mountain Forest Project HQ is located. Green longtail has been recorded in the tiny patch of forest alongside the HQ, forest swallow breeds here and oriole finch is found in the village. Opposite the HQ a trail leads through farmland (45mins) to the forest, which begins at 2,200m. Shortly after the school the trail splits into the gentle KA trail (right) and steeper KD trail (left) before reaching the forest. Bannerman's turaco, banded wattle-eye and Bannerman's weaver all occur here.

Other bird species at Mt Oku Western green tinkerbird, black-shouldered kite, short-toed eagle, gabar goshawk, red-necked buzzard, African hobby, African green pigeon, speckled mousebird, African cuckoo, grey, green-backed, Tullberg's and Elliot's woodpecker, MacKinnon's shrike, bar-tailed trogon, blue-breasted and white-throated bee-eaters, white-headed woodhoopoe, African thrush, Waller's and chestnut-winged starling, common stonechat, black-throated and grey apalis, willow warbler, garden warbler, black-crowned waxbill, yellow wagtail, tree pipit, baglafecht, black-billed and Preuss's weaver, yellow bishop, orange-tufted sunbird, yellow-fronted canary, thick-billed seedeater and red-faced crimsonwing.

MOUNT KUPE NATIONAL PARK (see page 131) An isolated massif, Mount Kupe is arguably the premier birding destination in Cameroon, not least because of the good infrastructure and excellent guides and information available from the local WWF office. Although only 25km² of primary forest remains, a list of over 320 species including some of Africa's rarest birds, such as Mount Kupe bush shrike (see page 37) tempt all manner of birders here. The forests are home to 27 Cameroon Mountain EBA birds including many scarce or threatened species that, despite having an extensive range, are difficult to see elsewhere in Africa. Diversity is high with eight kingfishers, eight woodpeckers, three trogons, seven honeyguides, 21 greenbuls, 14 shrikes, five wattle-eyes and 17 sunbirds. The most sought-after species are Cameroon olive and white-naped pigeons, Sjostedt's owlet, bare-cheeked trogon, western green tinkerbird, Zenker's honeyguide, grey-headed broadbill, mountain boubou, green-breasted bush shrike, black-necked wattle-eye, Crossley's ground thrush, mountain and white-bellied robin-chats, forest swallow, Cameroon mountain and grey-headed greenbuls, green longtail, white-tailed warbler, black-capped woodland warbler, white-throated mountain babbler, grey-necked rockfowl, Fernando Po oliveback, Cameroon and Ursula's sunbirds.

Birding Max's Trail Max's Trail is arguably the best trail for birding on Mount Kupe. It starts at the WWF project leader's cottage adjacent to the school. It passes through farms and secondary forest (farmbush) for the first 2km, up to 1,050m and then continues through primary forest right to the summit. Ignore the 2km of farmbush at your peril, as it provides diversity and good numbers of birds; it is possible to spend a day here without reaching the forest. The farmbush holds a number of 'lowland forest' species not found easily in the primary forest itself, including yellow-billed turaco, black bee-eater, many-coloured, fiery-breasted and grey-green bushshrikes, African and black-and-white shrike-flycatcher, yellow-footed and dusky-blue flycatchers, white-chinned prinia, green longtail, black-faced rufous warbler, black-throated, black-capped and buff-throated apalis, naked-faced barbet, rufous-crowned eremomela, violet-backed hyliota and Woodhouse's antpecker, pale-fronted and grey-headed nigrita.

In the primary forest the trail is steep in places. The forest on the trail at 1,050m and at 1,550m is highly productive and good for mixed species flocks with yellow-bellied wattle-eye, dwarf kingfisher, grey-green bushshrike and many-coloured bushshrike commonly seen. Zenker's honeyguide was regularly seen at around 1,050–1,150m in the 1990s, although records are increasingly scarce now. Other birds to be seen are black-necked wattle-eye, Bates's sunbird, bar-tailed and bare-cheeked trogons, black bee-eater, African piculet, Woodhouse's antpecker, grey-headed broadbill (1,350–1,450m), green-breasted bushshrike (1,400–1,600m), white-throated mountain-babbler (1,250–2,000m), black-headed batis and white-tailed warbler. At about 1,550m there is a clearing that has been used as a campsite; check this area, as red-thighed sparrowhawk, green-breasted bushshrike, African piculet, Fernando Po oliveback and red-faced crimsonwing have been recorded here.

Birding Shrike Trail

The Shrike Trail is very steep (not recommended to anyone who is either unfit or does not have sure footing) and very quickly reaches primary forest. It is located to the right-hand side of the pink building on the far side of the school campus, behind the dam. Most sightings of Mount Kupe bushshrike have been along this trail at an altitude of 950–1,350m. Grey-necked rockfowl has been seen a few times, although it is far from regular, and much luck is required, and white-throated mountain-babbler are often above 1,200m. Other specials seen regularly here include all the trogons, Crossley's ground thrush, Tullberg's woodpecker, chestnut-capped flycatcher, white-spotted wattle-eye, Bate's paradise flycatcher, Bocage's akalat, white-bellied robin-chat and the elusive olive long-tailed cuckoo.

Birding Nature Trail

The shortest and easiest trail is the Nature Trail, which despite being less than 1km long and being right at the edge of the village supports many of the specials, including grey-necked rockfowl (not seen now for several years). The entrance is reached at the south end of the school campus. Search for Bates's swift, grey-headed broadbill, forest swallow, green longtail and violet-backed hyliota here. In the evenings Fraser's eagle owl may be seen or heard here. The highly productive farmbush below the Nature Trail can be reached by going towards the Nature Trail, but continuing straight on over the stream instead of turning left at the small Mount Kupe signpost before the stream. A path goes up a hill, skirting the forest and then curves round to the right through nearly 180°, before dropping back down to the stream. The dead trees along here are exceptionally good for forest-edge hole-nesting species, particularly barbets and tinkerbirds, including bristle-nosed barbet, western green tinkerbird, red-rumped tinkerbird, yellow-throated tinkerbird, yellow-spotted barbet, hairy-breasted barbet and double-toothed barbet. Other specialities to be found include blue-headed wood-dove, fiery-breasted bushshrike, swamp greenbul and green longtail.

Other bird species at Mount Kupe

Palm-nut vulture, African harrier-hawk, lizard buzzard, red-thighed sparrowhawk, long-tailed hawk, black goshawk, Ayres'shawk-eagle, scaly francolin, white-spotted flufftail, tambourine dove, African green pigeon, speckled mousebird, Guinea and yellow-billed turaco, Klaas's, African, emerald and dideric cuckoo, yellowbill, blue-headed and Senegal coucal, black-shouldered nightjar, Sabine's and black spinetail, little swift, chocolate-backed kingfisher, white-crested hornbill, naked-faced and yellow-billed barbet, yellow-rumped tinkerbird, thick-billed and cassin's honeyguide, cardinal Woodpecker, african blue flycatcher, white-bellied and blue-headed crested-flycatcher, black-headed and rufous-vented paradise-flycatcher, shining and velvet-mantled drongo, western black-headed and black-winged oriole, grey, blue and Petit's cuckoo-shrike, red-eyed, pink-footed and large-billed puffback, brown-throated, chestnut and white-spotted wattle-eye, African thrush, brown-chested and fire-crested alethe, narrow-tailed and chestnut-winged starling, purple-headed glossy-starling, white-bellied and snowy-crowned robin-chat, barn swallow, lesser striped-swallow, common bulbul, Cameroon mountain, little, mountain, yellow-whiskered honeyguide, Sjostedt's, swamp, grey-headed, white-throated and icterine greenbul, Cameroon olive-greenbul, African yellow white-eye, chattering cisticola, white-chinned and banded prinia, grey-backed and olive-green camaroptera, white-tailed warbler, green hylia, black-capped woodland-warbler, yellow-bellied and violet-backed hyliota, grey-chested illadopsis, black-crowned waxbill, magpie mannikin, baglafecht, spectacled, black-billed, Vieillot's black and forest weaver, crested and red-headed malimbé, black-winged bishop, scarlet-tufted, green, collared, olive, Cameroon, green-headed, green-throated, Ursula's, northern double-collared, olive-bellied, Johanna's and superb sunbird, mountain robin-chat, tit-hylia, chestnut-breasted nigrita and green-backed twinspot.

SANAGA RIVER The Sanaga River runs near to the village of Edea and is an excellent place to see grey pratincole. It is possible to reach this site either by staying in Douala or at Edea. The forest about 50km south of Douala is excellent and warrants a few hours of birding.

Birding Sanaga River Driving in the direction of Yaoundé from Douala, one finds excellent forest after about 50km. Here pied, piping, white-thighed and black-casqued wattled hornbills can be found. Red-vented and blue-billed malimbé, splendid glossy starling, bristle-nosed and yellow-spotted barbets and speckled tinkerbird may also be seen. Watch overhead for Sabine's spinetail and Bates's swift. The Sanaga River lies some 60km east of Douala *en route* to Yaoundé (N3) near the town of Edea. Just before crossing the Sanaga River turn right on the dirt road to Dizangua and drive for about 10km until the road runs alongside the Sanaga River. From here follow the riverbank and check the sandbanks in the river for grey pratincole and African skimmer. The magical white-throated blue swallow can also occasionally be seen hawking up and down the river; check exposed rocks on the river as they sometimes perch on these. The sandbanks run for 5–6km depending on the water levels. It is possible to get fishermen to take you out on the river, so that you can walk on the sandbanks. These also hold Senegal thick-knee and white-crowned lapwing. It is worthwhile checking the bridge across the Sanaga River on the N3 near Edea; check the telephone wires for Preuss's cliff swallows and the reeds along the river for orange weaver.

Other bird species at the Sanaga River Grey and squacco heron, osprey, palm-nut vulture, common greenshank, common sandpiper, little stint, black-winged stilt, white-fronted plover, white-headed lapwing, black tern, palm and little swift, giant and pied kingfisher, little bee-eater, singing cisticola, tawny-flanked prinia, black-and-white mannikin, African pied wagtail, orange weaver, Vieillot's black weaver, black-winged bishop, olive-bellied sunbird.

MOUNT CAMEROON (see page 125) Although large sectors of the mountain have been deforested, the remaining natural vegetation supports Mount Cameroon francolin and Cameroon speriops, which are found nowhere else in the world as well as brown-backed cisticola, Cameroon pipit and Bates's weaver which are Cameroon endemics. Other special species on the mountain are Cameroon olive pigeon, western green tinkerbird, yellow-breasted boubou, green-breasted bush shrike, mountain robin-chat, mountain saw-wing, Cameroon mountain and grey-headed greenbuls, green longtail, Cameroon scrub warbler, white-tailed warbler, yellow longbill, black-capped woodland warbler, Fernando Po oliveback, Cameroon and Ursula's sunbirds.

Birding Buéa Approximately 70km west of Douala, the mountain is accessible from the town of Buéa. It is possible to walk up to 2,000m above sea level, where one can search for Cameroon pipit and the Cameroon speriops. Visitors need a permit from the tourism office in Buéa.

Birding Limbé The Botanical Gardens at Limbé can be very rewarding, and interesting species to be seen here include blue-headed wood-dove, African blue-flycatcher, rufous-vented paradise-flycatcher, MacKinnon's shrike, brown-throated wattle-eye, Cassin's flycatcher, grey-headed nigrita, slender-billed weaver, Vieillot's black weaver, western bluebill, Reichenbach's sunbird, green-headed sunbird and Carmelite sunbird. Tracks up the mountain can be reached from Mapanja, a village just above Limbé.

NGAOUNDABA RANCH (see page 198) Surrounded by forest–savanna mosaic, the lake and the remnant patches of gallery forest provide a perfect introduction to the birds of the Adamawa Plateau. Cool, forested gullies are interspersed with broadleaved woodlands. The gallery forests are in small valleys with banks that make viewing of the canopy easy. Ranch de Ngaoundaba is situated 40km southeast of Ngaoundéré, the only place to stay, with chalets, a great restaurant and private facilities.

Birding Ngaoundaba Over 200 bird species have been recorded at this ranch, although it undoubtedly holds more, amongst them a number of species difficult to see anywhere in Africa including Schlegel's francolin, brown-chested lapwing, Puvel's illadopsis, thrush babbler, white-collared starling, Bamenda apalis and Dybowski's twinspot. Some of the best birding is around the ranch buildings. The open woodland adjacent to the ranch supports brown-backed woodpecker, Senegal eremomela, white-shouldered black tit, white-collared starling, Emin's shrike (occasionally), white-breasted cuckoo-shrike, black woodhoopoe, spotted creeper, grey-headed bush-shrike, blue-bellied roller, marsh tchagra, Gambaga flycatcher, white-shouldered black-tit, yellow penduline-tit, sun lark and bar-breasted firefinch. In burnt areas watch for Heuglin's wheatear. The lake itself supports bittern, whistling cisticola and marsh tchagra. Brown twinspot is more easily found along the edge of the crater lake. Willcock's honeyguide and Bamenda apalis are seen regularly in the gallery forest in front of the chalets. The gallery forest near the ranch entrance is home to leaf-love, grey-winged robin-chat, grey-headed oliveback, red-faced pytilia, thrush babbler as well as two of Africa's star turacos, white-crested and Lady Ross's. Black-capped babbler, blue-breasted kingfisher, oriole warbler (moho), splendid glossy starling and white-crowned robin-chat are all residents here too. Night drives offer chances of plain, black-shouldered, pennant-winged, standard-winged and long-tailed nightjars. The mammals are no less spectacular with serval, civet and many others recorded.

Other bird species at Ngaoundaba Ranch Little grebe, long-tailed cormorant, African darter, spur-winged goose, little egret, grey and black-headed heron, great and cattle egret, squacco and striated heron, hamerkop, black-shouldered kite, black kite, palm-nut, hooded and white-backed vulture, brown snake-eagle, western marsh-harrier, Montagu's harrier, African harrier-hawk, gabar and red-chested goshawk, shikra, grasshopper and red-necked buzzard, Wahlberg's eagle, Eurasian and grey kestrel, red-necked falcon, double-spurred francolin, white-spotted flufftail, black crake, lesser moorhen, African jacana, common snipe, wood and common sandpiper, wattled lapwing, laughing, African mourning, vinaceous and red-eyed dove, blue-spotted wood-dove, namaqua dove, Bruce's and African green-pigeon, Senegal parrot, red-headed lovebird, speckled mousebird, western grey plantain-eater, Klaas's cuckoo, yellowbill, Senegal coucal, African palm-swift, horus swift, African pygmy-kingfisher, malachite, grey-headed, blue-breasted, striped, giant and pied kingfisher, red-throated bee-eater, African grey hornbill, yellow-rumped and yellow-fronted tinkerbird, Vieillot's and double-toothed barbet, lesser honeyguide, green-backed, cardinal, grey and brown-backed woodpecker, African blue-flycatcher, African paradise-flycatcher, square-tailed and fork-tailed drongo, piapiac, pied crow, African golden-oriole, red-shouldered cuckoo-shrike, common fiscal, yellow-billed shrike, northern puffback, marsh and black-crowned tchagra, tropical boubou, sulphur-breasted and grey-headed bushshrike, white helmetshrike, brown-throated wattle-eye, African thrush, violet-backed and wattled starling,

A3

purple, bronze-tailed, greater blue-eared, lesser blue-eared and splendid glossy-starling, pale and European pied flycatcher, northern black-flycatcher, common nightingale, snowy-crowned and white-crowned robin-chat, whinchat, familiar chat, barn swallow, common bulbul, simple and yellow-throated greenbul, African yellow white-eye, whistling, croaking, siffling and zitting cisticola, tawny-flanked prinia, white-chinned prinia, red-winged grey warbler, yellow-breasted apalis, grey-backed camaroptera, moustached grass-warbler, sedge warbler, greater swamp-warbler, olivaceous warbler, Senegal eremomela, northern crombec, willow and wood warbler, yellow-bellied hyliota, greater whitethroat, brown babbler, bush petronia, red-billed, black-bellied and African firefinch, orange-cheeked, common and black-crowned waxbill, bronze mannikin, variable indigobird, yellow wagtail, yellow-throated longclaw, plain-backed and tree pipit, baglafecht, spectacled, black-necked and village weaver, red-headed weaver, yellow-shouldered widowbird, western violet-backed, green-headed, scarlet-chested, variable, olive-bellied, copper and splendid sunbird, yellow-fronted canary and bronze-winged courser.

DANG LAKE (see page 200) Dang Lake is a large shallow lake located just north of Ngaoundéré (near the university, alongside the road north to Garoua) and is visible from the main road. It is best to visit this lake in the early morning when the heat haze is greatly reduced.

Species at Dang Lake This lake is good for waterbirds and may prove to be under-birded and hold many more interesting species. Thus far the following have been recorded here. Little grebe, long-tailed cormorant, white-faced whistling-duck, African pygmy-goose, yellow-billed duck, little egret, grey heron, great egret, squacco heron, black kite, hooded vulture, western marsh-harrier, lesser moorhen, African jacana, lesser jacana, wood and common sandpiper, spur-winged plover, pied kingfisher, woodchat shrike, sedge warbler and crested lark.

BÉNOUÉ NATIONAL PARK (see page 207)
Birding Bénoué The low rocky hills covered with orchard-like open forest support specials of this zone including Adamawa turtle-dove (drinking in river pools), white-throated francolin, Emin's shrike, rufous-rumped lark and white-fronted black chat. Some of the best birding is in the Campement du Bufflé Noir's garden along the Bénoué River. Prime specialities on the river are Egyptian plover (hippo pools) as well as three-banded and white-headed plover. At dusk check the terrace along the Bénoué River for bat hawk, northern white-faced owl and standard-winged nightjar. A walk along the river with a guard may be arranged in the morning, providing opportunities to see Bruce's green pigeon, grey kestrel, white-crested and violet turaco, giant kingfisher, bearded barbet, pearl-spotted owlet, white-breasted cuckoo-shrike, sulphur-breasted bushshrike, spotted creeper, yellow penduline tit, swallow-tailed bee-eater, little and black-headed weaver and cinnamon-breasted bunting. Other Guinea savanna specials include blue-bellied roller, grasshopper buzzard, stone partridge, four-banded sandgrouse, Senegal parrot, Abyssinian roller, Abyssinian ground-hornbill, Heuglin's wheatear, yellow-billed shrike, Senegal batis, Senegal eremomela, bush petronia, black-faced and black-bellied firefinch, red-winged pytilia and pygmy sunbird. The lucky may find brown-rumped bunting and west African (streaky-headed) seedeater.

Other birds species at Bénoué National Park Hadada ibis, African fish-eagle, white-headed vulture, brown snake-eagle, banded snake-eagle, bateleur, lizard buzzard, shikra, red-necked buzzard, Wahlberg's and booted eagle, Eurasian kestrel, red-footed, lanner and peregrine falcon, white-backed night-heron, Stanley bustard, Senegal thick-knee, bronze-winged courser, helmeted guineafowl, double-spurred francolin, green and wood sandpiper, laughing, African mourning, vinaceous and red-eyed dove, blue-spotted wood-dove, African green-pigeon, speckled mousebird, western grey plantain-eater, red-chested cuckoo, Senegal coucal, pearl-spotted owlet, African palm-swift, grey-headed, pied kingfisher, red-throated, white-throated and northern carmine bee-eater, rufous-crowned roller, African hoopoe, green woodhoopoe, African grey hornbill, Vieillot's barbet, greater honeyguide, fine-spotted and grey woodpecker, African blue-flycatcher, fork-tailed drongo, piapiac, pied crow, African golden-oriole, white-breasted cuckoo-shrike, brubru, northern puffback, black-crowned tchagra, tropical boubou, sulphur-breasted bushshrike, white helmetshrike, African thrush, purple, bronze-tailed and lesser blue-eared glossy-starling, swamp flycatcher, European pied flycatcher, northern black-flycatcher, whinchat, familiar chat, sooty chat, spotted creeper, grey-rumped, barn and wire-tailed swallow, common bulbul, croaking, siffling and rufous cisticola, tawny-flanked prinia, grey-backed camaroptera, olivaceous warbler, yellow-bellied eremomela, northern crombec, Bonelli's and willow warbler, yellow-bellied hyliota, brown babbler, white-shouldered black-tit, rufous-rumped lark, chestnut-backed sparrow-lark, black-bellied and red-billed firefinch, red-cheeked cordonbleu, bronze mannikin, African pied and yellow wagtail, long-billed pipit, little and village weaver, western violet-backed, scarlet-chested, variable, olive-bellied and splendid sunbird, yellow-fronted canary, west African seedeater, cinnamon-breasted bunting, speckle-breasted woodpecker, black-headed gonolek and Cabanis's bunting.

WAZA NATIONAL PARK (see page 216)

Birding Waza-Mora This area holds the richest birdlife in the entire Sahelian band, where the recorded list seems endless. The many small waterholes teem with waterbirds and also attract many dry-country species desperate for water in this harsh environment. The best birds at Waza include the highly sought-after Arabian bustard. Waterholes about 8–10km south of the park entrance on the road to Mora support river prinia and sennar penduline-tit. About 30km north of Mora there are flocks of Sudan golden-sparrow and anywhere where the feathery golden grass can be found is good for quail plover and is excellent habitat for the recently discovered golden nightjar. The entire district could yield scissor-tailed kite. Other range-restricted birds that are best looked for in the Waza–Mora area include Clapperton's francolin, black crowned-crane, black scimitar-bill, chestnut-bellied starling and black scrub-robin.

The park is open from mid-November to mid-June only and it is only possible to enter with a vehicle and the company of a guide. In the dry season nearly all the roads are navigable in a 2WD, although birding by 4x4 is much easier. There are three main areas to bird around Waza: Waza National Park, the pools along the main road south of Waza and the area around the village. Waza NP is one of the best parks in west Africa for observing mammals.

Other bird species at Waza Ostrich, white-faced whistling-duck, comb duck, northern pintail, garganey, grey, black-headed and squacco heron, hamerkop, hadada and sacred ibis, yellow-billed, Abdim's, woolly-necked, white, saddle-billed and marabou stork, African openbill, bat hawk, black-shouldered kite, black kite, Egyptian, hooded, white-backed, lappet-faced and white-headed vulture, Rueppell's griffon, short-toed eagle, bateleur, pallid and Montagu's harrier, dark chanting-goshawk, grasshopper and red-necked buzzard, tawny and Wahlberg's eagle, Eurasian kestrel, helmeted guineafowl, African jacana, green, wood and common sandpiper, black-winged stilt, spur-winged plover, black-headed lapwing, chestnut-bellied sandgrouse, European turtle-dove, laughing, African mourning, vinaceous and red-eyed dove, African collared-dove, namaqua dove, speckled mousebird, western grey plantain-eater, Senegal coucal, barn owl, spotted eagle-owl, African palm-swift, grey-headed kingfisher, green bee-eater, Abyssinian roller, African hoopoe, green woodhoopoe, red-billed and African grey hornbill, Abyssinian ground-hornbill, Vieillot's barbet, grey woodpecker, pied crow, woodchat and masked shrike, lesser blue-eared and long-tailed glossy-starling, yellow-billed oxpecker, whinchat, northern and Heuglin's wheatear, northern anteater-chat, sand and plain martin, barn, red-chested and Ethiopian swallow, red-pate and winding cisticola, tawny-flanked and river prinia, grey-backed camaroptera, melodious warbler, willow warbler, chestnut-backed sparrow-lark, grey-headed sparrow, bush petronia, red-billed firefinch, red-cheeked cordonblue, black-rumped waxbill, African silverbill, bronze mannikin, cut-throat, variable indigobird, northern paradise-whydah, yellow wagtail, white-billed buffalo-weaver, chestnut-crowned sparrow-weaver, little weaver, red-billed quelea, pygmy sunbird, white-rumped seedeater, cinnamon-breasted bunting, white-backed duck, secretary-bird, painted snipe, spotted thick-knee and lesser moorhen.

Appendix 4

FURTHER INFORMATION

BOOKS
Background/general

Scarecrow Press, US, has a series of African Historical Dictionaries.

Hachette and Jeune Afrique publish guides in French to Francophone African countries.

World Bibliographical Series from the Clio Press, Old Clarendon Ironworks, 35a Great Clarendon Street, Oxford OX2 6AT; ☎ 01865 311350.

Taussig, Louis *Resource Guide to Travel in Sub-Saharan Africa, vol. 1, East and West Africa* (Hans Zell 1994). Has very detailed information on Cameroon including lists of organisations, societies and conservation projects, and reviews of travelogues, guidebooks and maps.

Caufield, Catherine *In the Rainforest: Report from a Strange, Beautiful, Imperiled World* (University of Chicago Press 1984). Fact-filled tour by Caulfield of the ecology of the world's rainforests and the thorny issues relating.

Reader, John *Africa: A Biography of the Continent* (Penguin 1998). An introduction to the history of Africa.

Martin, Phyllis and O'Meara, Patrick *Africa* (Indiana University Press 1979). Covers the history, culture politics, religion, colonialism, arts and other aspects of the continent.

Beckwith, Carol and Fisher, Angela *African Ceremonies* (Harry N Abrahams 2002) A visual guide to the diversity of ritual and ceremony in modern Africa.

Murray, Jocelyn (ed) *Cultural Atlas of Africa* (Facts on File 1988) A cultural portrait of African history and culture.

Davidson, Basil *The Black Man's Burden: Africa and the Curse of the Nation-State* (Times Books 1993). Tracing the origins of Africa's independence movement, this book places the continent's current political instability in a historical perspective.

Boyle, T C *Water Music* (Granta Books 1998, Viking Penguin 1983) Lengthy humorous fictionalised account of Mungo Park's explorations 200 years ago.

Journalism about Africa

Marnham, Patrick *Dispatches from Africa* (Penguin 1980). A very insightful, entertaining book.

West, Richard *The White Tribes of Africa* (Jonathan Cape 1965). Fascinating examination of how white people integrated in 14 sub-Saharan countries in Africa.

Lamb, David *The Africans* (Vintage Book, 1987). Very readable and entertaining bestselling political and social survey of Africa in the early 1980s covering 46 countries, remaining relevant today.

Harden, Blaine *Africa: Dispatches from a Fragile Continent* (HarperCollins 1992). Harden was the African bureau chief of the *Washington Post* yet this is a disappointing read.

Gates, Stephan *In the Danger Zone* (BBC Books 2008). Accompanying the BBC TV series, *Cooking in the Danger Zone*, this terrific read includes a chapter about Cameroon.

History of Africa

Hugon, Ann *Exploration of Africa: From Cairo to the Cape* (Thames and Hudson 1993). Concise chronicle of 19th century exploration of Africa.

Fage, J D et al *History of Africa* and *A Short History of Africa* (Penguin 1990). Consisely written but comprehensive.

Pakenham, Thomas *The Scramble for Africa* (Abacus 1992). A very readable history of the Victorian land grab of Africa.

Oliver, Roland and Atmore, Anthony *Africa in the Iron Age, The African Middle Ages 1400–1800* and *Africa since 1800* (Cambridge University Press 1975). Detail of these important periods in African history.

Birkett, Dea *Mary Kingsley: Imperial Adventuress* (Macmillan 1992). Absorbing biography.

Afigbo, A E et al *The Making of Modern Africa, vol 1 Nineteenth Century, vol 2 Twentieth Century* (Longman 1986). A detailed history with illustrations.

Diop, Cheik Anta *Pre-Colonial Black Africa* (Africa World Press 1990). First published in the 1950s; Diop says that both African and Western civilisations started in Africa.

Davidson, Basil *Africa in History* (Scribner, 1995). Readable history focusing on the 19th and 20th centuries.

Davidson, Basil et al *A History of West Africa 1000–1800* (Longman 1977). Readable historical account.

Webster, J B and Boahen, A *West Africa Since 1800* (Longman 1980). A follow-up to the above.

McEvedy, Colin *Penguin Atlas of African History* (Penguin 1995, 1980). Historical overview of the continent.

Hibbert, Christopher *Africa Explored: Europeans in the Dark Continent 1769–1889* (Cooper Square 2002).

Manning, Patrick *Francophone Sub-Saharan Africa 1880–1985* (Cambridge University Press, 1988).

Davidson, Basil *The Story of Africa* (Mitchell Beasley 1984). A well-illustrated book that accompanied a television history of Africa.

Davidson, Basil *Modern Africa* (Longman 1983). Looking at African history since 1900.

History of Cameroon

Catchpole, Brian and Akinjogbin, L A *A History of West Africa in Maps and Diagrams* (Collins Educational 1984).

Delancey, Mark W and Mokeba, H Mbella *Historical Dictionary of the Republic of Cameroon* (Scarecrow Press 1994). This book examines the many groups that make up Cameroon and focuses on individuals who have played a notable role, delving into political, economic, social, cultural and other aspects.

Njeuma, Martin *Introduction to the History of Cameroon; Nineteenth and Twentieth Centuries* (Macmillan Education 1989).

LeVine, Victor T *The Cameroons: From Mandate to Independence* (University of California Press: Berkeley 1971).

LeVine, Victor T *The Cameroon Federal Republic* (Cornell University Press: New York 1971).

Politics, culture, environment and society in Africa

O'Brien, Donal Cruise *Contemporary West African States* (Cambridge University Press 1990). Includes a section on Cameroon.

Blakely, T D (ed) *Religion in Africa: Experience and Expression* (Heinemann, US 1994).

Church, R J Harrison *West Africa* (Longman 1980). Thorough; first published in 1957.

Rosenblium, Mort and Williamson, Doug *Squandering Eden* (Harcourt 1987). Proposals for stable African environments.

Caulfield, Catherine *Masters of Illusion: The World Bank and the Poverty of Nations* (Macmillan 1987). Exposing the huge inadequacies of this international development lending agency.

Timberlake, Lloyd *Africa in Crisis* (Earthscan 1985). Examines political and environmental factors contributing to drought and famine on the continent.

Cutrufelli, Maria Rose *Women of Africa: Roots of Oppression* (Zed Press 1983). Laborious study of women's position in contemporary Africa.

Politics, culture and society in Cameroon

DeLancey, Mark *Cameroon: Dependence and Independence* (Dartmouth 1989). Very thorough survey of the economics, politics and history of Cameroon.

Takougang, Joseph and Krieger, Milton H *African State and Society in the 1990s: Cameroon's Political Crossroads* (Westview Press 2001).

Pool, Robert *Dialogue and the Interpretation of Illness: Conversations in a Cameroon Village* (Berg 1994).

Denis, Alain *Beyond Legends: West Cameroon* (Beyond Sight: Cameroon, Editions du Damalisque).

Bjornson, Richard *The African Quest for Freedom and Identity: Cameroonian Writing and the National Experience* (Indiana University Press 1991).

Ngwainmbi, Komben Emmanuel *Communication, Efficiency and Rural Development in Africa: The Case of Cameroon* (University Press of America 1994).

Austen, Ralph A and Derrick, Jonathan M *Middlemen of the Cameroon Rivers: The Duala and their Hinterland* (Cambridge University Press 1999). About the Duala 'middlemen', who functioned as intermediaries between Europeans and their own hinterland for over 300 years. Originally traders in ivory, slaves and palm products, they then became colonial-era cocoa planters, and finally took a leading role in anti-colonial politics.

Burnham, Philip *The Politics of Cultural Difference in Northern Cameroon* (Smithsonian Books 1996).

Alexander, Lloyd and Hyman, Trina Schart (illustrator) *The Fortune-Tellers* (Dutton Books 1992). This original folk tale set in Cameroon is full of adventure and humour, telling of a young man becoming the village fortune teller.

Herrera, Susana *Mango Elephants in the Sun: How Life in an African Village Let Me Be in My Skin* (Shambhala Publications 2000).

Bocquene, Henri *Memoirs of a Mbororo: The Life of Ndudi Umaru, Fulani Nomad of Cameroon* (Berghahn Books 2002). Recounting the life of a nomadic Fulani and subsequently effectively shedding light on Cameroonian pastoral society. Ostracised because of his leprosy and befriended by a missionary, Umaru becomes a field assistant and searches for a cure for his leprosy.

Books about Cameroon for children

Grifalconi, Ann *The Village of Round and Square Houses* (Little, Brown 1986). For young children, the story of the village of Tos, where the women live in round houses and the men live in square ones.

Travel health guides

Dawood, Dr Richard *Travellers' Health* (Oxford University Press 2003). A very comprehensive yet readable book on the subject.

Schroeder, Dick *Staying Healthy in Asia, Africa and Latin America* (Avalon Travel Publishing 2000). A detailed, good all-round guide.

Werner, David *Where There is No Doctor* (Macmillan 1993). Geared to the longer-term visitor such as an expat or Peace Corps worker.

Arts

Bascom, William *African Art in Cultural Perspective* (W W Norton 1985). Covering African sculpture.

Laduke, Betty *Africa: Women's Art, Women's Lives* (Africa World Press 1997). Cameroonian pottery and bead-making are covered.

Caraway, Caren *African Designs of the Congo, Nigeria, the Cameroons and the Guinea Coast* (Stemmer 1986).

Denyer, Susan *African Traditional Architecture* (Holmes and Meier 1978). Includes many illustrations.

Blier, Suzanne *The Royal Arts of Africa: The Majesty of Form* (Prentice Hall Macmillan 1998). Includes a chapter on Cameroon.

Werner, Gillon *Short History of African Art* (Penguin 1991). Rather detailed instead of brief.

Willet, Frank *African Art* (Thames and Hudson 1994). A good in-depth overview of African art through the ages.

Picton, John and Mack, John *African Textiles* (Westview Press 1998). Includes numerous photographs.

Huet, Michael *The Dance, Art and Ritual of Africa* (Harry N Abrahams 1996). Engrossing photography.

Northern, Tamara *Art of Cameroon* (University of Washington Press 1986). Includes colour illustrations.

Fisher, Angela *Africa Adorned* (Harry N Abrahams 1998). Includes coverage of west African jewellery.

Etienne-Nugue, Jocelyne *Crafts and the Art of Living in the Cameroon* (Louisiana State University Press 1982).

Northern, Tamara *Expressions of Cameroon Art: The Franklin Collection* (Rembrandt Press 1986).

Natural history and field guides

Wheatley, Nigel and Helm, Christopher *Where to Watch Birds in Africa* (A & C Black 1995). A comprehensive chapter on Cameroon.

Borrow, Nik et al *A Guide to the Birds of Western Africa: An Identification Guide* (Christopher Helm 2001). An illustrated comprehensive guide to the region. Although bulky and pricey, it is often recommended by birders as being the best.

Van Perlo, B *Birds of Western and Central Africa: An Illustrated Checklist* (Collins 2002). Useful, convenient pocket-sized birders book.

Fishpool, L D C and Evans, M I (eds) *Important Bird Areas in Africa and Associated Islands: Priority Sites for Conservation* (Pisces Publications and BirdLife International 2002). Contains a chapter on Cameroon.

Serle, W and Morel, G *A Field Guide to the Birds of West Africa* (HarperCollins 1977).

Mackworth-Praed, C and Grant, C *Birds of West-central and Western Africa* (Longman 1970).

Urban, E K, Fry, C H and Keith, S *Birds of Africa* (Poyser 2004). A comprehensive six-volume set.

A Field Guide to the Butterflies of Africa (Collins 1969).

Guide des Parc Nationaux d'Afrique: Afrique de l'Ouest (Delachaux, Lausanne 1992). Francophone coverage includes some Cameroonian parks.

Alden, Peter *National Audubon Society Field Guide to African Wildlife* (Knopf 1995). Covering the landforms, wild areas, mammals, birds, reptiles and insects of Africa.

Kingdon, Jonathan *The Kingdon Field Guide to African Mammals* (Christopher Helm 2003). A well-regarded comprehensive field guide to African mammals covering more than 1,000 species, with excellent illustrations, although not the most user-friendly.

Haltenorth, T and Diller, H *A Field Guide to the Mammals of Africa* (Collins 1981). A classic, if a bit dated.

Stuart, Chris and Stuart, Tilde *Field Guide to the Larger Mammals of Africa* (Struik 1997). Excellently laid out, with over 400 photographs for easy identification.

Estes, Richard *The Safari Companion: A Guide to Watching African Mammals* (Chelsea Green Publishing 1999). An in-depth guide to the behaviour and habitats of large African mammals.

Lambertini, Marco and Venerella, John *A Naturalist's Guide to the Tropics* (University of Chicago Press 2000). Illustrated guide to the natural history of the tropics.

Giles-Vernick, Tamara *Cutting the Vines of the Past: Environmental Histories of the Central African Rain Forest* (University of Virginia Press 2002). The failure of conservation in Central Africa.

Lanting, Frans and Eckstrom, Christine *Jungles* (Taschen 2000). Stunning wildlife photographs.

Oakes, John F *Myth and Reality in the Rain Forest: How Conservation Strategies are Failing in West Africa* (University of California Press 1999). A study of national parks and conservation in west Africa.

African travel narrative/travelogues

Kingsley, Mary *Travels in West Africa* (National Geographic and other editions including Everyman 1993). A travel classic published in 1897, with Kingsley's cool, amused yet enthused account of her 1890s travels in the region including a trek up Mount Cameroon. There is an imperial tone yet the book is intelligent and Kingsley has no faith in colonialism or missionaries.

Park, Mungo *Travels into the Interior of Africa* (Eland Books 1983). First published in 1799, this absorbing account remains a classic.

Daniels, Anthony *Zanzibar to Timbuktu* (John Murray 1988, Century 1989). A very absorbing, entertaining account of a trip from Zanzibar to Mali, including Cameroon, by train, lorry, boat and canoe.

Stevens, Stuart *Malaria Dreams: An African Adventure* (Atlantic Monthly Press 1989). Rather uninformative travelogue about a trip from Algeria to the Central African Republic, passing through Cameroon.

Gide, André *Travels in the Congo* (Penguin 1986). This classic of travel literature, which covers Cameroon and which was first published in 1927, shows Gide an angry witness to the injustices of French colonialism.

Turnbull, Colin *The Forest People* (Pimlico 1994). First published in 1961, a study of the Ituri forest Bambuti 'Pygmies' in the Congo.

Turnbull, Colin *The Lonely African* (Chatto & Windus 1963). Turnbull's follow-up book examining the importance and meaning of the tribe in Africa.

Dickinson, Matt *Long Distance Walks in North Africa* (Crowood Press 1991). Despite the misleading title, this entertaining book has interesting accounts of a climb of Mount Cameroon and the Mandara Mountains.

Cahill, Tim *Hold the Enlightenment* (Black Swan 2003). Amusing romp through the Congo.

Biddlecombe, Peter *French Lessons in Africa* (Little, Brown 1995). One of a series of quite amusing and occasionally insightful books by this travelling businessman.

Huxley, Elspeth *Four Guineas* (1954). Huxley's trip through the four anglophone colonies on the eve of independence.

Watson, Pamela *Esprit de Battuta: Alone Across Africa on a Bicycle* (Aurum Press 1999). Travelogue that includes Cameroon.

Matthiessen, Peter *African Silences* (Random House 1991). About the author's travels in central and western Africa, with an ecological bias.

Naipaul, Shiva *North of South* (Penguin 1980). Compelling, entertaining, enlightening, disturbing account of Naipaul's travels through Kenya, Tanzania and Zambia.

Cameroon travel narrative/travelogues

Murphy, Dervla *Cameroon with Egbert* (John Murray 1989). Rambles a bit but the most popular travelogue by far about Cameroon in recent years.

Barley, Nigel *The Innocent Anthropologist: Notes from a Mud Hut* (British Museum Publications 1983, Penguin 1986). Absorbing, entertaining and insightful account of Barley's anthropological expeditions to a Cameroonian village populated by Dowayos, a pagan mountain tribe.

Barley, Nigel *A Plague of Catapillars: A Return to the African Bush* (Viking 1986, Penguin 1987). Equally good follow-up.

Durrell, Gerald *The Overloaded Ark* (1953, Faber 2001), *The Bafut Beagles* (1954), *A Zoo in My Luggage* (1960). Entertaining 1950s accounts by the well-known naturalist of his searches for various animals, evoking a very English colonial Africa that has long gone.

Deane, Shirley *Talking Drums: From a Village in Cameroon* (John Murray 1985). An absorbing account of Yaoundé-based English teacher Deane's experiences spending weekends working with the women of the village of Etam.

Sheppherd, Joseph *Leaf of Honey* (Bahai 1988). An account by an American anthropologist about the Ntuumu peoples of Cameroon.

African literature

Strathern, Oona (ed) *Traveller's Literary Companion* (In Print Books 1994, Passport Books 1995). More than 250 examples of literature from around the continent.

Maja-Pearce, Adewale (ed) *Heinemann Book of African Poetry in English* (Heinemann 1990). A good overview of poetry of the continent.

Moore, Gerald and Beier, Ulli (eds) *The Penguin Book of Modern African Poetry* (1998).

Allen, Benedict *The Faber Book of Exploration* (Faber 2002). Collates the words of many travellers and explorers through the ages, including west Africa.

Naipaul, V S *A Bend in the River* (Random Hous, 1989). Covers rural life in central Africa.

Boyd, William *A Good Man in Africa* (Penguin 1982). A lighthearted look at west Africa as seen through expatriate eyes.

Cameroonian literature

Oyono, Ferdinand *Houseboy* (1956, translated from *Une Vie de Boy*, Heinemann 1990) and *The Old Man and the Medal* (1967, translated from *Le Vieux Negre et la Medaille*, Heinemann 1982). Striking criticism of colonialism.

Bebey, Francis *Agatha Moudio's Son* (translated from *Le fils d'Agatha Moudio*, Heinemann 1971). Musician Bebey's debut novel about human relationships within a village.

Beti, Mongo *The Poor Christ of Bomba* (Heinemann 1971), *Mission to Kala* (1957, Heinemann 1964); *The Story of the Madman* (University of Virginia Press 2001), *King Lazarus* (Muller 1961) and other titles. Beti is probably Cameroon's best-known writer, covering social and political satire touching upon anything from dictatorship and democracy to basic human conflicts. *The Poor Christ of Bomba* cynically features the failure of a missionary to convert a village and missionaries are covered again in his novel *King Lazarus* while inter-tribal conflict is a theme of *Mission to Kala*.

Makuchi *Your Madness, Not Mine: Stories of Cameroon* (Ohio University Press 1999). Short stories by this enduring Cameroonian writer.

Beyala, Calixthe *Your Name Shall Be Tanga* (Heinemann 1996), *The Sun Hath Looked Upon Me* (Heinemann 1996). Chronicling the injustices of women in a male-dominant society.

Mokoso, Ndeley *Man Pass Man!* (Addison Wesley 1998). Entertaining short stories.

Kenjo Jumban *The White Men of God* (Heinemann 1980). Covers the country's colonial experience, where a Cameroonian village becomes divided when a white missionary arrives.

Asong, Linus *The Crown of Thorns* (Cosmos Educational Publishing 1990). Tribal society in the northwest.

Mbella Sonne Dipoko *Because of Women* (Heinemann 1975). A story about a river man quarrelling with his pregnant wife over another woman.

Guides

Hatt, John *The Tropical Traveller* (Penguin 1993). A well-written, absorbing and entertaining book full of advice on most aspects of travelling in the tropics: anything from money to flying, health, culture shock, animal and human hazards.

MAGAZINES

Travel Africa 4 Rycote Lane Farm, Milton Common, Oxon OX9 2NZ; ℡ 01844 278883; www.travelafricamag.com. An excellently designed and illustrated quarterly magazine with stimulating articles about all aspects of travel in Africa.

MAPS AND GENERAL INFORMATION The Cameroonian Embassy and Cameroon Airlines may be able to provide a small amount of tourist information on the country.

Buy a good map before you leave home as these can be difficult to obtain. International Travel Maps (ITMB Publishing) publishes a good one, with a scale of 1:1,480,000 and Macmillan publishes another (1:1,500,00), both with place-name indexes and city plans of Yaoundé and Douala. The Macmillan map has much better maps of Douala and Yaoundé, and on the national map indicates more touristic sites.

There is also a full colour sheet map published by Institut Geographique National (IGN), and an international road map from Freytag & Berndt Maps with a place-name index in several languages. The scale for both is 1:1,150,000. The former is not particularly detailed.

All the maps have considerable strengths and weaknesses and omissions, and if you are planning to go off the beaten track or travel extensively rurally, it may be worth buying two or three national maps and pooling their information.

In Cameroon, other maps are available at the Centre Geographique National (*Av Monseigneur Vogt;* ☎ *2222 29 21/2222 34 65*). It has national, regional and city maps, and publishes the national one for the Institut Geographique National, mentioned above.

SPECIALIST MAP AND TRAVEL BOOKSHOPS
UK

Africa Book Centre ☎ 01273 560474; www.africabookcentre.com. Its bookshop within the Africa Centre in Covent Garden, London, has sadly closed but it now operates as an online mail order bookseller.

African Books Collective Jam Factory, 27 Park End St, Oxford OX1 1HU; ☎ 01865 726686; www.africanbookscollective.com. Publications from many African publishers.

Blackwell's Map & Travel Shop 50 Broad St, Oxford OX1 3BQ; ☎ 01865 793550

Daunt Books 83 Marylebone High St, W1M 4AL; ☎ 020 7224 2295. Devoted to travel.

John Smith & Sons 57–61 St Vincent St, Glasgow G2 5TB; ☎ 0141 221 7472; www.johnsmith.co.uk

La Page French Bookshop 7 Harrington Rd, London SW7; ☎ 020 7589 5991. For francophone publications about Cameroon.

Stanfords 12–14 Long Acre, London WC2E 9LP; ☎ 020 7836 1321; www.stanfords.co.uk. Multi-storey travel bookshop emporium.

Stanfords 29 Corn St, Bristol BS1 1HT; ☎ 0117 929 9966; www.stanfords.co.uk

The Travel Bookshop 13–15 Blenheim Cres, London W11 2EE; ☎ 020 7229 5260; www.thetravelbookshop.co.uk

Republic of Ireland

Eason's 40 O'Connell St, Dublin 1; ☎ 01 858 3881; www.eason.ie

France

L'Harmattan 16 Rue des Ecoles, 5e, Paris. A great choice of African books published in French.

North America

The Complete Traveler Bookstore 199 Madison Av, New York, NY 10019

Globe Corner Bookstore 28 Church St, Cambridge, MA 02138; ☎ 1 800 358 6013; www.globecorner.com

The Literate Traveler 8306 Wilshire Bd, Suite 591, Beverly Hills, Los Angeles, CA 90211; ☎ 1 800 850 2665; www.literatetraveller.com

SPECIALIST MUSIC SHOPS
UK

Stern's 74–75 Warren St, London W1T 5PF; ☎ 020 7387 5550

France

Afric' Antilles Music 3 Rue des Plantes, 75014, Paris; ☎ 01 45 42 43 52

North America

Africassette Music PO Box 24941, Detroit, MI 48224; www.africassette.com

SPECIALIST LIBRARIES AND RESOURCE CENTRES
UK

Africa Centre 38 King St, London WC2E 8JT; ☎ 020 7836 1973; africacentre.org.uk. Library, reading room, restaurant, bar, bookshop, live music, etc.

Commonwealth Institute Kensington High St, London W8 6NQ; ☎ 020 7603 4535; www.commonwealth.org.uk. Library & exhibitions.

Royal Geographical Society 1 Kensington Gore, London SW7 2AR, ☎ 020 7591 3030; www.rgs.org. The Society has an expedition advisory service & lots of resource material. If you want a 150-page report on the plants of Mount Kupe, this is the place to come.

School of Oriental and African Studies Thornhaugh St, Russell Sq, London WC1H 0XG; ☎ 020 7637 2388. Large library.

North America

Center for African Studies Florida University, 427 Grinter Hall, Gainesville, FL 32611; ☎ 352 392 2183

Institute of African Studies Columbia University, 1103 School of International Affairs, 420 W 118th St, New York, NY 10027; ☎ 212 280 4633; www.columbia.edu

Council on African Studies Yale University, 89 Trumbull St, New Haven, CT 06520; ☎ 203 432 3436

WEBSITES
Government travel advice

www.fco.gov.uk British Foreign and Commonwealth Office
www.travel.state.gov US Department of State Travel Advisory Department
www.dfat.gov.au Australian Department of Foreign Affairs
www.dfait-maeci.gc.ca Canadian Department of Foreign Affairs

News

www.africanews.org
www.usafricaonline.com
www.allafrica.com
www.africaonline.com
www.africadaily.com
www.news.bbc.co.uk BBC World Service
www.panapress.com PanaPress

General

www.bbc.co.uk/worldservice/africa/features/storyofafrica BBC World Service site, section entitled the Story of Africa. Includes links concerning west Africa.
www.wwfcameroon.org World Wide Fund for Nature's Cameroon site
www.camnet.cm/mintour/tourisme Cameroon Ministry of Tourism, in French.
www.cameroun-plus.com Listings for hotels, restaurants, *agences de voyage*, touristic sites and other aspects of the country from a visitor's perspective.
www.irinnews.org Information on regional trouble spots and refugee issues.
www.africasounds.com Information on Cameroonian music.
www.cafonline.com African Cup of Nations (Confederation Africaine de Football) official website.

www.lespagesjaunesafrique.com African Yellow Pages, lists thousands of companies and services in Cameroon and other countries in Africa and is in both English and French.

www.sas.upenn.edu/African_Studies/Home_Page/Country.html University of Pennsylvania African Studies site includes information on Cameroon and links.

www.ecowas.int Economic Community of West African States (ECOWAS).

www.crawfurd.dk/photos/cameroon/htm Jacob Crawfurd's website has 100 excellent photos of Cameroon with informative captions.

www.africanbirdclub.org African Birdclub. Has information and links for those going to the region to birdwatch.

www.afrika.no Index on Africa. A Norwegian site containing information on cultural issues, language, etc.

www.nhbs.com Online natural history, environment and science bookstore; has a number of specialist publications about Cameroon.

www.weather.com and **www.weather.yahoo.com** Daily weather reports on various towns and cities in Cameroon are available from a number of websites including these.

www.zyama.com Online African Art Museum. Has examples of art from Cameroonian ethnic groups including the Bamiléké and Bamoun.

Online air ticket sellers
www.onetravel.com
www.sidestep.com
www.travelocity.com
www.travel.com.au For flights out of Australasia.

Index

Page numbers in **bold** refer to major entries, those in *italics* indicate maps

WIN £100 CASH!
READER QUESTIONNAIRE

Send in your completed questionnaire for the chance to win £100 cash in our regular draw

All respondents may order a Bradt guide at half the UK retail price – please complete the order form overleaf.

(Entries may be posted or faxed to us, or scanned and emailed.)

We are interested in getting feedback from our readers to help us plan future Bradt guides. Please answer ALL the questions below and return the form to us in order to qualify for an entry in our regular draw.

Have you used any other Bradt guides? If so, which titles? . . . .
. . . .

What other publishers' travel guides do you use regularly? . . . .
. . . .

Where did you buy this guidebook? . . . .

What was the main purpose of your trip to Cameroon (or for what other reason did you read our guide)? eg: holiday/business/charity etc. . . . .
. . . .

What other destinations would you like to see covered by a Bradt guide?
. . . .

Age (circle relevant category) 16–25   26–45   46–60   60+

Male/Female (delete as appropriate)

Home country . . . .

Please send us any comments about our guide to Cameroon or other Bradt Travel Guides. . . . .
. . . .
. . . .
. . . .

Bradt Travel Guides
23 High Street, Chalfont St Peter, Bucks SL9 9QE, UK
✆ +44 (0)1753 893444 **f** +44 (0)1753 892333
e info@bradtguides.com
www.bradtguides.com

CLAIM YOUR HALF-PRICE BRADT GUIDE!

Order Form

To order your half-price copy of a Bradt guide, and to enter our prize draw to win £100 (see overleaf), please fill in the order form below, complete the questionnaire overleaf, and send it to Bradt Travel Guides by post, fax or email.

Please send me one copy of the following guide at half the UK retail price

Title		Retail price	Half price
. . .	. . . .	. . . .	. . . .

Please send the following additional guides at full UK retail price

No	Title		Retail price	Total
. . .	. . . .	. . . .	. . . .
. . .	. . . .	. . . .	. . . .
. . .	. . . .	. . . .	. . . .

Sub total . . . .
Post & packing . . . .
(£2 per book UK; £4 per book Europe; £6 per book rest of world)
Total . . . .

Name . . . .

Address . . . .

Tel . . . .   Email . . . .

☐ I enclose a cheque for £ . . . . made payable to Bradt Travel Guides Ltd

☐ I would like to pay by credit card. Number: . . . .

Expiry date: . . . / . . .   3-digit security code (on reverse of card) . . . . .

Issue no (debit cards only) . . . . .

☐ I would like to subscribe to Bradt's monthly enewsletter.

☐ I would be happy for you to use my name and comments in Bradt marketing material.

Send your order on this form, with the completed questionnaire, to:

Bradt Travel Guides CAM2
23 High Street, Chalfont St Peter, Bucks SL9 9QE
☏ +44 (0)1753 893444   f +44 (0)1753 892333
e info@bradtguides.com   www.bradtguides.com